The Fragile Bridge

PATERSON SILK STRIKE, 1913

The Fragile Bridge

PATERSON SILK STRIKE, 1913

Steve Golin

Temple University Press
Philadelphia

Temple University Press, Philadelphia 19122
Copyright © 1988 by Temple University. All rights reserved
Published 1988
Printed in the United States of America

Library of Congress Cataloging-in-Publication Data

Golin, Steve.
The fragile bridge.

Bibliography: p.
Includes index.
1. Silk Workers' Strike, Paterson N.J., 1913.
2. Industrial Workers of the World—History—20th century.
3. Intellectuals—New York (N.Y.)—History—20th century.
4. Socialism—United States—History—20th century.
I. Title.
HD5325.T42 1913.P383 1988 331.89'287739'0974924 87-24356
ISBN 0-87722-534-6 (alk. paper)

A shorter version of Chapter One appeared as "Bimson's Mistake—
Or, How the Paterson Police Helped to Spread the 1913 Strike,"
New Jersey History 100 (Spring/Summer 1982): 57–86.
The first section of Chapter Three appeared as "The Unity and Strategy
of the Paterson Silk Manufacturers during the 1913 Strike," in *Silk
City*," ed. Philip Scranton (Newark: New Jersey Historical Society,
1985), 73–97.
Chapter Six appeared earlier as "The Paterson Pageant—Success or
Failure?" *Socialist Review* 13 (May/June 1983): 45–78, and is
expanded here.
Chapter Eight is expanded from "Defeat Becomes Disaster: The
Paterson Strike of 1913 and the Decline of the IWW," *Labor History*
24 (Spring 1983): 223–48.

For Alice

CONTENTS

ACKNOWLEDGMENTS

For providing me with information when I needed it, and sharing their experience or expertise, I thank Louise Branthwaite, Sophie Cohen, Delight Dodyk, Carrie Golzio, Sylvia Firschein, William Gerstein, John Herbst, Joseph Hoffspiegel, Helen Kehoe, Minnie Keller, William and Patricia Lievow, Phillip McLewin, Irwin Marcus, Jack Mandell, Ruth Muldofsky, Jerry Nathans, Robert Rosenstone, Jack Saperstein, Jack Saul, George Shea, Ben Stanton, Sol Stetin, Patrick Striano, and Rose Villano.

I thank the administrators of the New Jersey Historical Commission for two separate grants, and the administrators of Bloomfield College for two study leaves. I thank the secretarial and library staffs of Bloomfield College and the editorial and production staffs of Temple University Press for their generous and timely help.

For encouraging me in the project and for criticizing drafts of chapters or of the whole manuscript, I particularly thank Ron Aronson, Rosalyn Baxandall, Jon Bloom, Ann Botschon, John Cumbler, Jeff Escoffier, Clyde Ferguson, Doris Friedonsohn, David Goldberg, Howard Green, Martie LaBare, Rick Manning, Michal McMahon, Erika Miliziano, Philip Scranton, Patricia Sterling, and Nancy Wolcott.

All these people participated in the making of this book, and I am grateful to each of them. But only Alice Golin felt the excitement of 1913 as intimately as I did, or read each piece of the manuscript, as well as the whole, at every stage, with good humor, loving criticism, and seemingly endless curiosity. To her, especially, I give thanks.

INTRODUCTION

The Moment of 1913

In 1913, in Paterson, New Jersey, three vital groups of people came together: striking silk workers, organizers from the Industrial Workers of the World (IWW), and Greenwich Village intellectuals. Their collaboration was facilitated by the open and hopeful cultural climate of 1913 and became the fullest expression of that climate. This book tells the story of their collaboration in Paterson.

The 1913 strike is important because it challenges certain conservative assumptions about labor history that have become so widely held as to be shared even by many on the left: the elitist role of skilled workers, the bureaucratic function of union organization, and the irrelevance of intellectuals. But in Paterson in 1913, skilled weavers began the strike and successfully reached out to unskilled dyers' helpers; union organizers committed to the idea of workers' control successfully encouraged the emergence of rank-and-file leaders, particularly women; and intellectuals went beyond sympathy and support to participate successfully in the strike itself. Paterson is also important because it suggests possibilities of connecting economic, political, and cultural struggles, possibilities that have been lost—in part because the strike was not, finally, a success. The bridge that the IWW formed between the silk strikers and the intellectuals was fragile and did not last, but the memory of that bridge, however fragile, calls into question assumptions that have guided the left for seventy years.

The Fragile Bridge argues that the Paterson silk workers began the 1913 strike and controlled it themselves (Chapter One); that with the help of the IWW they created institutions that supported the strike and reinforced its radically democratic character (Chapter Two); that the need for a bridge to New York grew out of a deadlock in Paterson (Chapter Three); that the New York intellectuals and IWW organizers had become more open to each other

1

as a result of informal contact in the Village (Chapter Four); that the experience of the strike in Paterson changed the Village intellectuals (Chapter Five); that the Pageant which the strikers performed in New York with the help of the IWW and the Villagers was a success (Chapter Six); that the strikers were defeated because the mill owners were able to keep their annexes open in Pennsylvania (Chapter Seven); that the loss of the strike hurt the IWW more than it hurt the silk workers (Chapter Eight); and that through its effect on the IWW and the intellectuals the defeat became a major turning point for the American left (Conclusion).

The present study integrates the arguments into the narrative and in that sense is an exception to a current trend. Much of the best working-class and social history written recently in the United States has sacrificed narrative to analysis (despite the powerful example of E. P. Thompson in England). The arguments in this book are part of the story of the coming together of the silk workers, the IWW organizers, and the Village intellectuals. Their story is worth telling for its own sake, as well as for what it says about us on the left—about our history, its lost possibilities, and what may still be recovered.

FROM LAWRENCE TO PATERSON

The silk strike that began in February 1913 was one in a series of industrial conflicts that erupted in the eastern United States in the period from 1909 to 1913. New immigrants from southern and eastern Europe took the lead in these industrial conflicts: Jews dominated the New York garment strikes of 1909–10; Italians were crucial in the great woolen strike in Lawrence, Massachusetts, in 1912. When they struck, these new immigrants tended to form all-inclusive, industrywide unions that cut across traditional lines of craft and sex. Women in fact spearheaded the garment strikes of 1909–10 and played a major role in the textile strikes of 1912–13.[1] These tendencies—the militance of Italians and Jews, the aggressiveness of women workers, and the formation of an industrial union including skilled and unskilled workers—were reflected in the Paterson strike of 1913.

In other ways, however, the Paterson strikers were unique: the delicate nature of the silk thread, even in the twentieth century, demanded great skill on the part of the weaver. The Paterson silk weavers were more skilled and in some ways more sophisticated than the Lawrence weavers or the New York garment workers; they had come to Paterson with prior experience both in weaving and in labor conflict. The fierce struggles in Paterson's silk industry, begun by the first generation of weavers from western Europe in the 1860s and 1870s, were expanded by the later generation of skilled immigrants from northern Italy and Russian Poland. In Europe they had not been peasants, and in Paterson they were not striking for the first time. From Macclesfield, England, in the 1870s, Biella, Italy, in the 1890s, and Lodz, Poland, in the

1900s they brought a strongly cooperative and anticlerical bent, and a determination not to be pushed around by the mill owners.

"That's one thing my father always taught: no matter where you go to work, don't let them step on you," said Carrie Golzio. "That was instilled in me when I was a kid."[2] Golzio, a rank-and-file leader in 1913, had been trained as a silk weaver by her father in Paterson; both her father and mother had been woolen weavers in Biella. The refusal of skilled weavers to be stepped on by the manufacturers made Paterson notorious as a center of labor militance and radicalism during the last decades of the nineteenth century and the first decade of the twentieth. Throughout these years they struggled as well against their internal divisions by nationality, craft, and gender. Finally, in 1913, as a direct result of what they had learned from previous setbacks, they went on strike together: male and female weavers, English-speaking and Italian and Jewish weavers, skilled weavers and unskilled dyers' helpers.

Solidarity in Paterson, growing out of the history of the silk workers, was reinforced by the influence of the IWW. The Paterson strikers invited organizers from the national IWW to help them in 1913 because of its highly publicized success in organizing the new immigrants in Lawrence, Massachusetts, in 1912. Lawrence made the IWW famous. "To most Easterners, the IWW is merely a name," the New York *Times* pointed out, but "its successful management of the Lawrence strike focused the attention of the country upon it"; it had become "the most serious menace the present system of society has ever been called upon to face," because IWW strategy was "to work from the bottom up," in contrast to the "top down" approach to social change favored by many Socialists.[3]

The Wobblies, as they were called, attracted the attention of the press after their Lawrence victory because new immigrants had won under the leadership of an organization that sought revolutionary change from below. William D. ("Big Bill") Haywood, who in 1905 had helped to found the IWW as a revolutionary alternative to the American Federation of Labor (AFL), always emphasized its radical goal. Addressing a meeting in New York in 1911, Haywood had stressed that the "Progressives, or whatever they propose to call themselves," would not end class exploitation: "They will give you eight-hour laws, compensation laws, liability laws, old-age pensions. They will give you eight hours; that is what we are striving for, too—eight hours. But they won't get off the workers' back."[4]

The IWW wanted to end the class system. To conservatives, the effect of the IWW's revolutionary rhetoric on striking immigrants was unsettling. "We have had strikes aplenty in the past," observed the New York *Sun*. "But the first considerable development of an actual revolutionary spirit comes today at Lawrence among the un-American immigrants from southern Europe."[5] In the months after Lawrence more than eighty articles in magazines and major newspapers analyzed the strike and the IWW. Conservative commentaries, like those in the *Times* and the *Sun*, stressed the danger; radical commentaries stressed the possibilities. Lawrence was "the greatest victory in American labor history," said the *International Socialist Review*. "For the first time in America a method of organizing men and women of twenty different nationalities and leading them to victory has been found." Reflecting the growing optimism of left-wing Socialists, the *Review* expected industrial unionism to sweep the country in 1913. Before Lawrence, industrial unionism had been associated with violence, "but during 1912, the Industrial Workers of the World won at Lawrence. . . . And this victory was won by a courageous self-restraint that prevented all violence."[6] Neither conservative nor revolutionary, Progressive journals like the *Survey* suspected that the strike's nonviolence made it even more dangerous: "On all sides people are asking: is this a new thing in the industrial world? . . . Are we to expect that instead of playing the game respectably, or else frankly breaking out into lawless riot which we know well enough how to deal with, the laborers are to listen to a subtle anarchistic philosophy?"[7]

While reformers worried and some conservatives called for restricting immigration, the IWW organizers celebrated. "It was a wonderful strike, the most significant strike, the greatest strike that has ever been carried on in this country or in any other country," said Bill Haywood at a big Socialist meeting in New York, "because we were able to bring together so many nationalities. And the most significant part of the strike was that it was a democracy. The strikers handled their own affairs." Democratic and nonviolent, the strikers conducted their business in the open, Haywood emphasized, "even as this socialist meeting is being conducted."[8] The IWW celebrated Lawrence as proof of what women and new immigrants could do in a democratic strike when not divided and held back by craft unions. Sensitive to the media image of Lawrence as a strike of un-American immigrants guided by an un-American philosophy of revolutionary syndicalism, the IWW insisted on the native origins of the strike. "Whatever it may have in common with European labor movements," the IWW itself "is a distinct product of America and American conditions," said *Solidarity*, the IWW's eastern weekly. As for the strikers, "regardless of their birthplaces, THEY ARE AMERICANS in the true sense of the term."[9] Unlike later revolutionaries who adopted models of organization from abroad, the IWW organizers consistently claimed to embody the best of America. This was good politics; it was also the way they actually felt.

Elizabeth Gurley Flynn's later description of what she and Haywood said to the workers of Lawrence, recalling Jules Michelet's description of France in 1789, conveys the sense of being present at the rebirth of a nation.

We spoke to nationalities who had been traditionally enemies for centuries in hostile European countries, like the Greeks and Turks and Armenians; yet they marched arm-in-arm on the picket line. . . .

We talked of their own experiences, how they had come from Europe, leaving their native village and fields, their old parents, sometimes wives and children. Why had they come . . . ? Was it to be called "Greenhorns" and "Hunkies" and treated as inferiors and intruders? Heads nodded and tears shone. . . .

We talked of "Solidarity," a beautiful word in all languages. . . . It was internationalism. It was also real Americanism—the first they had heard.[10]

To Flynn, the more international the feeling at Lawrence, the more American it was. America was the place where all could become free together.

Flynn, Haywood, and their colleagues came to Paterson with real hope for America. The IWW had conducted occasional campaigns in Paterson over the years but had met with scarcely more success there than in the rest of the industrial East. "It remained for the Lawrence strike to boom the IWW in Paterson and vicinity," said *Solidarity* in 1912.[11] In Paterson, as in many New England mill towns, the news from Lawrence helped precipitate an immediate strike in 1912. But whereas New England textile workers generally succeeded, with or without strikes, in raising wages in 1912, the Paterson silk strikers of 1912 failed to achieve their main objective: halting the manufacturers' efforts at a speedup. Meanwhile, in Paterson and throughout the East, the IWW gained considerable support among Italians. When the silk workers next went on strike, in 1913, they followed the urgings of many Italians among them and invited the victors of Lawrence to Paterson. It was a good idea. From Lawrence, the IWW organizers brought democratic and nonviolent techniques of organization, innovative ways of actively involving women and immigrants, and a vision of America as the place where the working class of the world could come together.

Although smaller and weaker than it appeared in its inflated post-Lawrence image (the national IWW at the beginning of 1913 claimed only 70,000 paid-up members, of whom more than half were in the textile industry), the IWW at the time was not only revolutionary but also genuinely committed to the people with whom it worked. Looking back on 1913, what one finds most remarkable about IWW staff members (not only those who came to Paterson but also those working elsewhere) is how humane and intelligent they were in the midst of militant struggle. Humane: unlike moderate Socialists, they were not narrowly prejudiced against nonwhites, immigrants, or women; more than even left-wing Socialists, they tried to practice freedom and equality in the movement while fighting for it in society. Intelligent: they recognized and grappled with the contradictions their movement spawned between freedom someday and freedom now, between solidarity and individuality, between we-are-all-leaders and Haywood, Flynn, et al. as leaders. And they were capable of learning: in Paterson, despite an unfortunate tendency to imitate their Lawrence tactics, they finally responded to the new situation with new ideas. They could improvise: they were not so bureaucratically organized that their creative imaginations were smothered. It was not doctrinal purity that appealed to people in Paterson and Greenwich Village then or can appeal to us now; nothing in IWW theory led them to organize separate meetings for women in Lawrence and Paterson or to rely heavily on Socialists in both strikes. In fact, IWW principles strictly applied would have ruled out two of the most characteristic features of the Paterson strike: the leading role played by skilled workers, and the direct participation of intellectuals. The IWW organizers, uncompromising in their commitment to class struggle, proved surprisingly open in relation to almost everything else.[12] In Paterson they had the grace to trust the strikers and the democratic process of the strike, and the confidence not to try to force the revolutionary pace.

In Greenwich Village, as in Paterson, people were initially drawn to the IWW organizers because of their success in Lawrence. As rebels, Village writers and artists had been sympathetic to immigrant workers, but few really believed that such workers had a chance. If reformers were impressed by the IWW's victory, Village intellectuals were exhilarated. "What we saw in Lawrence affected us so profoundly that this moment of time in Lawrence changed life for us," declared Mary Heaton Vorse, a writer who lived in the Village. Vorse's description of her Lawrence experience again recalls Michelet's account of the magical moment when the connections between people became more real than the separations: "Speakers came, and for a moment in Lawrence speakers, visitors, spectators, strikers, leaders were outside themselves, swept up out of their small personal existences into the larger and august flow of the strike."[13] A similar image appears in Margaret Sanger's account. In 1912 Sanger was working as a nurse in New York and mixing with other bohemians in the Village and in her uptown apartment. One of her tasks during the Lawrence strike was to take charge of the strikers' children who were sent to New York. Waiting in Grand Central Station for the train, anxious because it was late, she was afraid that something would go wrong with the arrangements. Then she saw the children finally arriving and being greeted by the happy crowd, which carried them in triumph on its shoulders. "Singing, laughing, crying" herself, Sanger felt the pleasure of solidarity: "I, too, had the illusion of being swept from the ground." As a result of her Lawrence experience, Sanger joined the IWW and began working with it in local strikes.[14]

The Lawrence strike ended in victory in March 1912, and during the following year real relationships began to develop between the organizers and Village intellectuals. Greenwich Village was already a home for bohemian artists and radicals but was not yet the self-promoting tourist attraction it would later become. A new feminist luncheon club called Heterodoxy quietly began meeting there in 1912; Flynn was soon invited to speak and became an enthusiastic member. Mabel Dodge held the first of her weekly "evenings" at her Village apartment in January 1913; Haywood and other IWW organizers frequently joined in these free-flowing discussions of art and politics. Haywood also mixed with writers and artists at the open editorial meetings of *The Masses*. Max Eastman had taken over direction of *The Masses* late in 1912 and immediately aligned the previously respectable socialist magazine with the Village cultural rebellion and with the IWW. His first issue acclaimed the Lawrence triumph as "the biggest human victory of recent years in America."[15] Eastman moved the offices of *The Masses* to the Village and designed a masthead statement (with John Reed's help) that began "A REVOLU- TIONARY AND NOT A REFORM MAGAZINE: A MAGAZINE WITH A SENSE OF HUMOR AND NO RESPECT FOR THE RESPECTABLE." Reed and other poets who joined the staff under Eastman's leadership wrote warmly about the IWW. In turn, IWW leaders began to identify with *The Masses* and contribute to it. The growing contact and attraction between IWW organizers and Village intel- lectuals in the year after the Lawrence strike became the foundation of a bridge between the classes.

In Paterson more than anywhere else, the friendship of the Wobblies and the intellectuals was fruitful. Their cooperation was based not only on mutual attraction but also on mutual respect. There was not, in 1913, a fawning "cult of the proletarian" on the part of intellectuals, nor the corresponding need within the union to persuade intellectuals to endorse some party line. Writers and artists were able to observe the Paterson strike, to mix in it, to find their own way of contributing. Hence, the IWW was able to serve, for a moment, as a fragile bridge between the Village intellectuals and the Paterson working class.

1 9 1 3

"'Thirteen'—my own lucky number," the painter John Sloan wrote in his diary on January 1. For Sloan and his colleagues on *The Masses*, 1913 began full of hope. They were excited about the new tendencies in art and society. On January 15, when the latest issue of *The Masses* came out, Sloan noted in his diary that he and the other editors thought that the magazine was "coming on in splendid style," and that he liked Eastman's socialist editorials best. On January 16 Sloan was visited by a writer from *American Art News* and told her that the modern movement in art—"Matisse and the 'neo-impressionists' and Cubists, etc."—constituted "a bomb under convention"; despite the limitations of particular modern painters, "the explosive force is there—revolution it is."[16] In 1913 Sloan felt no contradiction between his artistic and political activities. As one of "the Eight," painters who had become known as the realistic or Ashcan School, he would help organize the Armory Show of modern art in February. He would also run for assemblyman in 1913 on the Socialist ticket. Sloan and his wife, Dolly, had been Socialists for years but had been unimpressed with the IWW until Lawrence changed their minds. In 1913 he and Dolly would become active participants in the Paterson strike. John Sloan's artistic and political hopes for 1913 converged on *The Masses*, to which he freely gave his art and his time. Unlike later artists, unlike his later self, Sloan believed in 1913 that his involvement in politics made him a better artist. "I met Kirby on the street and went with him to his studio," he had written earlier in his diary. "Says he don't see why I—how any artist—could be interested in Socialism. I told him that no man could do good work and *not* be."[17]

Sloan, Art Young, and Eastman committed *The Masses* to class struggle. Like the IWW, the magazine considered *how* to achieve a revolution, not *whether* there should be one. Asked how his publication could claim to be open and yet exclude various reform movements from its pages, Eastman answered that reform by definition aimed "to assuage and obliterate the class struggle," whereas *The Masses* hoped to intensify it.[18] Yet no merely political magazine could have been as alive as *The Masses*, which was driven by the creative needs of Eastman, Sloan, Young, John Reed, and other artists and poets and fed by the larger currents of the Village rebellion against conservatism of all kinds. A Village radical like Vorse, a founder of and contributor to *The Masses*, aimed at her own liberation as well as that of the working class. "I am trying for nothing so hard in my own personal life as how not to be respectable when married," wrote Vorse to a friend in 1913. "Up to now I have succeeded quite well."[19] As the rebellion of the new immigrants gave strength to the IWW, the bohemian rebellion gave strength to *The Masses*. And as young women were at the center of the revolt of the immigrants, so young women were at the center of the revolt in the Village, where they commonly kept their own names when married and where a couple would put both individuals' names on the mailbox, whether they were married or not.[20] The sense of convergence—between art and socialism, the women's movement and the industrial union movement, the personal and the political—defined the moment of 1913. Eastman, who was normally reserved, later described the atmosphere at a *Masses* editorial meeting: "The talk was radical; it was free-thought talk and not just socialism. There was a sense of universal revolt and regeneration, of the just-before-dawn of a new day in American Art and Literature and living-of-life as well as in politics. I never more warmly enjoyed liking people and being liked by them."[21] As Vorse said of the same meetings: "The flame was present here too, as well as in Lawrence."[22]

For their part, IWW organizers shared many of the wider hopes of 1913. They did not feel isolated as radicals. In Paterson they would be met by fierce public and official hostility. But in court, when the Paterson prosecutor tried to prove that they were un-American by citing their revolutionary goal of abolishing the wage system, Judge James F. Minturn responded—in the spirit of 1913—that some of the country's leading minds believed in abolishing the wage system.[23] In this fluid atmosphere, in which capitalism itself was open to question and revolution seemed a real possibility, the IWW thrived.

In Lowell, Massachusetts, following up on the Lawrence victory, Flynn and several other organizers went to eat in a Chinese restaurant and found it decorated with new flags and special signs. Smiling Chinese workers explained that Sun Yat-sen had proclaimed the Republic. "We rejoiced with them though we little knew the full significance of what was stirring in far-off Asia. But we were for freedom—everywhere—and their happiness looked good to us. They liked the IWW too. So we were all friends."[24] Like Eastman, Flynn enjoyed the camaraderie that came from being part of the universal revolt; like Vorse, she was succeeding quite well in not becoming respectable. In Lawrence after the strike she had met and fallen in love with the anarchist Carlo Tresca, who moved to New York in 1913 and lived with her and organized in Paterson alongside her. Flynn would later begin the Paterson chapter of her memoirs with the central fact of her love for Tresca, noting that although each was legally married to someone else, they "honestly and openly" showed their love for each other "according to our code at that time."[25]

Love and revolution, beauty and freedom: they were almost as closely connected in the minds of the IWW organizers as in the minds of Village intellectuals. Haywood visited the studio of an Ashcan artist, wrote poetry in Washington Square, and spoke to the Paterson strikers of the coming time when even the workplace would be transformed into a thing of beauty. *Solidarity*, the IWW weekly, noted that "twenty-five finishers in the E. T. Wright Company shoe factory at Rockland, Massachusetts, quit work because their view of the scenery surrounding the shop had been shut off. 'No scenery, no work,' is their slogan! Good for the finishers."[26] Arturo Giovannitti, one of the key IWW organizers in Lawrence, was equally famous as a poet; like the artists and writers of *The Masses*, whom he knew well, Giovannitti emphasized the "subversive" power of culture and saw the different spheres of his activity as two aspects of the same revolt.[27]

The overlapping of the separate energies of the IWW and *The Masses* created a new field of force in 1913. Many who were not part of *The Masses* or the IWW felt a similar sense of radical possibility and contributed toward making it real. From Massachusetts, Helen Keller sent money to IWW-led strikers in Little Falls, New York, asserting that "their cause is my cause."[28] In January 1913 she published a defense of Haywood against the moderate Socialists who had recalled him from the party's executive committee. For a radical like Keller it was not enough to comment on the class struggle from a position of safety; as much as she could she put herself on the line, because although everything was possible, nothing was inevitable. The radical, explained student intellectual Randolph Bourne in 1913, "feels himself not as an idle spectator of evolution, but as an actual co-worker in the process."[29] As a young theorist, Walter Lippmann cited both the feminist movement and the industrial union movement as the "big revolts" that were transforming America in 1913; IWW strikes and the battle for women's suffrage were "at once the symptoms and the instruments of progress." Lippmann singled out Lawrence as a model of radical social change: "The Lawrence strikers did something more than insist upon their wrongs; they showed a disposition to right them." As a result, "the Lawrence strike touched the most impervious: story after story came to our ears of hardened reporters who suddenly refused to misrepresent the strikers, of politicians aroused to action, of social workers become revolutionary."[30] Upton Sinclair had predicted some years earlier that America would be socialist by 1913. In 1913, living in the Village, Sinclair was encouraged by the "stirring among the foreign-born workers in our country" and sensed "the beginning of the change."[31]

Lippmann, Bourne, Sinclair, and Keller serve as witnesses to the moment of 1913. Although they are major figures in American cultural history, they played minor roles in the Paterson strike and thus appear only briefly in this book. Sanger, Reed, Eastman, Sloan, Mabel Dodge, and Hutchins Hapgood played significant roles in the Paterson story, and they are part of this book. In the moment of 1913 they were unusually responsive to the connections between the changes in public and private life, art and politics, the women's movement and the workers' movement.

"We are living at a most interesting moment in the art development of America," wrote Hapgood in the New York *Globe* on the eve of the Armory Show. "It is no mere accident that we are also living at a most interesting moment in the political, industrial, and social development of America. What we call our 'unrest' is the condition of vital growth, and this beneficent agitation is as noticeable in art and in the woman's movement as it is in politics and industry."[32] Four months later, Hapgood was the first to recognize the importance of the Paterson Strike Pageant as both revolutionary art and revolutionary politics. His friend Dodge was equally sensitive to the connections between movements, which she tended to see as connections between people: "It seems as though everywhere, in that year of 1913, barriers went down and people reached each other who had never been in touch before." In 1913 Dodge served the artistic and political movements as a kind of amateur communications expert, inaugurating her "evenings" in January, promoting the Armory Show in February, and suggesting the idea of the Pageant in April. Employing the same image that Sanger and Vorse used in describing Lawrence, Dodge wrote that in 1913 "the new spirit was abroad and swept us all together."[33]

Sanger, like Sloan, was involved in the radical movement in politics and the modern movement in art, but she was also committed to sex education and to what she would soon christen "birth control"; she brought a dimension of her own to Paterson.[34] Eastman was a feminist before he became a socialist; in *The Masses* he supported the women's movement, and the aggressive role played by women in the Paterson strike, as wholeheartedly as he supported industrial unionism. He later evoked his sense of the richness of the moment by remembering it as "that year of beginnings 1913."[35]

Early in 1913, Reed published a long satirical poem in which he acknowledged Lippmann as the intellectual leader of the young Villagers. He also made fun of Lippmann's tendency toward barren abstractions, describing him as one

Who builds a word, and leaves out all the fun,—
Who dreams a pageant, glorious, infinite,
and then leaves all the color out of it.[36]

In the Paterson strike, Reed and his friends would help create a pageant with all the color put back into it.

This book takes Reed, Flynn, and Carrie Golzio seriously, as opposed to treating them condescendingly or nostalgically. As it turned out, 1913 was not a lucky year for the Paterson strikers, or the IWW organizers, or their New York friends. This is the story of their disappointment as well as of their hopes. It is also the story of the silk manufacturers and their allies in Paterson, including the AFL, and of all the local people caught in the middle and forced to choose sides. But it begins, as the strike began, with the silk workers themselves.

CHAPTER ONE

Bimson's Mistake

On February 25, the first day of the 1913 strike, Police Chief John Bimson arrested three out-of-town speakers at Turn Hall. The last speaker that morning had been Elizabeth Gurley Flynn, who had warned the strikers not to be "tricked by racial prejudice, for they'll try to tell you that the Jews are going to work and then they'll tell you that the Italians have gone back."[1] After her speech the hall had begun to empty. It was eleven o'clock, and the strikers wanted to eat before picketing the mills during the noon lunch break. Patrick Quinlan, who arrived at Turn Hall too late to speak that morning but had spoken the evening before, saw Bimson and four detectives talking roughly to Flynn. Quinlan joined them, and Bimson asked whether he was another outside agitator. "None of your business," answered Quinlan. "I am an American citizen."[2] That was all, and it was enough. The four detectives hustled him out of the hall. "What right have you, an Irishman, to come here and speak to these wops?" one detective said.[3] At the police station, Quinlan demanded to know the charge. There was no charge yet; it would be filled in a few hours later. The years Quinlan would spend in jail on the trumped-up charge of advocating violence in a speech he had not made were intended by Bimson to make a point: everything in Paterson during this strike was his business.

Back at Turn Hall, Bimson gave the other out-of-town speakers a choice of leaving town permanently or also being arrested. Samuel Kaplan agreed to leave, but Carlo Tresca and Flynn insisted on their rights and were arrested. Bimson admitted that in a strictly legal sense he was exceeding his authority, but in a larger sense he regarded the arrest of outside agitators as "preventative medicine." With the IWW organizers unable to function, he was sure he would be able to keep the strike within manageable bounds.[4]

Bimson's assumption was that the Paterson silk workers were incapable by themselves of mounting an effective challenge to the power of the mill owners;

therefore, the way to control the strike was to control the outside agitators. But Bimson's assumption was false, and his strategy backfired from the very beginning. As his captives were led out of Turn Hall, "fifteen hundred strikers waiting outside nearly went wild at seeing Miss Flynn in the clutches of Bimson," and on the way to the police station "all the efforts of four mounted policemen, and the frightful clubbing meted out to the marchers, failed to disperse Miss Flynn's escort."[5] For Bimson, this was but a taste of what was to come. Partly because of his efforts, the strike spread uncontrollably in the next two weeks.

Bimson's mistake was widely shared. When John Fitch, a writer for the *Survey*, came to Paterson in May he talked with business and professional people about the way that they perceived the strike. "It cannot be without cause," he wrote,

> that working people numbering tens of thousands continue on strike, their incomes absolutely cut off, for a period of three months. Yet there is very little talk in Paterson today, outside the ranks of the strikers, about the grievances, real or imagined, of the silk workers. In the offices, stores and cafes, in the meetings of the ministerial association, in the Charity Organization, in most of the papers and at the firesides of the more comfortable citizens, there is but one topic of conversation—the I.W.W.[6]

Like Bimson, Paterson's business and professional class treated the strike as the product of outside influences.

After the strike, Captain Andrew J. McBride, who was Bimson's second-in-command, maintained that the majority of strikers had not wanted to strike. Testifying before the Senate Commission on Industrial Relations, Captain McBride insisted that the IWW organizers used violence and threats of violence to force the workers to leave the mills: "The leaders came here and declared a strike and adopted tactics to get them out." But then why didn't the police simply use greater force to protect the workers who wanted to stay at work? McBride's answer to this question drew on his experience: the police were "warned by people working in the mills if we stayed around there they would leave work; that they did not want to work in a mill which was considered a scab mill by the police being around it."[7] McBride knew what a silk worker feared most was the shame of being considered a scab by the community. Yet he continued to insist that the majority of silk workers went on strike only because they were forced to do so by the IWW.

Dr. Andrew F. McBride, the mayor of Paterson in 1913, was also questioned by the federal commission. Dr. McBride testified that the silk workers originally had walked out for a lark, that they had stayed out almost five months, and that during this time they had suffered, many of them greatly. William O. Thompson, lawyer for the commission, asked him why the strikers had not gone back to work when the strike ceased to be a lark.

MCBRIDE: The agitators preached if there was any break in the line . . . the bosses would become more arrogant and conditions would become more intolerable and finally they would be treated like slaves. . . .

THOMPSON: And these people had been working in the mills for some time before they went out on strike?

MCBRIDE: Yes.

THOMPSON: They were acquainted with their employers?

MCBRIDE: Largely, I believe.

THOMPSON: But in your opinion they preferred to take the word and say-so of outside agitators who came in at that time, and so they stayed out?

MCBRIDE: Why, many of them were absolutely influenced by the preaching of the outside agitators. They believed everything that was told them, and they worshipped them really as heroes, and you could not talk with them.[8]

What Captain McBride attributed to the use of violence, Mayor McBride attributed to the seductive force of words, but both located the cause of the silk workers' actions outside them and their history, in the tactics or propaganda of the IWW.

During the second week of the strike, Rabbi Leo Mannheimer met Bill Haywood, who had just arrived in Paterson. Mannheimer and some other members of the clergy were hoping to mediate the trouble.

MANNHEIMER: Oh, Mr. Haywood, I'm so glad to meet you. I've been wanting to meet the leader of the strike for some time.

HAYWOOD: You've made a mistake, I'm not the leader.

MANNHEIMER: What! You're not? Well, who is he?

HAYWOOD: There ain't any "he."

MANNHEIMER: Perhaps I should have said "they." Who are they?

HAYWOOD: This strike has no leaders.

MANNHEIMER: It hasn't! Well, who is in charge of it?

HAYWOOD: The strikers.

MANNHEIMER: But can't I meet some responsible parties somewhere?[9]

Mannheimer refused to believe that the silk workers were responsible for their own strike. Although Haywood explained to him that it was run by the strikers themselves through an elected Central Strike Committee, which met daily and openly in Turn Hall, Mannheimer continued to regard Haywood and the other IWW organizers as the parties responsible. For his efforts at mediation, Rabbi Mannheimer was later forced by the manufacturers to give up his position in Paterson, but he never gave up his assumptions. "I cannot refrain from paying tribute to the leadership of William Haywood, Elizabeth Gurley Flynn, Patrick Quinlan, Adolph Lessig, and Carlo Tresca," he wrote in May. "For 13 weeks they have held in check and directed an army of 25,000 men and women."[10] Despite his good intentions, Mannheimer failed to understand the silk workers who created and controlled the strike.

The strikers were controlled by out-of-towners: this was the common assumption of the mayor, the police captain, and the rabbi—even though each had been told the workers' version. The rabbi had been told by Haywood that the silk workers democratically controlled the strike through their own committee. The captain had been told even by nonstrikers that they did not want police protection, because they would not be scabs. And the mayor had been told by the silk workers that they regarded this strike as the decisive one, the one they had to win to prevent the manufacturers from making conditions intolerable. In his capacity as a physician, Dr. McBride had heard this version many times. "I have been in practice for 25 years and have treated many of them for years and years and was very intimate with them, but during the strike I could not talk with them. It got so I would not discuss it with any of my patients."[11]

Unable to grasp what they were told, the police captain blamed the disorder and violence of the strike on the IWW agitators; the rabbi credited them with its orderliness and peacefulness. Neither could accept what his own evidence suggested, that praise or blame for the strike belonged primarily to the silk workers themselves. Like the mayor, Paterson's manufacturers, clergy, and police officials had all had personal experience in dealing with silk workers. But before 1913 few had experienced the workers as equals. And when for five months in 1913 they were compelled to deal with the silk workers as equals, they could not accept the meaning of their experience. They attributed the strength and solidarity and staying power of the workers to the national IWW leaders.

Historians, while correcting contemporary biases toward the 1913 strikers on many particular points, have perpetuated the general tendency to devalue their achievements. The discipline, unity, and sophistication of the silk strikers have been acknowledged by scholars but attributed to the IWW.[12] Most historians continue to share Bimson's predilection for focusing on the articulate outside agitators.[13] One important though partial exception is James Osborne. In two articles on the strike and a dissertation on Paterson's silk workers up to and including 1913, Osborne has succeeded in placing the strike in the context of Paterson's history: the history of the silk industry, of immigration, and of class conflict. Seen in this context, the 1913 strike ceases to appear as the product of IWW activity. Osborne rightly concludes that historians, like contemporaries, have "glossed over the role of the millhands" and exaggerated the role of the IWW. In reality, "the I.W.W. exercised very little authority over the day-to-day functioning of the strike, partly because the I.W.W. ideology held that the workers were quite capable of managing their own affairs, and partly because the city's workers had their own deeply entrenched strike traditions." Osborne's permanent contribution is to take the history of the strikers seriously. But although he has assembled valuable information about the work habits and communal traditions of both the old and the new immigrants, he misses the chance to show the development of the Paterson working class from the older to newer immigration. Embracing a historical perspective that stresses the "primitive" characteristics of first-generation industrial workers, he underestimates the growing unity and sophistication of the Paterson labor movement. Osborne finally fails to break with the dominant view of the silk workers as incapable of helping themselves. Because over the years they had developed no permanent union organization to carry out collective bargaining, Osborne concludes that in 1913 they were "helpless" in the face of the determination of the police chief and mayor to crush their strike.[14] Anything but helpless, as we shall see, the silk workers were even able to turn the police offensive to their advantage in the first two weeks of the strike.

To grasp why the Paterson silk workers reacted as they did to Bimson's use of force, we need to understand their history better than he did. This chapter focuses on the history of the three major groups of silk strikers: the ribbon weavers, the dyers' helpers, and the broad-silk weavers. The ribbon weavers gave the strike a leaven of skilled workers with a history of militant struggle in Paterson and a sense of their rights as Americans. The dyers' helpers provided a core of disciplined proletarians ready to picket and go to jail, and able to rally the support of a vital immigrant community. The broad-silk weavers created the basis for unity across sex and nationality lines by achieving unity in their own ranks. From 1913 to the present, the notion has prevailed that the silk workers were a disorganized immigrant mass incapable of taking effective action. This chapter aims to show that it *was* their strike: their needs drove it; their hard-won unity made it possible; and their accumulated wisdom guided it.

THE RIBBON WEAVERS

The first ribbon and broad-silk weavers in Paterson owned their own looms and supplied the power with their hands and feet. These handloom weavers made their warps themselves; their wives and children did quill winding and other tasks, and helped them turn the loom when they were tired. They owned their homes in Paterson and expected to be treated with the respect due artisans. In Europe they had worked independently in their homes or in the small workshops of master weavers. From the silk centers of France, Germany, Switzerland, and especially England, they had come to Paterson in the 1860s and 1870s, bringing their traditional work habits and a sense of their traditional rights. In Paterson, although some weaving was done on a putting-out basis in the home, most of it was done in old mills that had become empty after cotton began to fail in the 1830s. (Given a chance by a high U.S. tariff placed on imported silk in 1861, the developing silk industry utilized both the abandoned cotton mills and the skilled machinists who originally had come to build them.) But despite the factorylike atmosphere of the workplace, the work itself was still done on handlooms, and the old artisan traditions of the skilled handloom weavers took firm root.[15]

In Dickens's Coketown (in his novel *Hard Times*) the circus embodied the preindustrial values of craft work and community, in contrast to the dominant values of industrialization. Similarly in Paterson, a customary circus holiday symbolized the persistence, in a modern mill town, of preindustrial ways of life and work. "No Paterson mill-hand, with a proper self-respect, can be kept at spinning frame, or loom, when a circus is in town—it has been tried thoroughly," complained the *American Silk Journal* in 1890.[16] In 1882 one silk manufacturer fired twenty-eight employees for taking the day off to see the circus. Other manufacturers tried locking the doors to keep the weavers in when the circus parade came by, but they climbed out the windows. By 1905 most manufacturers, acknowledging defeat, simply closed their shops when the circus arrived. Other holidays as well were claimed by immigrant weavers, such as the Macclesfield wakes celebrated by English weavers in Paterson from 1880. Given all the traditional European and American and circus holidays, said the *American Silk Journal*, "it is a poor week that Paterson silk and other operatives do not manage to get at least one day for recreation."[17] Drawing on artisan traditions, immigrant weavers imposed many of their own rhythms on life in Paterson instead of merely submitting to an established industrial routine.

As an industrial town, Paterson at the beginning of the twentieth century was something of an anomaly. It was unusual not because it depended on immigrant labor—that was hardly exceptional—but because it depended on *skilled* immigrant labor. And it was unusual because it had undergone the process of industrialization so recently and, indeed, incompletely. The industrial revolution started later and proceeded more slowly in the weaving of silk than in the production of other textiles, and the efforts of Paterson silk weavers to protect themselves against its effects were more successful. The power loom came to silk only in the 1870s. Equipped with an automatic device that stopped the loom when the silk thread broke, the new loom could be attended by women and girls, a less expensive and initially more manageable source of labor. In broad silk the male weavers fought a delaying battle against the power loom, which nevertheless gradually replaced the handloom during the 1880s. In ribbon weaving, however, power lagged behind. Ribbon weavers made the narrow and often fine silk used for ties, labels, and hat bands. For the very reason that power came to silk so much later than to cotton and other textiles—because, that is, of the delicacy of the thread and of the work—power came to ribbon weaving last.[18] Not until 1889, when a high-speed automatic ribbon loom was introduced, could embroidered designs on ribbon goods be produced efficiently by power looms. Throughout the 1890s some handloom ribbon weavers still worked the old way, but by 1900, or 1905 at the latest, the handloom had disappeared in Paterson. By using the latest technology, Paterson's manufacturers captured markets from the less mechanized European silk industry and also attracted capital away from Paterson's older industries; by 1900 they had succeeded in making Paterson into "Silk City," the "Lyons of America." But the new technology did not equally transform their work force; the habits and attitudes of the handloom weaver outlived the handloom.

In 1880 one manufacturer singled out the immigrant English weavers as especially troublesome: "They are generally a bad set, a very bad set. They are so tainted with a communistic spirit that we prefer to have nothing to do with them."[19] Weavers from Coventry and Macclesfield were proud of their skills and experienced in banding together to enforce their customary rights, in Paterson as in England. Usually, they came directly to Paterson from their hometowns because they knew from fellow townsmen who had previously emigrated that weavers were needed in the town's expanding industry and that they would be well paid. A boom in ribbon production in the late 1870s accelerated the migration from Macclesfield, which peaked in 1879–80 and continued at a steady rate throughout the 1880s. Richard Margrave, historian of the English emigration to Paterson, emphasizes that English weavers came to preserve and protect their hand-processing skills. He also points out, however, that the continual influx of skilled immigrant weavers to Paterson made it impossible for them to maintain the European apprenticeship system in America.[20] Their militance resulted from their knowledge that the market value of their skills—in the absence of a viable apprenticeship system restricting entry into the trade—could be maintained only by cooperative action.

For the next forty to fifty years, or as long as the industry was expanding, the manufacturers of Paterson continued to hire immigrant weavers and continued to complain about their militance. Long after the English and French migration had stopped and the power loom had completely replaced the hand-loom, weavers were still coming to Paterson because their skills were needed. And they were still troublesome, because only by causing trouble could they maintain the value of their skills. In 1907 the magazine *Silk*, a trade organ, acknowledged that "in hardly any trade is the labor question more dominant than in silk manufacturing." For weaving the finer grades, "skilled help, already trained, is imperative. This can usually only be obtained in proper quantity in the large silk centers, such as Paterson, N.J., and even then the supply is none too large and the cost is not low."[21]

Paterson manufacturers suffered the cost of hiring experienced, skilled help, with all its attendant labor problems, because they had no good alternative. As the advertisement of a bankrupt manufacturer put it tactfully in 1913, "While this labor is more or less of an agitative character and at times unruly, yet this is due to the fact of its skilled character."[22] Manufacturers preferred to hire young, native-born females for semi-skilled jobs like winding, doubling, and twisting, and sometimes for weaving plain broad silks. But the cost of training unskilled workers to weave even the plainer silks was very high because damage to the material was both frequent and expensive. In 1913 an industry expert pointed out that hiring inexperienced men or women who had to be trained as weavers meant "weary and discouraging work" for the silk manufacturer, "covering months and years, during which time the percentage of imperfect goods turned out is very great."[23] In 1913 it still took years to train a silk weaver properly. And even then, according to a Connecticut manufacturer, someone who had been taught weaving on the job would continue to do work inferior to that of someone who had weaving in the blood—or rather, in the hands.

> The hands of a silk worker are one of his important assets. Take a man from the fields of Siberia, from the plains of Austria, from Southern Italy, or from a farm in the United States . . . and it is a very different matter to make a silk worker of that man, a very different matter, from taking men who have been brought up in countries where silk is produced, where the very habits and occupations have developed the techniques and the kind of hand that makes the silk worker. . . . Machinery does not do away with the use of hands in silk manufacture. The hands still remain, and will always remain in my opinion, a very important factor in the operation. A man with clumsy, awkward hands handling silk warp is a very different factor from the man whose grandfather before him handled the silk fabric.[24]

Silk manufacturers were trapped: either they hired inexperienced people and took the consequences, or they hired experienced immigrant weavers—and took the consequences. In Paterson, which remained the center of fine silk work in America through the 1930s, weaving continued to be skilled work. The power loom did the weaving, but the weaver had to watch carefully and try to make adjustments without stopping the machine; once the thread broke and the automatic stop-motion went into effect, it might take hours to start up the loom, and this would be time lost in production. The trick was to anticipate the break and keep the loom running as much of the time as possible. This trick, it is true, might be learned by initially unskilled women and men with attentive eyes and nimble fingers. The greater skill, however—not easily learned—was in starting up the loom in the first place. "I don't know of any of them that can be started earlier than half a day," said a ribbon weaver in 1914," and that is what we call a remount, where the same class of goods goes immediately into the loom when the other side goes out."[25] Here multifaceted skills, often passed from father to son, were needed. In fact, it took several years of training to become a skilled weaver of fine and fancy ribbon. By 1913 the high-speed ribbon looms were usually run by women and girls who were paid by the week (and even they were skilled workers who owned their own tools), but the better grades of ribbon were still made by experienced male weavers on heavy German looms. Paid (and paid relatively well) by the piece, these highly skilled ribbon weavers spent about one-third of their time twisting in new warps on the loom or repairing broken threads in the warp.[26] In the ribbon trade, and to a lesser extent in broad silk, the male striker of 1913 was direct heir to a long tradition of artisan independence.

It was a militant tradition: in ribbon weaving and in broad silk, shop strikes were everyday occurrences in Paterson. Strikes of the entire ribbon trade (which became split into increasing numbers of medium-sized shops as the industry grew) were less frequent. The first time the ribbon weavers struck en masse was in 1877. Protesting against a wage cut at one mill, handloom ribbon weavers from all eight mills in Paterson struck together and succeeded in restoring their wages, despite the depressed economic conditions of that year. Afterward, the silk manufacturers complained that the mayor and the aldermen of Paterson had failed to provide potential strikebreakers with sufficient police protection. Convinced that the authorities were more sympathetic to the weavers than to the employers, the manufacturers threatened to raise a private militia.[27]

The second general strike by ribbon weavers was in 1894, and again they achieved at least a partial victory. In Paterson and in New York City they won a uniform piece-work scale. The 1894 strike displayed many of the features of the great 1913 strike: there was picketing when needed; strikebreakers were mocked as "scabs" and followed even to their homes; outside speakers— including socialists and anarchists—addressed the strikers, placing their struggles in a broader framework, and the speeches were translated into five languages. Rev. Joshua Gallaway and other prominent Patersonians also spoke at rallies. Strikers sang the "Marseillaise." At the climax of the strike, 550 ribbon weavers marched from New York to Paterson and held a demonstration there; several days later, 800 strikers from Paterson marched to New York, taking along several wagons of provisions and their own brass bands.[28] The mass picketing and verbal intimidation of scabs, the mixing of nationalities, the outside speakers, the international songs, even the climactic trip to New York—all these became part of the tradition of Paterson silk strikes and reappeared on a larger scale in 1913, when the ribbon weavers struck as a body for the third time.

Even Gallaway, the minister, was part of the tradition; in 1913 he was still speaking for the strikers. But in 1913 he would become the only clergyman, almost the only respectable citizen of Paterson, to defend the silk strikers. As one old-timer pointed out, a great difference between 1894 and 1913 was that in the earlier strike Paterson's authorities had not sided with the manufacturers.[29] The mayor defied them by refusing to request troops from the state to supplement the city's still inadequate police force; the aldermen had previously restricted the growth of the police department through their budgetary control. In an industrial city like Paterson, aldermen were often ex-workers; they were also, like the mayor himself, dependent on silk workers' votes. The neutrality of the authorities in the 1894 battle between the manufacturers and the strikers helped shape the future strategy of both sides. For the weavers, peaceful picketing of the mills and humiliation of anyone still working in them became the central strike strategy. "In the case of a strike," a silk manufacturer observed in 1897, "there is no move to protect loyal operators from taunt, infamy and intimidation. Absolute violence must be committed before the city authorities will interfere. Hands are followed through the streets, jeered at and maligned without hope of protection in any form."[30] Accordingly, the battle strategy of the manufacturers in the years from 1894 to 1913 had a double focus: to try to gain political control over the Paterson police, and—whenever possible—to move their mills out of Paterson.

The first objective continued to elude the manufacturers. As the twentieth century began, they were still unable to wield the city's police force as a weapon against pickets. Paterson in 1900 belonged as much to the workers as to the manufacturers. As if in recognition of that fact, the manufacturers began to flee the city: between 1890 and 1910 there was a great rush to build annexes in Pennsylvania. Although the absolute decline of Paterson's silk industry did not begin until the textile slump of the 1920s (in 1910 there were a record 276 silk mills in Paterson, employing over 20,000 people), the silk industry was nevertheless growing faster in Pennsylvania. The same improvements in technology that enabled Paterson manufacturers to hire inexperienced workers, usually women and children, also enabled them to move a large part of their business to the coal-mining towns of Pennsylvania. There, the local authorities did not have divided loyalties and were able as a rule to intimidate the miners' wives and children who constituted the work force in the new silk mills. The most skilled women still fought back,[31] but at least there was no tradition of resistance by proud and unruly artisans to deepen and legitimize such protests. More than simply the opportunity to pay lower wages was involved in the move to Pennsylvania, as a leading Paterson manufacturer acknowledged in 1901: the new locations were "less liable to labor troubles, which are incident to Paterson."[32]

Hard-silk or throwing plants (which prepared the raw silk for weaving by winding, doubling, and twisting) were moved to Pennsylvania first, following an improvement in the throwing machine. Many of the ribbon mills were moved next, after the development of a high-speed ribbon loom with an automatic stop.[33] This sequence, which preceded the 1913 strike by two decades, should have put to rest the endless local arguments about whether the 1913 strike caused the decline of the Paterson silk industry: its decline relative to Pennsylvania began with the exodus of throwing plants and ribbon mills. Skilled workmen, proud of their craft and aggressive in the pursuit of justice as they conceived of it, were central to the rise of Paterson—and to its fall. Their old independent habits, their constant strikes, and especially their many victories were costly to the silk manufacturers. By resisting with all their strength and wisdom the tendency of capitalism to turn improvements in machinery against them by lowering the value of their labor, the skilled male weavers inadvertently helped launch the flight of capital from Paterson. Whom we blame in a situation like this says more about us than about the people, on both sides of the class struggle, who lived through it.

The new ribbon mills in Pennsylvania employed women and children exclusively. But in Paterson in 1913, highly skilled males still constituted about half of the city's ribbon weavers. By 1913, it is true, all the gains won by the ribbon weavers in 1894 had been wiped out by the employers' counter-offensive: the heavy looms of the male weavers had been lengthened and a second deck had been added; at the same time, wages had continually declined. Restoration of the uniform price scale for piece work (which the manufacturers had reluctantly accepted in 1894 as a way of ending the strike) appeared as an almost utopian demand of the ribbon weavers in 1913.[34]

"The wages have decreased in proportion as the loom improved," insisted a striking ribbon weaver in 1913. Ribbon weavers believed that the value of their labor increased as their productivity increased; therefore, improvements in the loom should mean higher wages. As another striking weaver put it:

> We don't object to improved machinery. We welcome improved machinery, if we can get some benefit from it outside of making the work easier or making it possible to produce more goods; but as a rule we never receive any benefit from improved machinery they put into the mills. On the contrary, we get a cut in wages whenever there is a new method made on a loom. Instead of giving us a benefit from it the benefit is really taken away from us and the manufacturer gets the benefit instead of the worker. So that improved machinery does not help us. It only antagonizes the workers the more, because they can see themselves that they can produce more under the improved machinery; still they get less wages.[35]

The ribbon weavers refused to believe that the tendency of modern machinery to render their labor cheaper was irreversible; to them, the relationship between improved technology and falling wages seemed neither natural nor inevitable. By contrast, the attitude of the mill owners was expressed by Moses Strauss, who managed two Paterson ribbon mills, one employing male weavers on German looms, and the other, female weavers on high-speed looms:

> A good deal of trouble comes from the fact that the silk business is passing through a change, that it is gradually becoming a business for females; that in the next 15 to 20 years the males employed in the silk industry will be nil. The change is coming very fast. For instance, as far as ribbons are concerned, the high-speed looms are mostly being run by females. The German looms are gradually changing from male to female and, as I say, in 15 to 20 years, or possibly less time, the mills will mostly be run by female labor.[36]

To Strauss, the skilled male weavers simply had no future; all their protests and strikes could not change that fact.

The long struggle between the skilled ribbon weavers and the mill owners was never merely a dispute about wages. Rooted in a conflict between two ways of life, it came to reflect two fundamentally different views of social change. To the owners and managers, capitalism appeared given; within it, social change—"progress"—occurred more or less automatically as the result of the search for profit. To the ribbon weavers, social change could result from the conscious actions of people with similar interests, and there was nothing inevitable about capitalism. By 1913, socialism had in fact become the dominant ideology of the ribbon weavers. Their spokesman, Louis Magnet, was an active member of the Socialist Party, and most of their strike leaders were socialists.[37] By 1913 many skilled ribbon weavers had concluded, on the basis of their long history of struggle, that their problems could not be solved within the framework of capitalism.

On the shop level in the years before 1913, the ribbon weavers had experienced a new impotence.

> We asked the boss what are you paying for the job; if we did it would amount to an offense to the boss, and if you were to ask, "can you not pay a little more for this job?" it was almost equivalent to a discharge, so domineering did some of the employers—had they become—that the workers were afraid to go before the boss, almost afraid to state their grievances to one another, for fear that the employer would use the weapon that his economic position gives him in discharging them.[38]

Within the shop the balance of power had shifted sharply toward the employer. Able to employ increasing numbers of less skilled female weavers and to choose from an overabundance of male ribbon weavers consequently competing for jobs, the ribbon manufacturer appeared, for the first time in Paterson's history, as the dictator of the shop. If a weaver "individually went to the office and made complaints in regard to the price he was told that if he didn't like it he could quit; that there were lots of workers only too glad to come and take his place."[39] Some employers continued to negotiate piece rates with individual ribbon weavers or with their representatives, as they had been accustomed to do in the past. But, explained Magnet, speaking precisely, "if it should have reached the ears of some employers that a committee was going to be formed or there was even talk of a committee being sent to the employers, they would be singled out and systematically discharged."[40] Militant ribbon weavers, unaccustomed to such treatment, reconsidered their methods in the years before 1913. At the tactical level, they realized that they had to walk out as a group first and present demands afterward, when it was too late for the employer to intervene.[41] At the strategic level, they increasingly thought in terms of political power, on a larger and larger scale.

In Paterson, through the last two decades of the nineteenth century and the first three of the twentieth, militant weavers contested manufacturers for control over both the rate of technological change and the distribution of its benefits. Especially in ribbon weaving, their fight was not hopeless, because they knew that their skills remained an essential part of the productive process. Alan Dawley has contrasted the largely defensive labor movement in the New England textile industry with the aggressive labor movement in Lynn, Massachusetts, where shoe workers possessed a rich craft heritage. "The textile industry in New England began at the factory stage. . . . Consequently, labor had no opportunity to establish its household independence, to create pre-factory customs in the work process, or to develop the means to resist industrial capitalism as an encroachment on established patterns of work and life."[42] Paterson's labor movement, which superficially contradicts Dawley's point, actually tends to confirm it. Silk did not begin as a modern industry. The silk weavers of Paterson, especially the ribbon weavers, had brought with them to the modern mill a tradition of craft pride and independence and a sense of their rights as artisans and as citizens. Much of the aggressiveness of Paterson's labor movement and its growing orientation toward power in the shop and the nation was a result of the influence of these skilled weavers.[43]

THE DYERS' HELPERS

A separate tradition of militance, however, helped to shape the 1913 strike. If the skilled ribbon and broad-silk weavers gave the strike its upright posture and aggressively forward look, the dyers' helpers were its central nervous system.

Dyers' helpers were the proletarians of the silk industry. Working in teams of seven or eight under the supervision of a dyer, dyers' helpers added chemicals to silk yarn in large tubs. Their work was unskilled and could be learned in a week.[44] Their working conditions were the worst in the silk industry. The delicacy and value of the material caused silk manufacturers to provide their weavers with better lighting and generally cleaner conditions than those enjoyed by cotton or woolen weavers,[45] but workers in the dye houses did not share these advantages. "As everybody knows, the dye house is the most dirty and unhealthy part of the silk industry," declared a dye worker in 1913.[46] Dye houses were always filled with steam and fumes. In summer the steam was suffocating; in winter it could condense and freeze. No provision was made to drain off the moisture that collected on the ground, so dyers' helpers always wore wooden clogs, weighing three to five pounds, to protect their feet— which got wet anyway. As part of their job, they worked with boiling chemicals—sometimes skin came right off their hands—and even tasted the mixture to determine proportions.[47]

Silk dyeing was a modern chemical industry. Weaving flourished in numerous middle-sized shops, whereas silk dyeing had been housed in sizable plants ever since the 1870s, when it first split off from the silk mills and formed a separate branch of the industry. Mergers between dye houses followed, and dyeing became concentrated in a few large firms. In 1913 there were nearly 300 ribbon and broad-silk shops in Paterson but less than a dozen dye houses. And whereas the largest silk mill employed 1,000 people, the Paterson branch of National Silk Dyeing employed 1,400, and the Weidmann Company some 2,000. They paid their skilled employees—the dyers and master dyers—competitive wages, but they paid the unskilled dyers' helpers at rates comparable to unskilled laborers in other industries, about $11 per week. In practice, dyers' helpers made much less because the work was highly seasonal; before the 1913 strike they were averaging only $6.00 a week. In 1913, ribbon weavers were still making $3.00 to $3.50 per day in Paterson (despite the decline in piece rates) and, even when all their unpaid hours and days were included, were still averaging more than $14 per week.[48] Within the silk industry the ribbon weavers and dyers' helpers stood at nearly opposite poles. As craftsmen and English-speaking Americans, the ribbon weavers were struggling in 1913 to protect a whole way of life; as Italian-speaking proletarians, the dyers' helpers were fighting for a chance to live.

The militant tradition of the dyers' helpers was rooted not in a common craft but in community: namely, the Italian community of Paterson. During the great migrations from southern and eastern Europe, many textile towns fragmented into a myriad of ethnic communities. In Paterson, however, the Italians dominated the new immigration. Many who came in the 1880s were northern Italians who had worked as weavers in Piedmont or as dyers in Lombardy; they became skilled dyers and weavers in Paterson. After 1890, however, southern Italians with no experience in textiles began to arrive in great numbers to work as dyers' helpers. By 1910 there were 7,000 to 8,000 Italians working in the manufacture of silk in Paterson, making them easily the largest nationality in the industry. Although somewhat more than half were from the north, southerners already outnumbered northerners in silk dyeing by a considerable margin. Among northern Italians in the dye houses, 70 percent made less than $12.50 a week (when working); among the southerners, more than 90 percent made less than $12.50. As unskilled dyers' helpers, they became the focal point of Paterson's Italian community.[49]

The most remarkable thing about the Italians was that they became a community at all. They arrived in Paterson speaking widely varying dialects from localities in Italy that had very different historical experiences and frequently did not get along with one another. In Paterson they founded about twenty-five mutual-aid societies that tended to keep them separate, and patronized "the doctor, the grocer, the wine dealer and even the priest coming from their own place."[50] Especially between northerners and southerners the prejudices were very strong. As Carrie Golzio, whose family came from Piedmont, recalls, "If a girl came home and said she was going with a Napoli-tano, oh, her father almost killed her."[51] It is not clear how northern and southern Italians overcame these prejudices sufficiently to work closely together in 1913. Martin Mooney has suggested that religion in Paterson—or, rather, its absence—helped unite the immigrants.[52] Northerners were generally anticlerical and often politically radical when they arrived. Many southerners came to Paterson with much greater respect for clerical authority, yet before 1910 the Italian population of 20,000 had only one Catholic church. In Paterson, the church was Irish, like the police. Rejected by the church, previously religious Italians drifted toward anticlericalism. Fund-raising efforts among them to pay the mortgage on the one Italian church languished. "In the yearly parade of the Holy Name Society those who take part can be counted on the fingers," wrote an Italian observer from New York in 1911. "A fact is that a spirit of anticlericalism is in the air."[53]

We need to extend Mooney's hypothesis. Underlying the growing unity of northerners and southerners was a common experience of being mistreated in Paterson—and not only by the church. The public and the authorities made no distinction between northern and southern Italians but extended the same contempt to both. There was no night school (in English or Italian) for Italians, no reading room, no gymnasium. When a group of Italians organized in 1900 to establish night classes, the idea of their using a public school was so vehemently attacked by citizens fearing damage to the building that the Italians withdrew their proposal, citing public prejudice.[54] Northern or southern, skilled or unskilled, anticlerical or religious, Italians were treated especially brutally when they fought back. Conflicts with management in the dye houses and mills and with the police shaped the Italian experience and unified it.

Northerners, who had brought their own radical theories and agitators with them, were prepared to defend themselves against such treatment. During the 1890s Paterson became the international center of Italian anarchism. The anarchist group in Paterson published an Italian-language newspaper and a journal, and encouraged fellow immigrants to think in terms of class rather than of region of origin. It also encouraged them to think in terms of violence. In July 1900 an Italian master dyer at the Weidmann plant was killed by an anarchist. Later in the same month the king of Italy was assassinated by an anarchist from Paterson; the city's anarchists continued for years to celebrate the assassination date.[55] In 1902 a dyers' strike, with the help of the anarchists, became the bloodiest in Paterson's history.

Strikes by dye workers were infrequent. From 1888 to 1894, for example, there were thirty strikes by Paterson weavers and only two by dye workers. However, because dyeing was big business and the great majority of its employees were unskilled dyers' helpers who could easily be replaced by strikebreakers, the strikes that did occur tended to be big—and they tended to be violent. During the 1894 ribbon weavers' strike, 500 Weidmann dye workers formed a committee to make their own demands. When the committee was summarily fired, the dye workers went to the other dye houses and the ribbon shops still in operation, broke down the doors, smashed the windows, and threw the silk on the floor. In contrast to the ribbon weavers, who relied primarily on peaceful picketing and verbal intimidation, reserving the threat of violence for exceptional situations, the dye workers simply drove all hesitant workers out of the shops. "The only thing that prevented a bloody riot," commented the New York *Daily Tribune*, "was the fact that a mob everywhere controlled the situation and was too strong for successful resistance."[56] As if to confirm this analysis, in 1902 the forces were more equal, and there *was* a bloody riot.

The Italian dyers' helpers took the lead in 1902 when twenty workers from two dye houses began the strike on their own initiative. It spread rapidly; at one plant three Italian workers and one policeman were shot. The manufacturers pressed the mayor to request the militia from the governor, but in keeping with Paterson tradition, the mayor refused. The dye workers were successful in shutting down their branch of the industry but were unable to force their employers to give in to their wage-and-hour demands. The strike was stalemated, foreshadowing the long stalemate in 1913. The only way for the dye workers to break the deadlock was to precipitate a general strike of all branches of Paterson's silk industry. Calling a mass meeting, they invited leading Italian anarchists to speak, who urged the use of whatever force was necessary. Marching to the weaving mills, the dyers' helpers forcibly emptied them, and this time eight workers and one policeman were shot. For six hours the dye workers controlled the city. At that point the mayor did ask the governor to send the militia. The use of violence had boomeranged: the Italian dyers' helpers became isolated, as both the weavers and the English-speaking dye workers drew back from them, and the militia stayed in Paterson while the defeated dye workers drifted back to work.[57]

The 1902 strike proved a setback for Paterson's labor movement as a whole. Sensing that for the first time public opinion had swung in their favor, the dye plant and silk mill owners used the violence of the 1902 strike as a basis for renewing their counteroffensive against the political influence of Paterson's workers. This time they were successful. Aided by public hysteria over anarchists and prejudice against Italians, armed with the threat of moving even more of their business to Pennsylvania, Paterson's manufacturers won victory after victory. The old police chief, who for more than thirty years had guided the department along its moderate course in strikes, was suspended; his captain, previously known as a hard-liner and publicly denounced as such by the workers, was promoted to acting chief. This new chief was John Bimson, who had never respected the traditional right of Paterson's silk workers to picket peacefully. In 1877, as a young policeman, he had contested their customary control of the streets. In 1894, as a captain, he had drawn his gun to threaten angry pickets. In 1901, silk workers (who praised the old chief for refusing to prohibit their public meetings) had denounced this captain for "abuse of his authority."[58]

In 1906 John Bimson became permanent chief of police, and in 1907 a business-sponsored reform of the city's government freed him from popular control. The aldermen were shorn of power, and a nonelected Board of Commissioners, appointed by the mayor, became responsible for the operation of the police force. The new commissioners immediately made their intentions plain: they increased the size of Bimson's force by more than 50 percent. The reaction time of the police was shortened by installation of a telephone system that connected the patrolmen with headquarters. There was also a mounted division to accompany patrols and a new "Italian Division," for which Bimson hired two Italian detectives and established a precinct station in the predominantly Italian Riverside section. The following year those leaders of the Italian anarchist group who had not fled Paterson in 1902 were arrested, and their journal was permanently closed down.[59] Bimson came to power in the backlash from the dyers' helpers' strike in 1902. His specific mandate as police chief was to keep the Italians in line.

The defeat of the 1902 strikers changed the approach of the Italians as well. Treated like the enemy, the whole Italian community came together, its emerging unity expressed by the Sons of Italy. Founded in America in 1905, the Sons of Italy was intended to be a fraternal organization for all Italian-Americans, uniting the many local immigrant societies. In 1911 the convention of its New Jersey Lodge met in Paterson; in 1914 the national convention met there, reflecting the strength of the local organization. In 1913 Italian grocers and saloonkeepers united behind Italian dyers' helpers and broad-silk weavers; the entire community, including tradesmen, organized its considerable resources through the Sons of Italy and put them at the disposal of the strikers. "The success of the dyers strike up-to-date," explained the Paterson *Evening News*, "is largely due to the influence of the Sons of Italy, an Italian organization with nearly three thousand members in this city."[60]

The dyers' helpers emerged from their defeat in 1902 with pride in having shown "that patience has its limits, and that a popular furor is above the gun and sword," as an Italian observer put it in 1911,[61] but also with a chastened sense of the limits of violence. The influence of the anarchists within the Italian labor movement had declined even before their publications were closed down by Bimson. During the 1913 strike Haywood observed that the "Italians have showed a spirit seldom credited to their class in this city and they should be congratulated."[62] The restraint demonstrated by the Italian dyers' helpers in 1913, in contrast to their wholesale violence in 1902, has typically been attributed to the influence of the IWW,[63] in accordance with the widespread assumption that the union's speakers were the brains behind the strike. But the dyers' helpers listened to the advice of the IWW speakers only because it dovetailed with their experience. The calling of the militia in 1902, the promotion of Bimson, the expansion and modernization of the police force, and the administrative reform designed to give Bimson a free hand had visibly altered the balance of power in Paterson. After 1902 the dye workers could no longer hope to hold the city by force. From the beginning of the 1913 strike, Captain McBride liked to point out that the police, aided by their telephone system and automobiles, could reach any point in the city in five minutes and were prepared to finish anything the Italians might start.[64] Although straightforward violence could hurt the manufacturers and the police who now served directly under them, it could no longer win a strike. The disciplined militance of the Italian dyers' helpers in 1913, which Tresca reinforced, was their own response to the changed situation in Paterson.

Tresca, who was born in southern Italy, had come to the United States in 1904 as a revolutionary fugitive and remained an Italian revolutionary. He never became comfortable speaking English, but in Paterson he moved in and out of the Italian community with ease. Prosecutor Michael Dunn later blamed "the foreign element" in the strike for its aggressiveness and asserted that "the man who was at the bottom of inciting most of that disposition and that temper was this man Tresca. I think he is one of the worst men in the United States to-day."[65] In Paterson, Tresca—aggressive but disciplined—was arrested seven times and never convicted.[66] Combining traditional Italian activism with the industrial unionism of the IWW, he was the perfect person to express the mood of Paterson's fighting Italian community.

Among the major groups of strikers in Paterson in 1913, the dyers' helpers came closest to the popular image of near-starving workers who strike in the desperate hope of increasing their wages. But what needs to be emphasized is the extent to which their strike behavior went beyond the mere reflex of their economic condition. Dyers' helpers from Holland, who were purely agricultural in background and lacked any militant inheritance, were far more likely than the Italians to be strikebreakers in 1913.[67] The Italian dyers' helpers were inspired by an immigrant tradition of violent revolt which, in Paterson, was broadened by ethnic oppression and tempered by experience in battle. In 1913 they went beyond violence and made themselves into an effective strike force.

BROAD-SILK WEAVERS

Paterson's silk workers in 1913 were no raw mass, waiting to be molded by the IWW. Both the ribbon weavers and the Italian dyers' helpers had traditions of their own, which shaped their responses to the manufacturers, to the police, and to the IWW. Despite their great contributions to the strike, however, the dyers' helpers and ribbon weavers did not begin it. It was the broad-silk weavers who triggered the strike of 1913 and succeeded in transforming it into a general strike. In a sense they contained within their own history the militant traditions of both the ribbon weavers and the dyers' helpers. Like the ribbon weavers, broad-silk weavers were heirs to a craft tradition that went back to the handloom weavers. Like the dyers' helpers, broad-silk weavers were heirs to traditions of collective protest and radical ideology brought by new immigrants from southern and eastern Europe. Uniting the craftsmen's experience in shop struggles with the communal rebelliousness of Paterson's new immigrants, the broad-silk weavers were ideally situated within the silk industry to inaugurate its first general strike.

Most broad-silk weavers had been textile workers in Europe. In 1910, 85 percent of the immigrant Jewish men working in the silk industry in Paterson had worked with textiles in the old country, as had 78 percent of the men and over 50 percent of the women from northern Italy.[68] Joseph Hoffspiegel was born in 1889 in Lodz, Poland, where his father had woven wool "by hand. Over here, it was machines." Migrating to Paterson, Joseph and his father became broad-silk weavers, as did many immigrant weavers.[69] "Because the wool isn't any different: the picks are there, everything is there," explains Carrie Golzio; only "the handling of it" was different. Carrie's mother and father had worked with wool in Biella and became broad-silk weavers in Paterson. When she was ten years old, Carrie began to accompany her father to his Paterson mill, where he was a Jacquard weaver. "I went in there to learn how to weave . . . I remember he'd go up on the machine and he'd fix the needle and he'd say to me down at the bottom pull the string down there."[70] In Paterson in 1913 Joseph Hoffspiegel and Carrie Golzio were second-generation broad-silk weavers, whose parents had participated in labor conflicts on both sides of the Atlantic and who, as experienced weavers in their twenties, were themselves prepared to fight to advance themselves and their kind. The alliance between Jews like Hoffspiegel and Piedmontese like Golzio grew out of the similarity of their experience and became one of the great strengths of the 1913 strike.

The Jews, like the Piedmontese, were veterans of class struggle. As early as 1878, Jewish textile workers had participated in huge strikes in Bialystok, Poland. "In those quiet, still times," a Jewish socialist wrote, "when Jewish workers throughout Russia were sound asleep, dreaming of the Messiah and the world to come, we Bialystok workers were already waging economic battles, beating up the industrialists, breaking looms, striking, struggling."[71] Weavers from Bialystok tended to be secular, cooperative, and socialistic. Max Gerstein, a Paterson 1913 striker, had been a textile weaver in Bialystok; he was sent to Siberia for his political activity in the 1905 revolution, escaped, and emigrated to Paterson; there he became a broad-silk weaver, an active member of both the Socialist Party and the Workmen's Circle (a Jewish fraternal organization "steeped in the Socialist traditions" and strongly pro-union), and a founding member of the Purity Cooperative Bakery, which played a key role in the 1913 strike.[72] The Jews from Lodz had a reputation in Paterson of being even more radical than those from Bialystok. In 1905 a series of intense mass meetings, strikes, and growing demonstrations united Jewish and Polish textile workers in Lodz against Christian and Jewish manufacturers, until cavalry and foot soldiers violently crushed the movement. Fleeing the draft, the counterrevolution, and pogroms, Jewish textile workers carried their skills and revolutionary idealism from Lodz to Paterson.[73]

Like the Piedmontese and the English and French before them, the first Jewish weavers who came to Paterson maintained ties to their hometowns that made it easier for others to follow. Jews migrated to Paterson in large numbers only after the turn of the century; by 1910 there were between 3,000 and 5,000 working in the silk industry, mostly in broad-silk weaving. Class struggle, which brought the Italians together as a community, split the Jews in Paterson, as it had split them in Lodz. In 1913 there were actually not one but two Paterson Jewish communities. Those who had come from Germany in the late nineteenth century were often owners or managers of silk mills and formed a Jewish upper class; to the newcomers from Poland, the German Jews seemed more German than Jewish. As Polish Jews moved into Paterson's Jewish neighborhood, in the heart of the city—"Jewtown," as it came to be called—the German Jews moved out to the fashionable East Side. Jewishness no more united these older and newer immigrants than Catholicism united the Irish and Italians. Soon there was a "big shul" for the Jewish merchants and broad-silk manufacturers and a "little shul" for the Jewish broad-silk weavers and other working-class people.[74]

The Jews from Poland organized through the Workmen's Circle, just as the Italians were uniting through the Sons of Italy. In each case, the decisive experience for the new immigrants, shaping their sense of community, was the experience of ethnic and class oppression. As the latest comers to Paterson's broad-silk mills, Jews were generally given the plainest quality and lowest-paid work. "The Russian Hebrews were willing to work for lower wages and in worse surroundings than the English-speaking people, or even the Italians," reported the federal Immigration Commission in 1911, adding that "they are inferior to all of the other races now employed in the mills."[75] The leading role played by Jews in the 1912 broad-silk strike and by Italians and Jews in the 1913 general strike refuted their supposed willingness to be exploited. A spokesman for the 1913 strike explained that "the manufacturers of Paterson for years have been trying to get the Italians and Jewish workers into the silk because they could get them to work cheaper than the others"; now that they had proved to be the most militant of the workers on strike, "the manufacturers would like to get . . . them out of the silk but they will find that impossible."[76]

Once again, skilled immigrants were perceived as troublesome and unmanageable, as the English had been. Their skills were still vital in the twentieth century and not easily replaced: "The quality of production increases with experience," acknowledged a broad-silk manufacturer in 1924. According to data from his Connecticut mill, broad-silk weavers reached their highest quantity of production after ten to twenty years and attained their peak in quality only after a total of twenty to thirty years, maintaining that level of quality, "without a falling off worth mentioning," through their fiftieth year of weaving.[77] At the same time, unlike earlier immigrants, Jews and Italians faced discrimination on the job and throughout Paterson. The daughter of a weaver from Lodz noticed—and never forgot—how her first-grade teacher, who was Irish, singled out the Jewish and Italian children, putting a plaster across their mouths when they made a noise.[78] It was because the Jews and Italians refused to be silent that the 1913 strike took on the aspect of the rising of whole communities. The "Wops and Jews," as Bimson's police called them, had been treated as inferiors by the authorities, the manufacturers, and the AFL unions. Their militant background and their similar experience in Paterson encouraged them to draw together across ethnic lines.[79]

The powerful alliance between Italians and Jews and their somewhat shakier alliance with English-speaking weavers were initially forged in the crucible of the broad-silk industry, in response to the manufacturers' attempts to increase loom assignments. In Paterson the Piedmontese and Jews found themselves, for the first time, tending power looms in a technologically advanced industry and vulnerable to further improvements in the work process. There were no automatic silk looms that would change the shuttle or quill or bobbin by themselves. But the almost universal use of filling stop motion (which stopped the loom when the thread in the shuttle broke) and the increasing use of warp stop motion (which stopped the loom when a warp end broke) tempted broad-silk manufacturers to increase the number of looms assigned to each weaver.[80] Pennsylvania and New England broad-silk manufacturers had doubled the loom assignments in the years before 1913, and the Paterson broad-silk manufacturers were arguing that in order to compete on plain silks they would have to do the same.[81] This threat provided a basis for unity among all Paterson broad-silk weavers. Seeing their trade becoming progressively degraded, English, Piedmontese, and Jewish broad-silk weavers joined together in 1913 against the stretch-out.

The stretch-out, or increase in loom assignments, first became an issue for the broad-silk weavers in the early 1880s with the change from hand to power looms. The labor movement in broad silk began, before the coming of the Italians or the Jews, as a protest of the skilled weavers against the increase from one to two looms. This tradition of protest, and the system of values on which it rested, continued to inform the struggle of the broad-silk weavers. Their objection was not to improved machinery but to the fundamental inequality that enabled manufacturers to secure the benefits of improvements for themselves. In 1881 a skilled weaver noticed that "every month the bosses increase the . . . improvements in machinery and thus the workers can tend to more machines and produce more. But the general complaint in all mills is, that for producing two thirds more the workers only get one third more pay."[82]

The insistence on his right to be paid in proportion to his productivity was a trademark of the artisan weaver. In 1913, speaking in the still recognizable tones of the skilled weaver, the Central Strike Committee made the same point: "The manufacturers must realize that the improvement of machinery means something besides increasing the already swollen fortunes of a few unscrupulous and money-mad barons. That the toiler who feeds and clothes the world must have a fairer and more just share of the wealth he creates. This they demand as a right, not as a favor."[83] From the 1880s through 1913 there was a continuous thread of protest by broad-silk weavers against the manufacturers' attempts to monopolize the benefits of increasing productivity.

Beyond protest, the intellectual triumph of the broad-silk weavers was to grasp the logic of what had been done to them in order to prevent it from being done again. In the 1880s their resistance to the doubling of loom assignments had been ineffective for two reasons. Striking in isolated shops, they were easily defeated; the remedy for this was to strike together. But they were defeated also because they were tempted by the higher wages which, at first, resulted from working two looms. Even though wages fell behind productivity, they still rose; the weaver who worked two looms made more money than the weaver who worked one. But the wage increase was temporary, lasting only so long as the manufacturers were winning acceptance for the heavier loom assignments. Afterward, profiting from the higher productivity and the resulting surplus of labor, the manufacturers gradually reduced piece rates until weavers were running two looms for virtually the price of one. This problem was harder to solve. Its solution depended on the ability of the broad-silk weavers to analyze the long-term tendencies of increased loom assignments and to reject as a group the short-term advantages offered by the manufacturers. If some weavers agreed to work a larger loom assignment in return for higher aggregate pay, it would stampede the others to submit. A chance for successful opposition depended on a near-impossible unity of the more and the less skilled—among the English-speaking, Italian, and Jewish weavers. Between 1911 and 1913 the broad-silk weavers of Paterson achieved this seeming impossibility.

In 1910 one Paterson broad-silk manufacturer increased the loom assignment of some of his weavers to four. Henry Doherty had built a new mill—the biggest in the Paterson area—and equipped the looms with automatic warp stop motion, arranging them so that each weaver could tend two looms in front and two behind. Doherty received prior approval from the AFL's United Textile Workers (which had organized most of his weavers): he would use four looms only on the plain forms of broad silk, and four-loom weavers would make more money than two-loom weavers—though not twice as much. But when Doherty began to implement his plan, his weavers twice went out on strike. Ordered back by union officials, they turned to another union, Local 25 of the Socialist Labor Party. Striking again in 1912, they reached out to other broad-silk weavers and other issues.[84] When the new union's settlement of the 1912 strike left the original issue of four looms unresolved, the three- and four-loom system spread in Doherty's mill to less plain forms of silk and in Paterson to several other broad-silk mills. In January 1913 Doherty's broad-silk weavers went on strike yet again. This time they turned to Local 152 of the IWW. And this time they took out all the broad-silk weavers with them.

But why did Doherty's weavers repeatedly strike, against the dictates of their first union and despite the mistakes of their second? And why did the other weavers increasingly support them in resisting the four-loom system? It was not primarily a question of the difficulty of the work itself. Weaving was not heavy work; rather it was "tedious work," as one weaver put it, "and a man's nerves must be on the tense all day, and he has to be right there on the job with the work he does."[85] Tending four broad-silk looms in place of two made a weaver more tense and was harder on the eyes but was not impossible. Nor was it simply a question of wages: in the short run, four looms did indeed pay better than two. It was because they understood the long-term effect of the larger loom assignment that Doherty's weavers repeatedly struck and the other broad-silk weavers joined them.

With each weaver producing twice as much, fewer weavers would be needed. Adolph Lessig, a broad-silk weaver, explained the process to the Commission on Industrial Relations in 1914: "If the thing became general throughout the trade, the three and four looms, it meant the filling of the street with unemployed, which would mean a general reduction in wages, and that is what all the weavers realized." When asked by a commission member how the employers originally persuaded weavers to run two looms instead of one, Lessig answered: "By the same methods and process Mr. Doherty is using today, by appealing to the hungriest of the workers and making him believe that he is always going to continue on making that same amount of money." Drawing on their history in Paterson, the broad-silk weavers were able, as a group, to resist the lure of temporarily higher wages.

> THOMPSON: If the rates of pay offered to the workers who would remain had been sufficient, would there still have been a complaint that the weavers would have refused to use the new system?
> LESSIG: Well, the workers all realized that it was only a matter of time: that the wages must come down if they were going to have that army of unemployed. They were wise enough to see that.[86]

When a writer for the *Survey* visited Paterson in 1913, strikers told her that the four-loom system in broad silk would cause unemployment, "as did the installation of the two-loom system." They also told her, she reported, that "the logical consequence" of the new loom assignments and of the increasing employment of women and children would be "a forcing down of wages until the Paterson average . . . became as low as the Pennsylvania average."[87] Historians who contrast the long-range idealistic goals of the IWW with the supposedly short-range bread-and-butter goals of the striking weavers have missed this point. In the short run, many weavers stood to gain from the four-loom system, particularly those who embraced it first. Yet on February 25 both broad-silk weavers in mills already touched by the three- and four-loom system and those in mills not yet affected by it responded together to the call for the general strike. It is true that some of the Doherty weavers who were already working four looms were reluctant to strike; the single call for violence on February 25, later used to convict Quinlan, was uttered by a worried shop chairman from the Doherty mill.[88] But the broad-silk weavers in 1913 were able to subordinate their differences to their common and long-range interest. They were wise enough to do that.

Newspaper accounts of the outbreak of the 1913 strike denied that the broad-silk weavers showed wisdom. The strike was "a protest against new and improved machinery," wrote a New York *Times* reporter from Paterson on February 25. In fact, no improved machinery was involved in the speedup except the automatic stop motion, which was not new. But the reporter was eloquent in defense of the manufacturers' point of view. Improved machinery "permits fifty silk weavers to do the work that formally required 100." The weavers were blind opponents of progress, the Luddites of the twentieth century, according to the *Times*. Their strike call on the grounds that four looms would cause unemployment served only "to show how futile the strike is and how hopeless it is to expect that modern machinery can be eliminated because weavers don't like to lose their old positions." Explicitly following the lead of the Paterson Board of Trade, which was dominated by silk manufacturers, the *Times* concluded that "the introduction of the newest machinery was being opposed by the same protests which marked the introduction of the weaving machines in England in the last years of the eighteenth century."[89]

Against this version of the origin of the strike—the version of the manufacturers—should be set the version of the Central Strike Committee, published in April.

> The manufacturers endeavor with specious arguments to establish the system under the guise of progress. Let us see. In the broadsilk, with the same looms, without a single improvement under the same general working conditions, the weaver is today asked to operate four looms instead of two, as formerly. Is this progress?

The Strike Committee argued that broad-silk weavers would end up producing more goods, working harder, and making less money. In ribbon weaving "the same condition obtains in aggravated form, for, unlike the broad-silk loom, the ribbon loom in the last few years has increased in productiveness three hundred per cent, while the earnings of the weavers has decreased in about the same ratio, and still they ask why do men throw bombs?" Briefly turning (for the benefit of "the average citizen") to the history of the textile industry in New England, the Strike Committee sketched the continual improvement in machinery there and the corresponding increase in production and in cost of living, while "wages remain about the same as thirty years ago" and would be even lower if not for the "long, insistent and bitter warfare" waged by textile workers. What had happened in New England was now happening in Paterson, "but then, of course, there is progress. If four looms mean progress, then six looms. But what's the use?"[90]

The broad-silk weavers fought not against progress but for a progress that would not be against them. To have a chance of success, they needed more than unity among themselves; they needed unity among all the silk workers. In 1902 broad-silk workers had remained at work (albeit somewhat reluctantly) during the big dye workers' strike; during the broad-silk weavers' strike of 1912, the dye workers had returned the compliment. Amid rumors that they were going to join the broad-silk weavers in 1912, the dyers' helpers had been offered "an increase of wages of one dollar a week. In this way the talk of going on strike was abolished," explained a dye worker. "Many of the workers appreciated the generosity of employers, but there were amongst the wiser ones dissatisfaction and they considered it a great insult. They did not fail to see that the advance in wages was thrown at them as a robber would throw a bone to a barking dog."[91] In 1913, having seen their gain of the previous year whittled away, the dyers' helpers went out as a body in support of the broad-silk weavers. They had learned what the Jews and Italians within the broad-silk industry had learned and what the IWW speakers would never tire of repeating: that each trade or group within the industry as a whole could advance only if they all joined together, as a class.

THE DYERS' HELPERS AND RIBBON WEAVERS JOIN THE STRIKE

The unity between different nationalities, first achieved by the broad-silk weavers, was one essential ingredient of the 1913 general strike. The other essential ingredient was the achievement of unity between the different crafts. The basis for solidarity between dyers' helpers and broad-silk weavers was developed by militant silk workers in the months preceding the strike and centered on the movement for an eight-hour day. Resistance to four looms directly involved only broad-silk weavers, but the demand for the eight-hour day expressed in radical fashion the hopes of all silk workers for steadier work, more bargaining power, and better conditions and wages.

Weavers in Paterson worked a ten-hour day, and five hours on Saturday; workers in the dye houses often worked double shifts. The idea of eight hours was attractive to weavers and dyers' helpers not only because it meant more rest and leisure but also because it promised less unemployment. "There is no other way to give employment to those deprived of work except by reducing the hours of those employed," a Paterson labor leader had argued in the 1880s.[92] During the national campaign for the eight-hour day in the 1880s, some Paterson weavers had articulated the alternative political economy implicit in the demand. "The eight-hour system would give us steadier work," said a ribbon weaver, and a broad-silk weaver agreed that it would "give employment to unemployed workmen."[93] A quarter of a century later, in November 1912, Paterson Local 152 of the IWW appealed to fellow silk workers in identical terms. "THE EIGHT HOUR WORK DAY FOR ALL SILK WORKERS would compel the bosses to hire more workers to get the work done. The unemployed would find work, and you KNOW that with no workers looking for work we could compel the bosses to give us more wages, better treatment, better light, etc."[94]

This appeal, and the three months of organizing that followed, represented Local 152's contribution to the national campaign for the eight-hour day declared by the IWW in 1911. In fact, the national IWW never came near its goal of pulling together a countrywide demonstration for the eight-hour day, but the Paterson silk workers responded. In the 1913 strike, and for years afterward, they made a reduction in hours their central, unifying demand.[95]

Although broad-silk weavers and male ribbon weavers, who were paid by the piece, supported the demand for eight hours, it was the dyers' helpers— who were paid by the week and would profit directly from a reduction of hours without a reduction in wages—who took up the issue and made it their own. Prior to the strike, their shop delegates had already agreed that eight hours would be their key demand.

On Tuesday morning, February 25, broad-silk weavers went to work at the usual time of seven o'clock, then left work one hour later, as planned, and marched to Turn Hall. They were all encouraged as they listened to the shop delegates make their reports—a total of almost 5,000 broad-silk weavers had quit work that morning, according to the shop reports—but the biggest applause greeted the news that a few dye workers had already joined the strike.[96] On Wednesday and Thursday more dyers' helpers and dyers came out. But the big break came on Friday at the Weidmann plant, where a force of private detectives had been hired in an all-out effort to keep the men at work. After a few hundred dyers' helpers walked out and the gates were closed behind them to prevent anyone else from following, the men who had walked out came back to their jobs, hoping to win over more workers. "The boss then ordered several wagons full of frankfurters and sauerkraut to appease the men. The workers ate them, opened the gates and then, over a thousand strong, marched to the Union headquarters at Turn Hall."[97] The adherence of the dyers' helpers, Italian and unskilled, to a strike called by broad-silk weavers was tremendously significant; it was "one of the biggest achievements of the current struggles," said the Paterson *Evening News*.[98] In the next few days all the dyers' helpers joined the strike. By March 4, when they assembled en masse to formally adopt the eight-hour day as their central strike demand and to commit themselves to remain on strike until the broad-silk weavers won their demand for abolition of the four-loom system, it was already apparent that the remaining supplies of dyed silk would soon be used up and that the silk mills would not be able to reopen until the dyers' helpers went back to work.[99]

The IWW outside speakers did not create unity among the Paterson silk workers; the silk workers, including those in Local 152 of the IWW, created their own unity. Solidarity was a reasoned response to their prior experiences. This was what Bimson did not understand. He did not take the strikers' demands seriously. To him, as to the manufacturers and the New York *Times*, the strike was merely a disturbance. Strikers could not stop progress; their job was to make silk, not history. To limit the disturbance, he believed, he had only to separate the strikers from their out-of-town shepherds and herd them back to work.

In fact, the reaction of the silk workers to Bimson's use of force immeasurably strengthened the strike and brought the ribbon weavers into it. The response to the police action troubled the *Times* reporter on the very first day. The strikers allowed out-of-town speakers and pickets to be arrested, "but for many hours after the arrests the strikers moved in disorganized masses about the town, threatening the police and the Mayor, and denouncing the treatment accorded them." The agitation continued into the night: "Detectives on duty tonight in the district where the silk weavers live brought in word that secret meetings were going on in many of the houses and that the strikers seemed much agitated and alarmed. About 2,000 more had joined the strike tonight."[100]

Throughout the first week Bimson's tactics continued to agitate the silk workers. On Wednesday, February 26, he approached Turn Hall with fifty patrolmen and four mounted policemen. Inside, he climbed up on the platform to read the riot act to the assembled strikers, and to warn them that he would regard picketing as disorderly conduct.[101] On Thursday at Turn Hall the Socialist Party's New Jersey secretary, Wilson Killingbeck, challenged the ban on out-of-town speakers and denounced the repressive actions of the police, until Bimson had him pulled from the platform. Bimson was still insisting that "the strikers . . . will not be permitted to bring out-of-town men here."[102] On Friday morning the Passaic *Weekly Issue*, published by the Passaic County Socialists, was ready with a headline that asked, "Shall Police Chief Bimson override Constitution?" Bimson answered by ordering the patrol wagon to Socialist headquarters, where four policemen confiscated all 5,000 copies of the paper. That night, Alexander Scott, editor of the *Weekly Issue*, read his offending article to 6,000 silk workers in Paterson's largest hall. "When I got through, I was put under arrest by these two detectives and was taken to the police station through the streets, with a jeering crowd of strikers of about 3,000 following me. They were jeering at the policemen; not me."[103]

At the same big Friday night meeting, Killingbeck asked for a vote of thanks for Bimson, "the man who won our strike." Later, he explained that "when the constitution was abrogated by the authorities, in closing down the halls, arresting speakers and clubbing citizens, such a feeling of disgust arose among the workers that it became a very simple matter to call out shop after shop."[104] Flynn agreed with this analysis. The attempts at police repression, she told the strikers in March, had solidified their ranks; shops that originally had not wanted "agitators" to address them now called on the strike committee for speakers.[105] By the beginning of the second week of the general strike about 500 silk workers a day were joining Local 152; the dye houses and broad-silk mills were shut down; and Flynn, Tresca, and Quinlan were again addressing daily meetings of the strikers at Turn Hall and Helvetia Hall. Asked why he was not carrying through his threats about preventing the outside agitators from speaking in Paterson, Bimson looked "somewhat crestfallen," according to the New York *Call*. "What's the use," he said. "I did the best I could."[106]

Bimson's attempt to use force to prevent Flynn, Tresca, and Quinlan from speaking brought out the ribbon weavers, particularly. During the first week, while the dyers' helpers were joining the strike, delegates from the various ribbon shops were in contact with the Strike Committee. On Monday evening, March 3, and again on Tuesday evening, March 4, the ribbon weavers gathered by themselves in Helvetia Hall to debate the question of joining the general strike. The Tuesday meeting lasted late into the night and resulted in the decision to strike. What pushed the ribbon weavers over the edge was their outrage at Bimson's violation of their rights. Historically, Turn Hall and Helvetia Hall had been the meeting places of Paterson's workers. How could the police dictate who could speak there or under what conditions they might remain open? Veterans of Paterson's labor movement, the skilled ribbon weavers expected that their customary and constitutional rights would be respected during strikes. When Bimson violated these rights, he served notice that everything Paterson's silk workers had won over the years was under attack. Commenting on "the rapid spread of the strike," Louis Magnet, the spokesman for Paterson's ribbon weavers, asserted that "the action of the city authorities in trying to suppress the constitutional right of free speech had a great deal to do with inciting . . . those law-abiding, liberty-loving Americans who believe that the constitutional rights of each and every citizen should be preserved under any circumstances."[107] "The ribbon weavers, the aristocrats of the industry, decided to come out in support of the general strike," exulted *Solidarity*. "This almost unprecedented situation is largely the result of the resentment of the working class against the high handed and outrageous action of the police."[108]

During the second week, celebrating the remarkable spread of the strike, the New York *Call* gave credit where credit was due. Chief Bimson and Mayor McBride, it said,

> have seen the work of their hands in the tying up of the entire trade of the city, the idle silk mills and dyehouses, the impossibility of procuring scabs— there are heroes enough of the breed, but they haven't the necessary skill. . . .
>
> When the first move was made by a small number of strikers, [Bimson and McBride] persuaded themselves that it was more a foolish childish prank than anything else; that the workers had no grievance and that under the circumstances they should be caned like naughty children and sent back to the looms. . . . The outside agitators were rounded up. . . . Bimson was hailed by the local press as the savior of Paterson society. Leave it to old Bimson. Who said he was too old for the job? Had he been in command years ago, at the time of the previous trouble, there would have been no trouble. He knows how to handle these malcontents who give Paterson a bad name. He doesn't talk—he acts. . . .
>
> And Bimson did all that was expected of him—and a little more for good measure—and he succeeded—in tying up the silk industry of Paterson.[109]

Bimson had indeed miscalculated. His reliance on force and his focus on the outside agitators were based on the assumption—shared by the manufacturers, the ministers, and the mayor—that the silk workers could not act on their own behalf. This assumption would prove costly. The unprecedented unity forged by the broad-silk weavers, dyers' helpers, and ribbon weavers in the first two weeks of the strike would last for almost five months—despite the pressure of hunger and the increasing temptation of individual shop settlements—and would deprive the city of enormous funds and the manufacturers of their spring and fall seasons.

From the beginning, the strike belonged to the silk workers themselves. Before Flynn and Tresca said a word to them, the basic direction had been laid down. The calling of the strike, the aggressiveness of the workers, their intelligence and tactical flexibility all preceded the coming of the national IWW leaders to Paterson. And yet, when we turn from the national leaders of the IWW to the members of Local 152, the distinction between what belonged to the silk workers and what belonged to the IWW begins to break down. It was not Flynn or Haywood but Lessig who was a broad-silk weaver; he had been weaving cotton and silk since the 1880s. Moving to Paterson in 1902, he had belonged for a time to the AFL United Textile Workers, then joined the IWW shortly after it was founded. Lessig was a class-conscious union man. Asked his religion on the occasion of one of his numerous arrests, he replied: "None, except the labor movement."[110] In 1913 he was working full time as a broad-silk weaver in the David mill, heading silk workers' Local 152, and organizing for it.

Ewald Koettgen was the only full-time local organizer. Of German background, like Lessig, Koettgen had worked in Paterson as a ribbon weaver from the 1890s. In 1912, after the Lawrence victory, he was elected by the Paterson IWW locals as their paid organizer. His militance and commitment to the IWW (he had joined shortly after its creation and by 1912 was serving on its national board) resulted from his years of experience as a weaver in Paterson. In 1913 he was about forty years old, "a tall, gaunt man with deep lines in his face" who had the reputation of never resting; he was "out with the pickets at six in the morning and not home again until late at night."[111] In January 1913, he was elected chairman of the IWW's National Textile Union, partly in recognition of his success in building Local 152, which had grown to almost 500 members.[112]

Local 152 did not call the Doherty strike that began in late January 1912; like so many previous strikes in Paterson, it was called by the workers in the shop. In fact, the rapid spread of the 1913 strike from the Doherty mill to the entire silk industry took Koettgen by surprise. In January, reporting on the work of the IWW in Paterson, he emphasized the organization of Paterson's shirtwaist workers into Local 210 and Flynn's speech to its members. Only at the end of his report did he mention silk workers' Local 152, noting that it was continuing its campaign against the four-loom system and for the eight-hour day.[113] Like Flynn, he had no idea of the explosion that was about to occur in the silk industry. But the existence of Local 152 and its ties to militant workers in many mills, including the Doherty mill, helped focus the explosion when it came. The small IWW shop committees sounded out people in their mills and dye houses on the question of turning the Doherty walkout into a general strike. Encouraged by the favorable response, Local 152 organized a series of mass meetings, formed an Executive Strike Committee of fifteen to twenty silk workers, and assembled a Central Strike Committee of 125 silk workers (later almost 300), a majority of whom were not members of the IWW. It was these committees that called the general strike for February 25, arranged for the meeting in Turn Hall, and invited the national IWW to send speakers to encourage the strikers and instruct them in the techniques used so successfully in Lawrence.[114]

Local militants planned the general strike, organized it, began and controlled it. Most were not paid, as was Koettgen, nor were they officers of the local, as was Lessig. Unknown at the time, they remain largely unknown. One member of the Executive Strike Committee who testified before the Commission on Industrial Relations may have been fairly typical. Edward Zuersher was born in Yonkers, where his father was a ribbon weaver. The family moved to Paterson in the late 1880s, and Zuersher began weaving ribbon there around 1903. In 1913 he was a militant member of the IWW and (like many ribbon weavers) also a Socialist. During the 1914 hearings Zuersher surprised the commission by maintaining that local people possessed enough skill and practical knowledge to run the big strike; Haywood and the other national IWW leaders had been needed, he added, only to address the mass meetings.[115]

This was news in 1914—and is still news. Overemphasizing the importance of Haywood, most historians have overlooked the decisive role played in the strike by local silk workers like Zuersher, Magnet, Golzio, Lessig, and Koettgen. Haywood did not make the same mistake. "The silk workers are fortunate in having Local No. 152 as a nucleus around which to form their organization," he wrote. "This Local was largely composed of seasoned veterans of the labor movement"; as a result, the Paterson silk workers were able to organize in 1913 "without relying much on outside help."[116] Eventually, when the strike became deadlocked and food scarce, the Paterson strikers would come to depend more heavily on the outside speakers for their eloquence and their ties to other sympathetic groups. But in the crucial formative weeks immediately preceding and following February 25, the contribution of the outsiders was minimal. In a sense, their greatest contribution was that they recognized and encouraged the abilities of the silk workers.

When Haywood arrived in Paterson on March 7, he found the weaving mills and dye houses already shut down and the strike well organized. Because he could see that there was little for him to do, he returned for a while to Akron, to resume the more difficult task of trying to organize striking rubber workers there. During this brief initial stay in Paterson he stressed familiar IWW themes. "I have come to Paterson not as a leader," he told the strikers in Turn Hall. "There are no leaders in the IWW; this is not necessary. You are the members of the union and you need no leaders. I come here to give you the benefit of my experience throughout the country." And by way of emphasis, he added: "The union belongs to you." From the gallery, a voice cried out in English: "And we're going to keep it, too."[117]

CHAPTER TWO

The Strike as a Way of Life

The strike spread almost uncontrollably through Paterson's silk industry. Energy and momentum were on the strikers' side. Victory seemed inevitable and not far away. But this explosion of energy was in fact contained; the strike waves reached their outer limits within a few weeks and slowly began to recede, leaving the power of the enemy increasingly visible. Settling down, creating its own institutions, the strike became almost routine. By the same token, it became a way of life.

THE LIMITS OF THE STRIKE

"It is expected the silk production in and about Paterson will be completely paralyzed," wrote a correspondent for *Solidarity*, "and that the workers' demands will be granted in a short time."[1] Reporting during the first week of the strike, the correspondent was reacting not only to the successful walkout in broad silk but also to the growing support for the strike in other branches of Paterson's silk industry. Like many of the strikers, he thought it was going to be easy; the really difficult work of preparation was over, and everything was falling into place. When the dyers' helpers joined the strike at the end of the first week and the ribbon weavers during the second, optimism appeared justified. "The general impression is that the bosses will be forced to yield," observed the New York *Call*, "for they were badly hit during their busiest season."[2] The silk workers and IWW speakers believed that a complete shutdown of Paterson's silk industry would soon lead to victory; they assumed that the manufacturers would not be willing to lose their spring season. "In the opinion of every leader of the strike and many of those who are taking an active part . . . if the strikers remain out for another week they will have won their fight," noted the Paterson *Evening News*.[3]

The inability of the manufacturers and police, despite their frantic efforts, to halt or even slow the spread of the strike confirmed the strikers' optimism. Even the hard-silk workers, mostly unskilled boys and girls, joined the walkout during the second week, while the highly skilled loomfixers and twisters were forced out by lack of work. By the end of the second week, strike leaders estimated that 9,000 broad-silk weavers, 6,000 ribbon weavers, 6,000 dyers' helpers, 2,000 hard-silk workers, and 900 loaders, warpers, and quillers were out, for a total of 24,000. When mill-supply workers, their jobs hampered by the effects of the strike, decided at the end of the third week to join and make their own demands, Koettgen observed that "this will mean about 2,000 more, and will complete the chain from the time the silk reaches the city to the time the finished product leaves the city."[4]

This extraordinarily rapid extension of the broad-silk strike to all branches of the silk industry *in* Paterson, exhilarating as it was to the silk workers and Wobbly speakers, tended to give them an overly optimistic view of their power *outside* Paterson. "Workers never before on strike, in certain departments and mills, have this time joined the general movement, which it is expected, will spread to other silk centers and result in complete paralysis of the industry."[5] But the expectation of spreading the strike to other silk centers was never fully realized. The Paterson strikers and Wobbly organizers knew much more about conditions in Paterson than in the other centers; "complete paralysis of the industry" would in fact remain beyond their grasp.

The other silk center that mattered was eastern Pennsylvania. Rivaling Paterson in the quantity of silk weavers and dye workers, if not in the quality of the product, this region had been expanded by the Paterson mill owners precisely to counter the militance of Paterson's silk workers. In 1900 the secretary of the Silk Association had emphasized that silk manufacturers were developing Pennsylvania annexes of their Paterson businesses in order to "diversify" the silk industry "so that labor trouble in one place will not control the whole industry."[6] Therefore, as Koettgen later explained, a general strike in Paterson alone had no chance to win. "Now what is the result if the workers strike only in one locality? The work is immediately shifted to another locality."[7] Or, as Flynn put it, so many Paterson manufacturers had annexes in Pennsylvania that even with their Paterson mills shut down "they could fill a large percentage of their orders unless we were able to strike Pennsylvania simultaneously."[8] Accordingly, during the second week, IWW organizers left for Easton, Williamsport, and Wilkes-Barre, and a group of ten Paterson strikers and an IWW organizer went to Allentown.[9]

In Allentown they met with some immediate success, thanks to the police. "The strike was precipitated by the stupid use of the police who were placed on guard over the mill March 11th. The exploiters were afraid some Paterson men might get in and explode things," wrote an Allentown Socialist. As in Paterson, the police in Allentown helped produce the explosion they feared: "The men were furious at being guarded like convicts." And like the Paterson dye workers, the Italian dye workers walked out as a group, supported by the local Socialists. But unlike the Paterson weavers and dyers, Allentown silk workers had not developed unity among themselves: "Some of the silk workers, who were Socialists, came out, but the great mass would not move."[10] Though the Allentown strikers made the same demands as the Paterson strikers, though 500 of them joined the IWW, though Haywood and Tresca addressed mass meetings in Allentown, the Paterson strikers and the IWW were not able to shut down the silk industry there. The Allentown dyers' helpers supported the Paterson strikers, but their fellow silk workers would not support them.

In Pennsylvania as a whole, the silk workers were not as militant as the Paterson workers had been for decades. They had not created the same traditions of struggle or developed the same unity. It therefore proved more difficult for the Paterson silk workers to expand their strike to Pennsylvania than it had been for the silk manufacturers of Paterson to expand their businesses there. The manufacturers had indeed made a good move. Nevertheless, there were sympathy strikes throughout much of the Pennsylvania silk region, not only in Allentown but nearby in Easton, in the Scranton area, in Williamsport, and in Philadelphia. They were generally short, however; the Pennsylvania strikers were not nearly as determined or committed as their counterparts in Paterson and did not hold out for a general settlement throughout the industry.

The decisive conflict took place in Hazleton, about thirty-five miles northwest of Allentown. The Hazelton strike began not as a sympathy strike but for its own sake, even before the outbreak in Paterson. Early in February 1,200 workers of the Duplan Silk Company struck against the system of fines and for higher wages. Most were coal miners' children between fourteen and eighteen years old; many were Italian; and all were paid about half of what Paterson silk workers earned for the same work. The 1,200 strikers chose the IWW to be their union. Responding to a call from a Hazelton miner who was a Socialist and an IWW sympathizer, Koettgen and other IWW organizers visited Hazleton and gave direction to the strike. But early in March the United Textile Workers of the AFL intervened, challenging IWW leadership and appealing to the strikers' parents to support an AFL-sponsored settlement. Haywood came to fight the AFL, and Quinlan came twice. But the bulk of the strikers voted on April 2 to take the advice of the AFL and settle for a 10 percent wage increase. Because a minority continued to strike and to picket, however, Flynn came to Hazleton for several days to address meetings of the young workers and their parents, and Tresca spoke to the Italian workers. But the IWW was unable to sustain the picketing, and the strike collapsed. In Hazleton, as in Allentown, the Paterson strikers and their supporters failed.[11] With the exception of Philadelphia (an old textile center) and some dye houses in Allentown and elsewhere, the strike did not develop roots in Pennsylvania; there, silk strikers generally settled for what they could get and went back to work. Production in Pennsylvania did fall, as much because of the effect of the Paterson dyers' strike on the availability of dyed goods for weaving as because of the local walkouts. But the almost complete work stoppage achieved in Paterson could not be replicated in Pennsylvania. That fact constituted a serious check to the silk workers' hopes. They could not paralyze the silk industry after all.[12]

The strike news from New York was more encouraging. During the third week, Paterson strikers learned that 300 ribbon weavers of the Smith and Kaufman Company in New York City had gone on strike in sympathy with them. A few days later a delegation of ribbon weavers from Paterson attended a mass meeting of ribbon weavers in New York, and it was decided to pull all the New York shops. From its beginning at Smith and Kaufman, at West 132nd Street in Manhattan, the walkout spread rapidly to West 54th and West 55th Street mills, to College Point, to Brooklyn, and to Astoria (in Queens); by the end of March the ribbon industry in greater New York, encompassing 10,000 workers, was practically shut down. The New York strikers joined the IWW and adopted the Paterson demands—for an eight-hour day and a return to the 1894 price scale. All spring long they sent shop delegates regularly to Helvetia Hall, strike center for Paterson's ribbon weavers, to report on the situation in New York. Within the ribbon branch of the industry, the strike was a decided success. Although the IWW national organizers spent little time organizing in New York, the ribbon mills remained closed there.[13]

In New Jersey there was more good news. At a Paterson subsidiary in Summit (about fifteen miles away), silk workers asked for an organizer from Paterson during the third week of the strike; ten days later they shut down the subsidiary. Nearer Paterson, there were stoppages in Hackensack, Carlstadt, and Pompton Lakes, and 3,000 dyers' helpers walked out in Lodi. Strikes flared west of Paterson in Stirling and in Phillipsburg, and to the east (in Hudson County) in Hoboken and West New York. Months later, when word reached Paterson that silk was being woven for Paterson manufacturers in Hudson County, Flynn and Tresca toured Hoboken, Weehawken, Union Hill, and North Bergen, and with the help of a nucleus of 100 local workers, succeeded in calling out 8,000 employees.[14]

The strike spread also to silk mills even farther from Paterson. Weavers at the Miller Gloria Silk Company in Norwalk, Connecticut, walked out in April and, after meeting with an organizer from Paterson, decided to join the IWW. In May, silk workers in Boston joined the IWW, and a Paterson newspaper reported growing unrest in the silk mills of Buffalo, New York, and New London, Connecticut. In June, word reached Paterson that there were even strikes at the Weidmann dye plants in Europe![15] Carried away by such impressive evidence of solidarity, some participants exaggerated the success of the general strike. Writing in early April, when the defeats in Pennsylvania were not yet evident, Haywood asserted that 50,000 silk workers in New Jersey, Pennsylvania, New York, and Connecticut had joined the strike that the Doherty broad-silk weavers had begun, making it "the closest approach to a general strike that has yet taken place in an American industry."[16] Late in

May, with less excuse, one enthusiast claimed that "until this strike was called, no industry in America had ever been completely tied up by a general strike —the ideal weapon of the militant proletariat. Paterson has demonstrated the power of a general strike in an industry, New Jersey, New York, Connecticut, Pennsylvania, Rhode Island, and Virginia mills and dye houses being either entirely closed down or hopelessly crippled."[17] Had the Paterson strikers and the IWW really closed down or hopelessly crippled the silk industry in Pennsylvania, there would have been no need for sympathy strikes in May; the Paterson strike would have been won, and the victorious strikers would have been back at work.

Within Paterson itself, the strikers seized hopefully on stirrings among workers in industries other than silk, as the excitement of the silk strike and the demand for the eight-hour day touched workers generally. There was strike talk—and sometimes more than talk—among the streetcar men of Paterson, piano makers, hatband workers, molders, shirt-factory employees, machinists, coremakers, and jute mill workers.[18] Both sexes and various ages were involved, and most participants looked to the silk workers as the leaders of the strike movement. Koettgen was meeting with silk workers at Turn Hall on March 3 when he was told someone was waiting for him outside.

> He went out and found a delegation of boys and girls, averaging 14 years of age, who said that they had come over from the Dolphin Jute Mill. . . . "We want strike," eagerly whispered one of the youngest into Koettgen's ear. "We want fight boss: too much work." Similar sentiments were expressed by the girls. . . . They went back to their fellow workers with the message that they should plan to come out in a body, elect a strike committee and send them to the joint board.[19]

But little that was permanent came of these stirrings. Workers at two of the three jute mills did strike for a time, as did some shirt-factory hands, and the coremakers won a raise.[20] Outside the silk industry, however, the workers of Paterson were not bound to each other or to the silk workers by years of common struggle. Their solidarity was broad but not deep. Only the dyers' helpers and broad-silk weavers and ribbon weavers had learned, over the years, how much they needed one another. As the excitement of the first weeks of the strike subsided, they found—to their disappointment—that they could count on no one else.

Gradually, they realized that the strike would not be easily or speedily won. Daily reports from Paterson in the New York *Call*, a Socialist paper, reflected this change of mood. From unrestrained optimism as the strike spread throughout Paterson's silk industry and beyond, the *Call* in the third week implicitly acknowledged the staying power of the manufacturers and began reluctantly to describe the strike situation as "critical," "more intense," and finally "deadlocked."[21] On his first brief visit Haywood sounded a note of realism. Perhaps because he was not yet caught up in the day-to-day excitement of the strike, Big Bill saw the coming deadlock more clearly than those who were directly involved. On March 11, while Quinlan was announcing that "the strike is won," Haywood suggested that "this strike has only begun." It might last twenty weeks, he said prophetically.[22]

But official pronouncements continued to be optimistic, right up to the end. Like most leaders, the strike leaders generally felt obliged to be positive. Victory was almost always presented—at Turn or Helvetia Hall, in speeches at Haledon (a working-class suburb) or articles in the radical press—as a matter of holding out for only a few more weeks. To the strikers, these claims sounded reasonable. With the silk industry shut down in Paterson and plagued elsewhere by sympathy strikes, the manufacturers were clearly hurt. Surely the bosses would not sacrifice their fall season after losing so much of the spring? Even in Lawrence, as almost everyone knew, the wool trust had been able to hold out for only two months before capitulating to the strikers and the IWW. Yet despite official optimism about an early victory, the strikers gradually began to settle down in preparation for extended battle. It was going to be a long strike after all. Bertold Brecht once wrote of the exile whose actions belied his ostensible hopes. "When do you think you'll be going back? / Do you want to know what you really believe in your heart? / . . . Look at the little chestnut tree in the corner of the courtyard / That you carry your canful of water to."[23] In just this way, without ever renouncing hope of early victory, the Paterson strikers began to organize themselves for the long haul.

GETTING ORGANIZED

The police were already organized. During the first week, as the strike spread beyond their control, cots were installed at headquarters so that officers could be on duty twenty-four hours a day; in the third week, with the strike still spreading, more cots were brought in for reserves. Sleep-in police needed to be fed, so a cook was hired on March 3 to serve what the New York *Call* described, accurately enough, as "war rations," with new metal garbage cans used as cooking pots. The police also hired a barber.[24]

The strikers had similar needs: as personal savings became rapidly depleted, they needed to make arrangements for food and for rent; they also needed barbers, doctors, druggists, and lawyers. Food was first. On Tuesday, March 18, three weeks into the strike, the workers established a General Relief Committee. On the same day a local bakery offered to supply needy strikers with bread. The work of self-organization had begun.[25] The General Relief Committee took charge of staffing and running a store where families of strikers could get staple groceries—bread, potatoes, flour, rice—and three restaurants for the single men. Each mill also elected its own relief committee. The system was characteristically democratic, flexible, and time-consuming —but time was the one thing the strikers had in abundance. A request for relief would go to the chairman of the local committee, who verified the number in the striker's family and signed the request. The striker would take this slip to the General Relief Committee (which was also elected) and exchange it for a meal ticket good at one of the restaurants, or for a store order proportional to the size of his or her family. When the striker lived too far from the store, a horse-drawn wagon delivered the groceries.[26]

The bakery that offered bread was the Purity Cooperative Company. Founded in 1905–6 by immigrant Jews, the Purity Cooperative was Paterson's first Jewish bakery. The Workmen's Circle had distributed shares for $5.00 each to its members, who became the stockholders and elected the officers who managed the cooperative. As a Jewish and Socialist institution, the Purity Cooperative backed the strikers wholeheartedly; indeed, most of the support services came from Socialists, Jews, and Italians. The bakery itself donated the flour; its sixteen bakers volunteered their time to make the bread. During the life of the strike some 30,000 loaves of bread were distributed free each week.[27]

Other staples were not free; the General Relief Committee had to buy them wholesale. To feed themselves, therefore, the strikers constantly had to raise money for the committee. Fund-raising became, after meetings and picketing, the most common form of strike activity, involving thousands of people in a variety of roles. Male and female weavers at the two Frank and Dugan mills held a cake sale and turned over $90 to the relief committee. Female weavers from the Miesch mill collected $189 by holding a benefit dance at Helvetia Hall, and a ball sponsored by strikers at Turn Hall netted $600. Benefits like these, run by the strikers themselves, were organized regularly. Strikers also contacted sympathetic actors, musicians, and athletes, who were able to attract large crowds. There was a boxing exhibition, and a benefit football game between the two best teams in the area. A Jewish quartet raised money for the relief fund, and Italian strikers who played the mandolin or guitar toured Newark, Orange, and Union Hill. A gala benefit was organized in Paterson at the Orpheum, featuring movies and "mostly home talent": a juggler, a magician, an opera singer, an "armless wonder." Strikers bearing the official credentials of the Relief Committee solicited contributions and weekly pledges from individuals and businesses in Paterson. A clothier on River Street gave $25 to the strike fund and pledged $5 weekly; his employees together donated $5. Lists of hundreds of local contributors were published weekly by the Paterson *Evening News*, ranging from the twenty-five cents given by one Levi, Robattino, or McCann to the $34.65 collected one week by the employees of the hosiery mill or the $50 provided every week by the Purity Cooperative. The usual contributions of silk workers to local charities were so important and the strikers' efforts at drawing available funds from the community were so effective that the Ladies' Auxiliary of St. Joseph's Hospital decided in April to postpone its annual public appeal until after the strike was settled.[28]

The money raised through the efforts, talents, and sacrifices of so many strikers and their friends did not, however, come close to supporting the strike.

Mills in other parts of New Jersey took collections and sent hundreds of dollars to Paterson,[29] but to feed the strike, $3,000 had to be raised every week. What made this almost possible was the support of the Sons of Italy. Early in the strike more than 500 members of the order, representing nine different Italian organizations, met in Turn Hall to discuss the matter, and on March 16—two days before the formation of the General Relief Committee—the Order of the Sons of Italy voted to levy an assessment on its members sufficient to provide $1,000 a week for the support of the strikers. In the course of the next ten weeks alone, the Sons of Italy contributed $12,000. Like the Jewish Purity Cooperative, the Sons of Italy made it possible for the strikers to eat and to continue striking.[30]

Not that they ate well—all their efforts and the efforts of their local supporters could not raise as much money as they needed. One striking broad-silk weaver, asked years later whether the strikers ate only one meal a day, shook his head and tried to explain. "You ate what you had. It wasn't a question of sitting down and eating meals. You ate whatever you could get."[31] Hunger was the strongest, most constant enemy of the silk strikers—and the one with which they became most intimate in the course of the struggle.

Other, less urgent needs could be satisfied without money. The police department could hire a barber, but the strikers depended on good will and were grateful when James Meola of River Street offered to shave all strikers "every Thursday, free of charge at his place." The Relief Committee provided free medical and dental services (volunteered by a sympathetic doctor and dentist) and free legal counsel and shoe repair. Most strikers could not pay the landlord, but most landlords understood; in fact, the Association of Jewish Landlords formally voted not to evict silk workers while the strike lasted. When other landlords were less understanding, the wagons were available, free of charge, to help an evicted family move. Many families ordinarily kept a boarder to help with expenses. In 1913 most of the boarders were on strike, taking their meals at the restaurants for single men and unable to make their usual contributions to the family economy, but the families kept them anyway and continued to do their washing. In ways such as these—through patience, cooperation, ingenuity, and timely support from nonstrikers, especially Italians, Jews, and Socialists—the Paterson strikers were almost able to take care of their physical necessities.[32]

The long strike also generated other kinds of necessities, however—less tangible but just as real. Morale had to be sustained through months of frustration. Key decisions about strategy—should we settle shop by shop? should we permit open advocacy of sabotage?—had to be made, questioned, and remade. Splits between the different nationalities and different crafts had to be prevented. To meet these needs, the silk workers transformed their rudimentary and spontaneous strike mechanisms into institutions capable of sustaining a long struggle. Mass meetings, with speeches and music, became rituals of renewal. The shop meeting became the place for serious discussion and debate. Picketing, in addition to preventing breaks, became a way of maintaining morale. Uncertain, like Brecht's exile, when they would be "going back," the strikers stopped holding their breath and began to create a new way of living.

By the third week of the strike the walkout was virtually complete; the mills were shut down. But under the pressure of hunger, some people would be tempted to give up and go back to work. Picket lines were necessary to discourage them from yielding to the temptation. The primary function of picketing was to make people feel ashamed if they did go back to work by forcibly reminding them that the community of silk workers knew who they were and regarded them as traitors. Its secondary function was to provide the strikers with a chance to assert publicly their determination to outlast the boss and the police.[33]

Picketing was effective because even the minority of silk workers who wished to work during the strike feared to be identified and condemned as strikebreakers. This fear was not primarily one of violence, although violence—not near the mills, as a rule, but closer to home—did play a role. The deeper fear was of being publicly shamed. In Paterson, the word "scab" was the worst insult that could be flung at a silk worker. The forces of law and order, attempting to protect not only the body but the feelings of anyone returning to work, treated this insult as a crime. Joseph Feltman, a weaver, was arrested while on picket duty at the Stern and Pohly mill at 7:00 A.M. one Monday: "Feltman is being held as a disorderly person," explained the *Evening News*, "inasmuch as the officer claims that he called several of the persons going to work in the mill 'scabs.' "[34] Charles Zeleskie was sentenced to twenty days in the county jail for calling Annie Van Lenten a scab. Throughout the strike, anyone caught in the act of calling someone else a scab could expect to go to jail. Zeleskie himself thanked the judge and returned proudly to his cell.[35] Other strikers, unwilling to do time, resorted to strategems. A daughter of striker Sholem Goldstein recalls that he and several friends would go to the attic of their house on Cliff Street, where they could see strikebreakers going to work in the mill across the street. "They'd go to this attic window, they'd holler SCAB!—and I was little, I was standing there—and then put their heads in, that [the police] shouldn't know it's them." Almost seventy years later, the usually subdued voice of Goldstein's daughter rings out piercingly as she repeats the forbidden word. "That was always in my memory: going up the steps and looking through the window and hollering SCAB!"[36]

For those willing to go to jail, getting arrested became almost routine. "There have been so many arrests," said Alexander Scott, himself arrested many times, "that such things no longer arouse interest."[37] Strikers could be arrested for many things, but picketing itself was the most common cause. Bimson's attempt, at the beginning of the strike, to silence the out-of-town speakers had been defeated by the overwhelming response of the weavers and dyers' helpers. Undaunted, he shifted the target of his attack from free speech to free assemblage, from the halls to the streets. For the first time in Paterson's history the police mounted a sustained challenge to the silk workers' traditional right to picket.[38] Pickets walking in front of a mill were told by police to move on; if they did not, they were arrested. In the beginning the usual charge against them was disorderly conduct. Later, after authorities discovered a 1665 English law that seemed to fit, the charge became unlawful assemblage. Arrested pickets were brought in bunches before Recorder James Carroll, who ordinarily gave them a choice of ten dollars or ten days. In March, while they still had a little money, strikers often paid the fine; as the strike turned into an endurance contest, however, they increasingly chose to be supported by the local government instead of helping to support it. Crowding the jail in time-honored IWW fashion (past a certain point, no new arrests could be made until some strikers were released), the silk workers reaffirmed their right to picket. "When the police would swoop down on the picket-line the pickets would not wait until they were arrested, but they would rush to the patrol wagons and fill up one after the other and go to jail singing the International and other strike songs."[39] A local AFL craft unionist, disgusted with such theatrical tactics, noted that he had seen the police "arrest crowds of 30 or 40, and you would think it was arranged for a moving-picture show. It was such a burlesque, some being taken into the patrol wagons, and some jumping in the patrol wagons, some trying to get in."[40] For the silk workers, picketing and going to jail became a show of strength, a way of dramatizing their cheerful refusal to be driven off the streets or back to work. "And they all went willingly because they figured they were gonna win the strike anyway," remembers a striker who herself went to jail.[41]

Once convicted, pickets were transferred from the city jail to Passaic County Jail, also located in Paterson (the county seat). Meals were served there twice a day: the first was sour bread and acidic coffee; the main course of the second was soup that often had dead insects in it. After finishing their "dinner," prisoners were locked two by two into tiny cells for thirteen and a half hours. Ventilation and sanitation were poor. Each prisoner shared a cup and a tub with nearly fifty other prisoners, some of whom had dangerous diseases. Yet to this awful place—"it takes courage to face a term in the Paterson Bastile," said Haywood, who had had considerable experience with jails[42]—strikers who refused to yield the streets to the police willingly came. Inside, there "was almost a cheer when some comrade came down the steps," for as an Italian prisoner explained, "soon all get arrest', fill up-a jail—can't pinch no more picket. Fine!"[43] After being released, many strikers returned directly to the picket line. "Many cases were reported when the police threw the strikers out of the patrol wagon, saying: 'You get out, I don't want you today, you only came out yesterday.'"[44]

Gradually, the activities of the police and the strikers took on a rhythm of their own. At times, the police routinely urged pickets to move on, with no real animosity or desire to make arrests. At other times, when the order came down, they would aggressively round up bunches of strikers and arrest their speakers. Even then, however, there was little violence. The strikers followed a policy of deliberate and conscious restraint; they knew they only stood to lose if the strike erupted into the kind of bloody confrontation that had marked the 1902 dyers' strike. The police, too, were restrained. In contrast with the private detectives, who were outsiders, many Paterson policemen knew the strikers or even had brothers and sisters among them. They did not really want to hurt anybody; besides, the strikers usually obeyed their orders. As a result, the police never killed or permanently disabled a striker.

The strikers nevertheless felt aggrieved: they believed they had a perfect right to picket and to choose their speakers without interference. When the police bore down on them on horseback, or clubbed them, or called them Wops or Jews, they combined insult with injury. The police were equally aggrieved: they believed that the out-of-town speakers and the pickets should not have been there in the first place. To the police, jeers and stones aimed at them by the strikers, barbs aimed at them by the speakers when they were only doing their jobs, combined insult with injury. Yet the restraint was real on both sides. Warily, like two veteran boxers aware of each other's ability to inflict punishment, the strikers and the police danced around each other, jabbing but not going for the kill.[45]

The strike was not entirely peaceable, but judged by the standard of previous silk strikes in Paterson (like those of 1894 and 1902) or of other strikes during 1913 (like the West Virginia coal miners' strike and the Buffalo trolley strike), the 1913 war in Paterson was waged with relatively little violence. Picketing, calling strikebreakers scabs, serenading them, expelling them from benevolent societies, throwing snowballs or stones at the mills in which they worked, following them home, harassing them, warning their families, stoning their houses, beating up a persistent strikebreaker, and very rarely (and then only when confidence was dwindling, as in the last month of the strike) exploding a bomb next to a strikebreaker's house—the strikers used a full range of tactics of intimidation.[46] Because all these tactics were considered illegal, many contemporaries and some historians have unthinkingly lumped them together as violent.[47] Yet while sticks and stones broke some bones of strikebreakers and words certainly harmed them, no strikebreaker was ever killed or permanently disabled, even by the few bombs; no striker was ever found with a gun; and no policeman was ever maimed by a striker. For the most part, intimidation stopped short of violence because the attempts to shame members of the community were so effective in preventing strikebreaking. Only the dyers' helpers—the least skilled among the major groups of silk workers and therefore the most easily replaceable—used violent forms of intimidation against strikebreakers with any frequency. But even they never reached the point of all-out assaults either on strikebreakers entering a mill or on the police who protected them. When the police were unusually brutal in their clubbing, Koettgen or Haywood or Flynn would publicly warn them that the strikers' patience had a limit; if necessary, they would exercise their right to defend themselves.[48] These warnings may have encouraged the police to control themselves; in any event, pickets and police never allowed the conflict between them to degenerate into a bloodbath. Given the length and intensity of the struggle, what stands out is the restraint of both silk strikers and law officers.

The key to the restraint of the police was the restraint of the pickets. And the key to the restraint of the pickets was their success in shutting down the mills. At McKees Rocks, in 1909, the IWW had advocated violence to prevent the importation of strikebreakers, yet at Paterson the IWW speakers consistently and emphatically warned against such violence. Lessig was asked why, by the Commission on Industrial Relations. "Well, we considered we had things pretty generally tied up, about 95% was tied up good and fast, and . . . with such general solidarity we thought we could win our demands without any other methods being used." What about the few strikebreakers who persisted in going to work? "Well we told the strikers that, so far as committing violence on one or two working in a mill, that one or two simply would not do them any hurt; that one or two people could not run a shop; and we advised them during the strike to keep their hands in their pockets and do nothing."[49] After the strike this policy of restraint was criticized by some anarchists. Flynn attacked their logic: violence, she pointed out, would have served no purpose. "The mills were shut down as tight as a vacuum. They were like empty junk boats along the banks of the river. Now, where any violence could be used against non-existent scabs, passes my understanding."[50] As the dyers' helpers had learned in 1902—when they had used violence against the broad-silk weavers and police—and as the IWW had learned at Lawrence, the alternative to wholesale violence was solidarity. When few people were able or willing to be strikebreakers, mass picketing was the most effective way to fight.

During March and April the police alternated periods of aggressiveness in arresting speakers and pickets with longer periods of relative inactivity. Their efforts were frustrated not only by the size of the county jail but also by the fact that each new police offensive called forth greater activity by the strikers, thereby renewing the strike's original dynamic. Bimson, unable to learn from his mistake, kept repeating it. The arrest of Haywood and Lessig on the last Sunday in March led to greater attendance on the picket line and at meetings.[51] The arrest of Flynn, Haywood, Tresca, and Quinlan at the end of April led to a burst of indignant anger and to wider participation in strike activities.[52] Bimson's repressive tactics did succeed in straining the resources of the strikers, adding to the financial pressure on them. Money constantly had to be raised for bail and legal fees, especially in the more serious cases. But the police could not break the strike. In the streets pickets continued to discourage strikebreakers, who could not slip back to work quietly or anonymously; in the halls through March and April the strikers continued to meet daily and to make the decisions that shaped the picket line and their other activities.

As the strike settled down, these meetings became—even more than picketing—the most characteristic strike activity. "The fourth, fifth, and sixth weeks of the strike were uneventful," Quinlan said. "Mass meetings in the morning, shop meetings in the afternoon."[53] At these meetings one saw one's friends and found out what was going on. Every morning from ten o'clock till noon, except on Sunday, the ribbon weavers gathered at Helvetia Hall and the dyers' helpers and broad-silk weavers at Turn Hall. These morning meetings and especially the Sunday afternoon assemblages in Haledon became well known for combining analysis and inspiration; here the out-of-town speakers starred.

Less publicized by the press but equally important were the constant shop meetings, usually held in smaller halls without benefit of outside speakers. For example, on March 14 the Empire Silk Company weavers met in Probst Hall; Kettermann and Mitchell weavers met in the Union Athletic Club. On April 2 employees of the Frank and Dugan mills met in Degalman's Hall, and the Graef Hat Band workers met in the Workingmen's Institute. "The Paterson I.W.W. men believe in occasional big mass meetings as an agency of publicity during strikes," *Solidarity* had reported in 1912. "But they pin their faith to shop meetings" as the most practical way to involve and educate workers.[54] It was at shop meetings that strikers would decide whether to accept an offer to return to work, or whether picketing of their mill was necessary. It was here that delegates to larger bodies were elected and instructed, here that they reported back on the decision of those bodies, here that they were held accountable. The morning mass meetings were well reported; representatives of the press often took down, word for word, the colorful speeches of the out-of-town agitators, as did a stenographer hired by the police. Yet the mass meetings were effective in coordinating strike activities and maintaining morale only because of the essential work done quietly and continually in the smaller halls by the strikers themselves.[55]

Mass meetings in the morning, shop meetings in the afternoon, and, in the evening—more meetings! Women's meetings were held weekly in the evening; meetings of IWW Local 152, though less frequent, also occurred in the evening. The broad-silk weavers, the Jewish strikers, the German weavers, and many other groups met from time to time in the evenings.[56] These gatherings reaffirmed the ties that gave continuous strength to the strike. But in solving old problems, they tended to create new ones. The regular morning mass meetings and occasional evening meetings depended for their success on the presence of the out-of-town speakers. "The reason they stayed here," explained Zuersher, "was that we held large meetings, sometimes numbering into the thousands . . . which they addressed." As a weaver, Zuersher knew that few silk workers, even among the most active, felt comfortable making speeches to audiences of thousands. "There were local men at the front, but very few of them took the platform outside of the secretary [Lessig] and the organizer [Koettgen]."[57] Local men had indeed called the strike and remained "at the front." Some, like Lessig and Koettgen, or Louis Magnet of the ribbon weavers and Thomas Lotta of the dyers, regularly chaired mass meetings or addressed them. But the dependence of the silk workers on mass meetings, as the strike settled into routine, left them dependent on outside speakers. Without Haywood, Tresca, and especially Flynn, mass meetings were not as "enthusiastic," observed a Paterson reporter, "for Miss Flynn is very popular with the strikers and is able to hold their attention for hours at a time."[58]

Flynn was what the IWW called an experienced "jawsmith."[59] Addressing large meetings was a specialized job that required specialized training. It was not easy, before the days of microphones, to make oneself heard or understood by thousands, especially when their knowledge of English was rudimentary. Early in her career Flynn had learned from an old soapboxer how to bring her voice up from her diaphragm instead of trying to supply the power with her vocal chords, which would soon have become strained. From Haywood, in Lawrence, she had learned how to use simple words, short sentences, and repetition so that recent immigrants could follow what she said. She had also become expert at finding out details of local conditions and weaving them into her talk. Often staying overnight in Paterson, drawing on her relationships with silk workers (some of which went back to 1907, when she had spent a week organizing in Paterson), Flynn rapidly educated herself in the issues affecting the strikers and their families. She could capture and hold the attention of the Turn Hall crowd in the morning for an hour or more, repeat the performance with appropriate variations at Helvetia Hall, appear at several shop meetings in the afternoon, and provide direction and humor to women or the Strike Committee in the evening. A professional agitator, a veteran at twenty-two years of age, idealistic and practical, equipped with a sharp sense of humor and a natural dramatic flair (producer David Belasco had once asked her if she wanted to act in a labor play, but she preferred to act in the real world), Flynn could simultaneously educate, entertain, and arouse. She put her whole self into speaking, and her audiences responded. In Paterson she was in great demand; in one week she spoke seventeen separate times, often at great length. Once in March, when she was sick, a substitute speaker could not hold the Turn Hall audience. Speaking broken English and inaudible even to those near the stage, he struggled helplessly on as the dyers' helpers and broad-silk weavers filed out of the hall.[60]

On another occasion in March the audience in Turn Hall grew restless, listening to local speakers, until Haywood took over; a reporter noted that the strikers had come to expect outside speakers regularly. When Tresca was in jail, Giovannitti came to Paterson to replace him, on the explicit assumption that the Italian strikers needed at least one outside speaker at all times.[61] By the fourth week of the strike the outside speakers had become essential to the maintenance of morale. The silk strikers remained active in their own cause; it was not in their nature to be passive. At shop and committee meetings and on the picket line, they continued to take the lead. Even at the mass meetings, shop chairmen continued to report on the situation in their shops. As listeners, too, strikers made their feelings known, laughing and cheering, or becoming noisy and walking out. But the fact remained that as the strike became institutionalized, with large meetings as the central unifying ritual, the role of the strikers tended to become subordinate to the role of the out-of-town speakers.

The speakers themselves, committed as they were to the IWW principle that the strikers should conduct their own strike, were uncomfortable with their leadership role. Flynn carefully explained to the strikers that the advantage possessed by out-of-town speakers was that they could not be hurt by an employers' blacklist: "We have done the talking and borne the brunt of the battle and we have been able to do it because our jobs and our living does [sic] not depend on the results."[62] Another time she emphasized that "I have nothing to lose so I can say whatever I please about the manufacturers as long as I express your sentiments."[63] Flynn's conception of herself as a kind of mouthpiece for the strikers, expressing what they would have said if not for the blacklist, was intended to undercut the mystique surrounding her starring role in the strike. Denying that she was a leader, insisting that she preferred the term "agitator," Flynn consciously sought to counter the impression that she and Haywood and Tresca were in charge of the strike.[64]

Haywood had a more radical approach: he tried to lessen the distance between the speakers and the audience by having members of the audience become speakers. Inviting representatives of each nationality to come up on the platform and tell about the strike from their point of view and in their native language, Haywood encouraged strikers to get over the fear of speaking before large groups. At a mass meeting in the fifth week, responding to his urging, volunteers came forward to address the crowd in French, German, Dutch, Swiss, English, Italian, Polish, Hungarian, and Armenian. Many had difficulty speaking, but Haywood encouraged them all and urged the audience to be patient. If some spoke too softly, he repeated their words so that everyone could hear. "When a sweet-faced, child-like girl, the Italian delegate, almost ran off the stage in a fit of fright, Haywood, with the attitude of a father to his young daughter or of a courtier to a princess, came to her, took her hand and with a bow presented her to the audience. And the girl, feeling safe under the protection of the tall Cyclops, found something to say and the voice to say it."[65]

Haywood deliberately used experiences like this to help the strikers find their public voices and to encourage them to listen to one another. In early May he told them they were reaching the point where they could, if need be, provide their own speakers in place of the IWW outside speakers.[66] At a huge meeting in Haledon later in the month, strikers sought to counter reports in the press that various shops had resumed work. "The establishments specified were each dealt with in turn and the real condition of affairs was set forth to, and by, the audience. For the members working in the establishments in question gave much evidence as to real conditions, as well as the representative speakers from the strike committee."[67] The movement of strikers toward center stage, which was to culminate in their performance in Madison Square Garden in June, grew out of their spontaneous tendency to take responsibility for every aspect of the strike and was supported by the IWW speakers, who genuinely wanted—in this respect, too—to share the wealth.[68]

Meetings were more than reports and speeches; there was singing, too. Singing was an inherently democratic activity. It required no outside specialists, the strikers having plenty of talent in their own ranks. "At nearly all our mass meetings, we have a brass band, singing societies or quartets, composed of strikers, or the strikers sing all together."[69] No particular knowledge of English was required; everyone could join in the chorus of the "Marseillaise" or "Internationale." Everyone could also join in songs that the strikers made up:

> LEADER: Do you like Mr. Boss?
> EVERYONE (going up the scale): No, no, no.
> LEADER: Do you like Miss Flynn?
> EVERYONE: Yes, yes, yes.[70]

The IWW had discovered in Lawrence the integrating power of music. "We're going to learn how to sing in Paterson," Haywood announced on the second Sunday in Haledon, "and the next time we meet in Haledon we'll have bands and music. We are going to learn to sing, in many different languages."[71] Singing knitted the Paterson strike together, as one Jewish girl later remembered: "It made no difference. You didn't think. Everybody spoke broken English. . . . No one spoke perfect English, whether you were Italian or Jewish. And then when they sang songs, everyone sang, as best they could."[72]

The strike needed this knitting-together; at no point could unity be taken for granted. The alliance between the Italians and Jews held and strengthened, but throughout the strike there were signs of tension between the Italians and Jews on the one hand and the English-speaking strikers on the other. "If more English-speaking people would get on the picket lines there would be less breaking of heads and arrests," Flynn scolded the ribbon weavers. "The police know that they cannot railroad you to jail because you are a citizen and have friends in the city who will not permit any injustices to be done."[73] The more respectable, native-born strikers seemed less willing than the new immigrants to be arrested. It is true that the native-born weavers, as the most skilled group of workers among those on strike, had least reason to picket, since few strikebreakers could be found to take their places. Nevertheless, their reluctance to picket and be arrested heightened tensions. "What nationalities stick together on the picket line?" Reed asked strikers in jail.

> A young Jew, pallid and sick-looking from insufficient food, spoke up proudly. "T'ree great nations—Italians, Hebrews an' Germans"—
> "But how about the Americans?"
> They all shrugged their shoulders and grinned with humorous scorn. "English peoples not go on picket-line," said one softly.[74]

Mass meetings served to bring people together and to soften tension over issues like picketing; at once educational gatherings and revival meetings, they tended to strengthen the ties between different traditions and peoples. When Koettgen or Lessig addressed a mixed audience in German, or Tresca in Italian, or Flynn and Haywood and Quinlan in English, the emphasis was on what everyone had in common. "You didn't have to understand Tresca," observes a Jew. "He was a fiery speaker. Of course I couldn't understand him. But he was so fiery that you felt what he was saying."[75] Not everyone reacted this way, however. Some American-born people became impatient when Tresca or another foreign speaker was talking; some would even leave the hall, particularly if the meeting ran into their lunch hour.[76] Speeches might heal some conflicts but could exacerbate others. More than listening to speeches, singing helped the silk workers stay together despite the persistent tensions. In Paterson as in Lawrence, music became the universal language of the strikers.

THE WOMEN

The Paterson strike gave people a chance to show what they could do. This was true of recent immigrants, who took the lead on the picket line and elsewhere; complaints about the inactivity of English-speaking strikers reflected the greater enthusiasm of the Italians and Jews. It was true as well of women, many of whom, normally denied a role in public affairs, seized the opportunity to become historical actors.

One morning during the third week of the strike, twenty-three-year-old Mary Gasperano was doing picket duty. As picketing ended and the strikers formed a group on the corner, she and Simon Polowski began to address the crowd—"harangue" was the term used by the reporter who was there. Someone called the police, who rushed to the scene. Gasperano and Polowski, refusing to be intimidated, "demanded to know in loud tones just what the police wanted." The police answered by immediately arresting both of them.[77] Gasperano appears to have welcomed such confrontation. During the next month she was arrested twice more for "unlawful assemblage" (that is, picketing) and was once accused of biting the hand of Sergeant Ryan. On April 17 she was arrested for the fifth time—accused of slapping a woman strikebreaker in the face—and her bail placed at $1,000. Instead of trying to raise bail, Gasperano chose to await trial in the Passaic County Jail.[78]

Gasperano's readiness to take a leading role on the picket line, her aggressiveness, and her willingness to go to jail were not unique or even unusual among the female strikers. Of the 2,338 strikers arrested, about a quarter were females. What most surprised male observers, who thought they knew what to expect of these women and girls, was the change in their attitude and behavior. Shocked to find a number of young girls from his church serving a ten-day sentence, a minister immediately offered to pay their fines and was even more shocked when they turned him down and insisted on staying in jail.[79] Mounted policeman David Horridge underestimated the determination and resources of Felicity DiCoppa, who was picketing a ribbon mill in the sixth week of the strike. Horridge told DiCoppa to move on. She refused. He used his horse to push her against the wall and warned her to leave. She told him she had "a perfect right to walk along the sidewalk" and added that she wasn't afraid of any blue uniform. When he and his horse finally succeeded in driving her off, DiCoppa proceeded to Turn Hall, where, at the regular morning meeting, she was introduced by the chairman. From the platform, backed by other pickets who had witnessed the incident, she related the whole story to the mass audience, including the name of the officer who had bullied her.[80]

Employers, too, were unprepared for the behavior of women in the strike. Moses Strauss, who managed the two Frank and Dugan ribbon mills, employed highly skilled male workers on the old German looms at the Cooke mill and less-skilled females on high-speed looms at the Dale mill. Perceiving his female employees as dependent, in need of a guiding hand, Strauss treated them differently, instructing them on how to make their wages last, for instance: instead of each woman buying a five-cent pail of soup for lunch, he had suggested, two women could share it. The men at the Cooke mill left work on March 5 and 6. On Friday March 7 the 200 women and girls at the Dale mill walked out. The women had no reason to leave, Strauss complained; they had never told him that they had any grievances. But he did not know his female employees. Meeting with other striking ribbon weavers at Helvetia Hall, they expressed their anger at his paternalistic and insulting attitude.[81] The Dale mill ribbon weavers went out in solidarity with their trade, to protest police interference with the strike. But once out, talking with other ribbon weavers, they were able to voice their own grievances and to participate in shaping the ribbon weavers' demands.

When their shop committee returned to the Dale mill on the following Friday to collect back wages and present a list of demands (with the eight-hour day at the top) bearing the stamp of IWW Local 152, Strauss was astounded at the behavior of his "girls": "I handed it back and said 'I'll receive no paper with the stamp of the I.W.W. on it!' She handed it back to me, and I says, 'Bertha, you better take it,' and she shoved it to me and I tore it up and said, 'I will never have anything to do with it.'"[82] Used to managing the lives of Bertha and the others, Strauss was amazed that they would close the mill and associate themselves with the radical IWW. Nor were his surprises over. Three days later, on March 17, Frank and Dugan's female employees met as a group with Flynn to talk about becoming active in the strike. Months later, two young girls were arrested while picketing Frank and Dugan.[83]

In 1910 there were almost 8,000 girls and women working in Paterson's silk industry. Many of them prized their skilled or semiskilled jobs and did not want to give them up when they married. Paterson women, on the whole, were much more skilled and better paid than their counterparts in Pennsylvania, where the cheaper silks were made; female weavers in Paterson were paid at rates almost 40 percent higher than female and 15 percent higher than male weavers in Pennsylvania. Young women in the Pennsylvania silk mills, according to an investigator who worked among them, "regard their work merely as a stop-gap until marriage." In Paterson, by contrast, women did not automatically quit the mills when they married, or even when they had children; consequently, a number of the women on the picket line were mothers.[84] Instead of allowing family responsibilities to limit their activities, some mothers brought their families into the strike. One woman took five of her six children with her in the morning to the picket line. When she was arrested, she told the policeman, "I can't go to jail and leave my children"; picking them up one at a time, she put them into the patrol wagon before getting in herself. "If you see Freddie," she told another picket, "tell him to come to jail."[85] Another mother, with a nursing baby at home, was arrested and given the choice of ten dollars or twenty days. Refusing to take the easy way out, she chose jail, and demanded to have the baby brought to her there.[86]

Carrie Golzio was twenty-five years old during the strike, and her son was four. Before she went to the morning meeting, Golzio would leave her boy with her mother, just as she did when she was working. At Turn Hall, she would sometimes speak from the platform, drawing on her years of experience in the mills and in strikes to urge everyone to remain out and remain united. Her husband wanted her home: "What do you want to go out for? Stay home. You don't belong out." "I can't stay home," she'd say. "I got to go out and fight." Marching in a strike parade, Golzio saw her employer watching from the window of his mill, and she ostentatiously pointed to the red ribbon around her neck and waved it at him. Tough and confident even before 1913, Golzio experienced the strike as an opportunity not only to advance her class but also to enjoy herself. "Aw, that was a strike. I had a lot of fun though, I had a lot of fun. I'd go around and I'd laugh and I'd carry on. You know, you had to hold a meeting and they'd sing and they had dances. You always had a lot of fun. When you're young, you know, everything goes."[87]

Among all these courageous and militant female strikers, Mary Gasperano and Carrie Golzio stand out only because they came forward so early in the strike. Most girls and women achieved militance and self-confidence more gradually; their participation in the strike process gave them the opportunity for self-transformation—and it gave them the time. "Those days we worked all day from 7 to 6," recalls a ribbon weaver who was nineteen during the strike. "You had no time for shopping, no time for nothing, just work, work in the mills." At home after work, women had to sew and clean and cook. "You cooked for two days and one day a little rest." The strike gave this nineteen-year-old a chance to attend meetings and become active. Once, while picketing, she was charged by a policeman on horseback. To her own surprise, she threw herself over a school picket fence to escape from the horse.[88]

Young female strikers experienced themselves and their world differently during the strike. Some enjoyed it, at least for a while, as a kind of holiday.

Maria Costelli, who was eighteen, celebrated the first day by going directly from the Turn Hall meeting to a movie theater on Main Street.[89] "While I am on strike," said another girl, "I go around to the school yard to watch the kids play, and sometimes I play with them myself."[90] Even picketing offered new freedom, especially when it meant going out while it was still dark in order to reach the mill before 7:00 A.M. Rose Villano remembers that she "had a good time. I was a young girl, I was nineteen, I had a boy friend, and we used to picket every day. I was allowed to go out early because we had to picket the shop."[91] In April two young sisters, found walking through the city between three and four o'clock in the morning, were brought to police headquarters for their own protection. They explained that they were going to call on a friend and later do picket duty together. "They were warned about walking the streets so early, and were allowed to go on their promise to stay at home until the proper time to do picket duty."[92]

To young female silk workers, the strike seemed to suspend or weaken the many prohibitions that ordinarily restricted their activity. One girl was seen kissing a boy in Helvetia Hall during the morning meeting. When someone complained, "Mr. Chairman, there is love going on here," a vote was taken, and the majority decided to put the young couple out of the hall.[93] The strike, then in its fourth week, was already becoming serious business. But no matter how serious and difficult, it gave young female strikers a chance to play, to walk around their city at night, to kiss during the day, and to find out what they could do.

Hannah Silverman, a teenager, offers the most dramatic example of the gradual emergence of leadership from below in the Paterson strike. Employed at the Westerhoff mill on Van Houten Street, Silverman enthusiastically took part in picketing the mill. By the time of her first arrest, on April 25, she had become the captain of the pickets there. On that occasion the police asked the seventeen-year-old to disperse the crowd, before arresting her and then arresting forty-seven other pickets.[94] Being charged with "unlawful assembly" and spending the night in the city jail seemed to have the same effect on Silverman that it had on Gasperano: it made her even more determined to assert her rights and more confident in her ability to do so. She was arrested again, and again.

Once, she and five other girls, including her sixteen-year-old friend Carrie Torrello, were charged with following two female strikebreakers home from the mill. Recorder Carroll, in recognition of her militance and growing leadership, gave Silverman the unusually stiff sentence of sixty days in the county jail. "'Thank you, your honor,' said Miss Silverman, smilingly. Carroll did not quite like the way the girl took the sentence but replied: 'You're welcome.'" Silverman, Torello, and their friends, confident in both the rightness of their cause and their own abilities, could not be intimidated. Cheered by hundreds as they were taken away, "the girls responded by giving three cheers for the I.W.W. and by singing all the way down to jail."[95] In Haledon, Flynn joked that "while this meeting is going on here another meeting is going on in Paterson and the police can't stop it either. That meeting is a gathering of our sisters and brothers at the county jail and they have good speakers such as Tresca and little Miss Silverman."[96] Out after only two days—a writ having been filed on her behalf and $5,000 bail raised—Silverman threatened not only to take the case to the upper courts but also to bring suit for false arrest. The charge was quietly dropped, and she returned immediately to the picket line. At a monster Sunday meeting in Haledon she told the strikers that she'd been to the county jail three times already, but the police couldn't keep her away from the picket lines.[97]

Two weeks later, Silverman was back in court for trial on the original charge of unlawful assembly for picketing the Westerhoff mill. The assistant prosecutor demanded that she tell what the IWW really was and whether it was true that Bill Haywood was really the IWW. "Haywood is Haywood," she shot back. "The workers in the mills are the I.W.W." Described by her lawyer as a "mere slip of a girl, in fact, only a kid," Silverman was called the "little agitator" by the assistant prosecutor and an "impudent girl" by Recorder Carroll.[98] On the following day she was sitting in the rear of the court, waiting for her own trial to resume, when the recorder gave a brutally long sentence to a striker in another case. Some accounts say Silverman gasped and others say she hissed; in any event, the furious recorder slapped her with a twenty-day sentence for disorderly conduct. This time her fellow strikers were worried, because she was supposed to lead the big parade to Madison Square Garden on the following Saturday. But the lawyers secured her release from the county jail with another writ in time for her to take her place at the front of the procession. "One of the leading lights in the present strike" was the way the Paterson *Evening News* described the girl. Flynn called her "the heroine of this strike" and used her in an article two years later as an example of what women could do during strikes if given the chance.[99]

Flynn herself helped to give young female strikers like Silverman the chance. Because the style of IWW organizers like Flynn was intended to demystify leadership and because she herself was only twenty-two, her presence in Paterson made the possibility of becoming a leader more real. "Did you talk to Flynn?" a nineteen-year-old ribbon weaver was asked years later. "Oh yes. She was just a plain [i.e., ordinary] girl like we were, only she chose to be a speaker"—and, as an afterthought, "She was a good speaker too."[100] Other women who came to speak in Paterson included famous trade unionists and Socialists, but Flynn was always the most popular, especially among younger women. To them, she was an example of what a woman could be. She seemed afraid of no one and totally dedicated to the strike and to the IWW. Haywood spent on the average only three days a week in Paterson during the strike; Tresca and Quinlan were newcomers to the IWW. Only Flynn among the outside speakers was an experienced IWW organizer who was completely devoted to the strikers on a daily basis. This woman, more than anyone, was the leader of the Paterson strike. When she was arrested with Tresca, Haywood, and Quinlan late in April, women strikers sang outside the jail that after the strike, "Gurley Flynn will be the boss."[101] A woman striker wrote to the Paterson *Evening News* that "if I could be a second Miss Flynn, I would be more honored than if I could be a queen."[102]

Flynn launched and presided over an important series of meetings for women only. At the first, held on March 5 while the strike was still spreading, 600 women and girls responded enthusiastically to Flynn's lengthy and detailed explanation of how the strike affected women and what they could do.[103] This meeting and the many that followed were not for the female strikers alone but also — perhaps especially — for the wives, daughters, mothers, sisters, and women friends of the male strikers.[104] Female silk workers could hear news of the strike at the morning mass meetings, but wives would not participate in the strike unless expressly invited. Because the strike affected everyone in the striker's household and the other family members were never neutral, wives could hurt the effort tremendously if left out of it, or help tremendously if brought into it. By reaching out to the women in the community through frequent for-women-only meetings, Flynn helped them to become conscious of their strength. They did the rest. At the second meeting, only five days after the first, 3,000 women jammed into Turn Hall to hear Flynn and Haywood and to be together.[105]

The women's meetings became weekly events, among the most successful in the strike. Margaret Pollard, a striker who had lived in Paterson since 1886 and who did not join the IWW in 1913 or attend regular strike meetings, went out of her way to attend "the ladies' meetings." By April the time and place had become regularized, like everything else; the women met every Tuesday evening in Helvetia Hall.[106] Not only did these meetings build confidence in the women; they also broke down the resistance of male strikers to the equal participation of women in the strike. They allowed women to show how much they cared. In this way, almost as a by-product of the successful attempt to get wives to support their men, the women's meetings helped to create the kind of atmosphere in which it became possible for female strikers like Hannah Silverman to emerge as the leaders of men and women alike.

Committed to the class struggle, like all the IWW speakers, Flynn had always shown a special concern for the place of women in that struggle. Her first public talk, in 1906, had been "What Socialism Will Do for Women."[107] Throughout her early career as an IWW and Socialist speaker, Flynn had argued (for instance, in Newark in 1909) that working women could be emancipated only through the emancipation of the working class as a whole. In Paterson she accordingly focused the anger of the women on class injustice whenever she could; for example, she pointed out that these women could not afford to buy the silk that they or their husbands wove. Years later, a female striker recalled Flynn's question:

"Would you like to have nice clothes?" We replied, "Oh, yes." "Would you like to have nice shoes?" "Oh, yes," we shouted. "Well, you can't have them.

Your bosses' daughters have those things!" We got mad. We knew it was
true. We had shoes with holes, and they had lovely things. Then she said,
"Would you like to have soft hands like your bosses' daughters?" And we got
mad all over again.[108]

But unlike many Wobblies and Socialists, Flynn was unwilling to wait for
revolution to improve the lives of working-class women. "I feel the futility,
and know that many other Socialist women must, through our appreciation of
these sad conditions and our deep sympathy for our sister women, of extending
to them nothing more than the hope of an ultimate social revolution," she
explained in 1911. "I realize the beauty of our hope . . . but I want to see that
hope find a point of contact with the daily lives of working women, and I
believe it can through the union movement."[109]

Flynn found ways to bring Paterson women into the movement. When the
Board of Aldermen invited certain strikers to present their case as a step toward
a settlement, Flynn blasted them for not inviting even one woman. The success
of the strike could in great part be attributed to the women, she said, and they
had as much to say about the settlement as the men.[110] When the AFL's Sarah
Conboy came to Paterson at the request of the manufacturers, Flynn challenged
her to attend the regular women's meeting and debate the issues of the strike
with her.[111] At one meeting, she reported a specific example of the sexual
harassment of a female silk worker by her employer; at another, she urged all
female strikers to boycott the policemen's ball; at yet another, she invited the
wives of strikers to join the picket line.[112] She continually strove for the
"point of contact" between revolutionary hopes and the daily lives of women.
She believed that everything she did to involve women in the strike was good
for them and good for the strike. The proof, to her, was the growing militance
of the women. "The I.W.W. has been accused of putting the women in front,"
she wrote in 1915, thinking especially of Lawrence and Paterson. "The truth is,
the I.W.W. does not keep them in the back, and they go to the front."[113]

The truth was actually a bit more complex. In Paterson the IWW did
actively encourage women to come to the front. Haywood and Tresca, as well
as Flynn, had seen what women could do in Lawrence; they knew, too, of the
militance of women in the New York garment strikes. In Paterson they found a
capable male local leadership already in place—Koettgen, Lessig, Magnet,
Thomas Lotta, and others—so they appear to have taken responsibility, in their
role as catalysts, for developing female leadership. Flynn brought Tresca or
Haywood to the women's meetings to help her sometimes; she would have
preferred to have only women speakers, she said, but too many women who
spoke well in small groups got "stage fright" before an audience of 2,000.[114]
Haywood, with his unusual sensitivity to the sufferings of women and children,
was particularly well suited to the task; Tresca, with his more traditional
masculine style, was somewhat less so. On March 17 both Haywood and
Tresca came with Flynn, and it may have been on this occasion that their

famous exchange took place. According to Flynn, "Tresca made some remarks about shorter hours, people being less tired, more time to spend together and jokingly he said: 'More babies.' The women did not look amused. When Haywood interrupted and said: 'No Carlo, we believe in birth control—a few babies, well cared for!' they burst into laughter and applause."[115]

Haywood took the women seriously; they "have been an enormous factor in the Paterson strike," he wrote in May. "Each meeting for them has been attended by bigger and bigger crowds."[116] More than many Wobblies, Haywood knew that women could decide the outcome of a strike, that they made brave fighters, and that they could fight harder if they weren't worn down by raising large families. Despite its egalitarian theory, the IWW had many members, particularly in the West, who looked on women as inherently conservative and inferior, and on marriage as something that weakened a man's fighting resolve. Even in theory, the national IWW rejected the idea that women needed to develop committees or organizing drives of their own; thus it had no national structure to support Flynn's efforts to organize around women's issues.[117] But in Paterson, women met by themselves every Tuesday, and Haywood was as committed as Flynn to recognizing and publicizing their fighting spirit. "One woman is worth three men—I never knew it to fail," he told a male audience. "The women will win the strike at Paterson."[118]

THE REVOLUTIONARY TENDENCY
OF THE STRIKE

The active participation of women transformed both the Paterson strike and the women. Becoming conscious of their strength as persons and as members of a class, the women—especially the young women—embodied the revolutionary tendency of the strike.

The girls who worked at the Bamford ribbon mill were not concerned about revolution before 1913. Ostensibly apprentices who were learning how to become ribbon weavers, they were in fact the most tightly controlled and intensively exploited workers in Paterson's silk industry. Under their contract with Joseph Bamford, he withheld one-half of what they earned for a year; if they left before their year was over, Bamford kept the money. These girls were not interested in great social questions. They were interested in avoiding fines, which were levied for a great variety of offenses: talking, laughing at the boss, opening a window, looking for another job. They were interested in knowing the exact time, because latecomers after lunch could be locked out and docked a whole day's pay; on Saturdays, when everyone else got off at noon, Bamford's employees had to stay behind and clean up on their own time. They were interested in the weather, because rain meant getting wet while they ate lunch on the old dirty steps. Above all, they were interested in lasting out the year and collecting their withheld pay—which only a minority of them succeeded in doing.[119]

The Bamford girls were initially reluctant to strike in 1913 because it would mean forfeiting the withheld money, and they were regarded in the community of silk workers as strikebreakers. "Under police escort, they passed my home twice each day," remembers a Patersonian who was then a boy. "We always jeered at them, and on occesion [sic], threw snowballs at them."[120] But after a while fifteen girls did join the strike, and the ribbon weavers' investigating committee they talked with concluded (in Flynn's words) that "these girls, ranging in age from 14 to 17, WERE VIRTUAL SLAVES UNDER AN ABOMINABLE CONTRACT SYSTEM."[121] They also talked at morning mass meetings, explaining the conditions under which they worked. And they talked with Flynn, giving her the information she needed to write an indignant article for the April issue of *Solidarity* and for the program of the Pageant in June. "We want the fathers and mothers to earn enough money that they won't need to send their 14 year old daughters to work for $1.25 a week," thundered Flynn. To her and to many of the adult strikers, the Bamford girls were a particularly shocking example of the exploitation to which silk workers were subject, an example that could move public opinion and help in raising funds. "The Paterson strike is a struggle for shorter hours and more wages," Flynn wrote, emphasizing in her appeal the nonrevolutionary aspects of the struggle.[122] But to the girls themselves, the strike was like a revolution. No one had ever asked them about their work experience before, or sought their help. Brought gradually into the strike, they were transformed by it. At Bamford's mill they had learned and submitted to the hard facts of life. Now the strike taught them hope.

Teresa Cobianci was born in southern Italy and came to Paterson with her mother when she was four, to join her father, a silk worker. Her mother worked in the mills, developed tuberculosis, and went back to Italy to die. Eight-year-old Teresa went with her and then stayed with her grandfather in Italy until her father came to take her back to Paterson when she was twelve. One year later, with forged papers, she began work as a winder in a silk mill. She had done well at school in Paterson and had not wanted to leave, but in both Italy and America, Italian children were expected to contribute to the family income. (Another female Italian striker recalls leaving school to begin work at age eleven, with forged papers—"and I loved school, isn't that funny?")[123]

Teresa became a ribbon weaver at the Bamford mill, where she tended two looms and was continually subject to speedup. A veteran silk worker by 1913, with chronic stomach trouble ("The doctor said it was because I hurry so"), she was fifteen years old and knew her place. Once she had an accident:

> I was on the stairs one day eating my lunch. One of those big wheels with fire hose around came loose and fell on my head. And I don't know nothing after that for the whole afternoon. But they tell me I had fits. No, they didn't call the doctor—not on your life. They had a fear of a damage suit. They gave me a free ride home in their automobile that night.[124]

Teresa went back to work with her head still hurting, because her father needed the money and she had to make up the days she'd missed. So tiny that she had to stand on a bench to reach over the loom and put in the ends, she was badly underweight but "with a face like a flower," said Flynn.[125] Then came the strike. On strike, she gained eleven pounds in fourteen weeks. Encouraged by Flynn, she also gained confidence. "Teresa Cobianci and Johanna Byzani, two little strikers, delivered addresses [at Turn and Helvetia Halls] and told of the conditions under which they were compelled to work."[126] And she gained class consciousness. "I want always to go back to Italy, but since the strike I am more happy here. We are all together. We stand solid. My father says there will always be bosses. I say 'Yes? Then we shall be the bosses.'"[127]

"We shall be the bosses" expresses the revolutionary élan of the Paterson strikers. Encouraged by their united strength against all the forces of society, educated in self-management by the democratic process of the strike, and driven to make increasing sacrifices in the here and now, the strikers tended to focus their hopes on a revolutionary future in which they would be in charge.

More than most strikes, even most IWW strikes, the Paterson walkout was radical in its origins. The IWW strikes in Lawrence and Little Falls had begun when wages were reduced, following a reduction in hours imposed by the state legislatures; they were, at least in the beginning, primarily defensive battles. The Paterson strike began as an attempt by the workers to control the rate of production; significantly, the reduction in hours that quickly became its unifying demand originated not in the legislature but with the workers themselves. For each major group of silk workers, the objectives of the strike extended well beyond wages, or even hours. The broad-silk weavers knew that without apprenticeship their future depended on their ability to limit the number of looms they worked. The dyers' helpers, in their very first meeting, agreed to demand not only the eight-hour day and a new wage scale but also "closed IWW shops" in which "shop committees shall have absolute control over all matters."[128] From previous victories and humiliations, the ribbon weavers had learned that the decisive factor in the shop and the state was power; after the strike, many of them did indeed enforce job control through closed IWW shops, while continuing to vote Socialist at the polls.[129] For the broad-silk weavers, the dyers' helpers, and the ribbon weavers, the Paterson strike was from the beginning a battle for control.

During the strike about 9,500 Paterson silk workers joined IWW Local 152. They found the union congenial because it was in essence a vehicle for workers' control. In 1912, Local 152 had declared itself "organized for the purpose of uniting the workers on the job to get control of industry. . . . As we organize a little we will control industry a little, as we organize more we will control industry more until the workers of the world have full control of industry and run them [sic] for the benefit of the working class."[130] After the strike Koettgen summarized what he had learned as a silk worker in Paterson and brought to his position as organizer:

In a mill where there is no organization the boss is the absolute master. Whatever he says will be the law of that mill. He will determine what wages the workers shall receive, how long they shall work, under what condition they shall work, how the work shall be distributed, who shall be employed or discharged and so on. When the workers organize they will demand that they will have something to say as to what the wages shall be, how the work shall be distributed, what the sanitary conditions shall be, whether or not a worker shall be discharged or kept on, what the hours of labor shall be, etc.[131]

The IWW outside speakers did not need to introduce the idea of workers' control into the Paterson strike; the concept had been there from the start, in the orientation of weavers toward shop control and in the revolutionary program of Local 152, with its emphasis on workers' control of industry.

The notion of workers' control was integral to IWW strategy. Beginning with struggles for control of the shop, the Wobblies proceeded through strikes and industrial organization to the eventual management of the economy. "A strike is an incipient revolution," Haywood had said, in which workers begin to take active responsibility for running their lives. "If the workers can organize so that they can stand idle they will then be strong enough so that they can take over the factories. Now, I hope to see the day when the man who goes out of the factory will be the one who will be called a scab; when the good union man will stay in the factory, whether the capitalists like it or not; when we lock the bosses out and run the factories to suit ourselves. That is our program. We will do it."[132] Haywood and Flynn came to Paterson with this revolutionary program in mind. Nourishing their vision of the future were memories of the job control won in the Goldfield, Nevada, IWW strike and the shop organization resulting from the Lawrence strike.[133] It might therefore be natural to assume that they simply transferred this revolutionary vision to such silk workers as Teresa, but the truth is more interesting. In reality, the IWW outside speakers only occasionally talked revolution in Paterson. Increasingly perceiving the deadlocked strike as one that would make or break their organization nationally, they emphasized strike tactics rather than revolutionary strategy or goals. Tresca, Haywood, and especially Flynn cared more whether each silk worker was still on strike, attending meetings, picketing, willing to go to jail—that is, active in and committed to the struggle—than whether he or she believed in the eventual abolition of classes by the victorious working class. They made no attempt to hide their revolutionary perspective, but neither did they dwell on it in a daily way.

From time to time, outside speakers articulated the IWW program of workers' control and placed it in the context of the national and international working-class movement. "You are building the framework of a great governing and industrial organization," organizer Robert Plunkett told the silk strikers, "and in a few years you're bound to run the factories yourselves."[134] Predicting that a united working class would some day take power, Patrick

Quinlan emphasized, "You of Paterson are only part of a vast army of the rebellion, which, standing shoulder to shoulder, will sweep capitalism out of existence."[135] But Plunkett was only an occasional visitor to Paterson, and Quinlan was speaking early in the strike. They resorted to revolutionary rhetoric in part because they did not have much to say about local conditions.

Flynn, who was the most knowledgeable about the local situation, talked the least about revolution.[136] It was Tresca, not Flynn, who announced that "this strike is the start of a great revolution," and it was Tresca who was later prosecuted in part for having said so.[137] Flynn usually preferred to stick close to the business at hand rather than to express ideas that might divide the strikers, alienate potential sympathizers, or cause the speakers to be arrested. As much as possible, she avoided ultimate questions in favor of immediate ones—though sometimes it was not possible. Testifying during Quinlan's trial, she was asked by the prosecution whether the IWW recognized the legal distinction between masters and servants. Knowing what was at stake (five days earlier the prosecution had been delighted when two Italian witnesses confessed their belief in anarchy, thereby discrediting themselves with the middle-class jury), Flynn tried to sidestep the issue. "We are compelled to do that," she answered legalistically. "Well," insisted the prosecution, "would you like to do away with such a system?" "We prefer not to have any masters, of course," she replied.[138]

Only when she was pushed to the wall did Flynn articulate the IWW's revolutionary goal: no masters. Tresca and Haywood were not quite as disciplined or single-minded about winning the strike as she was. When Tresca was angry, he talked about blood for blood; when Haywood was angry, he talked utopian socialism. Released on bail in later April and angry about his most recent arrest, Haywood told the strikers that before long, silk mills would have nothing in common with the existing mills. The little mills would be abandoned, and the silk workers themselves would run a giant silk mill.

> It will be utopian. There will be a wonderful dining-room where you will enjoy the best food that can be purchased; your digestion will be aided by sweet music, which will be wafted to your ears by an unexcelled orchestra. There will be a gymnasium and a great swimming pool and private bathrooms of marble. One floor of this plant will be devoted to masterpieces of art, and you will have a collection even superior to that displayed in the Metropolitan Museum in New York. A first-class library will occupy another floor.[139]

Speeches like this were the exception in Paterson, however. As a rule, the IWW speakers focused on the present, expecting that the workers themselves would take care of the future. That is to say, the speakers trusted the process of the strike. And that is the main point: the IWW speakers did not teach revolution in Paterson as much as either their critics or their partisans supposed —because they didn't have to. The strike itself taught revolution. What the silk workers learned about their right and ability to run the mills for themselves they learned primarily from running the strike. The formal structure of the strike ensured that decisions would be made by the strikers. The outside speakers were valued advisors but had no vote on the Central Strike Committee. It was composed of one or two delegates from each shop, eventually totaling almost 300, and met daily during the first four months in order to make the day-to-day decisions. Final control remained with the strikers, organized in their shops. Delegates to the Central Strike Committee were elected—and could be recalled—at shop meetings, where they reported and received instructions regularly.

The entire system was designed to allow maximum participation by the strikers in decision-making at all levels. As Haywood explained in May, the strike was being democratically managed; the silk workers were "doing it for themselves." After the strike the democratic mechanism developed by Local 152 was actually applied to some of the ribbon mills. "All mills organized [in Local 152] hold regular meetings at stated times, not less than once a month. At this meeting questions relative to the work in the mill are discussed; also matters pertaining to the union," reported Koettgen in September. "Each mill elects a shop committee and they thrash it out with the employer. If they fail then it is submitted to the shop meeting and from there to the Central Committee of Delegates." The linchpin of the system, the locus of democratic control both during and after the strike, was the shop meeting. "All delegates are required to report to the Central Committee what transpires in their shops and report back to the shops what transpires in the Central Committee."[140] In this way, the democratic control of the strike led to the democratic control of the shop, which, in turn—according to IWW theory—prefigured the democratic control of industry and society.

Koettgen was optimistic that "when the workers act directly for themselves they can be relied upon to use the right methods to gain their point. They will learn by acting," he wrote several months later, thinking of Paterson, "and gradually gain more and more control over industry until finally they have full control" and the working class, having become "the dominant class, will establish a new society where there are no masters and no slaves."[141] The difficulty with this revolutionary plan was that the silk workers did not always do what Koettgen, Lessig, Haywood, or Flynn thought they ought to do. In the short run the strikers sometimes rejected the advice given them by the IWW speakers, choosing—democratically—a less radical path. Particular tactics such as sabotage, for instance, and Lessig's plan to darken the city by a blackout were rejected by the Central Strike Committee. As Louis Magnet pointed out in April, if the strikers decided to settle with their employers, "not all the Haywoods, Quinlans or Gurley Flynns in the country" would be able to keep the strike going.[142]

In the long run, despite the tendency of the strike to radicalize those who participated in it, thousands of silk workers never agreed with the IWW that they could or should control the industry. The revolutionary tendency of the

Paterson strike remained only a tendency; even during the strike it coexisted and competed with more conservative tendencies. Teresa Cobianci spoke for many strikers when she told her father that they would not always be subject to class domination, but her father spoke for many when he said in effect that classes were eternal. Both tendencies found expression through the democratic control of the strike by the workers, which made it possible for immigrant workers—even young female immigrants like Teresa or Hannah Silverman or Mary Gasperano—to move the strike forward but also for traditional leaders like Magnet to hold it back. The IWW's national leaders knew that democratic control of a strike by the strikers would not necessarily make revolutionaries of them. "Our revolutionary program is not embedded with crystalline clarity in the mind of every worker who goes through an IWW strike. Far from it," said Flynn afterward.[143] What the IWW leaders argued, at their best, was that there was no other way for workers to learn, no shortcut to revolution.[144]

Many Paterson strikers saw the goals of the 1913 strike simply in terms of looms, wages, and hours. "Don't you think you ought to own the mills and drive the boss out?" asked a writer for the *Survey*. "No, no, boss all right, if he only pay a little more," was the frequent reply.[145] Others, looking back years later after the particular issues had faded, remembered how they felt about the future in 1913. Flynn, Haywood, Tresca, and Quinlan "gave us hope," recalls an Italian striker. "They used to talk about owning the factories which I think would have been good." A broad-silk weaver for thirty-four years, she had been seventeen at the time of the strike. "When you're young and there are people like that it makes you think that maybe there's a tomorrow for me."[146] A Jewish girl who attended strike meetings with her father and later organized for the IWW in Paterson insists that the IWW "was not just a union": "We really thought we were building a new society. It wasn't only hours, it wasn't only an increase in pay. It was changing everything; that's what we felt."[147]

CHAPTER THREE
Deadlock

In April and May the strike entered a new phase. Matching the unity and determination of the strikers with unity and determination of their own, the mill owners tightened the pressure and developed strategies intended to break the strike. In addition, as class war engulfed the city and everyone became a participant, the clergy and small businessmen found themselves faced with the necessity of choosing sides.

THE BOSSES

Through April and May the manufacturers refused concessions, maintained unity in their own camp, rejected all attempts by third parties at mediation, and continued to insist that they would never deal in any way with the IWW or with the strikers as a body. Their unity and intransigence surprised and bewildered the workers, who knew that the strike had been timed perfectly. March was the busiest time of year, and 1913 had started profitably: after two mediocre years, silk was back in fashion. "There is a large volume of business to be had at the present moment, and buyers are much in need of the best spring fabrics, but manufacturers are not in a position to accept this business . . . due to the strike."[1] The strikers knew that the manufacturers had lost their spring season and—as the demand for silk ribbons and dress goods continued high through April, May, and June—that they were gradually forfeiting their fall orders as well.[2] Strikes in February and March, when the spring fashions were dyed and woven, had usually succeeded in the past because the manufacturers had not been willing to remain closed for long during their busiest months. Then why, during such a good year for silk, did the manufacturers refuse to make concessions or even to negotiate? How were they able to prevent breaks in their own camp? Anxiously, the strikers and their supporters studied the owners' united front and wondered whether it would last.

Throughout the strike there were rumors of developing splits between the smaller and larger silk firms. According to these rumors, the smaller manufacturers were eager to settle, while the larger ones wanted to continue to hold out. At the end of the first month the Paterson *Evening News* reported that some large firms hoped the strike would last another month and squeeze most of the small firms out of business.[3] Three weeks later the New York *Call* suggested hopefully that the smaller manufacturers, having been made "the cat's paw of the Silk Trust, have signified their intention of breaking away and of dealing with the workers. Many have declared openly that should they continue to strike for any length of time, they would be forced to the wall, and, rather than go into bankruptcy, they will probably deal with the workers."[4] But nothing came of it, though rumors continued to circulate. In early May, it was said that about fifty smaller silk manufacturers and several dye firms were going to break ranks with their colleagues; when the small manufacturers met separately a week later, however, a spokesman told the press that "we can do nothing."[5] The rumored break never came.

This solidarity of the manufacturers was as remarkable in its way as the solidarity of the silk workers. As the pro-business press speculated about the hold of the IWW agitators on the strikers, so the Socialist and IWW press theorized about the hold of the large manufacturers on the smaller ones.[6] The "silk trust" (conceived on the model of the woolen trust in Lawrence) was blamed for forcing the smaller firms to refrain from settling with the workers. A widely disseminated article—published in *Solidarity* and the New York *Call*, and printed as a strike leaflet in Paterson by IWW Local 152—argued that outside capitalists controlled the Paterson manufacturers. Pointing to "concentrated and giant capital in the hands of a few," the article detailed the national and international connections of firms like Doherty and Wadsworth; Dexter, Lambert, and Company; the Ashley and Bailey Silk Manufacturing Company; the National Silk Dyeing Company; and Weidmann Silk Dyeing Company. These firms dominated the Silk Manufacturers Association and the Master Dyers Association: "Through these combined associations they control the local situation." How did the big firms prevent the little ones from settling? "The big corporations threaten the small firms who accede to the strikers' demands. They will make slow delivery or no delivery when silks are to be dyed; and give poor ratings when raw silks are purchased."[7] In short, the apparent unity of the employers was entirely artificial, the result of force and threats by giant capitalists.

This analysis was self-serving and incorrect. Like most conspiratorial theories, including the manufacturers' theory that outside agitators kept the workers on strike by force and threats, the socialist explanation of the solidarity of the bosses was a way of denying more disturbing realities. The fact was that there was no "silk trust" or "giant capital" in Paterson, no huge company or companies that offered the key to the situation as the American Woolen Company had done in Lawrence. All the manufacturers in Paterson were small by the national standards of 1913. In their attitudes toward competition, workers, and unions, even Henry Doherty and the managers of the Weidmann Silk Dyeing Company had more in common with nineteenth-century entrepreneurs than with twentieth-century trusts. Socialist and IWW theorists might pretend that the answer to the question "Who has Paterson by the throat?" was "simple—a few big capitalists": namely, "the same brand of capitalists who have got the country by the throat."[8] But the truth was that silk was and would remain a genuinely competitive industry and that the Paterson manufacturers could not agree among themselves to fix prices. Moreover, practically the only thing they could agree on (all 300 of them), in addition to the importance of a high tariff, was the necessity of retaining complete control of their own businesses and of keeping them free of interference from unions. On the issue of the strike, even though on little else, the solidarity of the bosses was real.

In terms of where and how they lived and of whether or not they hired managers to run their shops, the larger and smaller manufacturers formed quite distinct groups; in wealth, status, and power they had little in common. Most of the larger, older manufacturers were English; many of the smaller and newer ones were Jewish. The English-born proprietors of large firms had gradually achieved acceptance among Paterson's social and political elite—though some preferred living in New York, nearer to the market—but they had originally worked their way up in the trade.[9]

Henry Doherty, for instance, had been a young weaver in Macclesfield, like his father before him. Coming to Paterson in 1868, Doherty had worked as a weaver before entering into partnership in 1879 with another Macclesfield emigrant; at that time they owned a single loom between them. Joseph Bamford, who was also the son of a Macclesfield silk weaver, similarly built up his business in Paterson from nothing but his skill and his knowledge of the trade. Catholina Lambert had begun work as a ten-year-old in a Yorkshire cotton mill; at seventeen he was an office boy in a Boston silk firm; two years later he purchased a partnership in the firm. He renamed it Dexter, Lambert, and Company and eventually relocated it in Paterson. There he made enough money from his five mills (including two in Pennsylvania) to pay for the English-style castle he built on Garret Mountain (now a museum) and also for his collection of some 400 original paintings by Renoir, Monet, Courbet, Rembrandt, and others. Lambert, Doherty, Bamford, and other English-born manufacturers had founded in the nineteenth century, and continued to dominate in the early twentieth century, the Silk Association of America and the Paterson Board of Trade.[10]

It was these owners who had led the fight against the Knights of Labor in Paterson and against every other union that had tried to organize among the weavers and dyers' helpers. In 1886, responding to a proposal for establishing a labor arbitration board in Paterson with Knights of Labor representation, one manufacturer insisted that "he would sooner sell at auction than be compelled to argue with his employees, not one of whom has any practical knowledge of the business." Another declared that "the silk manufacturers were not in harmony with any project that would allow of argument as to what was right and what was wrong in matters relating to employers and employed."[11] Over the years the manufacturers were remarkably consistent in fighting against workers' interference in the running of their business. Each fought for the power to decide by himself the number of looms worked, the hours of work, the piece rates, the schedule of fines, and the ultimate question of who got fired. In 1913 the silk association's midyear report declared that "the very life of the individual manufacturer depends upon running his own mill without interference on the part of his operatives. It is a basic principle of hiring and service that there must be a master and a servant. The master must direct and success must depend upon skilled directions based upon justice."[12]

If the manufacturers were passionately opposed to the 1913 strike, it was because that strike was the most determined effort ever made by the silk workers to organize themselves in a union. The fact that this union was openly revolutionary in its aims, repudiating the whole distinction between master and servant, only served to clarify the issue for the owners and make it easier for them to intimidate deviants within their ranks and to mobilize public support. During the strike a number of manufacturers were interviewed by John Fitch, who concluded that "it is not alone against the IWW that the employers have set their faces. Unionism, organization, under whatever name, is opposed whether its aim be 'reasonable' or 'revolutionary,' because it 'interferes with business.'" Fitch noted that the Paterson manufacturers had previously opposed the AFL as strongly as they now opposed the IWW: "the employers, if pinned down, admit that they are opposed to unionism as such, and not to the IWW alone."[13]

Unable to prevent their Paterson employees from arguing with them about what was right and what was wrong, the large firms had led the exodus to Pennsylvania. In 1891 the mills in Paterson averaged 151 workers; by 1914 the average was down to 58.[14] As the large manufacturers moved their less skilled work out of Paterson, new small mills specializing in plain work took their place. In 1913 it was still possible for an ambitious weaver to start a mill in Paterson with a few hundred dollars, employ his family members and close friends, and carry the product under his arm to the market in New York, making the best deal he could. Such newcomers were already known in 1913 as "cockroach manufacturers," and to them (despite socialist theory, which dismissed them as "the relics of a fast disappearing class") belonged the future.[15] Between these newcomers, who were generally Jewish, and the veteran English-born manufacturers who still dominated the trade there was an impassable gulf. Yet although it would not have occurred to either group to stress the fact, the Jewish and the English-born manufacturers shared a tendency to rely on themselves and to be fiercely competitive and independent.

Some proprietors, remembering their origins, tried to treat their employees fairly and were personally respected by them.[16] But none would brook interference by a labor organization in his own right to run his business as he saw fit. And all of them were caught in a profit squeeze which, as Philip Scranton has stressed, had gradually overtaken the industry since the 1880s; by 1913 they probably could not have afforded major concessions, even if they had been disposed to make them. As one veteran of Paterson's silk industry, who was sympathetic to its manufacturers as well as to its workers, put it, "Competition is what made them hurt the people."[17]

In 1913 the manufacturers would not budge. The rumored tensions in their camp, while real, never affected the outcome of the strike. In fact, the unity of the strikers tended to force the owners together. By mid-March the broad-silk manufacturers, ribbon manufacturers, and silk dyers associations were meeting together and taking common action, in contrast to the squabbling that usually divided them. Within the combined associations the large mill owners spoke for all the manufacturers and dominated their discussions.[18] A number of small mills did indeed go bankrupt.[19] They had no capital reserves and no annexes in Pennsylvania to sustain them. To avoid bankruptcy by ending the long strike, some small manufacturers would have agreed temporarily to anything, even an eight-hour day. But in addition to the pressure from the larger firms, there were two compelling reasons why these small manufacturers could not reach a settlement with their employees.

First, the strikers did not trust them. In 1912 seventeen smaller firms, with orders begging to be filled, agreed to the conditions of the Socialist Labor Party union; then, "as soon as the strike was settled and the slow season was on, these manufacturers repudiated their contracts."[20] To an ally of the big firms, the behavior of these small manufacturers was typical: "I will tell you frankly from past experience the employers—I am speaking of the smaller ones—they will make agreements with these labor organizations, and they will be breaking them the next morning; in fact, before they get downstairs they are trying to find a way to break them."[21] To many manufacturers there was nothing sacred about an agreement. Like the IWW itself, they regarded the breaking of an agreement as a legitimate tactic in labor conflicts. Therefore, the tentative overtures that some of them made in 1913 were not taken seriously by the strikers except as signs of weakness in the opposing camp. The second and more important reason why even those smaller firms that wanted to reach agreement could not have done so is that the silk workers were no longer making separate agreements with individual mills. As a result of their experience in 1912, and guided by IWW strategy, the 1913 strikers had decided not to settle with any firm until the overwhelming majority of the manufacturers agreed to terms. This hostility to piecemeal shop settlements was intended to maintain unity in the strikers' camp—and it did; however, it also cemented the unity of the bosses. With nowhere to turn, the individual manufacturer was practically forced to fight on to the end.

Arthur Price, who employed about fifty workers in his mill on Broadway, tried several times to work out an arrangement with his weavers. In March he offered to concede to their hour and wage demands, pending the outcome of the strike, at which time they would receive the benefits of the general settlement. His workers rejected the offer, and the manufacturers association denounced him. In May he made a similar offer; this time his now-hungry weavers agreed to return to work. The strikers picketed the Price mill en masse. The police, to Price's evident distress, attacked the pickets with clubs and arrested eighty-five of them one day and fifty-seven the next.[22] For Arthur Price and the others, large or small, there would be no separate peace. Defectors would be treated roughly by both sides; the solidarity of the workers and the solidarity of the bosses, which reinforced each other, left little or no ground for maneuvering. Fighting to preserve his business autonomy, each manufacturer had to merge his interests with the general interests of other mill owners, even if in doing so he might go out of business.

Some of the larger manufacturers, too, despite their superior resources, paid a price for not dealing with the strikers. Lambert was apparently one of these. At the beginning of the strike, the manager of his Straight Street mill moved to divide the weavers and intimidate the English-speaking into remaining at work. "The 'boss' went around to all the 'foreigners' and told them not to come in . . . until the trouble was over." On the following afternoon, with the Jews and the Italians locked out, "the power was stopped and a shop meeting called by the boss to determine whether the remaining weavers wanted to go on strike or not. Seventy-five voted 'no strike' and forty-one 'strike,' the boss taking tally. This was a rather remarkable showing in the face of the circumstances, and it must have required a considerable amount of courage on the part of that forty-one to stand up and vote as they did."[23]

Refusing to be intimidated, Lambert's English-speaking weavers soon joined the other strikers; refusing to weaken, Lambert himself stood firm with the other manufacturers. But though they won, he lost. Despite his vast private wealth, or perhaps because of it (so much of his income had been spent in economically nonproductive ways), Lambert could not recover from the strike and was finally forced to declare bankruptcy and to sell his famous collection of paintings.[24]

Stubborn and willful, self-made men like Lambert preferred to risk their life savings rather than to compromise with a union. In this they typified the attitude of the National Association of Manufacturers (NAM), to which many of them belonged. The NAM stood for militant opposition to all labor unions and for the open shop. By contrast, the more sophisticated National Civic Federation recognized conservative trade unions as a possible means of integrating workers into large corporations. Many of the largest corporations in the nation, especially those that enjoyed some protection from market conditions, supported the National Civic Federation position, whereas relatively small and middling manufacturers belonged to the NAM and identified with its anti-union hard line.[25] Essentially provincial, Paterson silk manufacturers had nothing in common with National Civic Federation employers but did business in the old ways. As Haywood understood, "Paterson manufacturers have an absolute monopoly on the finer grades of silk, like brocades, that are made on the Jacquard loom, and it would be easy for them to raise prices to meet wage increases, but because of the cut-throat competition among them, silk is cheaper, on the whole, than it was 15 years ago."[26]

In contrast to the national trend represented by trusts and the National Civil Federation, Paterson manufacturers preferred to meet each other, and their workers, head on. In the summer of 1913, after turning briefly to the AFL in the hope of breaking the strike, the Paterson employers returned to their starting point. Sensing victory in July, "eighty-six of the Paterson manufacturers, all of whom are members of the National Association of Manufacturers, issued what they called an ultimatum. . . . No union of any kind will be recognized, the shops to remain wide open."[27]

This picture of the small-scale, self-reliant entrepreneur, almost equally opposed to combination with other manufacturers as to combination among his workers, must be modified to fit the dyeing sector of the silk industry. Doherty and Wadsworth was not the largest employer in Paterson's silk industry in 1913. The Weidmann Silk Dyeing Company and the National Silk Dyeing Company were both larger, and they operated on a somewhat different basis. Silk dyeing, under separate ownership from the mills, had taken root in Paterson later than broad-silk or ribbon manufacturing, and from the beginning it tended to be big business. Jacob Weidmann, born in Switzerland where his father ran a silk-dyeing plant, had come to Paterson in the 1870s to manage the dye works of a large silk manufacturer. He stayed to build his own dyeing company, relying on the capital and connections of such prominent Patersonians as Garret A. Hobart (vice-president of the United States under William McKinley) and John W. Griggs (former governor of New Jersey and McKinley's attorney general), both of whom became officers of Weidmann's corporation. In 1909, ready to retire, Weidmann sold his company to French capitalists.[28] The National Silk Dyeing Company, second only to Weidmann in the number of Paterson employees, was even larger nationwide. Formed by a 1908 merger of four Paterson-based dyeing companies and one Allentown, Pennsylvania, plant, the firm immediately purchased a larger dyeing facility in East Paterson and continued to expand aggressively, buying three more plants: one each in Paterson, Pennsylvania, and Virginia.[29]

But the greater wealth, power, and readiness to combine of the larger dye works owners were not reflected in greater tolerance for their workers' attempts to organize. On the contrary, their profits came from the intense exploitation of immigrant labor—paying their Italian helpers a fraction of what master dyers were paid, subjecting them to unsafe conditions, and employing them sporadically according to the amount of work on hand. Under these circumstances unions could only limit the dye works' flexibility and lessen their profits. "We are ready to treat with our men at any time, but we will not treat with their union," said Jacob Weidmann during the 1902 dyers' strike. "We say that the men must come to work again before we can do anything for them."[30] In 1913 the dye-house employers took an identical stand and backed it by force.

The methods used to control Italian workers in the dyeing sector of the silk industry were exemplified by the hated O'Brien detectives employed by the Weidmann Silk Dyeing Company throughout the strike. The O'Brien Detective Agency of Newark supplied men at $5.00 a man per day or night to guard the plant and the homes of the employing dyers and foremen. Hired to enforce the claims of French and American investors, the "special detectives" were troubled by none of the mixed feelings of many Paterson policemen about hurting local people. The O'Brien detectives were hated as outside agitators: "We realize that the detectives were a despised body of men by the workers," said Captain McBride. "Even our own policemen despised them."[31] The battle between the detectives and the dyers' helpers, fought out daily in Paterson's Riverside section, epitomized the fierceness of class war in Paterson in 1913.

On April 17, at 6:30 P.M., an O'Brien detective guarding the Weidmann plant shot Valentino Modestino. The special detective, Joseph Cutherton, was putting a group of strikebreakers on a trolley car after they finished work, while an angry crowd of dyers' helpers watched and booed. Modestino, who had just come from the file works where he was employed, was standing on the front stoop of his home in the Riverside section as the familiar confrontation developed between the special detectives and the dyers' helpers. Shots rang out, fired by the detectives to intimidate the crowd, and Modestino was hit in the back. In Paterson General Hospital that night he told the police: "Those bums at Weidmann's shot me."[32] Three days later he died. "We never expected things like that . . . to be shot at, to be killed. Never," said a female striker.[33]

No one, not even the detective, claimed that the pickets had fired or even possessed guns when Modestino was shot, and six witnesses in the Recorder's Court—while Modestino was dying in the hospital—identified Cutherton as the man who had shot him. Although Cutherton (represented by Griggs, Weidmann's attorney) was arrested after the shooting, he was never indicted.[34] Amazed that Cutherton went free despite the evidence against him, State Supreme Court Justice James F. Minturn asked, "What power is there in this community that is greater than the power of the law?"[35] The answer, of course, was the power of the manufacturers.

As a result of their successful campaign for structural reform of local government after the destructive 1902 strike, the silk-mill and dye-works owners were able to work much more closely with the police in 1913 than they had ever been able to do before. One prominent silk manufacturer sat as a member on the police board, which had been created in 1907 to give Chief Bimson a free hand. During the strike the National Silk Dyeing Company lent its car to the police, to be used on patrol. Moses Strauss directed the police to arrest specific pickets outside one of the mills he managed. O'Brien detectives were authorized to serve as "special policemen" by Chief Bimson and as "deputies" by the county. Outsiders were shocked at this open collaboration between manufacturers and police. Two federal investigators noted in 1914 that sixty specials had been "clothed with the authority of the police and sheriff" and used "as a private army of the mill owners."[36]

The manufacturers also enjoyed the active support of the local courts. In New Jersey, where all judges were appointed, whoever controlled the local political authorities also controlled the courts. Recorder James Carroll had been chosen by municipal authorities who were open allies of the mill owners. On the day Adolph Lessig was sentenced by the recorder to six months in prison, he saw a silk manufacturer leaving the recorder's office.[37] The Passaic County grand juries that indicted pickets and IWW speakers but refused to indict the man who shot Modestino had been appointed by the sheriff. Decisions in the Recorder's Court and county court were so flagrantly partisan that conservative New York newspapers were frequently driven to protest against them. But again, what mattered to the manufacturers was that they received support when they needed it. Appeals to higher courts were slow and costly. For all practical purposes, during the period of the strike, the law belonged to the manufacturers.

As the federal investigators concluded, legal authority in Paterson was, "in effect, turned over to the mill owners."[38] Mayor Andrew F. McBride was a Democrat, whereas the manufacturers preferred Republicans; he was an Irish Catholic, whereas they preferred Englishmen or Scots. He was also, however, a trustee of the Paterson Board of Trade, which existed to represent and promote the interests of the business community, especially of silk manufacturers. For a while the strikers of 1913 seemed to hope that McBride would at least make a show of neutrality, in the tradition of earlier mayors and aldermen. But they soon realized that the assaults of the regular and special police on the pickets were authorized and encouraged by the mayor and his police commission. When in late March McBride personally offered them $2.00 for their relief fund, they voted to refuse the money, insisting instead that he curb the police. Speaking for the strikers, Elizabeth Gurley Flynn explained that they wanted justice from the mayor, not charity. In May the Central Strike Committee formally requested McBride to resign.[39]

Throughout the strike the Paterson silk and dye employers were very successful in using the combined force of public authority and private detectives against the strikers. Still, they could not break the strike. As a strategy, force failed. It had failed in the first days, when the police arrested the IWW speakers and tried to club the broad-silk weavers back to work; in response to these actions, the ribbon weavers had joined the strike. Force similarly failed in March when the arrests of Haywood and Lessig at the Lafayette Oval on absurd charges, which Minturn later dismissed, led to renewed activity on the picket lines and in the halls. The murder of Modestino in April resulted in the largest and most impressive demonstration of solidarity of all: strikers and their families marched silently through Paterson from the Catholic church on East 19th Street to the Laurel Grove Cemetery, where they dropped red carnations in the grave.[40] On balance, the owners' strategy of force proved counter-productive.

The tendency of the mill owners to underestimate their employees also hampered the effectiveness of their other strategies. At the beginning of the strike, Weidmann futilely tried to bribe the dyers' helpers to stay on the job by giving them frankfurters. The National Silk Dyeing Company similarly wasted its money when it hired Rodney Miller of New York as "organization engineer." Employed from February to August 1913, Miller was supposed to find out what was bothering the men, as he had done previously in labor conflicts in Brooklyn's clothing industry and Boston's shipping industry. If hiring him represented a gesture from within the Paterson silk industry toward the then fashionable concept of scientific management, it failed; Miller was no efficiency expert, as he made clear, and he made no time-motion studies in Paterson. On the basis of his investigations, Miller predictably concluded that the IWW was symptomatic of a disease of which immigrant labor was the cause.[41]

The problem, as the mill and dye-house owners conceived it, was how to separate their impressionable employees from the militant IWW. After Chief Bimson's initial attempt to drive the IWW leaders out of town resulted in an increase of union support, the manufacturers decided to appeal to a spirit of patriotism. Hanging large American flags over their mills and inviting the town's tradesmen to do likewise, they urged their workers to come back on Monday, March 17, which they designated as "flag day." The stage had been set by the local press, which stressed how un-American the IWW was and luridly featured Bill Haywood's reference to the red flag in his first Haledon speech. The theme of flag day was the necessity of choosing between the flag of socialist revolution and the American flag. Across Market Street a sign, equipped with a large American flag, pointedly proclaimed: "We live under this flag, we work under this flag, we will defend this flag." A similar strategy had been effective in 1909 at McKees Rocks, Pennsylvania, in separating American-born from foreign-born workers and the IWW; it had even succeeded at Lawrence after the 1912 strike. The Paterson silk manufacturers believed that patriotism might achieve what Bimson's scare tactics had failed to accomplish.

On that Monday, hopes were high: "With flags flying and the city decked out in gala garb, the great silk mills of Paterson reopened their doors." According to the Newark *Star*:

> The ending of the gigantic labor war was beautifully planned. The factory owners were going to forgive their erring workmen. Mayor McBride and the police saw the end of their trouble approaching. The ministers who had urged

the workers to return understood that their exhortations were to be obeyed. It was a very successful end of the strike, marred by only one thing—none of the strikers went back.[42]

Throughout the city on that day, strikers wore a card in their lapels—designed and paid for by local Socialists—picturing an American flag and explaining: "We wove the flag. We dyed the flag. We won't scab under the flag." At Turn Hall that morning Flynn met the charge of un-Americanism by pointing to the workers of different nationalities supporting the strike. "The IWW in Paterson has done what no other institution in this city can do. It has brought together men and women of all nationalities. . . . The IWW represents the ideal spirit of America."[43] As Flynn tried to explain the meaning of the red flag, a striking dyers' helper jumped to his feet. "I know! Here is the red flag!" he exclaimed, and held up his right hand, stained blood red from years of working with dyes. "For an instant there was silence, and then the hall was rent by cries from the husky throats as all realized that this humble dyer indeed knew the meaning of the red badge of his class."[44]

Flag day failed miserably. The assumption behind it, like that behind the force used repeatedly against the IWW, was that the majority of silk workers were passive people. The manufacturers perceived the strike as the result of IWW manipulation of their employees and therefore believed that some coun-termanipulation of their own could get the workers back on the job. Intelligent as they were in practical matters, they never understood the anger of the dyers' helper with the stained hand, of the broad-silk weaver forced to work four looms, of the ribbon weaver threatened with dismissal if he or she complained about a piece rate. The managers and owners of the dye houses and mills normally were protected from that anger by their power at the work-place and could explain the collective behavior of their workers in 1913 only as an aberration, a result of outside influence or bad magic. In search for the good magic that would return the majority of workers to their former selves, the manufacturers discarded stratagems that didn't work without learning why they had failed. As a result, they repeated their mistakes. By Monday, March 24, they had begun to take down the useless flags from the mills and to prepare for the next round.[45] In April they tried the AFL.

THE GOLDEN RULE

John Golden was in Paterson on flag day and saw it fail.[46] As president of the United Textile Workers of the AFL, Golden sensed an opportunity: in April he launched an all-out attempt to separate the silk workers from the IWW and end the strike. Golden was a member of the board of directors of the Militia of Christ, a conservative Catholic organization whose purpose was to stamp out radical unionism.[47] His mission in Paterson was to break the IWW strike.

Golden had tried to break an IWW strike at Skowhegan, Maine, in 1907, and Killingbeck recalled that at Lawrence and Hazleton, "Mr. Golden was imported to create dissensions in the ranks"; he predicted that Golden would try to do the same in Paterson.[48] Flynn and Haywood warned that Golden would claim credit for the victory if the Paterson strikers won anyway, or he would "claim credit for being a very noble and conservative labor leader" if he could help them to lose.[49] William Morris Feigenbaum, a moderate Socialist, in a column for the New York *Call* headed "Paterson and Lawrence—Some Inside Facts," recounted Golden's testimony in Washington during the Lawrence strike: he had blamed the women and children for the beating they received from police at the railroad station. "John Golden, union man, for his dirty work in Lawrence, in Washington and in Paterson, is a scab and a traitor," concluded Feigenbaum.[50]

If Golden was seen by many who knew his record as a traitor to the working class, he nevertheless came to Paterson clothed with the authority of the AFL, which, whatever its faults, was the oldest and largest labor organization in America. Feigenbaum and others felt they had to warn the silk workers against this "union man" precisely because he seemed to be on their side. His authority as a labor representative made him potentially useful to the manufacturers. Though Golden might "banquet with the capitalist class at night," Haywood observed, he could still "talk to working men in the daytime."[51] And he could claim to talk on their own behalf. "You have had many pitfalls to contend with and you have escaped them," Haywood told the strikers. "There were the police, the newspapers, the pulpit, the special deputies, but now you have the worst of all—John Golden. He is the strike breaker. He is worse than the detectives."[52]

In Lawrence in 1912, Golden had signed an agreement on behalf of a small number of strikers and sent them back to work while everyone else was still on strike. Afterward, he had written to Ralph Easley, founder of the National Civic Federation, that the Lawrence strike had been "a very rapid education" for the manufacturers and that "some of them are falling all over themselves now to do business with our organization."[53] Promoting the United Textile Workers as the conservative alternative to the radical IWW, he saw a chance to do business in Paterson, and at the beginning of April he received encouragement from the silk manufacturers to go ahead. Opening two recruiting offices in Paterson, the United Textile Workers reached out to the weavers and dyers' helpers, even offering to waive the usual initiation fee. Echoing the line of the manufacturers, Golden's union told the strikers that if they wanted to settle the strike they would have to repudiate the IWW. The manufacturers added that when the AFL union had enrolled about 5,000 strikers, talks to end the strike could begin.[54] The *American Silk Journal*, organ of the Silk Association of America, was hopeful: "The latest phase in the situation, and one which it is thought may possibly lead to a change for the better, has been the arrival in Paterson of the American Federation of Labor. . . . The strikers, divided, may be more inclined to mediate with the manufacturers."[55]

But Golden made few recruits. Although the Paterson press tried to create the impression of a stampede to the reasonable, responsible AFL, even those strikers who had not joined the IWW and did not agree with its revolutionary program kept their distance from Golden's union. The problem, as one of Golden's critics put it, was that "workers have memories."[56] Weavers remembered that over the years the United Textile Workers union had consistently subordinated their interests to the interests of the most conservative silk workers: namely, the loomfixers and warpers. Broad-silk weavers bitterly remembered how Golden had collaborated with Doherty in introducing the four-loom system in 1910.

Some contemporary observers said, and historians have repeated, that the silk workers turned to the IWW in 1913 because the AFL was not interested in them and made no effort to organize them.[57] This half-truth does a disservice both to the AFL and to the silk workers. The AFL did try to organize Paterson's silk weavers and teach them its concept of trade-union discipline. Golden estimated in 1913 that the United Textile Workers had spent over $10,000 on organizing in Paterson since 1905.[58] After several failures, the union had succeeded in 1908 in forming broad-silk weavers' Local 607, which in 1909 joined the loomfixers' and twisters' local and the warpers' local in a Paterson Textile Council. Council approval was required for any local desiring to strike; thus, the weavers could be held in check. In 1910–11 broad-silk weavers in Local 607 called five strikes but were forced back to work in three of them by the council, which was controlled by the two small conservative locals.[59]

The loomfixers' and twisters' local and the warpers' local were authentic craft unions that had existed in Paterson for years, in and out of the AFL, before affiliating with the United Textile Workers. Their limitations were inherent in the craft-union tradition and had little to do with John Golden's opportunism or with his professional IWW baiting. Loomfixers, twisters, and warpers were the most highly skilled and highly paid silk workers. Their power was rooted in their ability to control entry into their trades. In 1903 they withdrew from a struggling federation of independent unions because it was promoting a school that taught silk trades.[60] The warpers' local protected its male members by refusing to admit less-skilled women warpers, whose numbers were increasing.[61] Both craft unions charged a high initiation fee ($25 for the warpers, $30 for the loomfixers and twisters); both required a three-year apprenticeship; both delivered appreciable benefits to their members. Limiting their numbers and avoiding strikes, these craft unionists relied on quiet negotiations by their business agents to get what they wanted from the employer, who knew he couldn't do without them.[62]

The conservative craft unionism that suited the loomfixers and the warpers, however, had little to offer Paterson's weavers who, lacking apprenticeship, were both more vulnerable and more militant. Among his fellow silk workers the loomfixer was known as the "bosses' man."[63] Identifying with the manufacturers, the loomfixer often quarreled with weavers over the condition of the looms and the rate of production. According to James Wood, historian of

Paterson unionism, the broad-silk weavers "were accustomed to taking prompt action over unsettled demands. But this was precisely what the U.T.W. officials did not want. They desired that the membership of local 607 become disciplined in conservative trade-union principles and practices, that they emulate the examples set by the other two locals."[64]

The lessons the weavers learned from contact with the AFL and the sort of discipline they increasingly defined as being in their own interests were not the lessons the AFL hoped to teach them. At the Doherty mill in 1910 Golden had signed an agreement for the loomfixers and twisters at the weavers' expense, leaving the weavers nothing to do but wait impatiently for the agreement to expire. "Well," said Koettgen, "the agreement expired, and Golden came to Paterson, renewed the old one, and was gone again before the weavers knew anything about it."[65] At this point, angry weavers began to leave the United Textile Workers; more left after the Doherty weavers struck against four looms and were told—by the top officials of the loomfixers and twisters, of the warpers, and of their own local—that four looms were standard in Pennsylvania and inevitable in Paterson. When the Doherty broad-silk weavers defied the Textile Council and went out again, late in 1911, the loomfixers and warpers crossed their picket line. The split was complete. The broad-silk weavers of Local 607 had lived within the AFL and learned that the union was organized from the top down, that it collaborated with the boss and sided with the "bosses' man," that it would not protect them against the stretch-out, and that it prevented them from defending themselves by striking. The remnant of Local 607 repudiated the United Textile Workers before disbanding.[66]

The AFL craft unionists in Paterson also learned from the experience. From their side, too, the divorce was irreparable: the weavers were not the material from which responsible trade unionists could be made. Thomas Morgan, long-time head of the loomfixers and twisters, explained in 1914 that the failure of Local 607 and of similar experiments had demonstrated the undisciplined nature of immigrant weavers and the futility of trying to organize them. "We have tried and attempted it different times, but it seems almost an impossibility. . . . They seem to be antagonistic to organization unless they can form an organization that will give them instant action. They want something to strike right away, and seem to think strikes is [sic] the only thing to benefit them." For Morgan, the weavers' emphasis on direct action and conflict was a result of their immigrant background. Italians "don't seem to be willing to stick to any organization any length of time unless you have a strike." And it was practically useless to try to organize Jews because "they would all talk at once. I don't know what it would come to after you got them together."[67]

The head of the warpers, James Starr, drew similar but even more far-reaching conclusions from the failures of the AFL to train the broad-silk weavers in craft-union discipline:

We have tried a great many times since I have been in Paterson and have been connected with our organization to organize foreigners as we find them and to

make a good union man [*sic*] out of him, and also a good American citizen.
. . . The biggest majority, I should say, of the foreigners can't see a form of
organization whereby they won't be allowed to strike just as soon as they are
organized. They have got some radical ideas in their heads and until those
radicals have been supplanted with others by some kind of organization that
don't stand for such things as what they would like to have and like to have
carried out we are going to have trouble going right on with these people.[68]

Starr and Morgan were right: the silk weavers chose the IWW in 1913 not
because they had been ignored by the AFL but because they preferred an
organization that shared their "radical ideas" and did not try to prevent them
from acting on those ideas. The weavers, in short, had rejected the AFL as
much as it had rejected them.

After years of sporadic organizing in Paterson, the AFL entered the 1913
strike with no members among the weavers.[69] Golden's only allies in the silk
industry were worse than no allies at all. The loomfixers, twisters, and warpers
were already at odds with the mass of silk workers before Golden even tried to
intervene in April. On the eve of the general strike, loomfixers and twisters
told the Paterson *Evening News* that they were totally opposed to the strike call.
Drawing on their craft-union experience, they predicted that "six to seven
thousand silk workers on strike with not a dollar in the treasury" would quickly
lead to defeat for the strikers.[70] Although this prediction proved wrong, as the
strike spread beyond the broad-silk weavers and the strikers developed a
sophisticated system of relief, the loomfixers, twisters, and warpers continued
to reject the strikers' appeal to join them. In March the head warper of the
Holzman company threatened to resign from his leadership of the shop if the
Holzman weavers allowed Flynn, who was waiting outside, to come in and
address them—and after the shop voted in favor of meeting with Flynn, he did
resign.[71] Even when the lack of weavers and dyers' helpers caused the mills to
shut down, forcing loomfixers and warpers out of work, they generally kept
aloof from the strike movement and had no influence on it.

Outside the silk industry, Golden's allies in Paterson's labor movement
were almost equally useless to him. Machinists, skilled building workers, and
other AFL unionists, organized in Paterson's Central Labor Council, were
separated by many of their beliefs and practices from the majority of silk strikers. Like AFL trade unionists everywhere, they favored restricted entrance into
their trades and restricted immigration. Within the labor movement, they
occupied a relatively privileged position, which their unions protected against
women, blacks, immigrants, and the unskilled. E. B. White, secretary-treasurer of the Central Labor Council, explained in 1913 that the AFL in Paterson
"has always been willing to play fair with the manufacturers." In the case
of the silk industry, White volunteered, "lots of men now on strike were
getting plenty good enough wages before the strike." If the AFL could settle
the strike, he said, "I don't think there will be any demand for general increase
over the top notch wages before the strike."[72] Supporters like White would

have killed the AFL attempt at intervention if it hadn't been dead already. Given their experience with both unions, the broad-silk weavers, ribbon weavers, and dyers' helpers overwhelmingly preferred the IWW—with its openness, its bias toward direct action, and its emphasis on democratic control of the union and the shop—to the AFL, with its restrictiveness, its bias toward legislative action, and its emphasis on controlling them.

When John Golden came to Paterson in 1913 to organize the silk workers, he carried the double burden of his own history of strikebreaking in Lawrence and the history of the United Textile Workers in Paterson. He came with no local allies in the silk industry to help him except for the bosses and the "bosses' men." Golden was willing to impose on the workers his own notion of what was good for them. This willingness recommended him to the manufacturers, who were opposed to all unions, but alienated him from the silk workers, who would not support a union that would not support them. As a weapon aimed at the strikers, the manufacturers' appeal to the AFL was even less successful than their appeal to patriotism.

The climax of Golden's drive to break the strike came on Monday, April 21, five weeks after flag day. It took the form of a mass meeting in Paterson's largest hall—the 5th Regiment Armory, provided for the evening by the state government—called by the AFL to discuss its plan for settling the strike.

This meeting had been well-publicized; even the Paterson *Evening News*, the only local paper that did not openly support the AFL against the IWW, had contributed to the build-up. "It now remains to be seen whether the claim that has so often been made that the majority of the silk strikers are held out by coercion and fear is correct. Monday night will tell the story and the outcome will make history for Paterson."[73] But Golden and the AFL never had a chance. When the doors opened at 7:30 P.M., some 10,000 strikers filled the armory, with thousands more left waiting outside.

> While waiting for the A.F. of L. speakers the crowd amused themselves by cheering for the I.W.W. until one worker took out his membership book and holding it up in the air called for three cheers for the I.W.W. In a few minutes, you could see thousands of the little red books waved over the heads of the crowd and the cheering for the I.W.W. shook the building. . . . When Big Bill, Gurley Flynn, Tresca and Lessig entered the big hall . . . the crowd opened up before them and they walked all around the hall, the crowd closing again after them amid wild cheering. It looked like a motor boat plowing its way through the waves opening up in front and immediately closing after them.[74]

From this point it was all downhill for the AFL. At 8:30 the crowd was still cheering for the IWW and waving red cards and red handkerchiefs. The chairman, representing Paterson's Central Labor Council, was forced to ask Koettgen to quiet the crowd. Obtaining silence, Koettgen announced briefly that the meeting's organizers would not allow the IWW to speak: "So, let us all go home."[75] Koettgen and perhaps 5,000 strikers then left the hall, but others immediately rushed in to take their places. The crowd booed and jeered at the AFL organizers, who still could not start the meeting.

Some strikers had apparently hoped until the last moment that a real debate between the AFL and the IWW was going to take place; Louis Magnet, the spokesman of the ribbon weavers, had publicly called for such a debate several days earlier.[76] Once the AFL officials made clear there would be no debate, they forfeited any chance of controlling the meeting. Sarah Conboy, organizer of the United Textile Workers, tried to break through the boos by taking a large American flag from the speakers' table and waving it in front of the crowd. Instead of abating, the jeers were changed to good-natured cheers. Giving up, the meeting's organizers sent for Bimson, who entered the armory with about fifty policemen and silenced the 10,000 men and women by clubbing them out of the hall. By 9:10 the hall was empty, and the police, still eager to help the AFL, began readmitting strikers who wore no red. Even then, with about 4,000 strikers allowed to return and the police watching closely, the meeting did not go smoothly. When Conboy made personal attacks on Flynn and Haywood, strikers shouted out objections and had to be escorted outside by the police. When Golden rose to speak, denying that he was a strikebreaker, more people left. Conboy defended the settlement in Hazleton; a Hazleton girl, one of a group who had come from Hazleton to the armory, tried to refute Conboy from the floor but was ejected by the police.

An AFL official from Scranton, claiming that "waving red flags doesn't get you anything," argued that the strikers would not be relinquishing their rights if the AFL were allowed to set up a meeting between a committee of strikers and a committee of manufacturers.[77] The strikers thought otherwise and no committee of strikers was ever appointed under AFL auspices to negotiate with the manufacturers. Though Golden tried to recruit silk workers in the weeks after the meeting before finally admitting defeat, it was apparent on April 21 that his attempt at separating the silk strikers from the IWW was actually strengthening the IWW; those who, like Louis Magnet, had not joined the IWW were completely alienated by the AFL intervention. In 1902, representing the Socialist Trade and Labor Alliance, Magnet had been ejected from an AFL meeting by the loomfixers, twisters, and warpers, who had proceeded to order the AFL weavers back to work during the dyers' strike.[78] But in 1913 the loomfixers and the AFL could no longer order the weavers back to work; now it was Magnet's turn to speak for the majority in ejecting the AFL. Early in May, Magnet and the ribbon weavers issued a statement condemning the O'Brien detectives for trying to encourage silk workers to scab, and pointing to "another force infinitely more reprehensible, *viz*, the officers and organizers of the Textile Workers [who] have come into the strike to divide them, and are [as] hostile to the strikers as are the silk manufacturers." Citing the continued scabbing of the loomfixers and twisters as well as Golden's abortive efforts at intervention, Magnet and the ribbon weavers called on higher AFL authorities to punish the United Textile Workers for strikebreaking in Paterson.[79]

The weavers and dyers' helpers had transformed the AFL meeting in the armory into the most dramatic demonstration of support for the IWW up to that point in the strike. For the manufacturers it was a serious setback. Recapitulating as it did their appeals to the force of the policeman's club in February, to the American flag in March, and to the AFL in April, Paterson's armory show underscored the limits of the power of the employers. They could not get the strikers to abandon the IWW or the strike. Not even swallowing their own distaste for dealing with a labor union had been able to accomplish that.

Less dramatically but equally decisively, the struggle with the AFL also revealed the limits of power of the IWW. With the exception of Pennsylvania, the IWW was supreme in the silk industry. Ribbon weavers in a New York shop that had previously been affiliated with the AFL now joined the IWW to show their solidarity with the strikers; even some warpers in Paterson joined to signal their adherence to the strike.[80] In mid-April, ribbon weavers in Norwalk, Connecticut—who belonged to the United Textile Workers— received a warning from their union not to support the Paterson strike financially, because it was not an AFL strike and because "operatives have been prevented from going to work largely by fear." The Norwalk weavers responded angrily by sending a delegate to the Paterson ribbon weavers with a copy of this divisive letter. On the morning of the armory meeting, they produced a new letter written by Golden himself to the head of their local, expressing concern that "our people at Norwalk" might support the Paterson strikers. This letter did Golden no good either in Paterson, where it further damaged his credibility, or in Norwalk, where the 200 ribbon weavers of Local 428 repudiated the AFL and joined the IWW.[81] Other United Textile Worker locals defied Golden by sending funds to the Paterson strikers, and some other AFL unions also contributed.[82] As Haywood was careful to point out, "Golden isn't the whole A.F. of L."[83]

But if Golden found out in April that he could count only on the old AFL craft unionists to support his attempt to break the strike, the striking silk workers found out that they could not count on AFL unionists to extend the strike in Paterson beyond the silk industry. When the IWW organizers tried earlier in April to reach beyond their natural constituency to AFL electrical and streetcar workers, their efforts fell flat. Carried away by the strikers' wonderful response to the arrests of Haywood and Lessig at the Lafayette Oval, the IWW called for a general strike in Paterson of all union workers, whether IWW or AFL: "Fellow workers, if these vile deeds can be committed against silk mill workers fighting today for just demands, they can be inflicted upon electrical workers, railroad workers, teamsters, and any and all others." Urging all these workers to "meet us in Haledon, at 2 o'clock P.M.," the strike call concluded: "We hereby declare a twety-four [sic] Hour General Strike in Paterson—Meet us in Haledon on Thursday, April 3, 1913."[84] On Thursday the AFL members did not come. Though the silk workers and IWW appealed to them in terms of class solidarity, the AFL rank-and-file went to work as usual. Similarly, in May, an IWW appeal to the electric light workers to darken the city in retaliation for Quinlan's conviction was rejected by AFL members. Electric light workers did meet several times with IWW representatives but ultimately refused to alienate their employers or to risk their sick benefits and accident insurance by breaking their contract.[85] The silk strikers and the IWW could not darken the city of Paterson or shut down its other industries, even for twenty-four hours. Like the AFL raid into IWW territory, the IWW raids into AFL territory were easily routed.

By April the limits of action of both sides were becoming clear. Each major attempt by the manufacturers or the strikers to break the growing deadlock had failed: on the one hand the repeated police offensives, the appeal to the flag and to the AFL; on the other hand the attempt to spread the strike to the Pennsylvania silk industry or to other industries in Paterson. Neither side found itself in a position to win. Gripped by the growing intensity of their struggle, needing allies, the manufacturers and silk workers reached out to nonparticipants and drew them into their struggle. Under this pressure, virtually everyone in Paterson became a participant.

WHICH SIDE ARE YOU ON?

There was a "more direct relationship" between residents in a nineteenth-century mill town like Paterson than in a big city, Herbert Gutman observed. Consequently, "street demonstrations had a greater impact in Paterson than in New York or Chicago." In 1913 Paterson still resembled in crucial ways the town that Gutman described. "A big strike in New York is merely an incident. A big strike in Paterson means business paralysis and a state of uneasiness for every resident in this community," explained the Paterson *Guardian* at the beginning of the 1913 strike.[86] Paterson's 124,000 residents could not easily separate their private and public lives, as people in a large city might have done. With more than one-third of the working population on strike and the police force expanded for the emergency, everyone knew someone on strike or on the police force. The majority of Patersonians—roughly 75,000—lived in households directly affected by the hardships of the strike. The other 50,000 could not escape the general "business paralysis," nor could they evade the competing claims for their allegiance made by the two sides. Compared to New York, Paterson in 1913 was a small town, with nowhere to hide.

Something of the small-town atmosphere of Paterson during the strike can be gleaned from the cross-examination of a defense witness from New York at Quinlan's trial. Rev. Percy Stickney Grant had come to Paterson from his cosmopolitan parish in order to testify to his friend Quinlan's good standing in New York. Quinlan had been living in Jersey City for the previous two years.

Armed with this fact, Assistant Prosecutor Munson Force sought to discredit Grant's testimony. "You don't know where he has lived in the last two years, do you?" Force began his cross-examination. After some hesitation, Grant replied that he believed Quinlan resided in Jersey City.

> FORCE: So you don't know during that time what people he has come in contact with?
> GRANT: I know hundreds of people he has come in contact with.
> FORCE: In Jersey City?
> GRANT: The whole world is not in Jersey City.
> FORCE: Do you know any people in the neighborhood in which he has resided in Jersey City for the last two years?
> GRANT: May I say, my idea of neighborhood and yours may be different.

This was, of course, the point. But Force brushed aside Grant's "sermon," as he called it, insisting that he confine his answer about Quinlan's standing in the community to Jersey City. When Grant asked permission from the court to answer "in my own way," Judge Abram Klenert supported Force.

> THE COURT: Answer this question, if you can; if you cannot, say so.
> GRANT: I should like to remind my questioner that his idea of neighborhood and neighbor is perhaps different from my own.

There is more here than the usual bullying of defense witnesses that took place in Paterson courts during the strike. In refusing to be bullied, Grant unwittingly revealed the distance that separated Paterson from New York. Both the local man and the New Yorker seemed genuinely baffled by the other's concept of community. Backed by the judge, Force insisted that Grant answer his question about Quinlan's reputation in the community in which he lived.

> GRANT: I know the estimate in which he is held by his friends, hundreds of them, with whom he is associated in business.
> FORCE: No. In the neighborhood in which he has lived. . . . Don't you understand my questions? Are they too deep for you? Or what is the trouble?
> GRANT: Do you realize in New York people do not know who lives in the house next to them? What would be the value of their opinion?[87]

People knew who lived next door in Paterson in 1913 and cared about those persons' opinion. The intensity of the struggle and the way it involved everyone are impossible to imagine in a big city with a diversified economy and an anonymous citizenry. In a town in which strikebreakers were routinely followed home and humiliated by being called "scab," in which the name of each donor to the strikers' relief fund and the amount of the donation were regularly printed in the newspaper, the narrow meaning of neighbor and neighborhood still obtained.

Everyone who lived in Paterson had to make decisions in regard to the 1913 strikers, from simple questions of money (should I give to their relief fund? should I extend them more credit?) to complex questions involving fundamental loyalties. Helen Haenichen, for instance, had loyally served Prosecutor Michael Dunn as his secretary through March and April. With the consent of her father, a Socialist, she had been working for the prosecutor for three years, since she was sixteen. It was a good job. But in May she quit. The civil authorities, in a new round of repression, had just prohibited the owners of Turn and Helvetia Halls from allowing mass meetings. This was too much for Haenichen and her father. To the amazement of the prosecutor, she resigned in protest.[88] Similarly, Ardee Numie had been looking forward to a career with the city, after passing the examination for the police force. But when his name appeared on the list of new officers in April, Numie wanted it known that he was not going to join the force during the strike, even if it meant missing his chance; he would not be a strikebreaker.[89]

John Kennedy was expected to be on the manufacturers' side because he was a mill foreman. Observing seventeen-year-old Mary Haeusler picketing his ribbon mill, however, Kennedy was attracted to her. He joined Haeusler and her family on the picket line, remained loyal to their cause during the rest of the strike, and married her.[90] By contrast, Tony Antunuccia seemed to be on the strikers' side. A silk worker and a member of the Central Strike Committee, Antunuccia was called by the defense to testify at Quinlan's trial. Asked in routine cross-examination whom he worked for, he blurted out, "Jerry O'Brien," meaning the detective agency. Now it was the strikers who were amazed. Before they could do anything, Antunuccia disappeared. A month later his father Fedela was arrested while picketing a mill near his home. "According to the stories told in police court, the elder Antunuccia went on the picket line to make good the wrong his son had done."[91]

In ways like these the strike cut across loyalties to family and career, community and class, forcing individuals to choose. As the conflict intensified in April and May, it became impossible for residents of Paterson to support evenhandedly the claims of both the manufacturers and the silk workers. In reality, the process of choosing sides had begun in February and March. The Sons of Italy and the Purity bakers, the civil authorities and the AFL workers in other industries had already made their choices. In April and May, the struggle dominated and polarized the physical and emotional life of the city. For Paterson's middle class—for the well-meaning clergyman, frightened small businessman, and sympathetic newspaper editor—the time to choose had come.

Late in March a group of about fifty Protestant, Catholic, and Jewish clergymen designated a committee of one Catholic and four Protestants to talk with both the manufacturers and the silk workers in the hope of finding a basis for settling the strike. The leader of this effort at mediation was Father Andrew Stein, the lone Catholic on the committee and its spokesman. Earlier in March, Stein had joined in Rabbi Leo Mannheimer's attempt to arrange a conference between the strikers and manufacturers, an attempt that had failed when Mannheimer denounced the IWW and was himself denounced by the manufacturers for interfering in their business and for agreeing with some of the strikers' grievances.[92] Now, Stein himself took the initiative. One of the most influential clergymen in Paterson and one of the most sympathetic to the strikers, Stein thought of himself as "a sort of moral custodian of the city."[93] Pressed by the more conservative clergy, including some members of his own committee, to endorse the position of the manufacturers, Stein persisted in trying to find common ground between the two sides. But the strikers laughed at his committee's suggestion that they return to work if granted a 5 percent increase, leaving their other demands to arbitration; and the manufacturers told him that they refused even to meet with representatives of the strikers.[94]

By the first week in April the committee was ready to give up. Then an opening appeared. The Board of Aldermen called a public meeting in the high school auditorium for April 9, inviting the strikers, manufacturers, and clergy. Though deprived of power by the 1907 change to a commission type of government, the aldermen still enjoyed some of their old prestige from the days when they had really mattered. The Central Strike Committee overruled Haywood's and Flynn's objections to third-party intervention and decided that the strikers would attend the meeting, and even the manufacturers agreed to send a representative. Stein seized the opportunity. An overflow crowd of 2,000, a majority of whom were strikers, heard Stein declare that the clergy were sympathetic to the silk workers and wanted justice for all. But when Stein claimed that the strikers were "dominated by outside agitators" who prevented them from settling their strike, the audience booed so loudly that his further remarks could not be heard.[95] After representatives of the dyers' helpers, ribbon weavers, and broad-silk weavers had presented their demands and the spokesman for the manufacturers had repeated that they would not meet with the strikers except individually, Stein rose again to propose that legislative action on the state level be utilized to settle the strike. Magnet pointed out, however, that the legislature was not going to meet soon enough to be of much use. The clergy's proposal for a legislative solution was rejected, and the aldermen moved into the gap to suggest the formation of a negotiating committee composed of five strikers, five aldermen, and five manufacturers. This idea was enthusiastically adopted at the meeting but shot down the next day when the manufacturers announced that they would not participate.[96]

In fact, the April 9 meeting at the high school was the swan song not only of the aldermen, whose impotence it revealed, but of the clergy as well. Thenceforth, those clergymen who had hoped to act as a third force had to choose sides like everyone else. For Stein, the April 9 meeting marked not the limits of his power so much as of his imagination. Though sympathizing with the strikers, he could not imagine that they knew what they were doing. Like Rabbi Mannheimer, Father Stein assumed that the strikers were being misled and manipulated by the outside agitators. Like Mannheimer, too, he was frightened by the revolutionary program of the IWW.[97] More than Mannheimer, however, who criticized the employers for their intransigence, Stein respected the manufacturers' resolve to run their businesses by themselves; his notion of moral custodianship did not extend to a denial of their right to do so. "We met twice with them," he explained later. "Of course, they were very firm in their determination that the men should come back first and deal with them, and we felt that we had no moral right to interfere with that request."[98] In effect, Stein and the clergy abdicated, yielding their moral authority to the mill owners.

Stein never went as far in his partisanship as his colleague on the committee, Rev. W. C. Snodgrass, who preached the open shop. To Snodgrass, there were not two sides to industrial conflicts—or, rather, "the worker's side was generally fairly conducted by the owners of industry," who had more to lose than the workers and who, having invested their capital in a business, had the right to run it as they saw fit and fire whomever they pleased.[99] And yet, though Snodgrass was one of the conservative clergymen on the committee whom Stein blamed for driving him to a nervous breakdown during the strike, they were, finally, on the same side. Both rejected the very notion of class struggle; both conceded ultimate authority on the industrial field to the manufacturers themselves; and both therefore rejected the claims of the 1913 strikers, with their revolutionary tendency to challenge the mill owner for control of the mill. Between them, Stein and Snodgrass represented the vast majority of clergymen in 1913 who, following the collapse of their efforts to mediate on April 9, embraced—some shrinkingly, some wholeheartedly—the cause of the manufacturers. In the end, Stein endorsed the repressive actions of the civil authorities, praising them for doing their duty "conscientiously" and "with a great deal of wisdom."[100]

Only one clergymen who spoke on April 9 went in a different direction. Rev. Joshua Gallaway, pastor of the Third Presbyterian Church, was not a member of Stein's committee and was not trying to mediate. Rather, he was on the strikers' side. He told the audience that the workers had as much right to organize as the manufacturers. Denying that the IWW was preventing a settlement, Gallaway said he could remember when the manufacturers had refused in the past to meet with striking silk workers led by the AFL. In 1894 he had spoken at the mass meeting held in support of the striking ribbon weavers; over the years he had consistently defended the rights of silk workers. Now, in the high school auditorium, he told the strikers that "if I did not know that you would not get a fair treatment, I would advise you to go to each mill separately, but I now advise you to stand together for your rights and let no power break up your organization."[101]

Gallaway continued for the rest of the strike to speak on the strikers' behalf. In May he entered Turn Hall flanked by Flynn and Tresca and was greeted enthusiastically. From the platform he told the strikers that "many men are angry at you for holding out so long, but that is the only way you can gain anything in this world—holding out, holding out, holding out." And he added: "I want to say right here that I have never been in favor of strikes—strikes are awful things—they are a curse to the city and everyone connected with them, but without strikes the oppression of the workers of the world will never cease." When he finished speaking, there was wild applause (wilder than any yet in the strike, according to one reporter); members of the audience threw their hats in the air and tried to shake his hand."[102]

No revolutionary, Gallaway gave the silk workers something that outside speakers could not give them: continuity with the past in Paterson and his reluctant and therefore moving endorsement of the necessity of struggle. Gallaway was courageous and imaginative enough as a clergyman to take the anger directed against the strikers upon himself, thereby enabling them to feel less alone. His was an authentic local voice raised to defend them—almost the only one outside the Italian or Jewish communities or the Socialist Party—a voice that expressed, beyond politics and tactics, the fundamental humanity and morality of their struggle.

Choosing sides after April 9, a few members of the clergy followed Gallaway's lead, though not so publicly. One Catholic priest from a working-class parish secretly visited Flynn. "His main concern," she said, "was to learn something about the IWW. Were we as bad as the newspaper said? Were we really trying to help the workers of Paterson?" Satisfied with her answers, the priest returned to his church and told his parishoners to stick to their union and not to scab.[103] The vast majority of clergymen, however, either attacked the strikers directly, like Snodgrass, or else, in the manner of Stein, advised them to give up the strike, repudiate the IWW, and throw themselves on the mercy of their employers. Angered by militant behavior they could not understand, frightened by the strike's revolutionary tendencies, and frustrated by the manufacturers' refusal to negotiate, even sympathetic clergy began to preach against the strike and against the IWW, which they regarded as almost a rival church. For those who hesitated, there was the example of Mannheimer, the man in the middle, who lost his position in Paterson in April; even Gallaway, after thirty-three years as pastor of the Third Presbyterian Church, announced in April that he was going to resign.[104] The remaining middle ground disappeared; public opinion polarized further along class and ethnic lines; and contact with the IWW became taboo—even the honest priest having to hide his visit to Flynn.

Clergymen who had begun by trying to mediate ended by contributing to the hardening of the battle lines. In May the clergy held a public meeting at the armory, where the AFL had met, and posed the issue as God and country versus the IWW and the strike. The audience was relatively small, especially compared with the huge crowd that day at Haledon.[105] Late in the strike, when fifteen-year-old Teresa Cobianci was asked whether she considered herself a Catholic, she admitted that "these days I feel different." She was "still a Catholic," but she was troubled: "You go to confess and the priest he tries to find out about the strike and he scolds us that we belong to the union."[106] Taking sides, the clergy as a whole lent legitimacy to the power of the manufacturers, at the price of further weakening their own authority over the silk workers.

With the help of the clergy and the press, then, the manufacturers stepped up their campaign to portray the IWW agitators as revolutionaries who were godless, un-American, and immoral. Though useless in winning over strikers, this campaign was much more successful in reaching Paterson's middle classes. The manufacturers and clergy, for example, called attention to the sexual relationship of Tresca and Flynn (or "Mrs. Jones," as she was pointedly referred to). The publicity did the IWW no noticeable harm with the silk workers but did help to turn middle-class opinion against it.[107] More damaging to its reputation with the middle class was its revolutionary program, especially in the sensational form given to it by press and pulpit. As Flynn at times deliberately deemphasized the IWW's revolutionary goal, hoping not to prejudice the middle class against the strike, the manufacturers emphasized and distorted it. The IWW strategy of repeated strikes leading to workers' control of industry and society was portrayed as a violent assault on all property owners. The manufacturers formulated a publicity campaign stressing the harm done to Paterson by paid agitators who didn't care what the city suffered.[108] Paid advertisements in the newspapers warned that "the entire fabric of the city's business interests and the commonwealth itself is menaced."[109] The symbols employed by the IWW in dramatizing its appeal to the workers—the red flag, the threat of sabotage, the songs of internationalism—were all used against it in the battle for the allegiance of the middle class. An outside observer noted that "the IWW with its strange doctrines has put into the hands of the employers a weapon that they are not slow to use. By keeping these doctrines to the fore, and by charging them with many others that Haywood never has dreamed of, they have lined up the clergy and the professional and business men almost solidly in opposition."[110] Driven by their fears, the small businessmen of Paterson, like the clergy, tended to line up behind the manufacturers.

And yet, where the small businessmen were concerned, there were countertendencies. Linked to the manufacturers by ideological orientation, the tradesmen were linked to the silk workers by self-interest. "The worker is the man who supports the merchant," Flynn pointed out. "The manufacturers . . . are not your customers. The workers are!" Noting in March that "the business men . . . are opposed to the cause of the strikers," she insisted that they were making a mistake.[111] In speeches and in an article she wrote late in March, Flynn argued that the demands of the strikers, if granted, would benefit the tradesmen, whereas "if wages are reduced there is less money in circulation, with the usual result that merchants and business men report that their business is bad."[112] Defeat of the four-loom system would keep employment high, she noted; achievement of the eight-hour day would make it higher. "What does this mean to you, Mr. Business Man? Listen to the music of your cash register and hear it sing. . . . Then if you're wise, help the strikers, or at least don't interfere."[113]

Was Mr. Business Man listening? Not at first. But eventually, he did begin to hear the silence of his cash register. By the third and fourth months of the strike, the landlords of 1,200 tenants were receiving no rent; grocers and bakers were carrying on credit customers who, they knew, could never pay them back; Saturday department store sales were down 50 percent; and saloon-keepers and theater owners were desperate.[114] At the end of May a baker killed himself by swallowing carbolic acid. He had been carrying a large number of strikers and was unable to pay his own creditors or to buy flour.[115] Many merchants felt the same pressures. They wanted the strike over. "The first month they thought it was a joke," observed Flynn in June. "They are starting to feel the pinch of the strike."[116] Meeting as a group in June, the small businessmen resolved to petition the federal government to investigate the strike. Within a few weeks they had the signatures of more than 1,000 Paterson merchants and businessmen on their petition, which squarely blamed the manufacturers for blocking a settlement.[117]

The small businessmen never actively supported the 1913 strike. With the exception of Italian tradesmen, Paterson's saloonkeepers and shopkeepers generally withheld the kind of support that silk strikers had received in the nineteenth century.[118] They did not respond positively to Flynn's appeals or Quinlan's threats of boycotts and rent strikes, nor did they come in April when invited by the strikers to a public meeting for businessmen to hear Flynn and Quinlan present the strikers' cause.[119] Moreover, even Italian or other trades-men who initially supported the strike could be intimidated by threats from the other side. "There are scores of business men here who in the beginning were only too anxious to go to bail for the strikers and their leaders but things have changed," Alexander Scott explained. "Pressure has been brought to bear against these people. They have been given to understand that it would be bad for business to go the bail of anyone connected with the strike, and it has been bad for the business of some of them already."[120] But the businessmen did not finally, like the clergy, throw their whole weight against the strikers. Caught in a cross fire between growing pressure from the manufacturers and economic dependence on the strikers, they became almost paralyzed. Unwilling to take Flynn's advice to withhold the taxes needed to pay for the trials and the special police, unmoved by threats, the tradesmen were shaken by the near collapse of Paterson's economy. They finally defied the manufacturers when they tried for the first time as a group to get someone to settle the strike.[121] Too little and too late, their last-minute appeal for federal intervention was a sign of their desperation.

The businessmen produced no spokesman of their own and left few records of how they felt. One apparent exception was W. L. Kinkead, who was eager to go on record against the strike and the IWW, and in favor of the four-loom system.[122] But Kinkead's business was mill machinery; his direct dependence on the mill owners disqualified him from speaking for the business community in general. More representative, though not a Patersonian, was the owner of a tin-can factory near Passaic who was on the Passaic County jury that convicted Scott of subverting authority. After the trial, Scott's incredulous lawyer asked why he voted to convict Scott, especially given his own recent criticism of Scott's trial judge in connection with another matter. The businessman reluctantly answered that he had read an article in Scott's paper that had "criticized the police, criticized the United States Government for building new warships, and I could not stand for that, and therefore I voted to convict him on this charge."[123] He was expressing the righteous and almost hysterical reaction to Wobbly and Socialist ideas that underlay the confusion of many businessmen. In this regard the businessmen must be clearly distinguished from the silk manufacturers. The mill owners and local authorities opposed the strike simply because it was a strike. But the middle class of Paterson permitted the manufacturers and authorities to run riot out of fear of worse riot. What seems to have paralyzed the tradesmen—despite their economic ties to the silk workers—and thrown the clergy into the arms of the mill owners was the threat of "foreign" revolution. Fear of the notorious Industrial Workers of the World came together in their minds with fear of the new immigrants, foreshadowing the national Red Scare of 1919.[124]

And there was another fear. Those middle-class individuals who felt attracted to the strikers, respected their grievances, admired their restraint, and abhorred their treatment at the hands of authorities were kept in line by the fear of rejection within their own community and class. Just as fear of ostracism by the silk workers discouraged would-be strikebreakers, fear of ostracism by the business and professional classes deterred middle-class defectors. The realistic basis for this fear is suggested by the contemporary story of Grant S. Youmans, a banker in Minot, North Dakota. Horrified by the treatment of IWW free-speech fighters in Minot in 1913 and ashamed of the violence practiced or condoned by members of his class, Youmans violated the great taboo by giving money to the hungry workers and allowing them to post a sign in favor of free speech in his bank window. Ostracized, he lost everything, including his bank. At a public meeting he was told: "There are just two sides to this question, either a man is on the side of the business man or on the side of anarchy. Any man who is not on the side of the business man is a TRAITOR to his country, and should be driven out."[125]

In Paterson, the threat of ostracism was enough. No businessman was as naive as Youmans or went so far, although Dr. T. J. Cooper and Morris S. Grossman and Harry B. Haines went further than most. Dr. Cooper had seen a policeman brutalizing two strikers in jail and had filed charges against him. "Since that time I have been made the subjects of threats on the part of members of the police department and a systematic campaign is carried on to discredit me," he complained late in the strike. He felt it necessary to let the public know, in view of the rumors circulating about him, that he was not a member of the IWW or the Socialist Party.[126] Grossman was less defensive. He had played a leading role, as secretary of the Business Men's Committee, in circulating the petition calling for a federal probe. Attacked by the Paterson *Morning Call* for his remarks, accused of IWWism, Grossman stated publicly that he had nothing to do with the IWW, whatever his critics said, but added that "if they consider the remarks that I have made, which were in favor of the working men and business men of this city, which also means the welfare of the city of Paterson, as an I.W.W. speech, than I am proud to be called such."[127]

Haines, editor and founder of the Paterson *Evening News*, was sympathetic to the strikers and publicly contributed to their relief fund. Much more daringly, he put his newspaper at their disposal, regularly printing announcements of their meetings as well as the names of contributors to their relief fund. Editorially, he came out for the strikers' right to stuggle to improve their conditions, though he withheld judgment on the IWW and remained silent on the whole idea of workers' control.[128] Haines criticized the manufacturers for refusing to deal with the strikers and pointed out how the whole business community was suffering as a result of the manufacturers' selfishness; his own business, he said, was hurt by the cutback in advertising that had been forced on many local businesses as an economy measure.[129] Strikers praised the fair and detailed coverage of the strike by the *Evening News* and urged a boycott of the *Guardian* and (especially) the *Press* and the *Morning Call* for their hostility.[130] In March and April the *Evening News* was the official organ of the strike. Though his newspaper was alone among the dailies in its openness toward the strikers, Haines did not feel isolated. As the *Evening News* happily observed, some other businessmen were also critical of the manufacturers for their intransigence; the clergy and aldermen were trying to mediate; and the paper could still maintain that "the general public" was leaning toward the strikers.[131]

By the end of April, however, the lines were drawn: the stepped-up campaign by manufacturers, local authorities, clergy, and other newspapers to turn the IWW into the overriding issue of the strike made it impossible for the *Evening News* to avoid the issue, and Haines began to retreat. "One paper pretended to be in favor of the workers and tried to take a middle course," said Scott, "and, like all papers that do that, fell flat."[132] In May, Haines announced for the first time that the *Evening News* would choose Paterson over the IWW if it came to a choice. Briefly, he tried to carve out a middle position, pleading with both sides "to forget class differences and talk settlement," criticizing the IWW speakers for "denouncing the authorities of the law and preaching class hatred" and the manufacturers for pretending that they could not afford to grant concessions to the strikers.[133] But it was too late for this kind of evenhandedness. Within days, Haines declared editorially in favor of the three- and four-loom system, on the specious grounds that Paterson needed to keep up with Pennsylvania and on the more revealing grounds that union resistance to the new typesetting machines in his own industry had been overcome. Within weeks, he was urging the strikers to return to work and attacking "labor unions and the industrial workers of the world" for their advocacy of the closed shop.[134] Forced by the class struggle in Paterson to choose, Haines in the last analysis identified with the employers and their view of progress.

The decisive choice was the rejection of class struggle. Like Rabbi Mannheimer and Father Stein, Haines continued to sympathize with the silk workers and to hope that they would be treated fairly by the employers, whom he urged to meet them halfway. What Haines and Mannheimer and Stein could never accept, however, was the necessity of permanent struggle by the silk workers against their employers. A limited strike, as a way of calling the employers' attention to specific grievances, was one thing; an unending strike as part of an ongoing challenge to the power of the employing class was quite another. The dividing line in Paterson between those who merely sympathized with the strikers and those who actually took their side was articulated on the one hand by Mannheimer—whose longing for "permanent peace" was embodied in his hope that each side would reject extremists (the IWW, the NAM) and find mutually satisfactory ways of remedying conditions—and on the other hand by Gallaway, who knew that the manufacturers in their desire for "making their fortunes at the expense of the workers" would never give the workers what they wanted and who therefore came down in favor of "holding out, holding out, holding out."[135]

Caught between the silk workers and the manufacturers, all well-meaning and sympathetic Patersonians sooner or later faced the unpleasant necessity of choosing sides. It was fitting that the IWW, with its emphasis on class struggle, became the symbol of their choice. Gallaway and the priest who came to see Flynn urged the workers to stick to their union; Mannheimer, Stein, Haines, and Thomas Morgan (of the loomfixers and twisters) wanted them to abandon the IWW for their own good. To those caught in the middle, the IWW's ultimate revolutionary goal was finally less important than its rejection of the possibility of class harmony here and now and its consequent insistence that the workers rely on developing their own power through militant strikes. In this way the IWW expressed in theory what the solidarity of the workers and the solidarity of the bosses embodied in practice: namely, that there was no middle ground between the two contending parties. Haywood tried in March to explain this to an unbelieving Rabbi Mannheimer: "In an IWW strike there isn't room for anybody except the working class and bosses."[136] When Mannheimer in March, Stein in April, and Haines in May rejected the IWW, they were rejecting the necessity for class struggle. Choosing sides in the class war, these well-intentioned members of Paterson's middle class simultaneously denied the meaning of the choice they were making.

Not everyone was well intentioned toward the strikers, or agonized over choosing sides. To some wealthy and socially prominent Patersonians, the strike and the strike leaders were simply beneath them. One member of the elite recalled that "while the eyes of the world were on industrial Paterson being rent by Carlo Tresca and Elizabeth Gurley Flynn, social Paterson deemed it unseemly to take cognizance of the presence among us of those other-side-of-the-track characters, and no mention of them and their momentous and prophetic activities ever elicited further response than 'Oh, those Anarchists!'"[137] Other leading citizens urged the use of greater force to get the agitators out of Paterson and end the strike. In May, John Fitch was amazed:

> What has impressed me more than anything else is the attitude of the so-called "best people." They find it difficult to talk calmly about the I.W.W. More than once I have had Patersonians, wearing immaculate linen and irreproachable clothing, men who pride themselves on preserving the amenities, shouting at me, red-faced and gesticulating, their denunciation of Haywood and his fellows.
>
> "These people never should have been permitted to come here at all," said one; "but having come they should be driven out. It is to the disgrace of Paterson that they have been allowed to remain."[138]

Civic pride blended with patriotism in the reaction of these prominent citizens. One leading businessman and organizer of charity told Fitch that the police needed to take stronger measures to free the community of IWW influence, whether such measures technically violated the law or not.[139] A year later, defending his stand, this businessman explained that feelings had become "very strong" not just among strike participants but also "among those who were not directly interested in this trouble, but who were interested to maintain the good name and character of this city."[140]

Driven by fears for their city and their class, other prominent Patersonians recommended the formation of a vigilante group. The editor of the Paterson *Press* was the most consistent advocate of this position. In March he printed on the front page a letter from an anonymous Civil War veteran who called upon citizens to get their guns, "the first graves to be filled with Haywood and his crowd."[141] The editor also wrote to California, asking how citizens in San Diego and Los Angeles had driven the IWW out, and published the reply. He argued that while the police might feel bound by the law, citizens were entitled to do what they had to do to protect themselves. In April, acknowledging that "no violence of consequence" had been committed by the strikers, the *Press* nevertheless urged Paterson's citizenry to follow the example of Los Angeles and Akron, which had "kicked the I.W.W. out of town in short order."[142]

These open and repeated invitations to violence were tolerated by the same authorities who prosecuted Scott for criticizing the police and arrested strikers for saying "scab." By the first week in May, when the mayor appointed a committee of nonparticipants to settle the strike, talk of violence against the IWW was becoming respectable. Meeting in the council chamber of the city hall on May 7, the mayor's committee went through the motions of discussing a negotiated settlement until a minister, impatient at the lack of "action," reminded the other members that the IWW was the problem. Emboldened, a leading physician rose to speak. "No matter when this strike ends, as long as it lasts and much longer after it is forgotten," he said by way of preface, "the teaching of these people will remain planted in the memory of our citizens." He proposed that the citizens of Paterson band together like the citizens of Akron to drive the IWW agitators out of town. Even if the citizens lost the ensuing battle, it would be worth it: "If we have to go down and out, let us go down fighting."[143] The committee applauded the doctor's speech.

Though no vigilante group was ever formed, the public calls for violence in the mayor's committee and on the front page of the *Press* contributed to the hardening of thought and feeling in Paterson. After studying copies of the *Press* and the *Morning Call* later in May, State Supreme Court Justice Minturn concluded that no unbiased jurors could be found in Paterson or its surroundings to try Haywood, Tresca, Flynn, and Lessig; he granted them a "foreign jury" made up of jurors from another country. Earlier, after Modestino's death, Minturn had lamented the physical consequences of the struggle in Paterson: the loss of work, of business, of life.[144] Now, in granting the foreign jury, he acknowledged that the deeper destruction was at the level of thought and feeling. According to the defense attorney, Minturn explained that there was not one public opinion in Paterson but "two states of public mind, one for the strikers and one against the strikers. . . . It would be impossible to get anyone possessing a state of mind absolutely fair and impartial."[145] With the city split into warring camps, Minturn was in effect forced to move justice out of Paterson to preserve it. A foreign jury, rarely needed before, had been used in 1880 to protect the rights of a Paterson property owner who had shot and killed a May Day tresspasser.[146] But Paterson was no longer the kind of town in which public opinion automatically tended to oppose violence against workers. In 1913, as Minturn recognized, opinion was divided along class lines.

Ironically, Minturn—who lived in Hoboken—personally experienced the affects of this polarization several weeks later when he tried to attend a ribbon weavers' meeting at Helvetia Hall to see for himself how the meetings were conducted. But the enlightened judge who tried to rise above his class—"the Honest and Humane Judge, who would not have Crucified Christ," as Gallaway had called him[147]—could not entirely escape the consequences of class struggle in Paterson. "At the hall the justice was greeted by one of the strikers, who, believing that the well dressed man was a manufacturer, told him the meeting was for strikers only. Later it was learned who he was, and a number of workers tried to locate him, but to no avail."[148]

DEADLOCK

"The strike is won," announced an IWW speaker on April 25, adding with unconscious humor that "it is only a question of the manufacturers realizing this."[149] That same day a Paterson weaver went to Hackensack to beg his sister for money. When she refused, he lost control and began to beat her. He was arrested and taken to the Hackensack jail, where he tried to tear his cell to pieces and had to be held down by three policemen.[150]

The official line was that victory was assured by the unity of the strikers; the reality was that the strikers were growing desperate. Most managed to keep control and even a sense of humor. On April 26, strikers erected a tent on a vacant lot near Weidmann's plant: "They declare that since the police refuse to allow them to walk the street they propose to camp out."[151] The good nature of the Paterson silk workers was a great resource, enabling them to withstand their growing hunger and isolation. But every resource has its limits, and everyone has a breaking point. In May, as if sensing that many strikers were near that point, the manufacturers and their allies tightened the pressure.

The crucial events of May began with the trial of Quinlan. On April 25 Quinlan, Flynn, Tresca, Haywood, and Lessig had been indicted by a Passaic County grand jury on charges stemming from the first days of the strike. The prosecution chose to try Quinlan first. The choice was surprising, in one sense, because the case against Quinlan was extraordinarily weak; he hadn't even spoken to the strikers on the first day, when he was supposed to have incited them. In another sense, however, the choice was logical: Quinlan had consistently defied and mocked the local authorities. The very weakness of the case against him added to its importance. If he could be convicted, anyone could.

During the trial there was little picketing. Attention focused on the Passaic County courtroom. On May 7 thousands waited outside for the trial to begin, accidentally interrupting with their cheers a murder trial that was nearing completion, distracting students in Paterson High School directly across the street. During the next two days thirty witnesses testified that Quinlan hadn't advocated violence on February 25, and nine policemen testified that he had. On May 10, after twenty-two hours of deliberation and despite tremendous pressure to convict (the doctor's call for vigilante justice was made on the day the trial began), the jurors declared themselves deadlocked. They were denounced by the Paterson *Press* as a disgrace to the community. On Monday, May 12, new jurors were selected, and Quinlan's second trial began. This time the prosecutor told the jurors that failure to convict would render the county helpless. On May 14 the jury found Quinlan guilty.[152]

The New York *Times* described what happened next.

> The strikers in the courtroom had risen to hear the verdict. For a minute or two they stood still in their places, a few of them repeating to themselves in low voices the words of Foreman Space, "Guilty as charged."
>
> Then the tension broke. Little Carrie Torello, one of the busiest of silk mill pickets, who had sworn that Quinlan never uttered the words in the indictment, started to run out of the courtroom.
>
> In the streets and on the high school green outside the Court House about 500 strikers were waiting to hear the news. They were lounging about on the grass, and were ready to give Quinlan a great cheer when he appeared among them a free man, as they were certain to a man he would.
>
> "Guilty as charged. Guilty as charged!" shouted Miss Torello as she came running out of the Court House. In a moment she was surrounded by the strikers. They would not believe that it was true.[153]

Quinlan's conviction changed the strikers and the police. An observer on the day of the verdict noted that it "angered the strikers and increased their bitterness toward the police who were the chief witnesses." On the following day, during what may have been the best-attended meeting held at Turn Hall, strikers noticed police detectives scattered in the audience. "Go to them. Put them out," someone shouted, and many took up the cry. Only the intervention of Thomas Lotta, who was chairing the meeting, prevented violence.[154]

The police seemed to be inviting violence. The Quinlan verdict, which angered the strikers and made them touchy, encouraged the police to be more aggressive. Following the collapse of all efforts at mediation, the open calls by the press and respectable citizens for extreme measures, and the failure of the authorities to punish the O'Brien detective who killed Modestino, the Quinlan conviction gave the police license. Early Monday morning, May 19, they were unusually rough in arresting eighty-five pickets, including seventeen women, in front of the Price mill. Later in the morning a group of police detectives accompanied the official stenographer, Sidney Turner, to Turn Hall, where they stood in the back talking noisily. Frederick Sumner Boyd was speaking from the platform when Koettgen leaped up and shouted: "You detectives in the back of the hall had better keep quiet, and if you can't why we'll put you out!" From all over the hall came angry cries: women in the galleries yelled, "Put them out"; men suggested, "Throw them out the windows."

Then strikers spotted Turner sitting on a radiator in the back, taking notes. Earlier in the strike he had posed as a reporter from the Newark *Star*, but now he was known, and they told him angrily to get out. One of the detectives took out his revolver to protect Turner. Infuriated by the sight of a gun in Turn Hall, the strikers surged toward the detectives. The speakers on the platform could not control the disturbance, but Lotta and Tresca waded into the crowd; the strikers' band began to play; the strikers slowly began to sing; the detective replaced his gun; and the detectives left quickly with Turner, allowing the meeting to continue. When Quinlan was introduced, "pandemonium broke loose," and the speakers expressed the frustration everyone felt. Boyd called the police "ruffians," "a bunch of cowards," and repeatedly referred to Bimson as "Bumson"; Quinlan termed the policemen "low dogs" and reached a new height of rhetorical violence by asserting that "we are preaching class warfare and we want to end this matter between ourselves and the police once and for all." Outside, the detectives invited the strikers to start something, shouting, "Come here you yellow dogs and we'll give it to you."[155]

The greatest provocation was yet to come. On the following day, strikers arriving for the morning meeting found Turn and Helvetia Hall closed and surrounded by police. Stunned and furious, they were about to resist when Quinlan came by and shouted, "On to Haledon"; the workers reluctantly followed. "It is not the policy of the I.W.W. to run away," Quinlan explained, "but we want to avoid trouble and trouble is what the manufacturers want." Trouble tried to follow the strikers. Some Paterson detectives boldly crossed the town line into Haledon. This would have precipitated a riot had not a Haledon councilman taken the detectives to Mayor William Brueckmann, who told them that their continued presence in Haledon was a provocation and that he would not guarantee their safety for ten minutes. They returned to Paterson. Meanwhile, Magnet and other strikers went to Mayor McBride, demanding that he open the Paterson halls, but McBride replied that the speakers had abused the right of free speech and made the halls "disorderly houses." Leading citizens privately acknowledged that the closing was illegal but supported the action on the grounds that it could force the strikers back to work. When the hall owners sought an injunction against the police in order to reopen, the Turn Hall proprietors were themselves arrested on the grounds that they had permitted a situation of near-violence at the time the detective drew his gun; the angry words of Boyd and Quinlan were also included in the indictment. In order to keep their liquor licenses (their main source of income), the proprietors of both halls agreed in the end to allow no more mass meetings. Meetings of a single shop or of a single craft (such as the dye workers or the ribbon weavers) were permitted. But for the last two months of the strike no outside speakers addressed general strike audiences in a Paterson hall.[156]

For the strikers, it was a no-win situation. Had they fought to protect their right to free assembly, they would have given the manufacturers and police the excuse they sought for an all-out assault; perhaps the militia would have been brought in, as in 1902, or the riot guns brought out. By restricting themselves to verbal and legal forms of defense, the strikers lost their meeting places.

The loss was a serious one. The strikers and IWW speakers tried holding mass meetings across from Turn Hall in adjoining yards on Ellison Street, with members of the audience literally hanging off the roofs of the houses, and then—more safely—at the old Doremus Estate on Water Street. But the outdoor meetings were not as well attended, and their organizers kept moving meeting times around in an attempt to bring people out. At an Ellison Street gathering Lotta denied that the Italian dyers' helpers were going back to work and urged strikers to resist attempts by the bosses to play Americans off against Italians. Koettgen pleaded, "We must meet to compare what is going on. We must not believe the lieing [sic] newspapers." The newspapers had begun carrying reports of breaks in the strike, alleging that this or that shop or nationality was going back to work. "The authorities are very wise in concentrating their energies against the right of free assembly and free speech," a strike sympathizer realized early in June, "for as soon as the strikers [sic] cannot get the true information first hand he or she becomes prey to all the gross fictions which are palmed off by the newspapers." At Haledon on Sunday, representatives from the shops cited in the press told the rest of the strikers that the rumors were untrue. But rumors spread quickly and had to be combatted daily. Simultaneously, the Paterson *Evening News* turned against the strike, encouraging strikers to leave the IWW and return to work and featuring rumors of breaks in the strike. On Monday, May 26, about sixty women and girls did return to work at Frank and Dugan, "believing the stories that the strikers were breaking ranks, but when they found that the situation has been misrepresented to them they walked out again."[157] Thus, the closing of the halls, unlike previous police actions, did not increase the solidarity of the strikers but rather increased their tendency toward fragmentation. Deprived of their daily ways of letting each other know what was going on, they became much more vulnerable to rumors of breaks.

Hungry, lacking their usual means of communication, and increasingly isolated, the strikers found themselves under siege in Paterson. After three months, the strike as a way of life had exhausted local resources and was in danger of being unable to sustain itself. Circus day came on May 16, during the week between Quinlan's conviction and the closing of the halls. The parade was canceled because the police were too busy with the strikers to provide an escort. Besides, as the New York *Globe* explained, "the twelve weeks of enforced idleness has [*sic*] made most of the strikers feel the pangs of hunger and they haven't any money for food, much less for circuses." Three days later a housewife, Mary Procopia, was arrested and held on $2,500 bail.

> Carrying her six months old baby she was passing by a crowded corner on her way to do some washing to secure money to buy food for four hungry children when, she says, she saw a policeman arrest a man who was doing absolutely nothing. She protested and finally hit a detective with her umbrella.
> In court she was not allowed to take her baby to jail. Finally a woman in the crowd offered to look after it. . . . One of the youngsters at home is very sick, said the mother. The father has been on strike for the entire thirteen weeks.[158]

The pressure on the strikers increased in every area of life: eating, meeting, picketing, even health care. At the end of May an Italian striker took his sick wife to the hospital. General Hospital was supported by silk workers through shop collections and fraternal society donations—Italian societies alone donated $3,000 a year—and gave free treatment to anyone who could not afford payment. Yet after he learned that her husband was a striker, the head of the hospital insisted the sick woman pay. When the husband explained that they had no money, he told them to "go to Haywood and get the money." Several weeks later another striker was told to remove his mother from the hospital; he had worn an IWW button when visiting his mother and had acknowledged, when asked, that he was an IWW member. Meanwhile, during May almost 600 strikers were arrested, and the daily number of pickets was declining, despite the temporary surge after Quinlan's conviction. At the Doremus Estate, strikers were harassed by police and told, "If you don't like it, just start something." As a result of the growing pressure, a striker attacked Henry Doherty, Jr., and was sentenced to one year in jail. The pressure exacerbated tensions between the strikers' Executive Committee and the IWW speakers. Boyd and Lessig (who had threatened to darken the city) and other speakers had reacted to the conviction of Quinlan and the closing of the halls by violently berating the city and its authorities. The Executive Strike Committee partly blamed the increased isolation of the strikers on these verbal excesses and warned the speakers to tone down their remarks. For the first time, the manufacturers and the police had put the strikers on the defensive. With the support of middle-class opinion, itself driven by fear of the IWW and the new immigrants, the police had closed the strikers' halls and handed the manufacturers a real victory.[159]

And still the strikers stayed together. Though some people were working at Price's mill and a few other mills and dye houses scattered through the city, the overwhelming majority of silk workers remained on strike, and the industry as a whole remained shut down. Early in May a visitor to Paterson described the daily routine: "Picketing, singing, attending strike meetings, a walk to get the latest news of the trials going on in Paterson, and again more educational meetings—these things make up the day of the strikers." The visitor was most impressed by the strikers' ability to endure hardships, especially their ability to continue struggling, with "grim determination," on only one meal a day.[160]

The number of strikers needing food from the relief committee had already grown from the hundreds into the thousands. At the end of the month another visitor emphasized the physical suffering of the strikers (from encounters with O'Brien men and police, as well as hunger) and the financial losses on both sides, "yet to-day, more than three months since this industrial war began, a settlement seems as far distant as ever. The employers say that they will go out of business before they will yield to the demands of the strikers; the latter fervidly declare that they will starve rather than return to the looms."[161] Earlier in the month, *Solidarity* had recognized "the strike deadlock"; at the end of the month the Paterson *Evening News* spoke of "the present deadlock," and Mayor McBride told the New York *Times* that the "stubborn resistance" of both sides had "resulted in a deadlock."[162]

The deadlock was a result of solidarity on both sides. The struggle was not quite an equal one, however. In a war of attrition, Pennsylvania gave the manufacturers the advantage. The greatest resource of the Paterson mill owners—greater even than their control of the police, the courts, the local media, and most respectable opinion—was their ability to shift orders to their plants across the state line. "With plenty of cheap labor in Pennsylvania and extra looms the Paterson owners found a way to retain their regular clients," explained an industry insider, late in May. As orders from regular customers were received, "they were promptly transferred to mills in Pennsylvania."[163] In the busy season of a good year, nevertheless, the strike was hurting them greatly. "This is the turning point in the Paterson strike," said the New York *Call* after the halls were closed. "No matter how much the workers have suffered, the manufacturers can sum up their suffering in great financial losses. But this is the time when every weapon in the possession of the manufacturers is turned against the worker."[164] Pushed to the wall for the first time, the strikers and the IWW fought back by developing new resources and reaching out toward new allies. In May they transformed Haledon into their outside base where—like the manufacturers in Pennsylvania—they could reassert their control and find ways to sustain themselves. In response to the manufacturers' spring offensive and to the dwindling of its own resources, the Paterson strike entered its most creative phase.

CHAPTER FOUR

The Bridge: New York

The IWW served as a bridge between the Paterson strikers and the New York intellectuals. At first, in April, traffic flowed primarily eastward across the Hudson as emissaries from Paterson tried to alert New Yorkers to the strike situation. Then, in May, responding to the pull of the strike and especially of the Haledon meetings, New York intellectuals "went over" to New Jersey to see the strike for themselves. As their commitment deepened, they helped the silk workers to bring the strike itself to New York in June in the form of the Paterson Pageant.

There was nothing easy or automatic about the initial contacts or eventual collaboration between the New York intellectuals and the Paterson silk workers. Class differences tended to separate them. But the IWW had developed vital ties to both groups; victory at Lawrence in 1912 had won for the IWW the respect of both Paterson silk workers and New York radical intellectuals. Now, in 1913, the IWW brought its admirers together.

Going beyond admiration, some radical intellectuals learned in 1913 to see Wobblies as colleagues. As the IWW speakers in Paterson developed complex relationships with the strikers, so in Greenwich Village the same IWW leaders developed relationships rooted in mutual respect with writers and artists. These relationships began to take shape in the months before the strike, intensified in April and May, and bore fruit above all in the Pageant. Writing and fund raising in New York, speaking in Paterson and Haledon, serving wholeheartedly on the working committees that brought the Pageant into being, intellectuals participated directly in the class struggle. Their interest in the IWW and the strike was not "radical chic."[1] Radical chic implies a fashionable flirtation with revolutionary types on the part of a condescending elite. But John Reed, Margaret Sanger, Hutchins Hapgood, and many other Village intellectuals risked themselves—including their middle-class prejudices—in direct and personal contacts with Wobblies and silk workers. Joining their activity to the activity of the strikers, they were forced to question some of their own assumptions and biases.

Such rich cross-class ties are unusual today. What made them possible in 1913 was the separate vitality of the Paterson workers' movement and the Greenwich Village cultural movement; neither was parasitic on the other. More generally, genuine cooperation was facilitated by the open cultural and political climate of 1913, which enabled different groups to learn from experience and from each other. The intellectuals were able to appreciate the silk workers— and to learn that they, not just the IWW organizers, *were* the strike—because of the opportunities they had to mingle informally with the IWW organizers in Greenwich Village and to observe them and the strikers in action together at Paterson. This chapter analyzes the contacts in the Village; the next chapter examines the intellectuals in action in Paterson. Begun in New York, the bridge was completed in New Jersey. At both ends the openness and flexibility of the IWW's style made the bridge possible.

Like the intellectuals, the IWW speakers had prejudices of their own to overcome. Intellectuals were traditionally viewed with suspicion by the IWW, which was always tough on so-called intermediate groups: small businessmen, clergy, farmers, and highly skilled workers, as well as intellectuals. It was much easier for Lessig and Koettgen, themselves skilled weavers, to go beyond the IWW's narrow emphasis on unskilled workers than it was for them or the national organizers to see the necessity for working closely with writers and artists. Hindsight, based on the knowledge that such an alliance was achieved in Paterson, can cause us to overlook the difficulties. As a corrective, it is useful to note that there was another vital social movement in Paterson during the strike, one that the IWW neglected. In March and April large groups of farmers were arrested in Paterson for committing civil disobedience. Mayor McBride had decreed that the farmers' market be moved from its traditional location on Main Street; the farmers resisted. The silk strikers and IWW speakers, who made great and largely unrequited efforts to woo Paterson's other workers, ignored the embattled farmers. Nationally, IWW strategy identified landless farm workers as the revolutionary agrarian class and farmers as the enemy; IWW doctrine carried this anti-farmer bias to such an extreme that *Solidarity* editorially termed the Zapatista landowning peasants in Mexico allies of capitalism. Prejudice against farmers may have cost the IWW an ally in Paterson. The missed possibilities are suggested by the first ballot of the jury that eventually convicted Alexander Scott: only two members of the jury were farmers, and they were the only two who voted for Scott's acquittal.[2]

Like farmers, intellectuals frequently had been dismissed by the IWW as class enemies. Moreover, the IWW leaders in Paterson tended to rely on tactics that had worked at Lawrence, where the strike had been shorter and the support of intellectuals had never become crucial. If, in the third and fourth months of the Paterson strike, New York intellectuals were able to play an essential role, bringing their talents and connections to bear on the problems of the strike, it was only because in this area Haywood and Flynn opted for experience over dogma. The informal contacts between Wobblies and intellectuals in New York were as important for the IWW as they were for the intellectuals. It was in New York that they began to work out the forms of equality between them.

Three new Village institutions provided ideal settings for the exchanges between Wobblies and intellectuals: the pages of *The Masses*, where writers and artists created the basis of a common discourse with the IWW; Mabel Dodge's salon, where Haywood participated in the give and take; and the club called "Heterodoxy," where the emerging network of Village women supported Flynn. In these settings in the months before and during the strike, the foundations of the bridge were built.

THE MASSES AS MEETING PLACE

The Masses took the Village cultural rebellion and transformed it into a social and political rebellion as well, linking its struggles against the status quo with those of the IWW. True to its origins as the means of expression of artists and writers, *The Masses* under Max Eastman affirmed the reality of class conflict without attempting to deny the reality of other conflicts. In its articles, editorials, and cartoons the magazine brought the ideas of revolutionary unionism into contact with the ideas of bohemianism and feminism. In this way *The Masses* created a kind of meeting place for movements and ideas.

To the writers and artists of *The Masses*, the IWW was as exciting, as sexy, as the feminist movement and for the same reason: it provided an objective correlative for their rebellious ideas. To Reed, the Socialist Party was "duller than religion." The rebellion of young Villagers against religion and respectability, against the reigning wisdom and the dominant conventions in life and art, required a force to the left of the Socialist Party and below it. After Lawrence, many Village intellectuals tentatively located that force in the IWW. Visiting Lawrence after the strike, Reed felt that the IWW now "dominated the social and industrial horizon like a portent of the rising of the oppressed."[3] Shortly after the great victory at Lawrence, Max Eastman wrote a letter to the New York *Call* "denouncing respectability" and defending the IWW. Eastman's letter—his first public utterance as a socialist—attacked mainstream Socialists for wanting to reject Haywood and the theory of class struggle "just when the fight was getting hot."[4]

To young intellectuals like Eastman and Reed, the IWW seemed to embody the possibility of revolution from below. The mainstream tendency in the AFL, even more than the mainstream tendency in the Socialist Party, appeared respectable, cautious, accommodating—more a part of the status quo than a radical challenge to it. In *The Masses* Eastman frequently criticized the outmoded organizational ideas of the AFL, as he did—with characteristic humor and attention to detail—in a short piece he entitled "Crafty Unionism."

The American Federation of Labor decided that men who drive brewery wagons are "Brewers," and should join the Brewery Workers' Union, but men who drive mineral water wagons are "Teamsters" and should join the Teamsters' Union. The beer drivers, it was assumed, come into a closer relation with the article of manufacture than the water wagon drivers.[5]

The AFL separated workers from each other instead of combining their strengths, Eastman believed, just as the Socialist Party was as a whole neither proletarian nor revolutionary. By contrast, he later explained, "the I.W.W. was the only genuinely proletarian revolutionary organization that ever existed in America—one of the few that ever existed anywhere."[6] Eastman and *The Masses* needed the IWW for the hope of change from below that it represented. Without the revolutionary industrial unionism of the IWW, *The Masses* writers and cartoonists could still have made fun of society but could not have hoped to transform it.[7]

In the same way and for the same reason that *The Masses* embraced the IWW, it embraced the women's movement as an emerging social force that could transform dreams and desires into reality. Eastman was an active feminist even before he became a socialist. In stories, editorials, and especially cartoons, the writers and artists of *The Masses* articulated the logic of women's suffrage and extended that logic beyond political equality to sexual and economic equality. As Mari Jo Buhle points out, socialists had traditionally portrayed women as helpless victims. Now, "most of all in the *Masses*," women were portrayed as active agents in a revolutionary process. "In its prose and visual representations *The Masses* made woman and her liberation a major subject. Never before had Socialist journalists so avidly depicted the slum woman as oppressed but nevertheless capable of a profound resistance, offered so much subjective evidence of an awakening female sensuality, and devoted itself to the fondest expectation of woman's triumph. . . . Woman's situation became for these writers and artists a way of knowing and believing, a touchstone for revolution."[8]

Women and Wobblies, sexual emancipation and industrial unionism—this was the territory *The Masses* worked. It was *The Masses* that publicized Haywood's praise of the women in the Lawrence and Paterson strikes and quoted his conclusion that one woman was worth three men.[9] Chief editor Eastman was never happier than when the suffrage and strike movements converged. In 1913 he commented in the magazine on a small news item about Hazleton silk strikers. "Little working girls, lost in ignorance and industry, up in Hazleton, Pa. are carrying pictures of Emmeline Pankhurst next to their hearts. And with good reason. For Emmeline Pankhurst has not only lit the torch for women, but she has shot full of fire the revolutionary movement of the workers all over the world."[10] Eagerly, Eastman seized on signs of convergence between feminism and the revolutionary labor movement. But unlike the Wobblies, Eastman never subordinated feminism and suffrage to the class struggle. As a feminist journal, *The Masses* insisted that "the question of sex equality, the economic, social, political independence of woman, stands by itself parallel and equal in importance to any other question of the day." So Eastman announced in a January 1913 editorial, adding that "the awakening and liberation of woman . . . is not an event in any class or an issue between classes. It is an issue for all humanity."[11]

The genius of *The Masses* consisted in committing itself totally to class struggle without trying to reduce everything to an aspect of that struggle. Sex and class were equally sources of energy, fun, and hope. With women and industrial workers moving to liberate themselves, no privilege seemed secure, no truth eternal, and no dream impossible. Like Dodge's salon and Heterodoxy, the magazine under Eastman was open to the new currents and was borne along by them.

Founded in 1911 as a moderate Socialist monthly, *The Masses* was almost defunct when Eastman took over in the fall of 1912 and moved it decisively to the left, aligning the magazine with the most militant tendencies within the women's movement and the labor movement. Responding to its energy and openness, members of Heterodoxy and other feminists wrote pieces for *The Masses*, as did Arturo Giovannitti, Haywood, and Flynn; and the IWW press reprinted many articles from the magazine and defended it when it was attacked by the Associated Press.[12] Art Young's famous cartoons for *The Masses* were sometimes triggered by the speeches of Haywood, Tresca, Giovannitti, and especially Flynn; completing the circle, the IWW press reprinted a number of his cartoons.[13] Inspired by Lawrence and Paterson, *The Masses* helped shape the public image of the IWW as the organization of revolution and of the Lawrence and Paterson striker as "the prototype" of the revolutionary worker. On the night of the Pageant, it was the only magazine sold by the Paterson strikers and the IWW in Madison Square Garden.[14]

The writers and artists of *The Masses* were drawn to the IWW partly because of their own developing class consciousness. Even before they became involved in the Paterson strike, many of them had experienced exploitation as writers and artists. They gave their best work to *The Masses* for nothing because the only work the commercial magazines would pay them to do was not their best. Young, whose cartoons had been featured for years in the commercial press and who was very successful, was clear about the price of success. "I do not think of myself as having arrived at any degree of achievement commensurate with my potential talent and capacity for work," he later wrote. "It was my money-earning ability that determined my right to exist, and I got through in a way—but what a way! Having spent so much of my time maneuvering to make enough cash with which to live decently, I count most of that effort a hindrance to my development, both as a man and as an artist."[15] Young's work for *The Masses* expressed his anger not only on behalf of the unrealized potential of women and industrial workers but also on his own behalf as an artist. In a savage cartoon in the December 1912 issue he showed everyone bowing down to Mammon. Young titled the drawing "A Compulsory

Religion" and, in commentary beneath it, rejected the moralistic view that people were to blame for being greedy. Rent, clothes, food—everyone "must struggle to pay the cost." With a bitterness unusual for *The Masses*, Young's commentary concluded: "So bend your back to the lash, cringe, crawl, prostitute yourselves mentally and physically. . . . Under the circumstances, how can the average individual worship any God—but Mammon?"[16]

Young amplified his point in 1913 with another cartoon, one depicting a big man called "Capitalism" eating the fruit that a little worker had prepared. Responding to *The Masses*, Arthur Brisbane, editorial writer for the Hearst papers, defended capitalism by explaining that the man eating the fruit had a "wonderful directing brain," which enabled him to get the fruit and entitled him to it. Eastman answered with his own editorial:

> The people who own this country—speaking generally—do not possess "that wonderful directing mind." At least it is not to be found in their own skulls. They get the benefit of it, of course. It is a part of their capital. But it is inside of somebody else's head.
>
> Arthur Brisbane ought to know this too, for he is exhibit A in this department himself. He has a wonderful directing mind—no matter what we may think of the editorial—he has a wonderful directing mind. But in order to use it he has to hire out to the man at the top—the man who owns the machine.[17]

From the beginning, *The Masses* was a protest by intellectuals against what the existence of classes did to everyone, including to intellectuals. Young bloomed at *The Masses*. So did John Sloan: "*The Masses* gave Sloan his first opportunity to do the kind of illustration he believed in," said his biographer. "In its first two years he contributed several drawings to every issue. Freer and bolder in every way than his work for commercial magazines, they were the best illustrations he ever did."[18] Writers and artists gave *The Masses* their time (including the time for editorial meetings) and their best work because they felt they were liberating themselves. And the work they contributed expressed not only their anger at a society that deformed its citizens but also their joy at being able for once to be straight. By contrast, the *New Review*, the other new radical journal in New York, took a conventionally earnest view of the moral duty of uplifting the suffering lower class. In its first issue, January 1913, the *New Review* declared that the Lawrence strike "recalls once more to American Socialists the imperative need and duty of giving a helping hand to these downtrodden workers in their ever renewed efforts at organization and in securing political rights."[19] In contrast to this traditional and joyless notion of duty and uplift, the socialism of *The Masses* was energizing because it was grounded in self-interest and fun. Its artists and writers celebrated the revolution embodied in IWW strikes and the women's movement because it was their revolution too. They made the magazine unique on the left not only by their superior art and layout and genuine commitment to feminism but also by their underlying sense of being colleagues in the class struggle.

In January 1913 one of Mabel Dodge's first "evenings" featured aspiring artists of *The Masses* and became itself a miniature class struggle. To the "Magazine Evening," as it came to be known, Dodge had invited not only the young artists of *The Masses* but also Will Bradley, the powerful art editor of the *Metropolitan*. She was elated because "all of a sudden the guests were telling each other what they thought of each other, and not merely their opinions." Criticized by frustrated young artists, Bradley could not understand their anger. Didn't the *Metropolitan* give everyone a chance? "Chance? What chance?" replied Maurice Becker, a *Masses* artist. "We never get a chance to see you and show you our stuff. We hardly know whether or not it reaches you, for often we can't even get it back." Furiously and recklessly, Becker attacked Bradley for sitting safely behind his mahogany desk, protected by his outer offices and "telephone girl," while the artist was forced to accept the editor's unilateral decision about what his or her work was worth. Weakly, Bradley defended the *Metropolitan*'s pay scale for drawings, explaining that many artists were satisfied. This led to a new explosion from Becker. "How do you know they're satisfied? Has any single poor devil ever told you how generous he thought you? Do you know anything about what any of us think about you and your prostitute of a magazine? Have you any idea at all what we think of your 'pretty girl' and how we loathe ourselves for selling drawings to go inside your covers? My God!"[20]

In a sense *The Masses* was waiting for Paterson to happen. The same energy that exploded at the Magazine Evening and regularly gave life to the publication was the energy that its artists and writers brought to the Paterson strike. Reed (who had joined the editorial board of *The Masses* by March 1913) contributed his powerful "War in Paterson"; Young and Sloan pictured respectively the breakdown of capitalist law in Paterson and the triumph of socialist law in Haledon; Eastman kept up an editorial dialogue with the strike and the IWW, and (on Haywood's request) gladly reprinted a notice sent by Recorder Carroll to English-speaking strikers.[21] A historian of radical periodicals observes that "in some ways the Paterson strike was the central event in the life of the magazine and, in fact, in the pre-war Village rebellion."[22] Eastman indirectly explained why in 1914. One can't only and always criticize and be negative, he wrote; in spite of doctrinal differences, anarchists were drawn to the IWW strike program because it gave them "a chance for affirmation."[23] The same could be said for Eastman and his friends in 1913: the IWW, and especially the Paterson strike, gave them a chance for affirmation.

Eastman exaggerated only a little when he later boasted that he "backed up the rebels in every industrial or legal battle then in progress" and that in return "the militant leaders of the working class without a single exception took the magazine into their hearts." Haywood, Flynn, Tresca, Giovannitti, and "every agitator who really intended to overthrow capitalism . . . felt that he had a body of friends and colleagues in the writers and artists of *The Masses*."[24] The word "colleagues" expressed the formal equality which, from the beginning, characterized the relationship between IWW organizers and Village intellectuals. Or, as Eastman put it, "our magazine provided, for the first time in America, a meeting place for revolutionary labor and the radical intelligentsia."[25]

HAYWOOD AT DODGE'S SALON

If *The Masses* brought Wobblies and artists together intellectually and politically, Mabel Dodge's salon allowed them to meet face to face. In the pages and the offices of the magazine, Wobblies and intellectuals tended to possess respectful but stereotyped views of each other. Frequent intense discussions in settings like Dodge's salon helped break down the stereotypes and make the equality less formal and more real.

In the year between the victorious conclusion of the Lawrence strike and the May crisis of the Paterson strike, IWW leaders had begun to mingle, not always comfortably, with Village intellectuals. Gradually, these contacts became more substantial. Some of the IWW leaders outgrew a defensive anti-intellectualism, and some of the intellectuals talked and argued with the IWW leaders instead of idolizing and fearing them.

Informal discussions took place in a number of New York settings. At the Ferrer Modern School, Wobblies and New York artists and writers heard one another lecture and enjoyed one another's company. Organized by anarchists, the Ferrer School had moved uptown to East 107th Street in 1912; it consisted of a day school run on libertarian principles and an adult evening center open to most modern political and artistic creeds. Some feminists who were active in Heterodoxy, like Henrietta Rodman, Marie Jenney Howe, and Fola La Follette, lectured at the Ferrer Adult Center. Tresca, Flynn, Haywood, and Giovannitti were at home there, as were such *Masses* artists as Robert Henri, George Bellows, and Sloan. Many Ferrer regulars participated in the Paterson strike in the spring of 1913, including Harry Kemp, Carl Zigrosser, Sanger, Hapgood, Rodman, and Sloan.[26] Important as the Ferrer School was as part of the bridge, however, we don't know a great deal about the quality of the interactions that took place there. By contrast, the anecdotal material from Dodge's "evenings" is unusually revealing of the process through which Wobblies and Village intellectuals grew to trust each other.[27]

At Dodge's salon the emphasis was on openness and clarity—as it was at *The Masses*—and the most important rule was not to be bound by the rules. "It was the only successful salon which I have ever seen in America," said Lincoln Steffens. Exchanges between guests were public, serious, and extended, he explained. A single theme would be explored in depth from varying points of view. The guests focused their energy and attention on the process and became part of it. "Practiced hostesses in society could not keep even a small table of guests together; Mabel Dodge did this with a crowd of one hundred or more people of all classes." The mix of classes, and of ages, sexes, occupations, and artistic and political tendencies, provided an essential source of energy. In addition to the more or less random collection of artists and agitators, school-teachers and poets, young radicals and well-known reformers, Dodge would "invite, say, Bill Haywood especially. He would sit or stand near her and strike out, in the hot, harsh spirit of his organization, some challenging idea, answer brutally a few questions, and—that evening everybody talked I.W.W."[28]

From late January 1913, shortly after her return from nine years in Europe, Dodge held the "evenings" every Wednesday in her Village apartment. Except for the few special guests chosen in relation to the theme for that night, no one was formally invited; whoever came, came. It was the moment of 1913: despite their differences, the guests shared a belief that the world was changing in exciting ways, that they were part of the excitement and might yet influence the direction and extent of change. Artists and strike leaders were interested in each other. All Dodge did was to attract them with the prospect of good food and drink and provide them with a current theme to discuss and a comfortable space in which to discuss it.

Haywood, Tresca, Giovannitti, and less famous Wobblies attended regularly. "Cross-legged on the floor, in the best Bohemian tradition, were Wobblies with uncut hair, unshaven faces, leaning against valuable draperies. Their clothes may have been unkempt, but their eyes were ablaze with interest and intelligence," recalled Margaret Sanger. Like the other guests, the members of the IWW welcomed the chance to test out their ideas beyond their usual circle of associates. "Each knew his own side of the subject as well as any scholar," said Sanger with pride in her old IWW friends, adding   perhaps as a result of her own struggle to participate as an equal—that "you had to inform yourself to be in the liberal movement. Ideas were respected, but you had to back them up with facts."[29]

Reaching back in memory for a typical "evening," Sanger, like Steffens, chose one that featured Haywood: "Big Bill was the figure of the evening, but everybody was looking for an opportunity to talk." The theme was the IWW tactics of direct action, including sabotage. People competed for the floor, quick to interpose a "but" whenever the current speaker paused, until he or she was finally "drowned by the weight of interruptions" and someone new began to hold forth. "It could not exactly have been called a debate," Sanger observed.[30]

But Dodge had in fact intended this particular evening as a debate, and it was actually far from typical. She scheduled it for a Monday, instead of the usual Wednesday, and individually invited the guests so that "none but more or less radical sympathizers would be there." She invited Emma Goldman to speak for anarchists and William English Walling for moderate Socialists in the hope of provoking Haywood and other Wobblies to admit to their left-wing audience what they would never say publicly: namely (according to Dodge), that they "believed in killing" and, in particular, that they believed in sabotage "no matter what the risk might be to human life." But the evening was a failure from Dodge's point of view: the Wobblies made no confessions; the debate faltered, losing its focus and becoming too vague, as the debaters could not define their differences; Haywood himself seemed uncharacteristically inarticulate. Dodge attributed the failure to bad luck.[31]

Dodge's account tells more than she knew about herself, her evenings, and the moment of 1913. Unlike most of her guests, she was not well informed politically; she was primarily interested in and attuned to the flow of energy in her drawing room. Hence, she recognized that this particular evening didn't work but never saw how she contributed to its failure. Her first mistake was to overmanage. Her "evenings" worked best when people chose to argue with each other, not when they were assigned to do so. In addition, Goldman and Walling (who at the time was a left-wing, not a "moderate-minded" Socialist, as Dodge mistakenly thought) were too close to the IWW in 1913 to create much dramatic contrast.[32] The IWW was attractive to anarchists and left-wing Socialists because it seemed to represent the rebellion from below for which their theories called. For the moment, theoretical differences mattered less than common ground in concrete matters such as mass strikes. A year later, after the defeat of the Paterson strike, the same debate undoubtedly would have been far less general—and would have produced a lot more of the expected heat.

Dodge's third and most serious mistake was to assume that Haywood and the IWW cared little for human life and believed in killing. This widely shared and titillating assumption about what direct action and "sabotage" meant to the IWW was rooted primarily in middle-class fear, just as the assumption in the 1960s that "Black Power" meant violence was rooted primarily in white fear.

In reality, Haywood especially was nonviolent. Unlike many of the young intellectuals who romanticized him as a wild man of the West, he knew what violence was and was afraid of it. Growing up in cowboy towns, he had been told about a massacre of Indians by one of the killers and by one of the survivors; he had seen the lynching of a black; he had found the body of a young friend who had accidentally been shot to death; and on his way to school he had watched the deliberate shooting of an adult in a gun fight. As a young adult he had shot a man in self-defense and participated in brutal mining strikes.[33]

Haywood's nonviolence grew out of such experiences in the West. His strength as an agitator in Lawrence and Paterson was inseparable from his gentleness, which was a learned response. Mary Heaton Vorse recognized in Lawrence—as Sanger, Eastman, Reed, and even Dodge would realize in Paterson—that despite Haywood's generally intimidating manner and appearance, his one eye, his great bulk and gruff speech, he was a gentle and compassionate man. "He was always accessible. He always felt the labor movement in terms of the individual worker. . . . I've known very few leaders to feel continually the actual human thing, especially in relation to women and children. He could hardly bear it."[34]

Haywood had little to say at Dodge's apartment that he could not say in public. The IWW's official Lawrence strategy of peaceful picketing and hands-in-your-pockets, which sharply distinguished between damage to property ("sabotage") and violence to persons, accorded perfectly with his own internal growth.

In New York, Haywood was growing in other ways. Early in 1912 he seemed uncertain about what he had in common with people in Greenwich Village. The IWW drew on a rich working-class tradition of anti-intellectualism, reinforced by the expulsion of the superintellectual Daniel De Leon in 1908. Like other Wobblies and many members of more conservative AFL unions as well, Haywood simultaneously looked down on intellectuals as parasites and feared their abilities as manipulators.[35] Like other self-taught workers, Haywood was aware of his own intellectual deficiencies; he could be more gentle with striking men and women than with New York intellectuals because he was much more experienced in class struggle than in debate.[36]

Yet Haywood was sufficiently confident about his own strengths and sufficiently secure about his own identity to enjoy the give and take with New York intellectuals and to learn from it. His own intellectual aspirations were of long standing. Working as a child for a cruel farmer to whom he had been bound out by his mother, he had been beaten when he paused, out of curiosity, to examine mice uncovered by the plow; the scene anticipated by several years Thomas Hardy's description of a similar experience in *Jude the Obscure*. His next job included a chance to usher at the Salt Lake Theatre, where he first acquired a taste for Shakespeare. At fifteen, beginning work in earnest, he took to the mining camp a pair of boxing gloves and a chess set. Other miners shared with him their well-read copies of Shakespeare and Milton, Voltaire and Darwin; his efforts at self-education were not unique. It was in the *Miners' Magazine*, an organ of the Western Federation of Miners, that he published his first articles. For this man, prison was an opportunity. In 1906, when he was thirty-seven years old, unjustly imprisoned as an official of the federation and awaiting trial on a much-publicized murder charge, Haywood experienced "the most quiet, peaceful period of my life. I have never enjoyed myself better than the first months I was there. It was my first real opportunity to read. There I went through [Henry Thomas] Buckle's *History of Civilization*, and extended my acquaintance with Voltaire."[37] His prison tour of the Enlightenment also included Marx and Engels, studies of the French Revolution, English novels, and Upton Sinclair. And he remembered what he read during this precious sabbatical. Five years later, after giving a militant speech in New York on class struggle and the general strike, he was asked by a member of the audience about the revolution then taking place in Mexico; he responded by describing in loving detail the relevant geographic features, citing Buckle and other prison readings as his sources and adding a bit defensively: "Those I read while I was on my vacation, when I didn't have anything else to do but read."[38]

Haywood never entirely outgrew his defensiveness,[39] but the atmosphere of Greenwich Village was a healing one for him. As some intellectuals lost their fear of him, so he lost his fear of them. Stimulated by discussions with

Villagers, he went sometimes to Washington Square Park, where he sat and wrote poetry.[40] Once he visited the studio of the painter Robert Henri but was disappointed when Henri and his friends insisted on talking only about the IWW rather than about their paintings. At a dinner with famous writers and poets in mid-1912, Haywood was more satisfied; the talk was as much about poetry as about labor. In the *Globe* Hapgood noted that Haywood's definition of "People Useful to Society" was "growing broader." At the dinner, Haywood included actors and some writers as productive workers—everyone in fact who made things "that can be directly, or if he can see it, indirectly, enjoyed by the workers, in which they can have their share of pleasure and light and ease."[41] Treated increasingly as an equal by writers and artists, Haywood felt less uncertain about his intellectual abilities and acted less belligerent. André Tridon, a Village radical, noted early in 1913 that "Haywood in his spare hours reads books or looks at paintings, that his sympathy may flow more freely not only to those who work with their hands, but also to those who work with their brains."[42]

Like Hardy's Jude, Haywood had a real drive for education; luckier than Jude, he found the intellectual nourishment he needed in the Village of 1912 and 1913. Melvyn Dubofsky, in his history of the IWW, describes Haywood as "a labor leader who was at home with both wage workers and intellectuals (an unusual combination in America)."[43] The description is accurate and illuminating. But it is important to remember that being at home with intellectuals did not come easily to Haywood. Frank Walsh, chairman of the Senate's Industrial Relations Committee, watched Haywood handle questions fired at him by committee members and realized that Haywood was a "rugged intellectual" who had been "fortified by a lifetime of study; by years of association with thinkers and by countless arguments."[44]

Much of that association began during 1912 and 1913, and some of the arguments took place in Dodge's apartment. At one of her evenings Haywood directly confronted artists, and this time "Bill was at his best," according to Dodge.[45] From her point of view—that of the energy expert—the evening on proletarian art was a success. In his novel about the Paterson strike, Eastman conveys the spirit of what happened. Challenging his audience, which included such artists as Francis Picabia, John Marin, Marsden Hartley, and Andrew Darlsberg, Haywood argued that the interests of workers and artists were in conflict. In the future, after the revolution, each worker would have the time and energy to be an artist. But at present there was no working-class art; how could there be, when the whole of each worker's life was absorbed in earning a living? "He does not live. He just works. He does the work that enables you to live," insisted Haywood, as everyone listened closely. "He does the work that enables you to enjoy art, and to make it, and to have a nice meeting like this and talk it over." According to Eastman, Haywood's manner was open, showing "that genuine personal interest which is the only courtesy"; without irony, Haywood called the discussion "nice" because he really thought it was nice. Proletarian art, he told the artists, "will be very much kindlier than your art. . . . When we stop fighting each other—for wages of existence on one side, and for unnecessary luxury on the other—then perhaps we shall all be human beings and surprise ourselves with the beautiful things we do and make on the earth."[46]

As Haywood finished drawing his picture of a future where there would be no separation between workers and artists, where everyone would share the necessary work and be free part time to be creative, Janet Scudder, a sculptor, rose to her feet and confronted him: "Do you realize that it takes twenty years to make an artist?" she demanded in a rage. Dodge loved it. Against the truth of the class struggle, grounded in Haywood's experience, was set the truth of the artist's struggle, grounded in Scudder's experience. It was high drama. What Dodge also saw, however, was that it was the kind of explosion necessary to clear the air and make real dialogue possible: "In the end, we really had General Conversation and the air was vibrant with intellectual excitement and electrical with the appearance of new ideas and dawning changes."[47]

At their best, Dodge's evenings went far beyond radical chic. They enabled Wobblies and New York intellectuals to meet and argue face to face, and these confrontations helped build the bridge. To the extent that artists and writers came to see Haywood as life-sized they were prepared to participate as equals in the Paterson strike. And even when the argument fizzled because it was artificial, as it did in the "debate" on direct action, the evenings were valuable. Even then they allowed Village artists and intellectuals to begin to know Haywood and other Wobblies directly instead of exclusively through sensational press accounts. In that sense, the evenings were themselves a kind of direct action.

FLYNN AND HETERODOXY

Ida Rauh helped start Dodge's salon as a place where "men and women could eat, drink, and talk."[48] The excitement of women and men talking seriously to each other was part of the excitement of 1912–13; so was the excitement of women talking to women. Rauh and Dodge were active members of Heterodoxy (which was for women only), as were Vorse, Henrietta Rodman, Crystal Eastman, Susan Glaspell, Grace Potter, and other Village radicals, as well as a number of women who were neither Villagers nor radicals. Created in 1912 to serve as a free space in women's lives, Heterodoxy—like Dodge's salon—was a Village institution. But unlike Dodge's salon, which disappeared when the hopes of 1913 faded, the club remained vital through the 1930s, continuing its every-other-Saturday luncheon meetings long after the original Village core of the group had physically dispersed. Heterodoxy met a continuing need of its members and led to the formation of lasting ties.

Politically diverse from the beginning, the members of Heterodoxy— ranging from several Daughters of the American Revolution to many Progressive reformers and a number of left-wing Socialists—were united by their feminism. In what they called "background talks," almost sixty years before the advent of "consciousness-raising" groups, Heterodoxy members shared their stories of growing up female.[49] They also regularly shared their experience in women's rights struggles and other political struggles. "All could talk; all could argue; all could listen," explained one member.[50]

Heterodoxy invited women both from inside and outside its membership to address the club on controversial issues. Early on, probably in 1912, they invited Flynn to speak about the IWW's efforts to organize female textile workers. Flynn knew Heterodoxy chairwoman Marie Jenney Howe, whom she had met in Cleveland in 1907 while on a speaking tour, and she was close to Heterodoxy member Rose Pastor Stokes, with whom she and her baby had stayed in the summer of 1910. She had also met Vorse (in Lawrence) and some of the other Village Socialists. Yet the predominantly middle-class nature of the club and its all-female membership made it a new experience for her. And she was a new experience for many club members. When they liked her talk and asked her to join Heterodoxy, they took a step toward building a women's bridge between the classes.[51]

Other, more formal attempts to build women's bridges within the AFL and the Socialist Party were already failing. The Women's Trade Union League (WTUL) formed within the AFL in 1903, had mobilized middle- and upper-class women in support of the 1909 shirtwaist-makers' strike in New York and itself played a major organizing role in the strike. Yet the league was encumbered by its AFL ties. In the 1909 strike the AFL had withdrawn support when the rank-and-file, mostly immigrant Jewish women, refused to accept the compromise worked out by union leaders. In the Lawrence strike of 1912, the WTUL was prevented by its AFL affiliation from helping the striking IWW women; in fact, it became entangled in Golden's attempts at strike-breaking. Some activists left the league in protest, and many members in New York became more open to the IWW. But the position of the league as an organization hardened, and after Lawrence it simply withheld support from the Paterson strike and every IWW strike, regardless of how many of the strikers were women or how badly they needed help. Nor was the AFL the league's only problem. Its cross-class ties were unstable, and the middle-class component won out. Though in New York it tried to organize Italian women, even hiring a northern Italian man from Paterson as organizer, by 1913 it had given up and had begun to concentrate on protective legislation and women's suffrage. By 1913 those radical members who—like Rauh and Rodman—were still committed to supporting the struggles of immigrant working-class women had to go outside the WTUL to do so.[52]

The Women's Trade Union League, in its heyday, brought together trade unionists and feminists; the Women's National Committee of the Socialist Party tried to bring together Socialists and feminists. Created in 1908 by female Socialists who saw the struggle for suffrage as part of the struggle for socialism, and given grudging support by male party leaders, the Women's National Committee briefly articulated the hopes of women who were sensitive to issues of both gender and class. The two great traditions it sought to bring together, however, were already pulling apart. Increasingly, the mainstream suffrage movement was moving away from ties that compromised its striving for respectability, including ties to Socialists; in the shirtwaist-makers' strike of 1909, wealthy suffragists who had initially supported the strike abandoned it, publicly attacking its Socialist supporters. For its part, the Socialist Party was in the process of withdrawing from a serious commitment to suffrage and feminism because it could not integrate the new groups of socialist women. On the one hand there were immigrant Socialists like the women of New York's Lower East Side, who were militant on class issues but conservative on issues of sex. On the other hand, there were young and highly educated American-born feminists—such as those in Heterodoxy—whose radical definition of women's rights extended into the home. Pulled in opposing ways, the Socialist Party in 1912 had begun to retreat from its tentative effort to deal directly with issues concerning women, and by 1915 it had disbanded the Women's National Committee.[53] Unable to utilize the formal mechanisms within the party to reach out to their immigrant working-class sisters, Socialists in Heterodoxy began in effect to create their own connections.

These radical women needed Flynn. From the beginning they wanted to extend the suffrage movement beyond its middle-class origins. In a masterful satire of the anti-feminist position in 1913, chairwoman Howe described the power struggle between the sexes: "It comes down to this. Some one must wash the dishes. Now, would you expect man, man made in the image of God, to roll up his sleeves and wash the dishes? Why, it would be blasphemy. I know that I am but a rib and so I wash the dishes. Or I hire another rib to do it for me, which amounts to the same thing." The recognition that hiring another rib amounted to the same thing—that is, the recognition of class as well as sex—made the suffrage commitments of Heterodoxy unusual. In contrast with many conservative suffragists who advocated votes for women as a barrier against the immigrant working class, Howe's argument for suffrage turned on its importance for working class as well as middle-class women. Working-class women needed a share of public power to control the conditions of their work because so much of their work had moved outside the home. "The baking, the washing, the weaving, the spinning are all long since taken out of the home. But I say, all the more reason that something should stay in the home. Let it be woman." In the spirit of 1913, Howe advanced her most serious arguments by playfully allowing the anti-feminist position to destroy itself. Her sure touch faltered only once: significantly, in emphasizing the importance of the vote for working-class women, she fell back on stereotypes. "The babies in the slums . . . and the working women in the sweated industries, the underpaid, underfed women," needed help, she said. "Who knows what woman suffrage might not do for such as these."[54]

Rejecting the exclusively middle-class orientation of the mainstream suffrage movement, Howe and the middle-class radicals in Heterodoxy wanted to bridge the gap between feminism and the immigrant working class. What they lacked, to get beyond the abstraction of working women as victims, was contact with working-class struggles. Taking up where the WTUL had left off, Flynn provided that contact. A number of Heterodoxy members—including Rodman, Dodge, Glaspell, Stokes, and Potter—became involved in the Paterson strike. Flynn and the Paterson women helped Heterodoxy members see the importance of linking the struggle for the vote with the struggle for unions. In 1914, when Howe and four other Heterodoxy members held a feminist mass meeting at Cooper Union, they asked a female trade unionist to join them on the platform and speak on "the right to organize" as one of the fundamental rights of women.[55]

In turn, Flynn needed Heterodoxy.

> I had worked almost exclusively with men up to this time and my IWW anti-political slant had kept me away from political movements. It was good for my education and a broadening influence for me to come to know all these splendid "Heterodoxy" members and to share in their enthusiasms. It made me conscious of women and their many accomplishments. My mother, who had great pride in women, was very pleased by my association with them.[56]

Flynn's mother, Annie Gurley, was an Irish-born feminist who had insisted on having female doctors to deliver her children, had named Elizabeth after one of these doctors, and had continued working after the children were born "as long as she could get caretakers for her children."[57] Flynn's father, Tom Flynn, American-born but from a lower social stratum than his wife, was an often unemployed engineer, a Marxist, an IWW member and sometimes organizer, with a propensity for speech-making and no sympathy for feminism. Elizabeth was caught between them. Outwardly she had followed her father into the Socialist Labor Party and the IWW. The IWW was a man's world, her father's world, the world of meetings in streets and saloons to which he had introduced her when she was a little girl. Yet always there was a core of rebellion in her against her father. In taking the situation of women as the topic for her first public lecture, at the age of fifteen, "I tried to select a subject upon which my father would not interfere too much, something he did not consider too important."[58]

To Flynn, Heterodoxy was an antidote for the male-dominated world of the IWW, a "broadening influence" leading in the directions her mother had always wanted her to go. There, emancipated and educated women held wide-ranging discussions that included but were not reduced to social and political analysis. No wonder that her mother was pleased or that Elizabeth found it liberating. Heterodoxy was "an experience of unbroken delight to me!" she said in 1920. "It has been a glimpse of the women of the future, big spirited, intellectually alert, devoid of the old 'femininity' which has been replaced by a wonderful free masonry of women."[59] Years later, recalling the writers and actresses, social scientists and suffrage leaders whom she had met through Heterodoxy, Flynn emphasized that "all were people in their own right. . . . No one was there because her husband or her father was famous."[60]

Heterodoxy helped Flynn reconcile her conflicting heritage. More specifically, it helped her to affirm her organizing career and to fight against male conservatism within the IWW. The idea of woman as person, as mother and yet not limited to motherhood, was new, and the IWW circles in which Flynn traveled were not receptive to it. Indeed, her separation in 1910 from her husband, an IWW organizer and miner whom she had married when she was seventeen, was partly caused by his insistence that she "settle down" and raise their expected child. Influenced by her mother's belief that women needed to have "a life of their own," Flynn permanently left her husband, came home to have the baby, and continued her speaking and organizing work. "But it wasn't easy in 1910."[61] Tresca, her lover after 1912, criticized young mothers who went out to speak instead of staying home with their babies. As Flynn had complained in her first lecture, men "carry a little bundle or umbrella for a woman, but seldom carry a baby."[62] Even in the Village, where relations between the sexes were more nearly equal than anywhere else and where she and Tresca could be open about their relationship, it was assumed that babies were the responsibility of the woman. Heterodoxy could not make men take responsibility. But a series of "background talks" by members on their own efforts at raising children helped each mother in the group to feel less isolated. It was one of the ways these women supported one another.[63]

Members also supported one another's struggles for women's rights. For Flynn, the critical arena was the IWW itself; being a Wobbly and a feminist was not easy either. In 1916 she spoke of the problems: "I know a local where members forbid their wives speaking to an I.W.W. woman, 'because they get queer ideas!' I heard a member forbid his wife, who had worked nine hours in a mill, from coming to the meeting, 'because she'd do better to clean the house!' When I suggested an able woman as secretary of a local, several men said, 'Oh, that's a man's job. She couldn't throw a drunk out!'"[64] The only other woman who was a paid IWW organizer, Mathilda Rabinowitz, gave Flynn no support; privately she criticized Flynn for lacking domestic skills. As for the rank-and-file women of the IWW, they did not share the freedom of Flynn's life as an organizer or identify with her rebellion against traditional sex roles. She therefore confined her own opinion of sexual freedom to her private manuscripts: "What is the other alternative? slave-love? Then I believed in *free* love, at all costs."[65]

As an emancipated woman and a feminist, Flynn was isolated within the IWW. If she became, as Meredith Tax rightly calls her, "one of the more important voices for women's liberation in her time," it was largely because of the support she received from women outside the IWW, especially from the women in Heterodoxy. "All its members were ardent suffragists, some were quite extreme feminists," Flynn later observed.[66] Experiencing the "wonderful free masonry of women" in Heterodoxy, she came close to viewing the women's movement not merely as a subordinate aspect of the labor movement but as a separate source of revolutionary change. In an important article for *Solidarity* in 1916, summing up what she had learned, Flynn argued—against received IWW opinion and some of her own earlier ideas—that the two movements ultimately converged.

> Feminist propaganda is helping to destroy the same obstacles the labor movement confronts, when it ridicules the lady-like person, makes women discontented, draws them from sewing circle gossip and frivolous pastimes into serious discussion of current problems and inspires them to stand abuse and imprisonment for an idea. A girl who has arrived at suffrage will listen to an organizer, but a simpering fool who says "Women ain't got brains enough to vote!" or "Women ought to stay at home," is beyond hope.[67]

Earlier, before Heterodoxy, Flynn had simply rejected the suffrage movement on the grounds that it was middle class. In 1911 she deplored the way in which the striking shirtwaist-makers had been "made the tail of a suffrage kite in the hands of women of the very class driving the girls to lives of misery or shame." Her class analysis at that time reduced all the sufferings of women to the effects of capitalism. "In the final analysis, women's sufferings and inequalities, at least in the working class which is our only concern, are the result of either wage slavery directly or personal dependence upon a wage worker."[68] In 1911 Flynn had treated middle-class women almost as if they were another species. They were the enemy, and their suffrage movement was a weapon used to distract working-class women from the task of building, with men, the industrial unions which alone could set them free. But this was before the growing militance of middle-class British suffragists won her grudging respect ("I don't agree with them, but I like their spirit")[69] and before Heterodoxy. In Paterson, building on Lawrence, she met separately with the women, encouraging their pride and their anger and raising their consciousness both as women and as workers.[70] Haltingly, she had begun to move away from the IWW's view of the feminist movement. On a theoretical level she never broke with the IWW position that class alone was real and sisterhood was a sham; indeed, whenever she was angry at middle-class reformers or wanted to call attention to the IWW's unique emphasis on class struggle, she would fall back on her earlier position.[71] But on a practical level she was already, in 1913, using the resources of the women's movement in her work as a labor organizer and implicitly recognizing that "feminist propaganda is helping to destroy the same obstacles the labor movement confronts."

Haywood was changing in parallel ways. Touching awkwardly on women's rights in his famous Cooper Union speech in 1911, he had stressed that women's suffrage in Colorado had been used against the miners. But after Lawrence and his experience in New York, his tone changed. Chatting with Hapgood in April 1913, "Haywood talked with emotion about the women of the country. He thinks, what so many of us are beginning to think, that what is called the woman's movement is of the greatest social importance. It is they who, just now, are carrying on the world's progressive thought and feeling—they and, in Haywood's opinion, those . . . workers who are at the bottom of the industrial scale."[72]

Industrial unionism and feminism: by the spring of 1913, Haywood and Flynn on the one hand and *The Masses* on the other shared a common framework of discourse. Haywood still insisted, as Flynn herself would have insisted, that for working-class women it was "not a question of equal suffrage but of economic freedom." But sidestepping the difficulties inherent in opposing the suffrage movement while supporting the women's movement, Haywood joined Flynn in celebrating the changing consciousness of the women who came to her meetings in Paterson. In May he wrote with excitement about their ever-increasing number: "They are becoming deeply interested in the questions of the hour that are confronting women and are rapidly developing the sentiments that go to make up the great feminist movement of the world."[73]

Haywood's growing appreciation of the women's movement was an integral part of his openness to the moment of 1913; emotionally and politically, he was ready for bridge building. Flynn was neither so open nor so ready. The women's bridge was for her the exception; otherwise, she remained uneasy and somewhat defensive with intellectuals.[74] She seemed to need to insist on her working-class identity, on how different she was from middle-class intellectuals. In contrast with Haywood and most IWW organizers, she had never actually been a worker. She had left school voluntarily to become a star in the socialist movement, whereas Haywood had been forced, against his inclinations, to leave school in order to go to work. Secure in his working-class identity, Haywood wanted to meet people who were different and to resume his education. Less secure, a child prodigy who had inherited her revolutionary politics (and who, at the age of thirty-six, after twenty years of continuous activism, would suffer a breakdown and withdraw from her parents and politics for ten years), Flynn was in general much less comfortable with intellectuals than was Haywood.[75] Outside the IWW, the women's movement was the only movement to which she was drawn. Heterodoxy was the only bohemian or middle-class group that she took seriously; that is why it was so important. Heterodoxy reinforced her feminism and diminished her anti-intellectualism. For Flynn and the Paterson women whom she touched so deeply, the feminist movement was an opening to a wider world. For Flynn, Heterodoxy *was* the moment of 1913.

Heterodoxy, Dodge's salon, and *The Masses* under Eastman all took shape in 1912–13, influenced by the new radically democratic spirit. Older centers of cultural or political rebellion, like Alfred Stieglitz's 291 and the Liberal Club,[76] were less fully responsive to the Wobblies and contributed less to the Paterson strike. It was at Dodge's salon and the Ferrer School, at Heterodoxy and *The Masses* that Wobblies and Village intellectuals built the foundations of the bridge to Paterson.

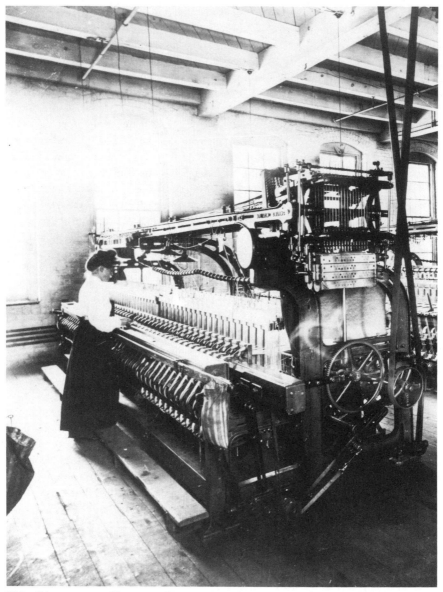

This ribbon weaver, like most silk weavers, has decent light in which to work. (American Labor Museum)

Dyers' helpers, working in steam, suffered from the heat of summer and the cold of winter. (Passaic County Historical Society)

Quinlan, Tresca, Flynn, Lessig, and Haywood were the main IWW speakers in 1913; Lessig was himself a Paterson silk worker. (American Labor Museum)

Lessig, Haywood, and Tresca, despite their frequent arrests, always returned to the streets and halls (Brown Brothers)

More than anyone, Flynn was the leader of the strike, delivering as many as seventeen major addresses in a week. Here she speaks to women and girls at the Lafayette Oval. (Courtesy of International Publishers)

Flynn (*on the right*) poses under the grape arbor at Botto house with Eva Botto and Mary Gallo, two of the many young women she inspired. (American Labor Museum)

O'Brien private detectives are protecting a small group of strikebreakers; the O'Brien men were more violent than the police. (American Labor Museum)

Chief Bimson's police close Turn Hall and bar the strikers from entering, as part of his attempt to separate the silk workers from the IWW. (American Labor Museum)

The funeral procession for silk worker Vincent Madonna fills the streets. He was shot and killed by a strikebreaker whom Mayor McBride had authorized to carry a weapon. (American Labor Museum)

SPEAKING OF ANARCHY.

Art Young's cartoon, in the June isssue of *The Masses,* protests the abuse of authority by the defenders of capitalism. (Tamiment Institute Library, New York University)

Drawn by John Sloan

WHEN KICKED OUT OF CAPITALIST PATERSON, N. J., A SOCIALIST HALEDON, N. J.,
HAS PROVED NOT ONLY CONVENIENT BUT NECESSARY.

John Sloan, in the July issue of *The Masses*, celebrates the rule of Socialist law in
Haledon. (Tamiment Institute Library, New York University)

At a meeting in Haledon in May 1913, a speaker addresses the crowd from the Botto house balcony, on the right. (American Labor Museum)

In May, hundreds of strikers' children were sent to live with strike sympathizers in New York as a means of combating hunger and of generating publicity. This group of Jewish children is ready to leave. (American Labor Museum)

On June 7, 1913, strikers march up Fifth Avenue on their way to the performance of the Pageant. (UPI/Bettmann Newsphotos)

The greatest effort to get publicity for the strike was the Pageant. This powerful design, by Robert Edmund Jones, appeared in advertisements for the Pageant and on the program cover. (Courtesy of American Labor Museum)

In Madison Square Garden, in front of John Sloan's painting of the giant silk mill, strikers enact a confrontation with the police in the second episode of the Pageant. (Courtesy of Tamiment Institute Library, New York University)

The Bridge: Paterson

In the spring of 1913, visitors from Greenwich Village came to Paterson, drawn by their desire to see the strike. Upton Sinclair "yielded to the temptation," encouraged to do so by "the intelligentsia of Greenwich Village," who were making "weekend pilgrimages" to Paterson "for strike-relief and oratory."[1] Wilbur Daniel Steele, who was finishing a work of fiction, wrote from Provincetown that he badly wanted to go to Paterson but couldn't "until I get that damn book out of the way. Goditsawful."[2] Most Village writers put aside their work and took the ferry and train to Paterson.

What drew them, as much as anything, was the nature of the strike. Like the Lawrence strike, the Paterson strike bubbled over with the songs and humor of many nationalities and was propelled by the courage of both sexes. More clearly than in Lawrence, however, where the strike began as a defensive reaction against cuts in wages, the Paterson strike aimed from the beginning at creating a human way of life. Flynn asserted again and again that Paterson was "more significant" than Lawrence, where "the strikers were forced to quit their work because they were down to starving working conditions"; in Paterson, the weavers were beginning at a higher material and educational level and aiming at a better way of life.[3] The silk workers' central demand for an eight-hour day was especially attractive to Village writers and artists. In a book finished just before the strike, Eastman argued that poetry was suffering from its separation from working people. "They who cherish hopes of poetry will, therefore, do well to favor in their day every assault of labor upon the monopoly of leisure by a few. They will be ready for a drastic re-distribution of the idle hours."[4] In 1913 one of the slogans which the silk workers carried on banners in Paterson and shouted on the streets of New York was "Eight Hours Work, Eight Hours Rest, and Eight Hours Pleasure."[5]

In the moment of 1913 the Paterson strike seemed to Villagers to be democratizing the right to pleasure. "As the train pulls in one sees long lines of closed mills, dark and gloomy," wrote Hapgood, arriving in Paterson on the first day of spring. "But as you step out into the street . . . you get into the atmosphere of life, and of joyous life." Despite the hardships of the struggle, "what would strike anyone is the widely spread feeling of joy, of a kind of happiness."[6] As visitors from the Village gradually became strike participants, the experience often changed them more than they had intended. Driving the process, even when it became uncomfortable, was their need for the Paterson strikers, which was as real as the strikers' need for them.

The silk strikers and IWW needed new allies to help break the deadlock in Paterson; the Village intellectuals needed to test their ideas and abilities in a practical situation, to prove to themselves that the world was changing and that they were indeed part of the change. To them the strike was the class struggle, not in a socialist textbook but in life, nearby, open to their intervention. Their energy and hope led them to participate, and the experience of participating fed their energy and hope. Though generally treated ironically by historians for their supposed innocence,[7] the radical intellectuals of 1913 saw the Paterson strike precisely as confirmation that their ideals were practical, rooted in actual historical processes. In helping the strikers, they were helping their own ideals become real.

THE EXAMPLE OF LAWRENCE

In March, the silk workers and their IWW speakers had concentrated on organizing themselves in Paterson. In April, they began to reach outside of Paterson for support. In New York the strike was hardly known; even on the left, it was regarded as a local affair.[8] The IWW itself considered it only one of a number of struggles nationwide. In mid-April, however, *Solidarity* published a "Special Paterson Strike Edition," with five articles (by Koettgen, Flynn, Haywood, two dye workers, and a ribbon weaver), a cartoon, and a photograph of a Haledon meeting.[9] The New York *Call* simultaneously recognized that outside support had become important to the strikers and the strike had become important to the left. The strikers "have received little outside help," observed the *Call* on April 21. "Their resources have been strained by the long conflict, and the end of it is not in sight. . . . But the winning of the fight means much not only to them but to others."[10] In accordance with the principle that united support for the strike should override tactical differences, the Socialist Party and the IWW cooperated in publicizing Paterson in New York.

The first mass meeting in New York in support of the Paterson strike was called for April 3 at the New Star Casino on 107th Street. The *Call* announced that "a New York audience will for the first time be told of conditions as they really are in the silk industry and what has been done in the present strike."[11] Jessie Ashley, secretary of the IWW strike-support committee in New York that sponsored the meeting, wrote a letter to the *Globe* urging the attendance of "those comfortable citizens in New York who want to hear a bit of the 'real thing' in the labor movement."[12] Though the strike was already in its sixth week, many of the 1,000 New Yorkers who came uptown for the meeting were hearing about Paterson for the first time. Haywood, who had been advertised as the featured speaker, was unable to appear because he was still in jail after his arrest at the Lafayette Oval, but Flynn, who chaired the meeting, saved the day by bringing two girls from the Bamford mill with her. Although William English Walling and Jacob Panken spoke at some length for the Socialists, and Giovannitti for the IWW, it was little Teresa Cobianci who was "the hit of the evening." In her untrained manner she told the crowd why she was on strike.[13] After Teresa spoke, a collection was taken to buy food for the Paterson strikers, and the audience gave over $100.

The April 3 meeting was only the first of a number of joint Socialist Party and IWW fund-raising events in New York during the month. An even larger meeting at the New Star Casino, with Haywood, Quinlan, and an English Socialist—a former member of Parliament—netted $225 for the strike. "Sentiment for the I.W.W. is on the increase in New York City," happily concluded *Solidarity*.[14] In fact, however, the IWW was only skimming the surface of potential support in the city. Haywood and Flynn were relying on their old ties to the Socialist Party; they had barely begun to utilize the vital connections they had been developing with feminists and other Village intellectuals.

One small event in April suggests the richness of those untapped possibilities. In the *Globe*, Hutchins Hapgood described a meeting of a women's club in Brooklyn: 175 women "of the comfortable and wealthy classes" listened as the wife of French painter Francis Picabia spoke on modern art and as Hapgood himself "talked about the relationship between modern art and the 'revolutionary' movement in literature, politics and industry." Sensitive to the emerging links between industrial unionism, art, and feminism, Hapgood glimpsed their practical importance for the Paterson silk strikers. "The president of the club, whose term has just ended, is actively working to collect funds to support the striking silk workers of Paterson, and is a great admirer of Haywood, Giovannitti, and Mrs. Pankhurst."[15]

The IWW was slower than Hapgood to appreciate the new possibilities it had helped to create. As the IWW's greatest victory, Lawrence had opened the East to its agitation and earned it an invitation to Paterson. But in Paterson, Haywood, Flynn, Tresca, Quinlan, and other Lawrence veterans approached the new strike in terms of its similarity to the old one, overlooking its unique problems and possibilities. Especially at first, the compelling example of Lawrence restricted the imaginations of the leading Wobblies.

Some uses to which the example was put were perfectly appropriate. On the first day of the Paterson strike, following on the heels of the Lawrence victory, Flynn congratulated the strikers on their timing: "I told them that the strikers of Lawrence had won because of careful and thorough picketing, and I advised them to emulate their example."[16] It was sensible advice. The tactic of nonviolent mass picketing, with a continuous moving chain of pickets, had supplanted in Lawrence the traditional method of small, isolated groups of stationary pickets that had been used, for instance, in the 1909 shirtwaist-makers' strike. The mass booing introduced in Lawrence also had application to Paterson, as Haywood pointed out: "Booes [sic] like those of Lawrence were now used by the strikers of Paterson against the police. The sound of 25,000 people shouting 'Boo, boo, boo' was like the blast of Gabriel's trumpet that shook down the walls of Jericho."[17] The important women's meetings, and children's meetings, too, were based on similar meetings held in Lawrence. It made sense to emulate these Lawrence methods. Nonviolent picketing and booing, for example, were effective ways for large numbers of immigrant strikers to participate actively in a strike and discourage would-be strike-breakers without giving the police any encouragement for violence. It was appropriate for the IWW to transmit to the Paterson silk workers what the Lawrence woolen workers had learned or created. In this way, too, the IWW served as a bridge.

Lawrence was relevant to Paterson in a very different way as well. The manufacturers themselves were thinking in terms of what had happened in Lawrence. Police repression of the Paterson strikers, even when they had broken no law, was defended by the manufacturers and their allies as a way of preventing Paterson from turning into another Lawrence. One prominent ally of the silk manufacturers, asked about the arrests of the IWW speakers and other violations of free speech, protested, "But we had the experience of Lawrence in front of us."[18] More specifically, the Paterson silk manufacturers borrowed tactics that had been used successfully against the Lawrence woolen workers. When in March they tried to use patriotism to break the strike, the IWW and its Socialist allies rightly interpreted the move as an attempt "to emulate the example set by the textile barons in Lawrence, Mass. recently."[19] When in April the manufacturers welcomed Golden and Conboy to town, Haywood correctly insisted that "they came to try to repeat the infamous strikebreaking tactics they attempted a year ago in Lawrence," and an indignant New York Socialist and former Lawrence activist warned that "history is repeating it-self."[20] Learning from history, the IWW and the strikers were ready for flag day and for the AFL.

At other times, however, the IWW applied the lessons of Lawrence somewhat mechanically. Giovannitti, denouncing the "silk trust" in March, was not seeing Paterson at all. Koettgen, warning the silk manufacturers in February (in terms imported directly from Lawrence) that "you can't weave goods . . . with the bayonets of the militia," and Quinlan urgently citing in March the presence of a few members of the state militia on the streets of Paterson, were looking for the enemy to take the same shape in Paterson that he had taken in Lawrence. Haywood, interpreting the destruction of railroad

tracks outside Paterson in May as "a scheme similar to the planting of dynamite in Lawrence," and *Solidarity* calling it "a plot, no doubt like that of the
dynamite 'plant' engineered in the Lawrence textile strike," were misreading
Paterson in terms of Lawrence.[21] As it turned out, the railroad tracks were
destroyed by boys on a lark, and the state militia was never sent to Paterson,
and there was no silk trust that could be brought down by a combination of
local and federal pressure. Paterson was different.

Paterson presented the IWW with unique difficulties and unique opportunities. The difficulties were rooted in the ability of the manufacturers to hold
out, as a result of their mills and dye plants in Pennslyvania. Flynn noted this
fact after the strike. She also noted another unique difficulty: "There was quite
a different situation from Lawrence. In Lawrence the halls were never interfered with."[22] Even in the Little Falls strike, where no picketing, parading, or
open-air meetings had been allowed, the halls were never closed.[23] The
closing of the halls (threatened from the first day of the strike and carried out in
May) and the staying power of the manufacturers (which had begun to become
apparent by April) necessitated different tactics from those of Lawrence.

Fortunately, Paterson offered new opportunities as well. The proximity
of both Haledon and New York was a great resource, one that the Paterson
strikers and the IWW gradually learned to turn to advantage. Haledon would
become the unique Paterson answer to the closing of the halls. New York
would become the unique Paterson answer to Pennsylvania. But at first these
opportunities were overlooked, partly because of the example of Lawrence.

The light from Lawrence partially blinded the IWW speakers to the unique
dangers and possibilities of Paterson. They had come, as Flynn later put it,
"with the aura of the Lawrence victories."[24] At first, or for those who were not
in Paterson every day, it was easier to preach from the text of Lawrence than to
listen closely to the silk workers. Boyd, as usual, carried this tendency to an
extreme. At Turn Hall, "in delivering his address he continually referred to
Lawrence, until Miss Flynn had to prompt him several times. It seems that
though he was rambling along in a trance, the speaker did not realize that he
had ceased his activities in Lawrence."[25] Living at times in the past, IWW
speakers not only looked for dangers in the wrong places but also recommended inappropriate solutions. In Lawrence a general strike called by the
workers to protest the imprisonment of Joseph Ettor and Giovannitti had proved
successful. In Paterson the general strike called by the IWW to protest the
imprisonment of Haywood and Lessig was a complete failure. Embarrassed,
Flynn explained that "in Lawrence a twenty-four hour general strike had been
called which practically won the cause for the workers there," and IWW speakers noted that "they were following the precedent that had been established in
Lawrence." The same powerful precedent misled Haywood into encouraging
hopes for federal investigation of the strike, as it misled Flynn into using almost the identical words she had used effectively in Lawrence to pressure the
small businessmen.[26]

Even when a tactic like mass picketing worked in Paterson, it did not necessarily work in the same way. Remembering Lawrence, the IWW speakers daily hammered away at the importance of getting out on the picket line. The Paterson weavers, more skilled than the workers of Lawrence and knowing they could not easily be replaced, tended to show up on the picket lines in large numbers only on Mondays or in times of crisis.[27]

The danger to the Paterson strike came not primarily from strikebreakers or militia bayonets or dynamite plots, but from hunger. Understanding Paterson in terms of Lawrence only increased this danger. At Turn Hall on March 13, Flynn invoked the example of Lawrence to show that hunger would not be a problem in Paterson. "Let me tell you that in Lawrence, when the strikers were in need of funds, $65,000 was raised within a month for their relief. The same can be done for the strikers in Paterson if the time arrives when this needs to be done. . . . The I.W.W. is not going to see anyone starve in Paterson."[28] Partly because the Lawrence strike lasted only two months, Flynn could not imagine on March 13 that the Paterson strike would go on for another four and a half months. Not until mid-April, after nearly two months on strike and with no end in sight, did Flynn and her IWW colleagues recognize the magnitude of the problem of helping the Paterson strikers to feed themselves. Only then did they begin to think seriously about New York as a resource. Flynn's and Haywood's first idea, however, was an old and borrowed one. Realizing that hunger was becoming the key problem and that publicity had to be the means of solving it, they fell back on another tactic that had proved decisive in Lawrence. They decided to send the children out of the city.

On April 14 Haywood announced that more than a hundred families in New York would be willing to take care of the children of Paterson strikers until the strike ended. Three days later Flynn campaigned for the proposal at a mass meeting at Helvetia Hall. After the meeting she explained that "if manufacturers are going to make this a starvation strike, then it will be necessary to get the children of strikers and send them to other cities, the same as was done in Lawrence."[29] On April 18 Flynn told the audience at Turn Hall that "we will do as we did in Lawrence. . . . Exile of the children from Lawrence practically won the strike."[30] But the idea had to be sold to the silk workers of Paterson. On April 25 Flynn and Tresca held a meeting of Italian mothers to persuade them to send their children away. Even in May, Flynn was still looking for willing Italian and English-speaking families; the first group of children had been mostly Jewish. Some parents apparently feared that the mill owners would retaliate against those who volunteered their children; others were proud of being able to feed their own. As a result, the demand from New Yorkers for children from Paterson continued to exceed the supply.[31]

In the end, the benefits of sending the children away from Paterson were modest. The operation went smoothly; the IWW established committees in New York and in Paterson. The New York committee, led by such veterans of the Lawrence experience as Sanger, Jessie Ashley, and Dolly Sloan, processed applications from families who wanted to take children, many of them the same New Yorkers who had cared for children from Lawrence.[32] The Paterson committee, under Flynn's leadership, worked with families willing to send their children away for the duration of the strike. On May 1 (the day was chosen to guarantee the widest publicity by coinciding with the International Labor Day celebrations organized by Socialists in both Paterson and New York) the first group of eighty-five children left Paterson.

The experience of the children themselves was mixed. They loved the trip to New York; for most, it was their first ride in a motor vehicle. Two big trucks took them from Helvetia Hall to the 42nd Street ferry, where they crossed the Hudson, and on to First Avenue to join the monster Socialist May Day parade. Afterward, families of strike sympathizers met them at the Labor Temple on East 84th Street and took them home.[33] Most children appreciated the food and clothing their New York families gave them. "My first meal there was a hot dog and a sugar bun. I thought, 'All this for me?'"[34] Some received more: one little Jewish girl was given the bedroom and the toys that had belonged to the family's own daughter, who had recently died. The parents had chosen "this little girl," as they said at the Labor Temple, and they made her feel at home. All summer long she did not miss her brothers and sisters "because I was having such a wonderful time in that house."[35]

Other children, however, were homesick the whole time. A Jewish boy of fourteen (one of the oldest children) felt exploited by his New York family, which made him get up at four in the morning to make deliveries of rolls and milk for its grocery store. After six weeks the New York children's committee, in a routine check, saw how he was being treated and relocated him with a doctor's family, but "if you can believe it, that was even worse. They were very cold people. They never spoke at any of the meals." He felt lonely and inferior: "I felt like the guy who knocked on the door and asked for a meal. I didn't know these people."[36] Another doctor's family picked a seven-year-old Jewish boy as a companion for their son, but though they were about the same age, the doctor's son "didn't want to play with me, so I just had to be on my own."[37] In general, the silk workers' children sent to New York stayed with families of a higher class than their own and thus experienced both a gain in physical comforts and a loss in warmth. Hutchins Hapgood and his wife, Neith Boyce, gave baths and toothbrushes, clothes and shoes, to an Italian brother and sister from Paterson. Asked by their solicitous hosts how they liked their new home, "they replied that they liked the baths, the clothes, and the eats; but that there was nothing to do in the evening except go to bed. They missed the life of the streets, the noises and excitement. . . . They were not sorry to leave."[38]

Financially, sending away the children did help the strikers. All together, as many as 600 children were cared for by families in New York (including many in Brooklyn) and more than 100 others by families in Elizabeth, New Jersey.[39] Fewer mouths to feed in Paterson provided the strikers some short-term relief. In the long run, however, the kind of publicity involved was a mixed blessing. By focusing on the plight of the children, the press releases and articles tended to reduce the Paterson strike to the least common denominator of suffering workers everywhere. The uniqueness of the Paterson strike, the wonderful resourcefulness, solidarity, and discipline of the silk strikers, tended to get lost among generalized appeals for sympathy.[40] In Lawrence and Little Falls the authorities had given valuable publicity to the IWW when they tried by violence to prevent the children from leaving the city. The Paterson authorities, having themselves learned something from Lawrence, made no attempt to block their departure. Instead, by publicly offering relief to the children of needy strikers through the city's charitable offices, Mayor McBride partially undercut the IWW's attempt to dramatize the heartlessness of the city.[41] In short, the tactic of sending the children away did not embarrass the Paterson authorities into doing something stupid that would have helped the strike.

In general, the uses to which the bridge was put in April—including the IWW/Socialist meetings in New York and the removal of the children—were shaped by the limited ways that cross-class ties had been utilized in Lawrence. Only in May, when the deadlock in Paterson had become apparent, would the IWW, Paterson strikers, and New York intellectuals together create a new model.

NEW YORK COMES TO PATERSON

In the last week of April, while Flynn was working hard on the details of the children's exodus, John Reed got involved in the Paterson strike. On May 1, when the children left for New York, Reed was in jail in Paterson. His involvement, which proved more important politically than the children's departure, was a casual outgrowth of the ties between Wobblies and Village intellectuals.

At a typical small gathering in New York of Wobblies, writers and artists, and the ex-member of Parliament, a few days after Modestino's death, Reed had heard Haywood describe Modestino's funeral and other fresh events of the strike. "Reed had never been to Paterson, but his imagination was stirred by the description," wrote Hapgood, who was there.[42] Two days later, on April 28, with a vague idea of gathering material for "a great labor drama" that might be put on in New York, Reed came to Paterson.[43] He came not to Turn or Helvetia Hall, but to the picket line on Ellison Street, where the action was, and he came early enough to be there for the expected confrontation with police at 7:00 A.M. Haywood had movingly contrasted the nonviolence of the pickets with the violence of the police and private detectives, and Reed wanted to see for himself. Arriving early, he entered into conversation with some of the pickets. (It was a Monday, so pickets were everywhere.) Standing with some pickets on a front stoop opposite the mills, like Modestino eleven days earlier, Reed watched strikers avoid confrontations with police by dispersing as ordered and then regrouping as soon as the policeman moved away. Reed was impressed by the resourcefulness of the pickets and by their restraint. When a strikebreaker appeared, they greeted him with boos but allowed him to go to work. When a policeman ordered the strikers on the stoop to move on, they temporarily retreated into the house. Reed himself, after a moment's hesitation, refused to move. Like Quinlan on the first day of the strike he stood on his rights as a citizen, and like Quinlan he was arrested. In court, before sentencing Reed to twenty days for disorderly conduct, Recorder Carroll asked the question frequently put to out-of-towners: "What's your business?" (meaning, what's your business here?). "Poet," Reed truthfully replied.[44]

The poet's arrest and sentencing were widely reported in the New York papers. The *Times*, the *Globe*, the *Call*, the *Sun* all carried details of how the popular young writer from the *American Magazine* had been arrested for standing still in Paterson. On Monday, wearing the washed-out blue and white uniform of prisoners in the Passaic County Jail, he was interviewed by the *Globe*. On Wednesday the New York *Call* devoted a playful editorial to Reed's arrest, pointing out that "he is the first magazine writer to take the educational course which Paterson is gratuitously supplying to all comers, and he will no doubt prove to be one of the most promising and influential pupils, and in the future will do full credit to his bonehead instructors."[45]

The *Call* proved right on both counts; for the Paterson authorities and for Reed, his arrest was a turning point. As the *Call* predicted ("No popular writer can really afford to overlook this great educational course"), other magazine writers followed Reed to Paterson. In Quinlan's words, "Paterson for a while became the mecca for magazine writers, photographers and settlement workers."[46] Part of the new surge of interest resulted from the death of Modestino, which continued to go unpunished. But some of it resulted directly from Reed's arrest. Mainstream writers who were not necessarily moved by the arrest of silk strikers, Wobbly agitators, or even Socialist editor Scott, took an interest in what happened to John Reed. Reed was a kind of bridge in himself. As Sanger observed, "Both right-wingers and left-wingers who ordinarily objected to those between loved Jack Reed, the master reporter just out of Harvard."[47] As a particularly humorous example of Bimson's policy of repression, Reed's arrest invited his friends in the media to make the Paterson authorities look silly. Three weeks after Reed's arrest, stung by the ridicule heaped on him and recognizing the impossibility of getting a favorable hearing in the New York press, Recorder Carroll retaliated by barring New York reporters from his court.[48] Though Reed spent only four days in jail, Captain McBride complained that "we had more inquiries about him than about Haywood all through the strike. That was, I claim, a good deal of the cause of the New York papers making a burlesque out of the action of the police on every occasion—the arrest of John Reed."[49]

For Reed himself, his arrest was decisive. During his days in jail, before an IWW lawyer had him released on a writ of *habeas corpus*, he continued the conversations with strikers he had begun on Ellison Street. His instinct of going directly to the picket line and to jail, rather than to Turn Hall to hear the same IWW agitators whom he had heard in the Village, proved sound. Getting to know the strikers changed him. For the first time he was talking with immigrant workers who were actively taking charge of their own lives. In a long poem about the Village written in 1912, he had devoted a few lines to immigrant Italians as seen from the distance of his Village apartment:

> There spawned the overworked and underpaid
> Mute thousands;—packed in buildings badly made,—
> In striking squalor penned,—and overflowing
> On sagging fire-escapes. Such to-and-froing
> From room to room we spied on! Such a shrill
> Cursing between brass earringed women, still
> Venomous, Italian![50]

This stereotyped view of immigrants did not survive Reed's stay in Paterson. From jail he wrote to his friend Eddy Hunt, who had come to Paterson with him, "If you saw the strikers in here, you would realize it is a great strike."[51] After his release, in an article for *The Masses*, he emphasized the courage and solidarity of the Italians and Jews whom he talked to in jail. Like many intellectuals, Reed had tended to romanticize the IWW leaders, especially Haywood, and to give them credit for molding the immigrant masses of Lawrence and Paterson. Now, though his earlier view lingered, he began to credit the "gentle, alert, brave men" he had met in person. "They were the strike—not Bill Haywood, not Gurley Flynn, not any other individual," he decided.[52]

Out of jail, Reed became a valuable ally of the Paterson strikers, making them the focus of his activities. On May 7 he spoke to a large, politically diverse audience at a new kind of meeting in New York. Sponsored by *The Masses*, chaired by suffrage leader and Heterodoxy member Inez Milholland, the meeting drew Republicans as well as radicals by offering a debate on socialism between a conservative clergyman and a well-known Socialist. The advertisement for the meeting promised that "JOHN REED, the 'Poet-Observer,' Will Relate His Experience in the Paterson Jail" and that Haywood would also speak on the strike. Introduced by Milholland before the debate, Reed emphasized the nonviolence of the strikers and the unfairness of the authorities; after the debate, Haywood made a successful appeal for funds.[53] Writing to the *Globe* five days later, Reed himself appealed to the public, asking that clothing, shoes, fruit, and canned goods for the strikers be sent directly to him at his Washington Square apartment.[54]

Reed's major essay for *The Masses* began with the essence of what he had learned.

> There's a war in Paterson, New Jersey. But it's a curious kind of war. All the violence is the work of one side—the mill owners. . . . Their paid mercenaries, the armed detectives, shoot and kill innocent people. . . . Their tool,

Recorder Carroll, deals out heavy sentences to peaceful pickets that the police net gathers up. They control absolutely the police, the press, the courts.[55]

With friends and acquaintances in New York he talked constantly about the strike. At lunch with a popular but apolitical columnist, Reed argued that the IWW was "sorely misjudged" when the press portrayed it as bloodthirsty. In October, Reed himself had written glibly to a friend that "I have become an I.W.W. and am now in favor of dynamiting."[56] Having gotten to know Haywood in New York and the strikers in Paterson, he was now both better informed and more serious. In fact, he was more committed to the strike than he had ever been to anything, and he wanted his Village friends to see it for themselves. He dragged Walter Lippman and Mabel Dodge and Robert Edmund Jones out to Paterson during May. He himself couldn't stay away. On May 19, during one of his many visits, Reed was introduced by Haywood to the audiences at Turn and Helvetia Hall, where he sufficiently overcame his genuine embarrassment about public speaking to say that "every man or woman who has been arrested is a hero," and that the strikers were making history for themselves.[57] By this time, three weeks after his first visit to Paterson, his vague idea of a play had begun to take shape, and he sketched for the strikers ten scenes that they themselves could enact in New York. On May 24, at Haledon, he led the strikers in songs for the picket line and the Pageant.[58]

Of all the New York intellectuals who took part in the strike, Reed gained the most from it and gave the most back. He was young and open enough to throw himself wholly into the experience and to be shaped by it. (It is no accident that Reed and Flynn, who at twenty-five and twenty-two were two of the youngest out-of-town participants in the strike, were the two most decisively affected by it.) For Reed, the democratic and nonviolent rising of silk workers against all the powers of the status quo confirmed his hopes of the possibility of social change from below. "Here was a drama, change, democracy on the march made visible—a war of the people," he wrote later.[59] His idea of the role he could play in that unfolding democratic drama was also shaped by his strike experience. He discovered in Paterson that he could help in the world's self-transformation. In the Pageant he connected his own activity with the activity of working people, helping them to tell the story of their revolutionary struggles to the larger world. Talents that before Paterson he had used primarily for experiment and fun turned out to be relevant to the struggles of working people. More than he yet realized (because he was still eager for fun), Paterson was where Reed's image of revolutionary change, and of his own role in helping to give form to that change, began to crystallize.

Hapgood, almost twenty years older than Reed, was not so deeply affected by the strike. In 1913 he already knew where he stood. For years he had looked to outside elements to revitalize the mainstream of American life; in sympathetic studies of immigrant Jews and anarchists he had sought alternative sources of value.[60] Now, in the Paterson silk workers, he located a major source of hope. Even more than Reed, he recognized and publicized the creative accomplishments of the strikers themselves.

Like many Village intellectuals, Hapgood became involved in Paterson through Haywood. Early in April the two men talked about the strike, and in his April 14 column for the *Globe* Hapgood reported on the impressive character of the IWW leader and his powerful description of the nonviolent resistance practiced by the Paterson strikers.[61] A week later, at the height of the AFL's challenge to IWW leadership, Hapgood went to Paterson. In his column titled "A Day at Paterson" he explained the importance of a bridge between New York and Paterson for both the strikers and the intellectuals. After reading "recent newspaper accounts," he had thought that perhaps the strikers were deserting the IWW for the AFL; many New York papers had insinuated that "this strike does not represent the feeling and initiative of the mill-workers, but has been forced on them by that dreadful I.W.W. organization." But firsthand contact with the strikers had dispelled this view, he said. At Turn Hall he had observed the "spontaneous enthusiasm" of the strikers for Haywood, Flynn, and Tresca. In a relief station he had watched seven strikers—all teenaged girls—running the store. Talking with one of them about her work as a weaver, watching her distribute the limited goods, he noticed her pleasure in taking an active part in the strike. Hapgood perceptively concluded that the much-publicized AFL challenge was empty because it was premised on the idea that the strike was controlled from above, by the IWW. "Anyone who comes in contact, however, with these mill-workers would be quickly undeceived. They themselves are running this strike."[62]

In this column, written a week before Reed went to Paterson, Hapgood was already becoming the advocate of the bridge. Contact between New Yorkers and strikers was important not only because it would help strikers expose the lies of the press but also because it would help New Yorkers renew their "sense of the dignity of human nature." Paterson was a democratic tonic: "I wish that everybody could spend a day at Paterson feeling the spirit of the silk strikers."[63] A few days after this first visit he spoke at the National Art Club on modern drama, one of his favorite subjects, but found the evening dull. "I could not feel as much sympathy for the subject as I would have felt, probably, if I had not recently been in Paterson and attended the strikers' meeting. There was the real thing."[64]

Everything Hapgood wrote about Paterson in the *Globe* was pervaded by this sense of the strikers taking charge of their own lives. He saw in the strike "the realization of our much abused conception of democracy."[65] And that was why he found Paterson so hopeful. Watching the strikers actively participating in a meeting in Haledon, he felt in them "the dawn of a hope that they may be co-operators in their own destiny."[66] This hope he shared, and wanted other New Yorkers to share. Hapgood's columns in the *Globe* helped create a key point of contact between strikers and intellectuals. To him, the strike in its most profound sense was a struggle toward self-expression. When rehearsals for the Pageant began in May, he was the first to appreciate its significance. "The big thing, and incidentally the difficult thing," he wrote in the *Globe*, "is that the strikers themselves are going to present the spectacle."[67] It would be "the real thing" on a modern stage. In a column he wrote on the eve of the Pageant, he was even more specific. This "effort of thousands of workers not only to realize their 'creative liberty' in industry, but also to get it over into drama, this is a democratic act of almost unprecedented interest."[68] For Hapgood, the radically democratic thrust of the Paterson strike opened up possibilities of freer expression for everyone. He seized on the Pageant, even before it was performed, because it exemplified his sense that the democratically run strike was breaking down the barriers between life and art, between workers and intellectuals, offering a vision of liberation to all.

Within the limits of his self-defined role as observer and publicist, Hapgood helped to shape the bridge and the Pageant. Reed *was* the bridge; in his intensely active way he personified the cooperative relationship between the Village intellectuals and the Paterson strikers. But more than Reed, more indeed than anyone, Hapgood understood that what the strikers had to offer to intellectuals was the hope of democracy. It was fitting that having begun with Haywood, he ended by judging Haywood and the other IWW leaders in terms of their responsiveness to the fact that the strike and the Pageant belonged to the workers. "The silk workers struck independently of the I.W.W.," he observed a few days before the Pageant. "The I.W.W. leaders have, for the most part, been conscious of the fact that it was the strikers themselves who took the initiative and their spirit that maintained the strike." But the Pageant was being advertised as if it were an IWW production, whereas "it should be regarded as the pageant of the striking silk workers of Paterson, and not of the I.W.W., except that their leaders for the time are of the I.W.W."[69]

Some Village intellectuals who began with Haywood never got beyond him. André Tridon—a writer, photographer, and secretary of the original *Masses*—came out to Paterson to see the strike a number of times, but he saw nothing but Haywood.[70] To Tridon, Big Bill was "almost seven foot tall" (actually, he was slightly under six feet), and Paterson was an opportunity for Tridon to build up his hero. When there, he was blind to everything else, as he cheerfully confessed in an article titled "Haywood," which he wrote for the *New Review* in May: "I was going to devote my attention to strike crowds, strike tactics; at the end of the day I found that I had observed closely and studied exclusively . . . Haywood."[71] Tridon was interested in the strikers only as props for his hero. When he observed Haywood inviting strikers from each nationality, including the Italian girl, to come up on the platform at Turn Hall and tell everyone about the strike in their own words, he was moved only by the proof of Haywood's genius. Haywood, he maintained, "trusts the crowd to follow him."[72] In his book *The New Unionism*, published in 1913, Tridon celebrated "capitalism's iron discipline," which had "lifted" the mass of workers "out of their original sluggishness and anarchistic individualism."[73]

He did not allow the proud and skilled Paterson weavers, who had resisted capitalist discipline at every point, to challenge his assumptions. To him, the workers were passive; his hero alone actively made history. Tridon's work demonstrates that one didn't have to be a policeman to commit Bimson's mistake.

Tridon gave little to the strike, and his flattery certainly did Haywood no good. One may only wonder about its effect on Flynn, who was in Paterson more than Haywood and was more intimately involved in the daily struggles of the strikers. Did she resent the focus of Village radicals like Tridon on Haywood's role in the strike? Did the tendency of male intellectuals to make Haywood larger than life—for Tridon represented only an extreme form of this tendency—increase Flynn's suspicions toward male intellectuals and confirm her doubts about the usefulness of the bridge?

Female intellectuals who participated in the strike were somewhat more critical of Haywood. At least in their memoirs, both Sanger and Dodge sought to deflate his image as a charismatic hero. Dodge in particular mocked his need to be the center of an adoring group and derided his typically male tendency to hold forth like an "eminent man."[74] It is true that Dodge and especially Sanger were disappointed in Haywood's nonviolence, and their criticisms of him reveal confusions of their own. Yet IWW organizer Mathilda Rabinowitz, who observed Haywood closely at Little Falls and who visited Paterson during the strike, also commented bitterly on his need to be a star.[75] And Mary Heaton Vorse, who thought well of Haywood, wrote that Flynn "is almost the only public character that I have ever known who has nothing of the prima donna about her."[76] In so far as female intellectuals seemed less prone than the men to worshipping Haywood, they may have given some comfort to Flynn and helped her remain open to the value of the bridge.

Flynn worked particularly closely with Sanger, whose role in the strike has been obscured by her later attempts to downplay it,[77] but in fact she was the only New York intellectual besides Reed who went to jail as a result of participating in the silk strike. Sent to Hazleton by the IWW as an organizer, in the difficult days after the AFL settlement, Sanger walked the picket line with the striking girls. For three days Flynn visited her there, helping out with speeches. When Flynn returned to Paterson, Sanger stayed in Hazleton, encouraging the strikers and trying to fight against the AFL and the police. On Tuesday, April 8, she and twenty-five other pickets were arrested outside the Duplan Silk Works.[78]

In jail she wired Flynn about the situation and continued her organizing. Refusing to pay the fine, Sanger was glad when most of those arrested joined her in choosing the alternative of five days in jail. Out on bail and still leading the picketing, she was arrested (but not imprisoned) again, this time for attempting to hit a policeman.[79] Though some of the strikers' parents complained that she was too militant, she wrote a hard-boiled piece for *Solidarity*, concluding with the wildly optimistic advice to "keep your eye on Hazleton, fellow workers, and watch results." "Fellow workers" was the standard IWW greeting; a middle-class radical like Reed would not use it. But unlike Reed, Sanger tried to immerse herself in the IWW. Indeed, by an effort of will, she tried to obliterate class distinctions and become one with the working class. "Twenty-six of us altogether were arrested," she wrote in *Solidarity*, as if the class differences between herself and the coal miners' children had disappeared in the heat of battle.[80] In contrast to Hapgood, who was most comfortable as an observer, Sanger held back nothing from the class struggle and seemed to want to participate not only as a Wobbly but as a silk striker. Denying the fragility of the bridge between the classes, she did violence to her own nature and prepared herself for a backlash reaction against the strike, the IWW, and the bridge.

That came later. Having fought the losing fight in Hazleton, Sanger was back in Paterson on April 21, helping Flynn organize the exodus of the children. New York families who wanted to take Paterson children sent their applications directly to Sanger, and she herself took one group of seventy-seven children to New York.[81] She had played this role before, in Lawrence. But in Paterson, for the first time, she worked with Flynn at strike meetings in the brand-new effort to publicize the notion of family limitation. Sanger and Flynn believed that sending the children away was only a stopgap solution; having fewer children would in the long run enable working-class men and especially working-class women to take control of their own fate and become more powerful. (Sanger was already something of an expert in this area: her popular and provocative series of articles for women on sex education, including birth control, had been published by the *Call* in 1912 and was issued in book form in 1913—for twenty-five cents a copy, with large discounts for 100 copies or more.)[82] According to Tresca and Boyd's wife, Sanger spoke on birth control at regular strike meetings and at women's meetings, drawing a warmly enthusiastic response.[83] Although the national campaign for birth control had barely begun, and the role of Sanger and Flynn in the campaign would not be clearly defined until the winter of 1914–15, Sanger helped build the women's bridge in 1913.

In May, Sanger also threw herself into the preparations for the Pageant. She made her uptown apartment into headquarters for the Pageant committee of New York intellectuals, which met there nightly for three intense weeks. On the day of the Pageant, in recognition of her leading role, she and Quinlan led the Hudson County and New York silk strikers in the great parade.[84] Like Reed and Hapgood, Sanger played a significant role in the strike and the Pageant. But unlike Reed and Hapgood, she never found a comfortable way to use her talents in conjunction with the strikers' talents. She seemed to ask too much of herself and of the strike. In his autobiographical *More Miles*, Harry Kemp has Sanger speaking passionately in Paterson to a mass meeting of strikers, provoking "jeers at the silk mill owners"; complaining angrily in New York about the "nonsensical lies" the Paterson clergy were telling about the

role of New Yorkers; raging against "the stupid, well-fed bourgeois" who senti-
mentalize poverty ("pain and suffering have never been good for anybody, and
whenever I hear any old fogy say so, it throws me into a rage"); and becoming
critical of Haywood and convinced that speakers like Boyd were right to
advocate sabotage and provide details of how to destroy silk and machinery.[85]
Sanger was frustrated by the continued suffering of the strikers and impatient
with their nonviolence. She tried with desperate energy to break the strike
deadlock. In the end, despite her organizing in Hazleton, her work with Flynn
in Paterson, and her contributions to the children's exodus and the Pageant,
Sanger emerged from the strike feeling good neither about the strikers nor
about herself.[86]

What she attempted to do, and why it was so difficult, can best be appreciated when her response to the silk workers is set beside the response to the
Pennsylvania silk workers of another middle-class woman. In 1909 Florence
Lucas Sanville, an official of the Consumers' League of Philadelphia, adopted
a working woman's clothes and speech and gained employment in a variety of
silk mills in the Pennsylvania coal country, investigating the working and
living conditions of female employees. When Sanville wrote up her experience
for *Harper's*, she reported that "the exaggerated chasm which is supposed to
separate a college-trained woman from a factory-bred one shrank out of sight";
superficial differences of clothing and language notwithstanding, she stressed
"the essential similarity which exists between women of the working and the
so-called 'non-working' class."[87]

In the end, however, Sanville was controlled by her biases. She discovered a "distinct tendency" for "evil factory conditions and a lower type of
worker" to go "hand in hand." By evil, she meant dirty. Foreign-born girls,
whose homes were generally "untidy and poorly conducted," were especially
prone to "accept and accentuate the dirt and untidiness" of the mills.[88] Sanville
helps us understand what Sanger was struggling against in herself. Aware of
the gap between the middle class and working class, afraid of imposing her
middle-class values on the silk workers, Sanger fell into the opposite error of
trying to merge herself with the working class. Though her effort to negate
herself led to a sense of emptiness and despair, she commands respect for
rejecting the assumption of moral superiority that so many middle-class reformers brought to their attempts to help the working class. Like Sanville, she tried
to collapse the differences between herself and the silk workers. But unlike
Sanville, Sanger tried to help them to become what they wanted to be.

Most female intellectuals were content to assist in smaller, less ambitious
ways. A number of women from the Village who participated in the strike did
so by helping the strikers distribute food in the relief stations in Paterson.
Henrietta Rodman was only one of many who worked quietly in this way.[89]
Mabel Dodge, according to her friend Carl Van Vechten, spent "almost half of
every day" in Paterson for a while, helping in various ways, including driving
pickets from place to place in her automobile.[90] Many women contributed so

quietly that we have no record of their activity. A prominent artist's wife, when arrested in Paterson, gave a fictitious name. Was it Dolly Sloan? We don't know.[91] An anonymous woman from "the wealthy class" attended the tumultuous meeting at the armory, where the strikers overwhelmingly repudiated the AFL, and told Hapgood that "it was one of the greatest experiences of my life," but she didn't allow him to use her name in the *Globe*. Might this woman (who had previously shown no interest in labor matters) have been Dodge?[92] Inis Weed and Louise Carey, two women about whom we know nothing but their names, came to Paterson and conducted an excellent interview with Teresa Cobianci, which they published in *The Masses*.[93] Though she never made a speech, Jessie Ashley contributed her time, money, and legal expertise in Paterson and in Hazleton and—like Dolly Sloan—helped make the arrangements for receiving the children and for putting on the Pageant.[94]

Some women contributed in ways that were more public and more like those of the men. From Massachusetts, Helen Keller sent a check for $48.90 to the striker's relief committee; in an accompanying letter intended for publication, she asserted that "it is a duty of the plainest kind for everyone of us to hold out a helping hand to our comrades in Paterson."[95] Helen Schloss, a heroine in Little Falls, spoke in Paterson early in the strike, as did Theresa Malkiel, a labor activist among New York's garment workers. Dr. Maud Thompson of Orange, New Jersey, spoke with Flynn at a women's meeting early in the strike; Sarah Goldstein, a New York Socialist, spoke in Yiddish at Haledon, late in the strike.[96]

Occasional speakers, both female and male, were at a disadvantage compared with the regular IWW leaders because their knowledge of Paterson was so much less concrete. The gap between them became more noticeable as the weeks passed. In the ninth week of the strike Rose Pastor Stokes addressed a large public meeting of silk strikers and interested Patersonians. She urged the latter to help the former and encouraged the strikers to stand firm until their demands were met. "In the lower Eastside in New York Mrs. Stokes is idolized for the fine charitable work she has accomplished," commented a Paterson reporter, "but here in Paterson she is unfamiliar with the general existing conditions and was forced to talk very generally of the Paterson strike. Mrs. Stokes is a very fine speaker, but she was not as popular with her audience as Miss Flynn."[97]

Stokes, like Keller, nevertheless brought to the strikers the encouragement and blessing of a wider world. Famous male Socialists played a similar role. Jacob Panken, a leading New York Socialist who later became a judge, spoke in March to Jewish strikers at an evening meeting in Turn Hall; in April he helped organize meetings for publicity and strike support in New York. A Socialist ex-assemblyman from Providence and a Socialist ex-mayor of Milwaukee also spoke in Paterson.[98] Ernest Poole, a Socialist who wrote popular plays and fiction, came to Paterson more than other prominent Socialists and took more away with him. Poole often accompanied Haywood to Turn Hall, where he found "an abundance of life and color." His most popular and effective work, his 1915 novel *The Harbor*, transmitted to a wide audience the dynamic of a radical strike that he had grasped at Turn Hall and Haledon.[99] Upton Sinclair spoke in Haledon, to the largest audience he had ever addressed. "I just could not stand it any longer," he told the crowd, "and I let my books go and came down here to congratulate you. Yours is the finest exhibition of solidarity ever seen in the Eastern States." He spoke briefly, urging the silk workers to vote Socialist so that the Paterson police would be "at your mercy."[100]

Socialist speakers like Sinclair could not help being impressed by the powerful solidarity they experienced at Turn Hall or in Haledon. By coming as Socialists to support an IWW strike, at a time of growing hostility in the nation between the Socialist Party and the IWW, they made their own contribution to solidarity. Though a Sinclair or a Stokes may have had little to say beyond Socialist pieties, his or her presence helped the strikers to understand the importance of what they themselves were doing, and the speaker in turn carried back to the wider world an impression of surprisingly disciplined strikers.

The Socialist Party encompassed many contradictions in 1913, and Socialists consequently brought to the strike a variety of positions and challenges. The most controversial speaker in the five-month strike, aside from the Socialist Fred Boyd, was the Socialist Hubert Harrison. Harrison came from New York to give the major address at Turn Hall on April 17. In May he spoke in Haledon. He was controversial for two reasons: he was black, and he was aggressively anti-capitalist. The Paterson *Evening News*, describing him as "a gentleman of color" and a "colored Socialist," found his Haledon speech out of character with the usual IWW speechmaking and "unfit to print"; it suggested that he "should be left in New York."[101] Flynn, however, stuck up for Harrison: "He tells plain facts and the bosses don't like them," she explained.[102]

Almost as provocative, in his own way, was a Socialist minister from New York. Rev. Irwin Tucker spoke in Paterson and Haledon during the first week of the strike; in April he appeared with Flynn and Tresca at a women's meeting in Helvetia Hall and again in Haledon. Meanwhile, in New York, Tucker presided over a meeting of the Socialist Forum at St. Mark's Church on the Bowery, where Quinlan spoke on the strike and in May his church doubled as a school—complete with Socialist teachers—for the Paterson children who were living in New York. Tucker was provocative because, as a minister, he gave his blessing to the spirit of the strike, especially when that spirit was most revolutionary. In his Haledon speech in April he likened the strike to "the spirit of '76, a spirit that laughs at jails, courts, and judges that prostitute their powers."[103] During the summer he published an article in the *Churchman* on the "spiritual regeneration" engendered by the Paterson and other revolutionary strikes: "When this revolution of the spirit is brought about, the worker looks on the world differently. There is a new heaven and a new earth. He looks on the workshop, formerly his prison, as his rightful possession, and sets to work to regain it for his class. 'Class-consciousness' is the name given to this transforming force."[104] As Harrison's presence on the platform in Paterson challenged the racial prejudice of many Patersonians, so Rev. Irvin Tucker's enthusiasm for the revolutionary tendencies of the Paterson strike must have challenged the conservative version of Christianity practiced by many Patersonians.

Unlike Harrison and Tucker, most New York Socialists who participated in the Paterson strike did so along fairly conventional lines. Socialist support for an IWW strike had been tested at Lawrence and had proved effective. Despite the subsequent warfare between the two organizations at the national level, it was to the Socialists that the strikers and the IWW turned for outside support, especially at the outset. Many strikers, particularly the ribbon weavers, were Socialists. Quinlan was a Socialist. The local Socialists, led by Killingbeck, were heavily involved in the strike from the start. Mayor William Brueckmann of Haledon was only one of many Passaic County Socialists who immediately responded to the appeals of their comrades in Paterson. In turn, the ribbon weavers, Quinlan, and Brueckmann had connections with Socialists in Manhattan and Brooklyn.[105]

Generally, these connections operated informally, but during the second week of the strike the Socialist Party's Passaic County local actually advertised (in the New York *Call*) for Socialist speakers from New York to address shop meetings in Paterson, day or evening.[106] More than any other established connection—including the anarchist connection, which also provided important strike support, though on a much smaller level[107]—the Socialist connection provided a ready mechanism for recruiting outside support throughout the strike. By the same token, however, most New Yorkers who participated in the strike as Socialist recruits already had well-defined political views. Not only did their speeches often echo standard Socialist themes, but they tended to perceive the strike through the lens of received doctrine and therefore to be less galvanized by it than were relative newcomers to class struggle.

In contrast to the Socialist connection, the connection between the IWW and the Village intellectuals was new, experimental, and explosive. The Socialist Sinclair was impressed by the strikers; the Villager Reed was transformed into a radical by them. Stokes talked about the strike from the outside; Sanger lived it from the inside. Panken did his Socialist duty for the strike; Hapgood experienced the strike as opening new possibilities of self-expression for everyone. The connection to the Village was less well defined and took longer to develop. Socialists from New York were already helping in Paterson in February and March. By contrast, Sanger, Hapgood, and Reed did not come until April, and the Village intellectuals generally did not become a real factor in the strike until May. But then they made a great difference, because the strike made a great difference to them. Energized by the strike, Reed and Hapgood,

Rodman and Dodge, Eastman and Sanger, and many other Villagers brought to it new ideas and resources.[108]

As a rule of thumb, strike supporters who were young, part of the Village, and critical of the mainstream Socialist Party—like Reed and Sanger—were more open and responsive to the experience than Socialists who were older, more established, or respectable, like Panken and Sinclair. Walter Lippmann was an exception. Only twenty-three in 1913, one of the minority of Socialist Party members who had defended Haywood within the party—"young and revolutionary," he described himself in 1913—Lippmann nevertheless did not let the experience of the Paterson strike affect him deeply. In the same piece in which he described himself as "revolutionary," he announced that the IWW and the Paterson strikers were nonrevolutionary: "When the silk strikers in Paterson say that they should own the silk mills, they are simply urging the creation of a large number of workmen-capitalists." His own vision of the socialist state as a giant consumers' cooperative was, he said, much more radical than the IWW's vision of society as an association of producers. Haywood's goal of workers' control allowed no mediating or directing role for a socialist government, and so, whether he knew it or not, "Haywood stands for private capital." The workers' self-management that Lippman saw in Paterson might have challenged his statist preconceptions. Instead, side-stepping the challenge, he concluded that such strikes taught only the "virtues of warfare" and were therefore "poor training for the tasks of civilization."[109] Workers were useful for shaking up the old society and precipitating change, but intellectuals would be needed to manage the socialist civilization of the future.

Lippmann demonstrates that the response of New Yorkers to the Paterson strike was not finally determined by age. Poole, who was nine years older and had been involved in Socialist politics much longer, proved far more responsive to the strike than Lippmann. But Poole went to Paterson to see for himself and improve his work, whereas Lippmann went because Reed dragged him. Lippmann saw the strike only as training in the negative virtues of class war, whereas Hapgood—nearly twice his age—saw it as training in self-management. Like Tridon, whose anti-democratic assumption about Haywood and the strikers rigidly governed his perceptions, Lippmann learned little from Paterson. What determined the quality of response by each visitor was, more than anything, the extent of his or her belief in the possibility of democracy.

Some New Yorkers who knew less than Lippmann learned more. Motivated primarily by the desire to see for themselves, most visitors from New York were not famous and left no record of their impressions. The testimonies of a young student and a crime reporter may stand for many of these. The student, Daniel McCorkle, came out to Paterson on a Wednesday in May, following the closing of the halls. Because his sympathies were "divided," he made a point of talking not only to strikers and IWW leaders but also to wealthy businessmen, to Mayor McBride, and to Sheriff Amos Radcliff.

In response to his questions about the conduct of the authorities, Radcliff informed him that "foreigners" were "a lower order of animals, unfit for free speech." Repelled by the prejudices he observed, McCorkle chose sides, writing a sharp letter of protest to the *Globe* to inform other New Yorkers about the treatment of immigrant workers in Paterson.[110]

Unlike the student, the crime reporter came with leftist leanings, though he had no organizational affiliations. Art Shields, later a well-known labor reporter, was twenty-four years old in 1913 and a crime reporter for a New York news service controlled by the Associated Press. Initially, Shields heard Haywood talk about the strike at a public meeting on the Lower East Side. He was struck by Haywood's claim that "all the king's horses and all the king's men can't put those looms to work again without meeting our demands." That Sunday he visited the strike. In Haledon, standing in the crowd, he heard Flynn tell the many different nationalities about the need for solidarity so that one day "you will run these plants for yourselves." On his next visit, working his way deeper into the fabric of the strike, he observed supplies from New York being unloaded at the relief station in Paterson, saw the picket line form in preparation for the noon lunch break, and spoke with Koettgen, the local IWW organizer who had come up through the mills. Koettgen sketched for him the way that skilled and unskilled workers, united as in Paterson, would one day run industry. (Shields asked about joining the IWW, but Koettgen told him that reporters did not qualify as industrial workers.) He spent most of his third visit with a German dye worker to whom Koettgen had introduced him. Sitting on the dye worker's front steps at 6:00 P.M. opposite a big mill, Shields watched strikers shout insults at a handful of strikebreakers on their way home. He was almost arrested when the police dispersed the pickets and stoop sitters; only his press card saved him. (Perhaps the publicity caused by Reed's arrest had taught the Paterson police something.) Other men and women were clubbed and arrested, and Shields rushed from the scene to get word of the police action not to his news service—which wouldn't have been interested—but to the New York *Call* in time for the early edition.[111]

From Haywood in New York to Flynn in Haledon, to Koettgen in Paterson, and finally to a dye worker on his front stoop, Shields had made a genuine pilgrimage from interested observer to involved participant. Now, he was reporting the crimes of the police. The individual initiatives taken by this reporter and this student, culminating in the public protest that each made, express the vitality of the bridge and suggest the rich variety of experience available to the hundreds of anonymous New Yorkers who came to Paterson to see class struggle for themselves.

Like Shields and McCorkle, other New Yorkers who came only to observe the strike process ended by becoming part of it. George Middleton, husband of Heterodoxy member Fola La Follette and already a successful playwright in 1913, met Haywood at Mabel Dodge's salon but first heard the "beautiful, dark-haired, blue-eyed, eloquent Elizabeth Gurley Flynn" in Paterson, where in the end "I, too, gave my bit in protest."[112] Harry Kemp, another Villager, also found himself speaking in Paterson when he had intended only to observe. Kemp came frequently with Rodman, Sanger, and other Village residents. He was a poet, and it was as a poet that he visited Paterson. On the last Saturday in April he reluctantly came forward to speak. "I only came here to look the situation over and write a poem," he told the strikers. "I find that the situation would make a stone speak."[113] Stirred by the excitement of the struggle, he frequented the back rooms of Paterson bars in May, "trying to write revolutionary poems, but the poems wouldn't come." Unlike Reed, Kemp never found a way as a poet to connect with the strikers. Almost in spite of himself, because the knowledge gave him little pleasure, he learned in Paterson that whether they won or lost, the real point of the strike was for the silk workers to learn "how to manage the next step—better!"[114]

An interesting example of someone who held back from the strike yet was changed by it is Max Eastman. In contrast to Reed and Sanger, who threw themselves into the strike, Eastman preferred to watch it from a distance. On his first visit to Haledon he "stood in the crowd alone," clinging to the critical intelligence that protected him from religious, patriotic, and even revolutionary enthusiasms.[115] His only previous direct contact with labor had been at an AFL national convention, where he had despised Samuel Gompers not only for his conservative policies but also for "the solidity of his stance, and the dirtiness of his teeth." IWW leaders were different; meeting Giovannitti and Haywood in New York, Eastman experienced feelings of "admiring inferiority." Whereas he himself only theorized about class struggle in *The Masses*, IWW agitators were its "disreputable and real heroes," and he tended to regard them as beings apart. Then he came to Haledon and saw his heroes "on the job." There they seemed less disreputable and more real, less romantic and more human. In short, they seemed more like Eastman himself. Haywood, Tresca, and Flynn spoke with anger (Tresca passionately—it was May, the strike was deadlocked, and Quinlan had just been convicted), yet to Eastman they were no longer larger than life but part of the life of the strikers. The decisive speaker, for Eastman, was Flynn. "When Elizabeth Gurley Flynn came out and began giving earnest and sensible advice to the strikers, I felt again and strongly the likeness of all human beings and their problems. I felt at home."[116] Flynn gave the strikers "explicit and detailed directions" about using the relief stations, remaining nonviolent despite provocation, picketing, distributing literature to counter the lies of the Paterson papers, and sending away more children to New York. In contrast to his stereotyped view of labor agitators, she "seemed instead of agitating the crowd, to take charge of it."[117]

Hearing Flynn talk to the strikers changed Eastman. On May 25 he himself spoke in Haledon, joining his former heroes on the balcony. Eastman told the strikers that their daily efforts had importance beyond themselves, that their battle against violence and illegal arrests and closed halls was becoming front-page news all over the country. As Eastman spoke, Hapgood watched the faces of the strikers and saw "a solemn, timid, but deep pride" in their importance.[118] Speaking to the crowd altered Eastman's view of himself, as standing in it had altered his view of the world. (As he himself noted, "One learns more sometimes by making a speech than listening to one.")[119]

From his listening and speaking Eastman gained a new sense of working-class power and of his own ability, in a small way, to increase that power by making it more aware of itself. For the first time in his life he felt connected to an actual class struggle. After Reed's arrest, Eastman had challenged the readers of *The Masses*: "You don't believe in the Class Struggle? Just go out to Paterson and make a noise like a free citizen. See what happens to you."[120] Now, having made some noises of his own in the protected borough of Haledon, he clarified his own thinking about class struggle. Specifically, he revised his ideas on the relative importance of the IWW's struggle for economic power and the Socialist Party's struggle for political power. Clearly, both were important. But for the first time he gave priority to strikes and the IWW, concluding that the road to power was through the Paterson strike and others like it. "Just as soon as you deliver the power on the economic field, the party will deliver results on the political field."[121] In another piece he meditated on the gap between the IWW's reputation for encouraging mob violence and the reality of Flynn's speech: "Personally, I never saw so much mob-lawfulness as I've seen out there." Then why did the editorial writers of most papers in New York and other cities harp hysterically on the IWW's violence and lawlessness? Eastman located the answer in the IWW's single-minded commitment to the working class. The crime of the IWW leaders was that they really meant it when they said that the product of the work belonged to the worker—"both the mills and their output."[122]

Still, Eastman kept his critical detachment. Forgetting what he had heard in Haledon, he sometimes described the spirit of the IWW as "wholly belligerent, somewhat negative and unresponsible." In his later accounts of Haledon he stressed Flynn's sturdiness ("perhaps a little too sturdy, a litle four-cornered"), whereas everyone else simply stressed her beauty.[123] It was as if he needed to find fault to preserve his distance. But this need makes what he learned, and what he gave, all the more valuable, since much of it was against his grain. In a way, Eastman was typical of many of the visitors from New York: he gave something of himself, and he held something back. No Hapgood or Reed, identifying himself with the strike, neither was he a Lippmann or Tridon, protecting his anti-democratic preconceptions against the experience of the strike. On the contrary, Eastman's delight in experience forced him to move past his easy conviction of his heroes' bigness and his own littleness, and of his remoteness from them and from working people. Haltingly and protestingly, he came to feel the humanity he shared with the strikers and their leaders.

GO TO HALEDON

Middle-class intellectuals like Eastman, Reed, and Hapgood, who came from old American families, had to wrestle with their own class and ethnic prejudices when they became involved in the Paterson strike. They could not help the silk workers without first helping themselves. It was one thing to admire Haywood in the Village; it was another to mix with ordinary silk workers in Paterson. Reed and Hapgood—and Sanger, Shields, Rodman, Weed and Carey, and the many whose names we do not know—went all the way to Paterson: they talked personally and directly with rank-and-file strikers. Like Eastman, many others made it only as far as Haledon, where they watched the crowd or spoke to it. For them, Haledon functioned as a halfway house, an almost neutral territory where they could mingle with the strikers and feel the excitement of the strike without making themselves overly vulnerable.

But even Haledon challenged their prejudices. Insofar as they had unconsciously shared the prevailing assumption that workers were passive and leaders were active, they could not witness the self-transformation of the strikers without carrying out, to some degree, a self-transformation of their own. Eastman's honesty enables us to glimpse his inner struggle, as Haledon enabled Eastman and others to glimpse the dynamics of the strike. In this sense, Haledon was the ideal place for New York intellectuals to begin their involvement in the strike. The New York *Call*, when it ran a column in mid-May urging New Yorkers to participate in the class struggle, did not title it "Go to Paterson." Instead, and for good reason, the column was headed "Go to Haledon."[124] Haledon became a crucial link in the bridge from New York to Paterson.

It didn't start that way. At first Haledon was used by the strikers to escape Paterson's blue laws and Bimson's police. The first meeting there was held on the first Sunday of the strike to protest against the police activity of the previous week: arrests, clubbings, refusal to grant permits for parades, confiscation of literature, threats to close the halls. This meeting could not have been held in Paterson. In Paterson, Sunday belonged to the clergy; city law banned all other public business. Sundays in Paterson were days of enforced quiet even when there was no strike. A Jewish girl who was nine years old in 1913 later recalled that since there was nothing else to do in Paterson on Sunday, she and her friends would go to the local YWCA, where "we would hold our breaths for a little while, because you weren't supposed to breathe Christian air!"[125] On the first Sunday of the strike the silk workers went to Haledon to breathe socialist air. Killingbeck and other Passaic County Socialists had suggested Haledon as a safe place, an oasis of free thought and assemblage, and Socialist Mayor Brueckmann had immediately responded with an invitation to the strikers to come to his borough on Sunday.[126]

Haledon had only one policeman; he weighed only ninety pounds ("a little pink-cheeked fellow," "a little bit of a policeman," Alexander Scott called him); and he took orders only from the Socialist mayor.[127] Paterson's Captain McBride complained that the Haledon police force was "one man; and whenever deputies were appointed they were all Socialists and attempted to lock up our detectives for being in the borough."[128] Throughout the strike, even after Haledon had taken on many other functions, it always retained its original meaning as a place where the strikers, without fear of harassment, could gather and express their anger against the way they were treated by the Paterson authorities. In Haledon they were free men and women. The allies of the manufacturers might rule in Paterson, but the allies of the silk workers ruled in Paterson's streetcar suburb.

From March to July, Haledon was used every Sunday, but not only on Sunday: whenever the Paterson police intensified repression in Paterson—as in their arrests of Haywood and Lessig at the end of March or their closing of the halls in May—weekday meetings would be held at Haledon to let the strikers protest and regroup. At the moment of greatest provocation, when real violence seemed inevitable, someone would invariably say, "On to Haledon."[129] Haledon functioned as a safety valve, enabling the strikers to maintain the discipline of nonviolence; like any good retreat, it sent the strikers back into the fray with renewed commitment and energy. At the conclusion of the second Sunday in Haledon, thousands of strikers marched back to Paterson and down Main Street, successfully defying Bimson's ban on parades and asserting their rights in Paterson.[130] Throughout the strike the Paterson authorities were furious at Brueckmann for providing this refuge to the strikers and tried by various unsuccessful means to coerce him into backing down; they sensed that Bimson's policy of repression and provocation would have more chance of success if the strikers had nowhere to go.[131]

After witnessing the first Sunday in Haledon, the New York *Call* reporter noted ironically that "owing to the absence of the Paterson bluecoats no disorders occurred."[132] Twelve thousand men, women, and children came to Barbour's Grove in Haledon that afternoon, braving muddy streets and March winds. Most walked; some rode the overcrowded trolley, which belatedly added special cars to accommodate the unprecedented traffic. By the time Brueckmann had completed his brief introductory remarks, there were too many people for a single meeting, and the crowd split into three separate groups. Barbour's Grove had no platform from which speakers could address the entire crowd. Quinlan, succeeding Brueckmann, spoke from a makeshift speakers' stand erected on a hill. Tresca, on a nearby hill, addressed one overflow meeting from a hugh rock; at the other an automobile served as a speaker's stand. Even after dividing into three groups, the strikers found it difficult to see and hear their speakers. Some men and boys climbed trees but were soon forced down by gusts of up to seventy miles an hour. On the edge of the crowd, latecomers waited patiently for those who had come earlier to be worn down by the elements and withdraw.

The biggest event was a speech by Flynn, who was already tremendously popular with the strikers. "The mention of her name . . . as the next speaker was the signal for hurrahs and a rush for vantage points by the shivering crowds."[133] Always attentive to local news, which at the time included a reported merger between the sewer systems of Haledon and Totowa, Flynn drew a laugh when she said that Paterson would be allowed to merge with Haledon only if Paterson became "civilized up to the standard set by the borough."[134] But Haledon itself was not yet Haledon. The March weather, the lack of a natural speaker's platform, the necessity for multiple meetings, and the absence of music meant that the first Sunday in Haledon, which was judged successful at the time and repeated with even bigger crowds on the following Sunday, was only a bare beginning compared with the meetings of the spring.

Haledon bloomed in May. Grass and dogwood blossoms replaced mud and bare trees. The strikers, who had stood shivering in March, began to picnic on the grass, bringing bread and wine with them. Singing became as important as listening to the speakers. And the speakers themselves found a way to be heard by everyone, thereby unifying the vast crowd in place of fragmenting it. One month after the first Haledon meeting,

> the I.W.W. leaders took possession of the house of Pietro Botto, at 83 Norwood Street, where they were able to address the great throng of strikers. An upper porch furnished an excellent platform from which the speakers could make their addresses and still be heard by the crowds. In front of this house thousands of people, men and women, evenly divided, gathered long before the speakers arrived. At 2:30 o'clock strikers were coming from all directions, and it was by far the finest demonstration that has been held during the strike.[135]

High on a hill overlooking a large green, which was almost enclosed by a semicircle of woods, the second-story balcony of the Botto house provided the speakers (in Flynn's words) with "a natural platform and amphitheatre."[136]

For the first time the Paterson strikers were able to meet as one. In Paterson they were split into Turn Hall and Helvetia Hall, with the dyers' helpers meeting separately from the ribbon weavers. But at the Botto house in April, May, and June, all the groups of silkworkers—together with their families and out-of-town supporters—sang the same songs, heard the same speeches, and were part of the same demonstration of solidarity. Bilingual individuals in the crowd quietly translated Italian, Yiddish, German, Polish, Dutch, or English speeches for the benefit of those around them. People who became too boisterous would be shushed by their neighbors. Speakers enjoyed the attention and responsiveness of the enormous crowd. To Haywood it "seemed as if the whole population of the northern part of New Jersey was present. To speak at such meetings," he added, referring to Turn and Helvetia halls but especially to Haledon, "is worth a lifetime of agitation."[137] Toward the end of each meeting, someone—often Flynn herself—would go through the great crowd, taking a collection for the relief fund; in May the sums ranged from $100 to $260. When at last the meeting was breaking up, Paterson police would hopefully station themselves on the border between Paterson and Haledon, as they did on April 3 after the first meeting at the Botto house, "but the strikers walked along in an orderly fashion, and all were in a good natured mood."[138] During that first meeting at the Botto house, a striker playfully called out "What's the matter with the Haledon Police Department," and the crowd instantly responded: "He's all right."[139] Freed for a while from the tension and discipline that were features of their struggle in Paterson, basking in the celebration of their unity and strength, the Paterson strikers rediscovered their good humor in Haledon.

The Paterson strike came into its own at the Botto house. Contemporary accounts and memoirs written by participants represent the Haledon meetings of May and early June as embodying the spirit of the strike. The size of the crowd kept increasing every Sunday. The May 18 meeting, at which Sinclair was one of many speakers, was the largest to that point. "The meeting was not planned to start until 3 o'clock this afternoon, yet at least two hours before that time every road and every lane leading to the green of the little village was crowded with men, women and children, all heading for the open space."[140] On the next Sunday, May 25, the crowd was even larger. *Solidarity*'s correspondent was excited. "The injunction 'Go to Haledon' seems to be followed by an ever-increasing number of persons. The attendance of this afternoon surpassed even that of last Sunday in size. One estimate is 30,000 present." An admittedly "conservative estimate" by the New York *Call* put 20,000 people at the May 25 meeting; the hostile New York *Times* said 25,000.[141]

The presence of so many people was, in and of itself, an impressive demonstration of working-class power. Speaking from the balcony of the Botto house on May 25, Haywood contrasted the immense numbers with the much smaller number of strike opponents who, on that same Sunday, attended the God-and-country meeting held by the clergy at the armory in Paterson. Haywood's point was that the Christian and Jewish capitalists who met at the armory illustrated the underlying unity of capital, whereas the workers of the many nationalities meeting in Haledon illustrated the unity of labor.[142] We might add that the two May 25 meetings symbolized the fact that in 1913 there were two Patersons, of which the larger by far was living in exile in Haledon. And although the speakers at the armory were clergy, the speakers at the Botto house — including Haywood, Flynn, Eastman, Reed (who led the singing), and many others — perhaps ministered more effectively to the spiritual needs of the people. Flynn liked to compare Sundays in Haledon to churchgoing, and IWW speakers to clergy who helped people forget their immediate physical suffering by reviving their long-range hopes.[143] Except for its misleading suggestion of passivity on the part of the strikers, Flynn's metaphor is apt. By the end of May, after three months on strike, most families of silk workers were having real difficulty feeding themselves, let alone paying the rent. Actively renewing their faith each Sunday in Haledon, men and women transformed their daily struggles into a living testimony to resilience, courage, and hope.

That is why Haledon had such an impact on visitors. There New York intellectuals saw the working class at its most hopeful and most united. One New Yorker, coming to visit the strike for the first time, arrived in Paterson on a Sunday and found the streets deserted; when he asked someone why, he was told, "Everyone's in Haledon."[144] Another newcomer took the trolley from Paterson to Haledon "and was just about to ask the conductor where the strikers were meeting when he happened to look up this little street. No questions were necessary." Standing in the crowd, this visitor saw that "many of the faces showed traces left by hungry days and supperless nights. But there was hardly a face among them which showed the slightest sign of desperation."[145] One New Yorker observed "a young woman standing near me with her face all pinched and drawn by malnutrition. But when she sang, what a sparkle in her eye, what a ring in her voice." According to this observer, the tens of thousands were anything but passive; "by singing, by cheering, by passing laws, and by arranging stage spectacles," they continually gave expression to their tremendous "creative energy."[146] Another visitor from New York was struck by the fact that the huge crowds, which sometimes overflowed the hillside and surrounded the Botto house, were always careful not to trample Maria Botto's lawn. As he listened to speakers assert that "these half-fed and desperately-handled men, women and children" gathered at Haledon were wonderfully patient and gentle, he realized that "I didn't need previous knowledge to be sure that they were right. The spectacle before me was enough."[147]

The spectacle was enough for many visitors. In the 1940s one New Yorker still remembered looking down from the balcony of the Botto house at "a crowd that brightened with sharp colors several areas of the grassy slopes around it"; another recalled how "on a lovely spring afternoon at a meeting out of doors, from the porch of a small frame house, where I stood with Jack Reed and the strike leaders, I looked on a whole hillside massed with men and women and children, more than twenty thousand in all."[148] The prevailing tone of those who recorded their impressions of Haledon was one of joy at the power of the working class. One transplanted New Yorker and strike participant said simply that "Haledon was always like a picnic, and it was a joy to go there."[149] A more analytical account, by the visitor who had taken the trolley from Paterson, tried to explain the magic: in Haledon, New Yorkers saw "visible evidence" of the ideal of the solidarity of the working class, "and the ideal itself, fine and inspiring as it is, pales before the fact."[150] For many New York intellectuals as for many Paterson silk workers, Sundays in Haledon in May were the nearest they would come to living in a world of solidarity and joy.

Back in New York, the intellectuals spread the word about Paterson, both publicly and privately, and joined in the serious task of fund raising. The round of fund-raising meetings begun in April continued in May, with their typical combination of Wobbly and Socialist speakers.[151] But the Village connection was already adding a new dimension to the drive to develop strike support in New York. By the third week in May, many New York writers and artists were hard at work on the Pageant.

CHAPTER SIX
The Paterson Pageant

In most modern drama, the best conclusion is: yes, this is how it was. Only an occasional play goes further, with the specific excitement of recognition: yes, this is how it is. Brecht, at his best, reaches out to and touches the necessary next stage; yes this is how it is, for these reasons, but the action is continually being replayed, and it could be otherwise.[1]

The Paterson silk workers took over Madison Square Garden on Saturday night, June 7. All contemporary accounts agree that the Pageant they staged, with the help of the IWW and village intellectuals, was a tremendous dramatic success. But the Pageant of the Paterson Strike was intended, by the workers and the intellectuals, to be a means of winning the strike. Eventually the strike was lost. All historians maintain that the Pageant failed, at least financially: it failed to raise money to buy food.[2] Many accounts, especially the recent ones, go further: the Pageant, they say, caused the failure of the strike; it demoralized the strikers by taking some of them away from the picket line, by creating jealousy among the rest, and by disappointing all their hopes for a big profit.[3]

The verdict of history has been pronounced: however exciting artistically, the Pageant was an economic and political failure. This chapter appeals that verdict. It maintains that in the Pageant the silk workers of Paterson and the radical intellectuals of New York together created a new form of economic and political struggle, one ideally suited to the needs of the strike and of the wider movement for workers' control of which the strike was a part.

THE PURPOSE

In its own terms, the Pageant was a success. By the middle of May the Paterson strike was deadlocked and the strikers had been placed for the first time on the defensive. People in Paterson were hungry, and there was no end in sight. Unless the strikers could receive substantial financial support from workers in the New York region, they would be starved back to work. "Strikes to be successful need more than the mere solidarity of the workers directly interested in the strike," *Solidarity* had pointed out just before the Paterson strike. "They also need the assistance of the workers throughout the country. The only way to get this assistance is through publicity."[4]

The purpose of the Pageant was publicity. Skillful publicity by the IWW had been an essential part of the Lawrence victory.[5] The resulting contributions from workers throughout America had helped feed the Lawrence strikers, and an aroused public opinion had broken the resistance of the woolen manufacturers after two months. But Paterson was not Lawrence. Paterson's silk manufacturers were in a position to fight on through the spring and the whole summer, if necessary; consequently, publicity was an even greater necessity than it had been in Lawrence. Yet good publicity was harder to come by. The Lawrence victory had raised the stakes: by triggering strikes throughout the textile industry and dramatizing the IWW's revolutionary threat, Lawrence had frightened editors in the East. Newspapers in the New York area gave little precise information about the Paterson strike, especially about the active role played by the silk workers themselves. They preferred to blame Paterson's labor troubles on the now notorious IWW. Mayor McBride was pleased with the coverage of the IWW. "The people of New York, through the great New York daily papers, have had a very favorable opportunity to study at close range the I.W.W. and their tactics since their arrival here in Paterson," McBride told the New York *Times* late in May.[6] The IWW was not pleased. "If we are to judge by the New York capitalist papers," said *Solidarity* on May 31, "the capitalist class feels instinctively that the strike is either going to make or break their ascendancy. . . . They are intent on utilizing the Paterson strike to defeat the I.W.W."[7]

During May the IWW expanded the publicity and fund-raising activities, aimed at New Yorkers, that it had begun in April, and a relief office for the aid of the Paterson strikers was opened in New York.[8] Flynn, Tresca, and Haywood tried with little success to get New York newspapers to carry appeals for relief of the strikers.[9] Also in May 100 Paterson strikers walked the sixteen miles to the ferry to take part in a demonstration in New York.[10] A Paterson ribbon weaver wrote to the New York *Globe*, begging for funds from New Yorkers, and two Paterson weavers carrying an American flag literally begged all the way down Broadway, until they were arrested for using the flag for commercial purposes.[11] The IWW and the Paterson strikers needed to find better ways to tap the financial resources of workers or potential middle-class supporters in New York. So long as the public image of the strike continued to be shaped by the hostile New York press, the situation in Paterson could only get worse. It was in this context that Haywood, Reed, and Mabel Dodge created the idea of the Pageant.

The Pageant began at the apartment of a schoolteacher who was an intimate friend of Haywood's, at the end of April. Her apartment was near Washington Square, and the mixture of guests was a typical one in the spring of 1913: Haywood and one or two other strike leaders, Hapgood, Dodge, Reed, a few novelists, a sculptor, an editor, the teacher, and the ex-member of Parliament. Haywood later summarized the results of the evening: "At a small gathering in the home of a New York friend of mine, it was suggested that it would be an excellent idea to stage the strike in New York City. I conveyed this suggestion to the strikers and it met with their approval."[12] Haywood did not say why he and the strikers responded so favorably to the suggestion. However, in an essay about the strike, which he had written earlier in April, he pointed to the need for publicity. "Through their control of outside newspapers, the Paterson silk manufacturers were able to bring about a general conspiracy of silence. The New York papers, for example, after the first few days in which they gave prominence to the strike, were warned through subtle sources that unless there was less publicity they would be made to suffer through loss of support and advertising."[13] The Pageant began, then, as a way of breaking the conspiracy of silence in New York.

This interpretation of the origins of the Pageant is confirmed by fuller accounts of the same "small gathering." Hapgood described what happened after he brought Dodge to the teacher's apartment. According to Hapgood, "Mabel's imagination was lit up" by Haywood's description of the strike and by his emphasis on "the impossibility of getting the New York newspapers to tell the story of the strikers." Dodge suggested bringing the strike to New York in the form of a large-scale drama, and Reed volunteered to take charge of the production.[14]

Dodge's own description further illuminates the purpose of the Pageant.

[Haywood] was telling about the long, unremitting strike over in Paterson, New Jersey. . . .

"But there's no way to tell our comrades over here in New York about it," he growled. "The newspapers have determined to keep it from the workers in New York. Very few of them know what we've been through over there—the drama and the tragedy. . . . I wish I could show them a picture of the funeral of Modestino. . . . Every one of the silk mill hands followed his coffin to the grave and dropped a red flower on it. . . . The grave looked like a mound of blood. . . . By God, if our people over here could have seen it, we could have raised a trunkful of money to help us go on. Our food is getting mighty scarce over there."

"Can't you get any reports of it into the papers by hook or crook?" someone asked.

"Not a damned word," answered Haywood.

Moved by his words, Dodge suggested, "Why don't you bring the strike to New York and *show* it to the workers?"[15]

Dodge's account, published in 1935, clarified two crucial aspects of the

Pageant idea. First, as Haywood realized, the strike was inherently dramatic. There was no need to invent drama; the drama of Modestino's funeral, for example, had already been enacted in Paterson by the strikers themselves. The Pageant would bring the strikers to New York, where they would reenact their drama. Second, by so doing, the originators of the Pageant hoped to break the control of strike news exercised by the enemies of the IWW in the New York press. On May 21 Dodge told the New York *Times* that "the Pageant was arranged because the newspapers have never let the people get a fair impression of the I.W.W. The actors in the pageant will bring out the fact that the I.W.W. is made up of the workers themselves."[16] By showing the audience the active role that workers were playing in Paterson, the originators of the Pageant hoped to reach out to the hearts and pocketbooks of workers in New York. They even hoped to force the New York newspapers to tell the real story of the strike. Reed himself, according to Kemp's autobiographical *More Miles*, spoke optimistically of this purpose: "I believe there's enough left of the old American spirit in the peoples' hearts to mold overwhelming public opinion in the strikers' favor—through the medium of the Capitalistic Press itself."[17]

In the end, Reed, Haywood, and Dodge proved justified in their hopes. On June 7 an overflow crowd of almost 15,000 people watched the silk workers enact the major events of their strike, including the funeral of Modestino. On Sunday, June 8, hundreds of thousands of New Yorkers read about the key events of the strike in detail in their newspapers. On Monday, Haywood announced that the newspapers had been saying that the Paterson strike was broken, but now the Pageant had shown the people of New York the truth.[18] And later in the month, sure enough, outside contributions to the strikers' relief fund in Paterson began to grow.[19] In terms of its original purpose of publicizing the strike, the Pageant was an overwhelming success.

But the Pageant lost money, says the chorus of historians. In making this charge, they flatten out the complex strategy of the Pageant's creators—to generate publicity, which would in turn lead to increased financial support —and reduce the Pageant to a simple fund-raiser. This misreading of the evidence has its roots in contemporary press accounts. Haywood, Reed, and Dodge were forced to use the press to advertise the Pageant. They needed willing workers in Paterson and New York, as well as an audience large enough to fill Madison Square Garden, and they had only three weeks to get it all done. Inevitably, the process of spreading the word about the Pageant resulted in distortions. Having begun as a way of letting potential supporters in New York see what was happening in Paterson, the Pageant sometimes appeared, in the same press whose influence it was meant to offset, as merely a fund-raiser.[20]

Hapgood, responding to this confusion, insisted in the New York *Globe* that "the Pageant to be given by the silk workers of Paterson is not a money-making idea. . . . It is intended to give the whole of New York an idea of the meaning of the great industrial and social happenings which are taking place in

Paterson and all over the country."[21] But as momentum developed in Paterson and New York, culminating in the standing-room-only crowd at the Garden on June 7, the hope of making money that very night became widely shared. When it finally became obvious, more than a week after the performance, that it had made no money (and that indeed a small amount of money would still have to be raised in New York to finish paying the debts incurred), the newspapers were quick to condemn the Pageant as a failure and even to accuse the IWW or New York intellectuals of stealing the profits.[22] Historians who say the Pageant failed because it did not make money for the strikers on the day of performance are perpetuating a confusion that developed in the press during the gestation of the Pageant idea.

Did the strikers themselves believe what they read in the papers? Did they come to expect the Pageant to raise a great deal of money directly, in addition to raising it indirectly through publicity? Under the pressure of hunger, many of them did. *Solidarity*, in an optimistic article on relief efforts written a few days before the Pageant, said that "the strikers hope to derive the largest lump sum of all from 'The Pageant of the Paterson Strike.'"[23]

In New York those who were close to the financial details always knew better. Members of the Pageant Executive Committee, which Reed and Haywood pulled together in the middle of May to manage the production details, were afraid of losing money on the performance. During its first week of operation, the committee held an emergency meeting at midnight and "seriously debated whether or not to drop the whole thing on account of the many difficulties that had then become apparent, among them the likelihood of a financial loss." During the second week, with only about ten days left, the committee "called a meeting in the Liberal Club of the members of the various working committees to propose again that the Pageant should be called off, in view of the enormous expense that they were quite unable to meet. . . . In other words, if the Pageant could be produced at all a financial loss seemed certain."[24] The working committees finally decided to go ahead, not because they believed money could be made from a single performance — especially not one aimed primarily at working people—but because New York silk strikers who were present at the meeting insisted that the Pageant simply had to be put on and themselves lent money to offset production costs.[25] The New York ribbon weavers knew what most historians have forgotten, that the real purpose of the Pageant was to publicize the dramatic class struggle then taking place in Paterson, in the hope of influencing the outcome.

THE POLITICAL EFFECT

The success of the Pageant, however, was not limited to achieving its original purpose. Conceived as a publicity event whose ultimate goal was economic, the Pageant grew during the three weeks of preparation into a political event whose goal was revolutionary.

As a political event the Pageant made its most obvious impact on the New Yorkers who saw it. More subtle but also more profound was its effect upon two of the groups that created it: namely, the Paterson silk strikers and the Village intellectuals. To appreciate the full extent of the Pageant's success, we need to see how it tended to radicalize all those who participated in it: the strikers, the intellectuals, and finally the audience.

The strikers first heard about the Pageant from Haywood on Friday morning, May 16. Quinlan had just been convicted. Driven by the new sense of crisis in Paterson, Haywood picked up the idea of the Pageant (conceived three weeks earlier at his friend's apartment) and brought it into the strike. Speaking at a regular strike meeting, he described the purpose and noted that about one thousand strikers would be needed to play the parts.[26] In Haledon on Sunday, repeating that "as one of the means of showing what this strike means we are going to move this strike to New York City," he sketched some scenes, asked for volunteers, and specified that 500 women and 500 men would be needed.[27] On Monday morning Haywood introduced the strikers to Reed, who described possible scenes. Reed, who had led the songs of the cheering section at Harvard football games, became "so enthused that he took off his coat" and rolled up his shirt sleeves. Rehearsals had begun.[28]

From the first rehearsal to the last, the strikers actively transformed the Pageant. At the beginning, some strikers were talking with Reed. "We were frightened when we went in," said one young woman, describing the first day of the strike, "but we were singing when we came out." Her account gave shape to the first episode of the Pageant.[29] Other episodes developed similarly: "Responding to Reed's enthusiasm, the strikers evolved the details of each scene, lost their self-consciousness, and felt themselves re-enacting the stirring events of their own drama."[30] Rehearsals continued each day at Turn Hall, with Reed using a megaphone to direct the singing and acting. From the galleries, hundreds of strikers watched "as, under their very eyes, are enacted the scenes through which they have been and are living in the great strike."[31] The Pageant was as real to them as their lives. Asked if she would get stage fright at the Garden, one performer replied that playing "fancy ladies and gentlemen" might be difficult, but the roles in the Pageant would be easy. "We know we can make a strike pageant because we're strikers. We're rehearsing every day, in the strike."[32] Hapgood understood, better than anyone, the unique relationship between the strike and the Pageant. He saw that the Pageant could not have been successfully staged after less than three weeks of practice "unless there had been much preliminary training. This preliminary training came from this long strike itself—the meetings of the strikers, their growing understanding of themselves and their cause and their situation. They were unconsciously rehearsing all through this strike of three months and a half."[33]

So close were life and art that at times they became indistinguishable. On Sunday in Haledon the performers sang to a crowd larger than any that Madison Square Garden could hold. Was this the strike or a rehearsal? The strikers' roles were eagerly sought, but no one wanted to play the strikebreakers or the police, and for a time it was rumored that New York intellectuals would have to take these parts.[34] During one of the last rehearsals, after strikers had filled all the roles—including the police—a New York reporter walked into Turn Hall and saw twenty big men charging a crowd of women and men and actually beating them, while the hall rang with boos. The reporter thought the police were breaking up the rehearsal and said so to a male weaver, who laughed and replied: "Police? Police nothing! They're just rehearsing the second tableau for the Pageant—that's all." A female performer nudged the reporter and proudly revealed the real bruise she had received on her arm in a previous rehearsal.[35] Completing the circle, a boy who was caught booing a real Paterson policeman claimed in court that he was only rehearsing for the Pageant.[36] In ways like these the life of the strike flowed into the Pageant, and the Pageant—more than the story of the strike—became the strike itself.

For the final rehearsal on the afternoon of the performance, dressed in their work clothes rather than their Sunday best, with everyone wearing or carrying something red, 1,147 strikers took a special train to the Lackawanna ferry. In New York—led by Hannah Silverman, released from jail just in time—they marched through streets lined with cheering people to the Garden, where they fell ravenously on food that had been prepared by New Yorkers for their lunch. Then "Hannah Silverman, together with John Reed, got their troupe together and rehearsed their parts."[37]

Silverman and other strikers were co-directors of the Pageant. Reenacting the drama they were living, they clarified its meaning not only for other people but for themselves. In this way the Pageant helped them claim the strike as their own. Planning and rehearsing, the silk workers raised their strike activity, previously performed more or less spontaneously in the heat of battle, to a fully conscious level. Linda Nochlin, in an important recent article on the Pageant, describes it as "a potent instrument in raising political consciousness." She explains that "the choice of significant moments—the walkout, the martyrdom, the funeral of the martyr, the May Day Parade, the sending away of the children, the strike vote—the repetition of the speeches of the strike leaders and the dramatic simplification and compression of events which may have been unclear when experienced in actuality, all made the striking workers conscious of their experiences as self-determining members of a class that shaped history."[38]

Abstracting from the actual elements of the ongoing strike, the Pageant was the strike as class struggle. This was its unifying theme. "No such spectacle, presenting in dramatic form the class war raging in society, has ever been staged in America," claimed the Pageant committee.[39] Indeed, the unique thing about the Pageant as public relations was that its interpretation of the strike emphasized the revolutionary elements. This consistently revolutionary thrust came partly from outsiders, especially Reed. Probably only outsiders *could* have gathered from the strikers the pieces of their experience and helped them to find the pattern of class struggle. The Pageant revealed the power of the strikers, especially to themselves. By uniting and concentrating the disparate revolutionary elements of the strike in a single drama, the Pageant encouraged the strikers to affirm the most radical meaning of their own experience.

For the intellectuals, too, the Pageant deepened a process begun earlier. They had already participated in the strike as sympathizers and spectators, occasional speakers or fund raisers. Now, the Pageant gave them a chance to show what they could do. Journalists like Hapgood and Steffens, writers like Sinclair, Stokes, Walling, and Inez Haynes Gillmore did publicity work for the Pageant. People with theatrical experience such as Poole, Thompson Buchanan, Edward Hunt, and the young stage designer Robert Edmund Jones planned the logistics of production. Jones made the powerful poster advertising the Pageant. Sloan painted the imposing 200-foot backdrop of a great silk mill flanked by a number of smaller mills. Jessie Ashley, Dodge, Boyd, and Sanger served with Reed and Haywood on the Pageant Executive Committee, and dozens more served on the working committees, meeting nightly in Sanger's apartment and helping Reed with rehearsals in Paterson.[40] Altogether, "a group of twenty or thirty men and women slaved day and night for several weeks," Sinclair later recalled.[41] Haywood estimated more broadly that "80 or 90 people with radical tendencies in New York" gave their time to the Pageant.[42] In return, the Pageant gave them a chance to test their beliefs through action and to use their creative skills in alliance with the labor movement. Working with the strikers, the radical writers and artists glimpsed the revolutionary role they themselves might play. The Pageant had been made possible by the bridge that Haywood and the IWW had built from Paterson to New York, and it confirmed the value of that bridge. It confirmed, too, what the intellectuals had previously only hoped—that art could become an integral part of the revolution. For many in their generation the Pageant would remain, as it did for Hapgood, the highest point "of self-expression in industry and art."[43]

It was precisely because the Pageant invited the creative participation of the intellectuals that its impact upon them was so great. In contrast to the passive or supportive roles often played by intellectuals in strikes, the Pageant enabled them to become fellow workers in a common cause. Like the strikers themselves, the intellectuals as a group were aggressive, energetic, and confident. Nothing suggests that in their relations with the Paterson strikers they were either patronizing or humble. It was this remarkable collaboration between two classes of strong, independent, self-confident people that made the Pageant revolutionary both as art and as politics.

But to make the Pageant revolutionary, the intellectuals had to revolutionize pageantry. Nowhere is the active role they played more evident than in the way they transformed pageantry into a radical art form. In 1913, historical pageantry (or "civic theatre," as pageant-master Percy MacKaye had dubbed it) was enjoying a revival. Dodge and Reed could spontaneously suggest staging the strike in New York because, in their cultural circles, the idea of historical spectacles performed by casts of thousands was then in vogue. But there was nothing radical about that pageant tradition; on the contrary, pageants were being used throughout the United States to promote patriotism and civic pride by dramatizing the integration of immigrants and other workers into American society. In a book entitled *The Civic Theatre*, published in 1912, MacKaye advocated pageantry as a democratic art form because it was essentially participatory. But he explicitly rejected the possibility of extending democracy to industry. Regarding the alienation of workers in modern industry as inevitable, he proposed only to make that alienation more tolerable.[44] His reformist and patriotic aims, and the aims of the pageant movement as a whole, were therefore diametrically opposed to the aims of the movement for workers' control of industry and society, spearheaded by the IWW.

But in 1913 American radicalism was vital, capable of appropriating aspects of the established culture for its own use. A radical reviewer of MacKayes' book had pointed to the potential of pageants for "expressing the art side of the struggle of Socialism against Capitalism."[45] In the Paterson Pageant, as Nochlin shows, the Village intellectuals seized the pageant form and made it over to fit the experience of the strikers.

> Reed may be said to have turned the patriotic rhetoric, the well-meaning "melting-pot" psychology of the do-gooder civic-theatre leaders, back upon itself, revealing the idealistic vision of the immigrant workers' place in their new land for the sentimental cant it was. The patriotic pageants were all too often merely spectacular rationalizations of the status quo. . . . In the Paterson Strike Pageant, it was made dramatically clear that the "new citizens" were contributing more than their dances, their songs and their folk traditions to this country: they were being forced to contribute their health, their hopes, their honor and their children.[46]

"Hail the new pageantry! Hail the red pageant—the pageant with red blood in its veins," wrote Stokes, who herself helped with rehearsals in Paterson and with publicity in New York. Rescuing pageantry from fancy costumes and long-ago events, the Paterson Pageant "gives us history fresh from the hands of its makers—and more thrilling marvel still—with the makers themselves as actors in the play."[47] Utilizing their talents, radical writers and artists like Reed and Stokes subverted the pageant form. In the process, they became more than mere sympathizers or supporters of the efforts of working people to better their condition; they became active participants in the class struggle.

Indeed, that was the Pageant's secret—the secret of how it radicalized almost everyone who touched it. From conception to realization, the Pageant invited active participation by the performers, by writers and artists, and even by those who only came to watch. The audience's active involvement was deliberately built into the staging. Robert Edmund Jones, catching the spirit of the project, made the long center aisle of the Garden into a street through the middle of the audience, thus breaking down the distance between the performers and the spectators.[48] In the sense of passive onlookers, there would be no spectators on Saturday night, June 7.

THE PERFORMANCE

When the doors were finally closed at nine o'clock by order of the police, every seat in the Garden was taken, 1,000 people were standing inside, and many thousands more were left outside in lines stretching for blocks. By that time almost 15,000 had crowded inside. Only about 12,000 of these had paid, however. The rest were silk strikers who had been admitted free, including 800 who had walked the twenty-three miles from Paterson to the Garden and a larger contingent from Hudson County, New Jersey.[49] The audience as a whole was overwhelmingly working class.

At 9:01 P.M. the ceiling lights were turned out, and the lights over the stage went on. Specially built for the performance, extending from the 26th Street side of the Garden all the way to the 27th Street side, the stage was dominated by Sloan's huge silk mill backdrop. A member of the audience described the scene:

> First we saw the mill, stretching its black stoves menacingly to the sky. Its windows were lit, its whistles blowing. We watched the still sleepy men, women and children, with their coat collars turned up to keep out the chill of the early morning—it was in February the strike began—we watched them swallowed, one by one, through the mill's hungry door. Then the unending whirr of iron-hearted machinery began. It seemed to us, waiting out there in the audience, that the machinery was grinding those workers to pieces. We thought of industrial accidents and diseases, of how terrible toil sucked all life, all initiative out of the workers. They were dying, and it was the same all over the world. We held our breath. And then—something happened. The machinery stopped grinding. A faint free cry rises slowly, to deafening hosannas from a thousand throats as the workers rush from the mill. They wave their hands, they shout, they dance, they embrace each other in a social passion that pales individual feeling to nothing. They are a mad mob, glad and beautiful in their madness. They sing the Marseillaise. The strike is on! . . . Here and there, from the balcony, the boxes and the great main floor, the sound of sobbing that was drowned in singing proved that the audience had "got" Paterson.[50]

Leaving the stage, the thousand silk workers marched down the entire length of the center aisle, "cheered all the way," said the *Independent*, "by the sympathetic audience of 15,000 workingmen and their families."[51] As they went through the audience, the actors shouted "Strike! Strike!" The audience, according to *Solidarity*, experienced "the onrush of a stupendous force," suggesting the power of labor. "It seized the imagination with a grip that was expressed, after a short pause, in which its significance was grasped, in an outburst of cheers and applause that was prolonged and deafening."[52] Another witness noticed that no one remained quietly seated, once the machinery stopped and the songs began. "The people on the stage had long ago forgotten the audience," he explained. "The audience had long ago forgotten itself. It had become a part of the scene."[53]

From this opening episode to the sixth and final one, the audience became part of the Pageant. One reporter was surprised that "everybody was on his feet all the time, men and women were humming—if they didn't know the words," and even the few wealthy members of the audience were crying. As for the applause, it "was one chronic roar."[54] Another New York reporter, also struck by the extent to which the audience participated in the production, recalled that "the Garden has held many shows and many audiences, from . . . Taft to Buffalo Bill, but it is doubtful if there ever was such an assemblage either as an audience or as a show. . . . In fact it was such a mixed grouping that at times they converged and actor became auditor and auditor turned suddenly into actor."[55] The critic for *Solidarity* agreed: "The audience was frequently as much a part of the Pageant as the strikers themselves."[56] Harry Haines, of the Paterson *Evening News*, acknowledged that "the entire audience was in sympathy with the movement which the Pageant portrayed, and joined in the applause, boos or cheers, as the occasion demanded."[57]

Each succeeding scene made new demands on the audience. In the second episode the strikers were picketing the big mill—its windows now darkened —when a strikebreaker appeared, heavily guarded by police. Booed by the pickets, he reached the mill and disappeared inside; now the pickets began to boo the police. Finally the police—"those in the show," a reporter specified —charged the pickets.[58] Forty were arrested, including Silverman. Leading their captives off down the long center aisle, the police were booed not only by the strikers but also by the audience. In the melee, the program added, a private detective employed by the mill owners had fired a shot, killing Modestino. But at the end of the episode, after the violence, the audience saw that the mill was still dark and quiet. "The Mills Dead—The Workers Alive" emphasized the program. The first episode had dramatized the power of the striking workers; the second dramatized the corresponding impotence of the authorities, even when they used violence.

The third episode explored the effects of that violence. This time there was no shouting, no singing, no booing, either on stage or by the audience. After brief speeches at Modestino's grave by Haywood and Tresca, there was no applause. Except for the funeral march and speeches, this episode was silent, "enacted with a repressed intensity on the part of both players and audience."[59] Portraying working-class solidarity, the thousand strikers fol- lowed Modestino's coffin down the center aisle to the stage, where one by one they dropped their carnations or red ribbons on the coffin "until it was literally buried under the colors of the I.W.W."[60] The funeral scene, observed the New York *Tribune*, "worked the actors themselves and their thousands of sympathizers in the audience up to a high pitch of emotion, punctuated with moans and groans and sobs."[61] For the moment, class consciousness ceased to be an abstraction to the audience and became a simple fact of its experience. "The funeral procession marched right through it," remembered Dodge, "so that for a few electric moments there was a terrible unity between all these people. They were one: the workers who had come to show their comrades what was happening across the river, and the workers who had come to see it. I have never felt such a high pulsing vibration in any gathering before or since."[62]

The fourth episode, a Sunday meeting in Haledon, featured songs by the strikers. The actors on stage and the members of the audience were "carried away" by the lilt of a song in Italian, with choruses in English, mocking the silk manufacturers and praising Haywood and Flynn. The German quartet, the Italian quartet, and the English octet led more songs. "Again and again the audience demanded repetitions of these strange, wonderfully musical chants, composed and sung by the strikers themselves."[63] Then everyone on stage and in the audience sang the *"Internationale"*: "Arise, ye prisoners of starvation" —could the audience forget that the performers on stage had been literally starving for weeks? " 'Tis the final conflict," proclaimed the refrain. "Let each stand in his place / The Industrial Union / Shall be the human race." Many must have wondered whether the Paterson strike was indeed the beginning of the revolution. Even the reporter for the Paterson *Evening News*, who noticed nervously that "there were red I.W.W. emblems everywhere," came away convinced that "the era of a social revolution is approaching."[64]

Revolution was a theme of the last two episodes. In the fifth the Paterson strikers recreated their celebration of May Day—"international revolutionary day," the program emphasized.[65] Led by their twenty-six-piece band, the strikers paraded up the aisles, through the audience. On stage, Flynn described to the strikers how their hungry children would be fed and cared for by families in New York for the remainder of the strike, and hundreds of children, dressed in red, were affectionately sent off. Underlining the potentially revolutionary role of New Yorkers in the strike, Flynn told the audience how she hoped that in New York the children would get "the rose put back in their cheeks and class solidarity in their hearts."[66]

Four of the first five episodes of the Pageant used the center aisle as a way of involving the audience. The sixth and final episode employed an additional device. Haywood was at the rear of the stage, facing the audience. The strikers stood on stage in front of him "with their backs turned to the audience, transforming the setting into a vast meeting"[67] and further dissolving the distance between strikers and audience, Paterson and New York. Speaking to the actors and the audience as if they were all part of one huge strike meeting at Turn Hall, Haywood urged them to adopt the eight-hour day. The workers were already in control, he explained, as he had explained in Paterson. If they decided to work only eight hours, no power on earth could make them work more.[68] As he spoke, the dead mills behind him emphasized the revolutionary power of workers and the impotence of manufacturers and their governments. The two audiences, which had become one, listened to Flynn, Tresca, and Quinlan. Then everyone sang the "Marseillaise," and the Pageant was over.

Newspaper reports of the Pageant on Sunday and Monday were generally accurate, detailed, and sympathetic. The New York *Tribune* gave a careful scene-by-scene narrative and commented:

> The I.W.W. has not been highly regarded hereabouts as an organization endowed with brains or imagination. Yet the very effective appeal to public interest made by the spectacle at the Garden stamps the I.W.W. leaders as agitators of large resources and original talent. Lesser geniuses might have hired a hall and exhibited moving pictures of the Paterson strike. Saturday night's pageant transported the strike itself bodily to New York.[69]

Newspapers that had condemned the IWW's role in Paterson and its emphasis on class struggle recognized that the Pageant gave effective publicity to the strike. The Paterson *Evening News*, in an editorial headed "The I.W.W. Pageant," concluded unhappily that "there was nothing to criticize."[70] Even the New York *Times*, while editorially damning the Pageant, implicitly acknowledged its subversive power: "Under the direction of a destructive organization . . . a series of pictures in action were shown with the design of stimulating mad passion against law and order and promulgating a gospel of discontent."[71] A writer for the *International Socialist Review* summed up the effect on public opinion: "No spectacle enacted in New York has ever made such an impression. Not the most sanguine member of the committee which made the preparations for the Pageant believed that its success would be quite so overwhelming. It is still the talk of New York, most cynical and hardened of cities, and will remain so for many days."[72]

Impressed with the Pageant, the New York newspapers tended to give the IWW credit for it, as they tended to blame the IWW for the strike. They could not deny the power of the performance, but they were unable or unwilling to see such power as an expression of the real or potential power of the workers. Reviews in national magazines more thoughtfully put their emphasis on the workers in the cast and in the audience. The *Independent* observed that the important device of having the actors parade through the center of the audience had been used several times on Broadway "but never with more effect than in this performance, where actors and audience were of one class and one hope."[73] The *Survey* praised the Pageant's creators less for using sophisticated devices than for enabling the strikers to tell their own story: "In fact, the offer of theatrical producers to help in 'putting it on' was declined by those who wanted the workers' own simple action to impress the crowd." The speeches of the IWW organizers, according to the *Survey*, "added nothing to the effect which the workers spontaneously gave." The power of the Pageant was that "it gave a real acquaintance with the spirit, point of view and earnestness" of the strikers themselves.[74] One magazine perceptively judged the Pageant in terms not only of the effect on the audience but also of "the effect upon the performers." *Current Opinion* contrasted the static and symbolic suffrage pageant produced at the Metropolitan Opera, which had similarly attempted to publicize a cause, with the Paterson Strike Pageant, which succeeded in emotionally involving both the audience and the performers. *Current Opinion* concluded that the Paterson Pageant was politically successful—"even tho it may be, as the *Times* has pointed out, a dangerous weapon for subversive propaganda."[75]

The Pageant did not impress all critics of the IWW or of the strike. Predictably, the anarchists of *Mother Earth* and the *Social War* were critical. *Mother Earth* held that the Pageant had educated outsiders but not the strikers themselves, because "good as it was," the production "was unfortunately too locally photographic, too lacking in the revolutionary spirit of active resistance to tyranny."[76] The criticism was hardly surprising, since *Mother Earth* had already, in May, called for the strikers to use violence against the police; by "the revolutionary spirit of active resistance," it meant the willingness to use violence.[77] After the defeat of the strike, the anarchists were less guarded in their criticism of both the strike and the Pageant. According to the *Social War*, in September, "emotional mass meetings, mass picketing and pageantifying have been weighed and found wanting."[78]

The AFL's criticisms were equally ideological and predictable. Like the anarchists, Samuel Gompers attacked both Pageant and strike; unlike the anarchists, however, he was not restrained by any respect for the strikers or for the IWW. "Unhampered by experience with theatrical pitfalls and financial losses, like children the Paterson workers gleefully fell in with the idea. Dazzled by the glamour of the footlights, they journeyed to Madison Square Garden, New York, expecting to bring back barrels of gold." The phrase "like children" summed up Gomper's viewpoint. He assumed that the purpose of the Pageant was to make money at the gate. Writing in July, when it had become apparent that all the proceeds had gone to pay the Pageant's bills, Gompers took the financial figures as proof of the "ignorance of these workers, mostly from foreign lands, and the terrible consequences from reckless inculcation of false principles and unworkable methods!"[79] Gompers was not alone; many of the papers that had originally praised the Pageant as a form of propaganda now either damned it for not making money or hinted that the IWW or New York intellectuals had made off with the profits. "Fearful of the immediate sympathy that we had raised, orders had been given to the write-up men to take away the glory," suggested Dodge, "but it was too late."[80]

FLYNN AND HISTORIANS

It is, however, never too late. In the long run, it was historians who took away the glory. Despite abundant evidence that the Pageant achieved its original purpose of publicizing the strike in New York, and that in addition it galvanized the people who saw it and transformed the strikers and intellectuals who created it, historians nevertheless agree that the Pageant failed. Their unanimous verdict cannot have resulted from such transparently biased sources as the AFL or the anarchists. Even the understandable confusion that developed around the Pageant's long-range objective of raising money through publicity cannot explain the unanimity of the verdict subsequently reached. The fact is that even in 1913 another voice besides those of Gompers and *Mother Earth* was being heard, a powerful voice that apparently could not be dismissed as biased and that condemned the Pageant as a disastrous failure.

The voice belonged to Elizabeth Gurley Flynn. In Haledon, the day after the Pageant, Haywood expressed the general excitement. "This was the biggest thing that the Industrial Workers of the World ever attempted," he told the strikers. "We have obtained publicity what [*sic*] could not be bought at any price. That was the idea." Flynn was more restrained. "I congratulate you on the splendid debut you made in Madison Square Garden last night. I have no doubt that David Belasco will take every one of you; and just think, if he does you will never have to go back to work in the mills again." She added that if the strikers were as good at dyeing and weaving as they were at acting, the mill owners would be foolish not to settle with them. And that was that. "Now, this is all I have to say about the big show."[81]

Flynn's joking had a serious side. She doubted whether "the big show" would help win the strike; she regarded acting in New York as a diversion from the real business of picketing in Paterson. By the beginning of August the strike had been lost, and her doubts hardened into certainty. As her friend Vorse explained:

> Elizabeth Gurley Flynn always believed that the Pageant had much to do with the failure of the strike. She felt that this disillusionment over not making a profit, together with diverting the workers' minds from the actual struggle to the pictured struggle, was fatal.
>
> We discussed the pros and cons of it during the summer and fall, when several of the strike leaders, including Haywood and Jessie Ashley, took a house in Provincetown.[82]

Opposed by Haywood and the great majority of Wobblies and radical intellectuals, Flynn voiced her criticisms wherever she went. Returning to Paterson, she told a meeting of silk workers that the Pageant had caused the break in the strike by taking them away from the real picket line.[83] In New York she directly attacked the intellectuals who had helped to create the show. Reading a lecture about the strike in January 1914 at the New York Civic Club Forum (uncharacteristically, she had written the speech out beforehand), Flynn admitted that "what I say about the Pageant tonight may strike you as rather strange." She acknowledged that it was "a beautiful example of realistic art" and even "splendid propaganda for the workers in New York." But she insisted, with the authority of a Paterson strike leader, that the Pageant had "started the decline in the Paterson strike," that it had undermined strike activity, morale, and solidarity. Activity declined because "in preparation for the Pageant the workers were distracted for weeks, turning to the stage of the hall, away from the field of life. They were playing pickets on the stage. They were neglecting picketing around the mill." Morale suffered because "the Pageant promised money for the Paterson strikers and it didn't give them a cent." Solidarity was injured because only 1,000 strikers were able to be in the Pageant, and the rest were jealous. "I wonder if you ever realized that you left 24,000 disappointed people behind. The women cried and said, 'Why did she go? Why couldn't I go?'"

"I wonder if *you* ever realized": Flynn meant the New York intellectuals in the audience. They especially were the target of her anger. If there was any credit due for the Pageant, she said, it belonged to the New York silk workers who had advanced the necessary money, not to "the dilettante element who figured so prominently, but who would have abandoned it at the last moment had not the silk workers advanced $600.00 to pull it through." Bitterly disappointed by the defeat of the strike, Flynn tried her best to be fair. "I don't mean to say that I blame the people who ran the Pageant. I know they were amateurs and they gave their time and their energy and their money. They did the best they could and I appreciate their efforts. But that doesn't minimize the result that came in Paterson."[84]

In her autobiography, published in 1955, Flynn summarized her three charges concerning picketing, profits, and jealousy.[85] With the publication in 1964 of her 1914 speech, these charges against the Pageant have come to dominate the historical record. But are they true? The evidence on picketing shows that there were significant differences throughout the strike between the IWW organizers and the weavers as to how much was necessary; that the organizers—including Flynn—were not satisfied with the amount of picketing even before rehearsals began; and that after the Pageant many strikers were still out on the picket line, despite the increased aggressiveness of the police.[86] Moreover, Flynn's reasoning on this point tends to undercut her larger argument. "The best ones, the most active, the most energetic . . . went into the pageant and they were the ones that were the best pickets around the mill," she complained.[87] By drawing the most active strikers into the process of rehearsals and performance, however, the Pageant concentrated their energy and propelled the radical thrust of the strike. To these militant silk workers, the Pageant, far from being a diversion from the realities of class struggle in Paterson, represented an intensification and extension of that struggle.

The evidence regarding profits is more ambiguous. Buoyed by the overflow crowd at the Garden and the rumors of thousands of dollars of profit at the gate, the Paterson strikers were indeed disappointed to learn, ten days later, that the Pageant had made no profit. Reed returned to Paterson on June 18 to tell the strikers the bad news. Then he "tried several times to get the gathering to sing the song that he had taught them, but with the announcement that money had been lost on the pageant it took the heart out of them, and had it not been for the children that were near the platform he probably would have had to finish the song himself."[88] Yet in blaming the Pageant for this disappointment ("the Pageant promised money"), Flynn was oversimplifying. The optimism about profits originated not with the Pageant organizers but "with the papers clamouring that tens of thousands of dollars had been made," Flynn said, while the Pageant committee was trying to explain "what was very simple, that nothing could have been made with one performance on such a gigantic scale."[89] She also knew from the committee's report that the real explanation why the receipts at the gate were somewhat smaller than expected was that the audience was solidly working class. The Pageant Executive Committee had not foreseen how many seats would have to be sold cheaply to workers or given away to silk strikers. As it explained afterward about the strikers who had been admitted free, "many of them had walked from Paterson, West Hoboken, Astoria, College Point, the Bronx and Brooklyn. The Pageant was theirs more than anybody else's."[90] In short, the Pageant did not make a profit precisely because it was not an amusement for middle-class dilettantes, because it was an enactment of solidarity not only *by* the workers but *for* them as well.

According to Flynn, however, solidarity in Paterson itself was hurt by the Pageant. Not everyone, of course, was able to participate; nevertheless, Flynn's perception of the jealousy felt by those left behind is a highly colored one. Even before the performance she told the strikers they were going to be jealous. "She stated that rather than pick out the 1,000 persons who are to take part in the Pageant, she would rather take a term of ten years in jail, as all were anxious to serve and those not selected would feel aggrieved."[91] Flynn's view of the strikers in this instance, as jealous children misled by Pied Pipers from New York, seems embarrassingly similar to Gomper's view of them as ignorant children misled by flashy outside agitators. In any event, there is no evidence to confirm her charge that the Pageant caused jealousy and dissension; all other accounts agreed that immediately after the performance the Paterson strikers seemed more enthusiastic than ever. Elsewhere in her 1914 speech Flynn cited the "friendly rivalry" among the Pageant performers as to who would get his or her picture in the paper as evidence of their growing class consciousness; on the opening day of the strike, out of fear of being recognized, the strikers in Turn Hall had refused permission to a newspaper photographer who wanted to take their picture.[92] Yet in judging the Pageant, she turned friendly rivalries into destructive jealousies and did not mention the growth of class consciousness.

Why did Flynn read the evidence so selectively? Why did she deprive the Pageant of the context that gave it meaning—namely, the need to break the deadlock in Paterson by finding new allies in New York—and then blame it for the defeat of the strike? We can only speculate. If the Pageant caused jealousy, the jealousy may have been Flynn's. In Paterson, and in speaking to the strikers in Haledon, Flynn shone. She had been in Paterson longer and more consistently than Haywood (who was involved for a while in the strike in Akron) and was at least as popular with the strikers as he was. An article in *Solidarity* during the strike said that "she has proven herself to be the most penetrating, analytical, courageous and eloquent of the I.W.W. speakers in her handling of the Paterson strike situation."[93] But the Pageant turned public attention back to the relationships with the New York intellectuals and to Haywood, who was stronger in those relationships.

Haywood had done more than Flynn to build the bridge from Paterson to New York. Increasingly, the connection with intellectuals appeared to him to be an alternative to electoral politics, a way of avoiding isolation in strikes and other militant IWW activities without having to depend on the Socialist Party. In discussion with radical intellectuals, Haywood shone; in their journals (the *International Socialist Review, The Masses*, the *New Review*) he was normally pictured as the leader of the IWW and of the Paterson strike.[94] Talking with writers and artists in Greenwich Village, Haywood had developed his position that industrial workers, given the time and opportunity, could create great art. In the Pageant, with the workers acting out their own drama, Haywood "was demonstrating his brand of aesthetics to New York," wrote his biographer.[95] Or, as a fellow Wobbly later put it, "the Paterson Pageant . . . was Bill Haywood's show—his greatest personal triumph."[96] Not part of the discussion that created the project and never excited by it, Flynn chose to regard the Pageant as she and Haywood sometimes regarded electoral politics—as an epiphenomenon that reflected the strength of real forces but could not affect them. Hence her emphasis, beginning the day after the Pageant, that it was only playacting. When the strike was defeated, Flynn lashed out at the New York intellectuals for having interfered in a strike that she regarded as not their business but hers. Her provocative speech at the New York Civic Club Forum seemed designed to blow up the fragile bridge that Haywood had done so much to build.

From the beginning the debate about the Pageant has been a debate about the value of the bridge. Initially, Haywood appeared to be winning. Within the IWW a consensus took shape that the collaboration of intellectuals and strikers had brought the strikers valuable publicity. In Haledon, on the day following the Pageant, a reporter for *Solidarity* observed that "the strikers are all elated with its success. It means publicity that counteracts the lies of the press; and more defense funds." *Solidarity* underlined the importance of the publicity: "Once the truth about Paterson is widely known, the strike will be won."[97] Two weeks later, after the expenses associated with the Pageant had been tallied and made public, Lessig acknowledged on behalf of the IWW that there had been some criticism of the Pageant because it produced no immediate financial results. But, he said, "while the strikers did not benefit by the pageant, every newspaper in the country made some comment on the same. This has resulted in donations coming in to the relief fund from all over the country, and there is now plenty of money on hand."[98] At the IWW's national convention in September, six weeks after the end of the strike, the Pageant was hailed as a great success. Koettgen reported to the convention that "the great Pageant in Madison Square Garden in New York City, where 1,000 strikers from Paterson enacted the scenes from the strike, made more publicity for the I.W.W. than anything ever attempted before."[99] Two years later a writer theorized in *Solidarity* about the "new drama," citing the work of Ibsen, Synge, and Shaw and calling for a workers' theater. As if to clinch his point, he pointed to the Pageant: "What good will the new drama do? What good did the Madison Square Spectacle of the Patterson [*sic*] strike do? Did it not raise funds to continue the strike, break down prejudice, arouse sympathy and cement the ranks of the strikers?"[100]

A great contribution to the strike, to class struggle, and to the drama: this view of the Pageant was the dominant one not only among Wobblies but also among Villagers. Randolph Bourne, despite a certain ambivalence, paid homage: "Who that saw the Paterson Strike Pageant in 1913 can ever forget the thrilling evening when an entire labor community dramatized its wrongs in one supreme outburst of group-emotion. Crude and rather terrifying, it stamped into one's mind the idea that a new social art was in the American world, something genuinely and excitingly new."[101] Like Bourne, a young woman who had moved to the Village from a small New England town not long before was sure that "no one who was in Madison Square Garden on the night of June 7 will ever forget the exhilaration of that mass meeting." More than Bourne, Bernadine Kielty saw that the Pageant broke down abstractions of the working class: "No one who saw the Paterson strike pageant was likely ever again to think of the working class as an indefinable mass. It was the tragedies of individuals that were enacted before our eyes. It was a glimpse into another world, only a glimpse, it is true, but an important one for many. It opened our minds."[102] Hapgood made a similar point, and carried it further. The Pageant overcame the stereotyped view of workers as incapable of managing their own affairs:

> I think that many persons who saw that spectacle must have felt that workers who are capable of emotional organization must also be capable of practical and material organization. Many persons must have felt, in the presence of this gentle and intelligent mass, that there is here a possibility of social development, which need not be feared.[103]

Reed himself showed his opinion of the Pageant's success by trying to repeat it. After the Bolshevik revolution, for instance, he talked about the need for pageants in the new Soviet Union.[104] In 1916 he had tried to extend the idea in the United States. Helped and encouraged by Grace Potter, who had seen the Pageant and written powerfully about it, Reed wanted workers throughout the country to create plays about their local struggles, with the best ones brought every May Day to New York. He, Potter, and others raised money for the initial expenses, but the project fell through.[105]

One reason the plan failed was that times had changed. By 1916 the

IWW, which had served briefly as the bridge between workers and intellectuals, had collapsed in the East. Without that bridge, radical theater came necessarily to mean drama produced by radical intellectuals for other intellectuals. The prototype of such groups, and one of the best, was the Provincetown Players; founded in 1915, the Players themselves owed a debt to the Pageant, and acknowledged it. Susan Glaspell, a key founder, recalled her experience as a member of the Pageant's audience; that night, inspired, she and her friends "sat late and talked of what the theatre might be."[106] Wilbur Daniel Steele, another Players founder, had written of the Pageant to Vorse, who was abroad, "I wish you could have been there. It was tremendous." On the following Sunday morning Steele had gone out to Haledon with Flynn; afterward he had eaten dinner with Flynn, Haywood, and Giovannitti in a little Italian restaurant. In his letter to Vorse he summed up his overall impression of the effect of the Pageant on the strike, after having talked with both Flynn and Haywood: "The Pageant was a big thing and I think turned the tide."[107]

But if Flynn failed to convince the people who had been there, she had greater success with those who had not. Historians of the radical intellectuals, of the IWW, and of the strike have followed her slavishly. In his study of radical intellectuals, Daniel Aaron admits that the Pageant was inspiring to them; however, "to the strikers, the Pageant was an exciting but disappointing fiasco" that "failed in its primary purpose—to raise money for the strikers." The only source Aaron cites for his judgments as to the purpose and failure of the Pageant or the disappointment of the strikers is Flynn's autobiography.[108] Melvyn Dubofsky, in his detailed history of the IWW, agrees that the Pageant failed. His description of its disastrous effect on the strike also follows Flynn: finances and picketing were hurt, and jealousy was aroused. Dubofsky's sole citation for this interpretation is Flynn's 1914 speech.[109] James Osborne, in a comprehensive study of the strike, sees that the purpose of the Pageant was "to break the deadlock" in Paterson, yet he too succumbs to Flynn's interpretation. The Pageant was a failure; as a result of it there was less picketing, less money, and more jealousy. All three of Osborne's citations are to Flynn's 1914 speech.[110]

In short, Flynn's version of the Pageant has prevailed. Even Reed's and Haywood's biographers follow her, and the best biography of Reed actually criticizes him for taking the pageant idea seriously. Robert Rosenstone follows not Reed but Flynn and the historical consensus in dismissing the Pageant: "Carried away in the feverish preparations for the Pageant, Reed may have believed momentarily in the power of art to affect history," forgetting that "such an effect could be marginal at best," that "the Pageant was at best peripheral to the grim business of class struggle."[111] Similarly, Haywood's biographer prefers Flynn's view of the Pageant to Haywood's view. Blaming the Pageant for hurting the strike, Joseph Conlin relies exclusively on Flynn's 1914 speech. He mentions picketing, money, and jealousy and notes that in addition, "the Pageant caused dissension among the strike's leaders"—that is, between Flynn and Haywood![112] In other areas Conlin has done much to puncture misconceptions about the IWW, but here he perpetuates the version of the Pageant that Flynn created. Why does he follow Flynn? At bottom, Conlin shares Flynn's assumptions about the place of art in a labor struggle: "What Flynn saw which Haywood did not (or at least never admitted), was that the romantic allure of the Pageant briefly diverted Haywood from one of his own principles—that the workers' fight was at the point of production."[113] In this way Haywood's biographer dismisses the notion, held not only by Haywood but by much of the IWW after 1913, that publicity was needed to win IWW strikes and that the Pageant had been the best possible publicity for the Paterson strike.

Historians, then, agree that the Pageant failed. The one important exception is Linda Nochlin, whose 1974 article emphasized the participatory nature of pageantry and the impact of the Pageant on the strikers themselves. As an exception, Nochlin illuminates the rule. She too has read Flynn; she begins and ends her essay with quotations about class consciousness from the 1914 speech. But when it comes to the Pageant itself, Nochlin wisely ignores Flynn. An art historian, Nochlin published her article in *Art in America*. Working at some distance from the practical questions that concern historians of the strike and of the IWW, Nochlin is able to distinguish the forest from the trees. The strength of her article is that it is informed by a commitment to radical art; its limit is that, insofar as it touches on immediate issues, it must yield to the experts. The Pageant, she says, "although it evidently failed in its fund-raising mission, was nevertheless a potent instrument in raising political consciousness and forging a sense of working-class solidarity."[114] As her use of "evidently" suggests, she yields only grudgingly, even on the fund-raising issue. Sidestepping Flynn's arguments and trusting her own sense that the Pageant was great politics *because* it was great art, Nochlin helps us to remember why so many different people in Paterson and New York were moved by the Pageant and changed by it.

Within the fields of labor and intellectual history, however, there has been no history of the Pageant; there has been only Flynn's myth of the Pageant. Most historians maintain that the strike was defeated not despite the Pageant but because of it. This chapter has argued, on the contrary, that the Pageant succeeded in publicizing the strike in New York and in drawing additional support to the hungry strikers. Growing out of the deadlock in Paterson, it was an integral part of the strike process and, like the strike itself, a tremendous force for the political transformation of all those who participated in it.

But to complete the argument, we need to explain why historians of the strike, the IWW, and the Villagers have followed Flynn on the Pageant. Part of the explanation lies in the current academic divisions of history. Social historians view the Pageant in the context of the organization of immigrant workers; cultural historians view it as an expression of the rebellion of New York intellectuals. But the Pageant defined the moment in which social history and cultural history became one. Its essence was both politics and art, a strike tactic and a cultural revolution. In their monographs, historians focus either on Paterson or the Village, on the IWW or the New York intellectuals. No one focuses on the bridge between New York and Paterson.

Narrow specialization, however, can provide only a partial explanation for the failure to come to grips with the Pageant and may itself reflect a wider loss of connection. Inside and outside academia, very few people today—even among those of us who think of ourselves as radical—believe in the possibility of an equal and creative collaboration between intellectuals and workers. Yet the Pageant demonstrated that possibility. Its power today is as an example of what can happen when workers who are moving left and intellectuals who are moving left come together. But powerful as it was, the Pageant cannot compel belief. Unable to change historians, it has been changed by them. Today we call Haywood and Reed romantic and naive because they relied on the bridge; we know that art is irrelevant to politics and radical politics largely irrelevant to the business of strikes. The connections have been lost, and we have grown up in a world that cannot admit that the Pageant actually happened. Hence, we maintain that the Pageant may have been great art but hurt the strike; it was fun for the intellectuals but a fiasco for the silk workers and the IWW. The deeper reason, perhaps, why historians have followed Flynn is that if they lack her passion, they share her cynicism.

The cynicism is protective: for her and for us, it conceals the pain of loss. In 1939, during the heyday of Stalinism, Hapgood reread his contemporary account of the Pageant and recorded "a sense of disappointment, after such high hopes." What he had found so "inspiring and hopeful" in 1913 was that "this Pageant was really the work and the recorded life of the striking mill workers of Paterson. That is the great thing about it, the almost unprecedented thing."[115] Hapgood was right in 1913 and right in 1939: the great thing about the Pageant was that it enabled the strikers themselves to tell their story; the most modern theatrical sensibilities and techniques were put at the service of the working class. And the disappointing thing is that this great example has, so far, led to nothing. But "the action is continually being replayed, and it could be otherwise."[116] We could yet learn to make the Pageant a success, not in its own terms alone but as precedent for the fusion of radical imagination with radical action. Today our imaginations operate usually either as ends in themselves, without external direction, or as strictly subordinated means to predetermined ends. The special thing about the Pageant was that the imaginations of hundreds of people in New York and in Paterson came together around the necessity of telling the story of the strike and transformed the telling into a political action. Under the pressure of time and money, they created a new form of art, of class struggle, and of doing history. If we could learn to trust ourselves as they trusted themselves, workers and intellectuals in the 1990s might join imaginatively around a renewed commitment to democratic control of industry and society. Because the Pageant is our history, it is not too late to reclaim it for the future.

CHAPTER SEVEN

Defeat

After the Paterson Strike Pageant the manufacturers were still united; their annexes in Pennsylvania continued to operate, and their allies in Paterson continued to increase the pressure on the strikers. Great as it was, the Pageant could not win the strike. Though more money came into the relief fund from New York, more and more strikers needed relief. Nevertheless, having strengthened themselves financially and politically by putting on the Pageant, the silk workers were able to go on fighting. For the next month they continued to respond creatively to the increasing pressure, looking for ways of minimizing damage to the strike and of keeping it alive. But there was no way out, and some of the new creative initiatives actually heightened the tensions they had been designed to lessen. Finally, more than seven weeks after the Pageant, the silk workers returned to the mills. Attempts by the IWW in the next year to revive the movement failed. The silk workers and the IWW had lost. For the IWW, Paterson was a devastating defeat; for the shaky alliance of the IWW with the Socialist Party, defeat proved fatal. But for the silk workers themselves the results of the strike were much more mixed.

AFTER THE PAGEANT

In May, hunger had become the primary problem of the strikers, and repression for the first time had been effective against them. With the use of the halls for big meetings having been prohibited and the Paterson *Evening News* having turned against the strike, the strikers had lost their two best means of combatting rumors of breaks. Some small breaks had occurred in May, as hungry silk workers yielded to the temptation to settle independently with their firms. In June repression intensified, becoming both more focused and farther reaching;

hunger pushed people to seek an end, one way or the other; and the question of individual settlements finally forced its way onto the strikers' agenda.

Infuriated by the strikers' persistence against overwhelming force, the manufacturers and their allies experimented with selective intimidation in June. They announced that they would blacklist everyone who engaged in regular picketing and threatened to use photographs to identify the individuals.[1] Recorder Carroll sent individually addressed letters to English-speaking strikers, saying that he wished to talk to each of them; those who accepted his invitation were warned against any further picketing.[2] Judge Abram Klenert, giving Hannah Silverman a suspended sentence, informed her that if he saw her again he would put her in the State Home for Girls at Trenton until she was twenty-one.[3]

Nor did the judge and the recorder confine themselves to threats. In June, Klenert picked Harry Hagerdon out of a group of thirty-seven strikers charged with picketing and sentenced him to six months in jail; Hagerdon had been a leader among Hollanders in the strike and had frequently spoken in both Paterson and Haledon meetings.[4] In July, Carroll gave Thomas Coppers three months in jail for calling a dye worker a scab; Coppers had been arrested five times previously and released each time because of insufficient evidence.[5] Standards of evidence, never high, reached a new low. John Marone was accused of insulting Mary Walsh, a strikebreaker. "Marone denied insulting the girl but after she had told her story the Recorder lost no time in finding Marone guilty." He was sentenced to 200 days in jail.[6] Although no striker had ever been found with a gun, Mayor McBride authorized strikebreakers to carry revolvers for their own protection. At the end of June, Vincenzo Madonna, a broad-silk weaver, was fatally wounded in a scuffle with strikebreakers. The man who killed him, who was freed without a trial on the grounds of self-defense, had a permit from the mayor for his gun.[7]

The local authorities also effectively utilized the resources of Passaic County to extend their reach. On June 13 the Paterson police crossed the city line into Prospect Park to rescue O'Brien detectives from an angry crowd of 4,000 strikers. The police could legally cross the city line now because all Paterson police had just been sworn in as deputy sheriffs of Passaic County by Sheriff Radcliff. Pleased with the results of the action, in which forty-eight strikers were arrested and brought back to Paterson, the sheriff announced his intention of taking similar steps in Haledon. About twenty special deputies under the sheriff's control remained stationed in Haledon and Prospect Park for the rest of the strike.[8] Meanwhile, in Paterson itself the authorities moved with unprecedented speed against individuals from out of town who had come to the aid of the strikers. Alexander Scott, editor of the *Weekly Issue*, was convicted; Boyd was arrested; Mayor Brueckmann was indicted; Flynn was put on trial; and Quinlan (who had remained free after his conviction in May touched off protests) was sentenced. Except in the case of Boyd, who really had advocated the destruction of property in an earlier speech to the strikers, the charges were absurd. Scott, for example, was convicted of subverting authority by criticizing Bimson; Brueckmann was charged with allowing disorderly meetings on Sundays in Haledon, appointing IWW members as deputies and marshals, and joining a picket line outside a Haledon mill.[9]

The new legal offensive put IWW and Socialist strike supporters literally on the defensive, turning their attention from the strike itself to their threatened comrades. Desperately needed money and energy were diverted from strike relief to legal maneuvers and protest meetings. Repression still could not break the strike, but it stretched the already thin resources of the strikers even further. The attacks on Scott and Brueckmann were especially significant. Only Scott's little paper still continued to support the strikers; only Brueckmann's Haledon still gave them the space to meet all together. The conviction of Scott and indictment of Brueckmann, coupled with the permanent stationing of Paterson police in Haledon, put the strikers on notice that they no longer had anything they could call their own.

Except hunger: hunger was becoming the strikers' own territory. On the first Sunday in June, Haywood told the strikers that they would win even if they had to stay out ten more weeks, but a visitor saw that at the idea of ten more weeks "they winced for a moment."[10] Two Sundays later Haywood was more realistic, discussing what the strikers could do "if starvation drives us back."[11] At a shop meeting of Ketterman and Mitchell employees later that week, a weaver spoke up. "We are starving," he said; "let's go back to work."[12] On June 20 the strikers' Relief Committee published an appeal to New Yorkers, pointing out that police, private detectives, and courts had "failed to break us" but that "the whip of hunger" could drive the strikers back.[13] At the end of the month the committee distributed in New York a leaflet emphasizing that the strikers were "determined to win. Only one enemy threatens, looming up at their very doors: HUNGER."[14]

New York was, in fact, the strikers' best hope. A group of strike supporters in Brooklyn, responding to a plea from the Relief Committee, issued an appeal to Brooklyn workers to donate a day's wages to the Paterson strikers.[15] On the first Monday after the Pageant, a women's conference called by the Consumer League of Greater New York voted to give "the utmost assistance" to the Paterson strikers and chose a special committee to approach potential female donors.[16] The committee also followed up on the publicity generated by the Pageant through more direct means. Silverman led a group of fifteen Paterson strikers, girls aged fifteen to seventeen, on an overnight fund-raising trip to Coney Island. Each girl wore a white linen dress, a red sash or scarf, and an IWW button; each carried a little metal bank.[17] Twenty-five young female strikers toured the Lower East Side in four trucks supplied by New York garment workers, stopping at the bakeries and delicatessens as well as tenements, collecting not only money but also bread and potatoes, clothing and shoes. But the food collected in New York and the funds raised by strike supporters in Brooklyn had to be shared with the New York ribbon weavers, who were still holding out.[18] These imaginative efforts demonstrated the continuing vitality of the Paterson strike but could not drive hunger away for long.

The problem was that no matter how much money came in, more was needed every week. All the resources of the strikers—their savings, their credit with store owners, and the help they received from local supporters—were exhausted. The cost of feeding the strike soared in June as the number of strikers needing relief of all kinds continued to grow. On the average, during the four months of its existence, the Relief Committee raised almost $500 a day, but by late June it needed almost $1,000 a day just to meet immediate needs.[19] In addition, the collapse of Paterson's economy as a result of the long strike undermined all local sources of support and created a multiplying effect. For instance, small landlords, who were not receiving rent were unable to pay their own expenses, including their water bills; as a consequence, the water company began to turn off the water.[20] The Relief Committee itself, unable to afford the rent, had to move out of Turn Hall into IWW headquarters; angry at not being paid, the proprietor of Turn Hall sued the IWW and seized the furniture of the Relief Committee, threatening to sell it.[21] The committee somehow managed to function, distributing whatever provisions it had with remarkable fairness and efficiency while making heroic efforts to locate new sources of aid, especially in New York.[22] And in fact, more money was coming in.[23] But it was a losing struggle, as this letter from the Relief Committee to the strike supporters in Brooklyn suggests:

> As is only natural our bread line is growing longer and longer day by day. Clothes are becoming more threadbare, toes are sticking out of shoes, tears and sighs are increasing . . . as father and mother stand in line to get what we can give them. No money for shoes, impossible to pay for rent or gas, we can only give them food, and it grieves me to say not much of that. Just imagine, on one particular day our funds were so low that we could only give bread, 5,000 loaves at three and one-half cents each ($175), not to mention dinners to be paid for to keep all those who are single, at the rate of 28 cents per day.[24]

Unable to banish hunger, the strikers themselves began to leave Paterson. In May, there had been an exodus of the children. In June, there was an exodus of the single men. But whereas Flynn had advocated and planned the sending away of the children, she tried to block the departure of the young men. Overriding her opposition and drawing on a long tradition of mobility among weavers—they had always gone where there was work and had originally come to America for that reason—the Central Strike Committee advanced carfare to any single man between the ages of nineteen and thirty who would seek work in another city until the strike was over. The idea was to lighten the strain on the Relief Committee so that "the strikers with families would not have to go hungry."[25] The three restaurants for single men were expensive to run. With thousands of young men gone, the Relief Committee estimated that it would save almost a quarter of what it took to feed the strike. A group of fifty weavers left Paterson for Detroit, where they expected to work in the automobile factories for $9.00 per week. More weavers were recruited by agents from New England cotton and braid mills. Others simply took their chances. By June 19 a total of 4,497 young men had left Paterson, according to the Executive Committee, and Lessig, as secretary of Local 152, was encouraging more to go.[26]

Flynn continued to disagree. On June 18 she sharply criticized Lessig and the strikers' Executive Committee. This was not the time for strikers to leave the city and the battle: "Don't be a coward," she told the young men.[27] The disagreement between Flynn and Lessig reflected the diverging responses of the outside speakers and the Paterson weavers to the growing pressures. Flynn and the national IWW still wanted nothing less than a complete victory, as in Lawrence; they argued that by holding out, the strikers could still achieve that victory. The weavers, who had fought many battles in the past—winning some, losing some, and always surviving to fight again—were beginning to look for ways to cut their losses. They too still hoped to win, but their emphasis was increasingly on survival. As a long-time Paterson weaver, Lessig knew that 1913 was only one battle in the continuing class war within the silk industry. Though he himself partly backed down in the face of Flynn's repeated criticisms, the Executive Committee as a whole stuck to its guns and for the first time publicly expressed anger at Flynn for her uncompromising attitude.[28]

The dispute over the departure of the single men was immediately overshadowed by a much more important and destructive dispute over the Central Strike Committee's plan for settling the strike shop by shop. In a shop-by-shop settlement, strikers would return to work at those firms that granted their demands, without waiting for the manufacturers as a whole to capitulate. Again, hunger made the idea attractive. Those who went back to work would not have to be fed and could contribute a portion of their wages to the support of those who were still out.

When the Central Strike Committee first tentatively endorsed the idea on June 17, calling for each shop committee to choose delegates to meet with the boss and explore the terms of a possible settlement, Flynn held her fire. She was already embroiled in the dispute over the departure of the young men, and (as she explained) she had just been criticized by a member of the Central Strike Committee for exerting too much influence. Withholding public criticism, Flynn and Haywood confined themselves to advising against the shop-by-shop plan. But when on June 20 the committee disregarded their advice and decided to put the idea of a shop-by-shop settlement to a vote, Flynn and Haywood actively campaigned against the plan. The shops that went back, they pointed out, would do the work of those that remained out and would in effect be scabbing on them. They also reminded the strikers that the manufacturers had reneged on individual agreements in the past. These arguments prevailed. By a vote of 3,789 to 1,007, in a referendum that typified the democratic process of the strike, the silk workers decided to reject the shop-by-shop settlement.[29]

But the idea remained tempting to those responsible for relief. It was tempting also to individual strikers. Many weavers were too proud to accept relief, even from their own strike committee; though Flynn and Haywood (as committed revolutionaries and inheritors of an IWW tradition of contempt for skilled workers) probably could not understand their attitude, many weavers perferred to leave town or—if an honorable way could be found—return to their old jobs rather than accept relief.

Significantly, the unskilled dyers' helpers had voted overwhelmingly against the shop-by-shop plan, whereas the ribbon weavers had approved it by about 800 to 600. Adding to the temptation to seek a settlement was the knowledge that many small manufacturers were as desperate to reach an agreement as the weavers were. It was difficult for the strikers to maintain unity while many hungry men and women knew that their old jobs were waiting for them, at reduced hours and increased pay. Despite the vote, five days later a number of broad-silk weavers did return to work at the Aronsohn mill after they were granted abolition of the three- and four-loom system, a nine-hour day, and an increase in pay ranging from 5 to 25 percent. During the period of public debate on the referendum, other weavers had already returned to work, often as a direct result of the meetings with management that had been mandated by the Central Committee. Meeting with the delegation of strikers, Moses Strauss (of Frank and Dugan) announced that he was willing to make concessions and then pointedly asked the delegates whether they had the power to settle; when they answered that they were obliged to report back to the Central Strike Committee, he dismissed them. The move was effective. By the following week, a number of Frank and Dugan weavers were back at work; they were also complaining that whereas Strauss had originally promised eight hours a day, he was now requiring ten. At a number of shops where the manufacturer reneged on his promises, weavers indignantly walked out again. But the damage to solidarity had been done. As Flynn and Haywood feared, the referendum had added to the confusion and rumors of breaks. By the time of the vote, which took place on the first day of the fifth month of the general strike, 2,500 silk workers had gone back to work. A seemingly practical idea for reducing the pressures on the strikers and exploiting the tensions within the manufacturers' camp had backfired, increasing the pressure on the strikers and exposing the tensions in their own camp.[30]

After the Pageant, the strikers had seized the initiative, devising new approaches to the growing problems of hunger and repression. Rejecting the advice of the out-of-town speakers, they sent the young men out of the city and explored the possibility of shop-by-shop settlements. Similarly, responding to the increasing aggressiveness of police and courts, they developed a new approach to picketing. On the day after the Pageant, a tremendous crowd in Haledon heard Flynn urge everyone to go on the picket line the following day, but few followed her advice. Picketing was very light on Monday, but "strangely enough, very few are reported to have returned to work this morning," noted the Paterson *Evening News*.[31] In May, the strikers had picketed heavily only on Mondays. In June, picketing was usually light even then, and the strikers' reasoning was an extension of their earlier logic: with or without picketing, few weavers would go back; even if they did, there would be little for them to do so long as the dye workers remained out. By mid-June, both rank-and-file strikers and local leaders were explicitly arguing that heavy picketing was not necessary at the mills so long as the dye workers remained firm. The typical pattern now was for large contingents to picket a mill only when many employees had recently returned or were expected to return; five to ten strikers would picket the other mills, just to keep track of who was going to work.[32]

In practice, the new approach took pressure off the weavers, who were now less likely to get arrested, and put it on the dyers' helpers. For the first time, the whole weight of maintaining solidarity and keeping the strike alive fell on the dye workers. On Monday, June 16, and Monday, June 23, picketing was light at the broad-silk and ribbon mills and heavy at the dye houses, especially at the crucial Weidmann plant. Not surprisingly, the police directed increased efforts at breaking up the picket line outside the dye plants and in protecting the few strikebreakers who were already working there (the raid across the city line into Prospect Park was on behalf of strikebreakers who were returning home from a Paterson dye house). Feeling the pressure, the dye workers held an outdoor meeting at the old Doremus Estate on June 21 and heard their chairman, Thomas Lotta, plead with them to continue to stand together for at least another week; the bosses were about to give in, he explained, because they needed to get the silk dyed for their fall orders. In the following week the Weidmann workers responded magnificently. On June 25, 1,649 Weidmann dye workers jammed into Riverside Turn Hall and voted unaminously against the shop-by-shop settlement, reaffirming their earlier commitment to remain out until they won the eight-hour day and could all go back together. A member of the shop committee proudly announced that none of the fifty-six strikebreakers who were working in the plant were local men; all had been imported from Long Island and New York. And later that day strikers all over Paterson were "jubilant" to hear that the Weidmann plant had been shut down tight again; one striker, pretending to be a scab, had gone into the plant and persuaded all the strikebreakers to quit. The dye workers were still responding positively to pressure, but how long could they go on? There were increasing reports of violence directed by dyers' helpers at individual strikebreakers.[33] In the end, despite their immense courage, it would be the dye workers who would go back to work first.

In retrospect, we can see that the Paterson strike was in decline by the end of June. Signs of deterioration were everywhere: while the Central Committee and the outside speakers disagreed, the mills were starting back up with skeleton crews. At the same time, however, the strikers exhibited continued determination and resilience: for every silk worker who had returned to the job by the end of June, there were eight who remained out. At the beginning of the month, in the Pageant, the strikers consciously reaffirmed the insistence on collectively controlling their own destiny, which had been implicit in the strike from the beginning. During the rest of June, despite overwhelming problems, they continued to control their own fate. They sent away the single men in an organized and planned way rather than allowing them to drift back to work or into violence. In an equally coordinated fashion they explored the terms of a possible settlement with their respective bosses and reported back to the Central Strike Committee; the ensuing debate and referendum reinforced the democratic process of the strike. Observers were impressed by the almost four to one rejection of a shop-by-shop settlement. They were impressed, too, by the fact that despite the absence of heavy picketing, relatively few weavers returned to the mills, thereby giving the lie to the manufacturers' repeated claim that the majority of weavers stayed out because of intimidation.[34] Only in retrospect is it clear that even the Pageant was unable to break the deadlock and that the strikers' best efforts later in June only deepened their difficulties. Notwithstanding hunger, repression, and real internal divisions, their strike at the end of June was still full of life.

This life was visible in Flynn's trial, which began on the last day of June. The courtroom was packed with reporters, witnesses, and supporters and friends of Flynn, and many were turned away. In a group at the rear of the courtroom on the first day, Tresca, Silverman, and Lessig with his wife Margaret sat chatting quietly while the assistant prosecutor made his opening remarks. On the following day Margaret Lessig was the first witness for the defense; in "simple, forceful language" she summarized what Flynn had actually said on February 25 when she was supposed to have advocated violence.[35] Women played a major role at all levels of the defense. In New York seven prominent women, including three Heterodoxy members and Jessie Ashley, issued a statement calling attention to the exploitation of women in the silk industry, claiming that Flynn was being framed for exposing that exploitation, and urging that "all women rally to her defense."[36] In a courtroom dominated by a male judge, male prosecutors, and an all-male jury, Ashley consulted frequently with Flynn and offered suggestions to her counsel. Flynn herself behaved with her usual dignity and intelligence, showing her anxiety about the outcome only by bringing her three-year-old son and her mother to court. During the second day of the trial, confirming its appeal to women, a group of Paterson schoolteachers obtained seats and eagerly "discussed the merits of the witnesses in whispers as the trial proceeded."[37] Witnesses were routinely subjected to insult and abuse by Prosecutor Dunn, especially if they evinced an uncertain grasp of English, but sixteen-year-old Carrie Torello refused to be intimidated and proved an effective witness.[38]

On the third day of the trial, Torello and twenty other strikers stayed behind in the courtroom during a recess and staged a mock trial of their own. Despite the seriousness of the occasion—Quinlan had already been convicted in May of the same charge of inciting to riot now brought against Flynn—the playfulness and good nature of the Paterson strikers could not be contained: they tried Quinlan on the charge of not getting a haircut and a shave and sentenced him to fifteen years in a brewery. As their impromptu play ended, a deputy sheriff rushed in and, according to the New York *Times*, demanded that Quinlan and the strikers stop "making a 'show' of justice in Passaic County."[39] Paterson justice had been upstaged again. Having begun June by playing a tragedy in Madison Square Garden, the strikers and the IWW began July with a farce in the courthouse. Their spirit could not be broken by repression.

At the same time, however, they could not win. On the following morning (the final day of the trial, since the Hudson County jury admitted later that it was unable to reach a decision on Flynn and was discharged), as Quinlan entered the courtroom, the enraged judge suddenly ordered him seized and sentenced him to two to seven years in state prison in Trenton, effective immediately.[40] The Emperor was naked, but he carried a big stick.

THE END

What finally won the strike for the manufacturers was their ability to outlast the strikers. Their dramatic efforts to break the strike—the arrests and trials of the outside speakers, the appeal to patriotism on flag day, the AFL meeting in the Armory—had been rooted in their misconception of the silk workers as easily misled and had inspired greater resistance. Their quieter efforts, including the sustained campaign to win public opinion in Paterson, had been more successful. By May the manufacturers had rallied the support of the press, the clergy, and the small businessmen of Paterson for such extreme measures as closing the strikers' meeting places. But what sealed the employers' victory, more than any strategies for breaking the strike, was their capacity simply to hold out longer than their employees. "Terror wasn't what defeated the silk strikers. They were starved—literally starved—back to work," wrote the crime reporter from New York. "I think the reason we lost was we had no money. They just drained us," said an Italian man. "A lot of [mutual aid] societies paid two dollars a week for relief, but that was practically nothing if someone had children to feed and had to pay rent. Winter was up ahead, and people began to give up."[41] The strikers succumbed to hunger after five months and returned to work, many under the old conditions. The most effective strategy for the manufacturers was endurance.

Two factors enabled the manufacturers to endure the strike. The minor factor, which was fortuitous, was that their fierce competitiveness and lack of monopolistic control had created a market glut in previous years. Normally, manufacturers shipped goods to commission agents who, as middlemen, warehoused them for sale and allowed the manufacturers to draw cash on account at interest against the future sale of these goods—frequently 60 percent of the expected market price. Having accumulated large surpluses as a result of competition in the industry, the commission houses were able to unload them during the strike, to their profit and that of the silk manufacturers. As the *American Silk Journal* noted, "The labor troubles and a scarcity of many lines in quick demand have, in a way, been a boon to the selling houses having stocks of goods to move. As a direct result of the situation and the demand for stock goods the market is cleaner, and with less jobs being available buyers have shown a willingness to pay prices to secure anything like what is desired."[42] The strike, in that sense, proved a "blessing in disguise for the producer" by cleaning out inventories and transforming the market "from a buyer's to a seller's market."[43] Even though their mills were closed, Paterson manufacturers could still make some money when their middlemen sold, at high prices, goods that were otherwise going to waste.

Their losses in Paterson were nevertheless tremendous. But here the major factor—which was by no means fortuitous—came into play. Those manufacturers who had moved much of their business out of Paterson before the strike were able to keep operating in the outlying areas, albeit at reduced capacity. Particularly in Pennsylvania, the Paterson silk strikers and the IWW proved unable to keep the mills closed; as a result, Paterson manufacturers with annexes in Pennsylvania were able to limp through the strike. Decentralization of their operations had become a conscious policy in the preceding years. At the beginning of 1913 the *American Silk Journal* had approvingly quoted advice given at the cotton manufacturers' convention: "Those corporations which have divided their mills among different localities have avoided the dangers of over-concentration by the operatives, so disastrous in Lawrence and Fall River."[44] The movement of plants from Paterson to Pennsylvania and the opening of annexes there, continued and accelerated during the strike. What proved decisive, in the end, was the ability of the manufacturers to keep their businesses going in Pennsylvania. An industry insider told the New York *Globe* in May that "the strikers never had a chance to win," largely because of the manufacturers' access to Pennsylvania. As Flynn recognized, "we were sort of playing a game between how much they could get done in Pennsylvania balanced off with how great the demand for silk was and how close they were to bankruptcy."[45] The winning moves in the manufacturers' strategy had been made before the strike ever began. Ironically, although the employers continually underestimated the strikers, their deeper respect for the militance of Paterson's silk workers had led them to become as independent as possible of their employees. Despite Bimson's mistake, Pennsylvania and hunger gave the manufacturers the victory.

"The dyers were the first to break under the pressure . . . followed by the broad-silk weavers," observed Quinlan. " The ribbon weavers held out for a week or so longer."[46] Because dyers' helpers were much less skilled than weavers, it was easier for their employers to replace them and harder for them to find work elsewhere. Consequently, they were more vulnerable to the pressure of hunger and more likely to stampede. By July 1, only a few days after a striker had persuaded everyone working for Weidmann to quit, about 100 men were working and living at the plant. There was little the strikers could do about this live-in work force except watch it grow. By July 12 there were some 400 workers at Weidmann's, and more at the Simon and Auger plant and other branches of National Silk, according to the dye companies. The strikers still emphasized that most of the dyers, dyers' helpers, and finishers who were working in Paterson had been imported from outside. But this fact gave little comfort. The longer a Paterson dye worker held out before going back, the more likely he was to find that someone else had taken his job. In addition, the manufacturers' ultimatum of July 7 made it clear that those who returned last would be regarded as troublemakers and not rehired. In an attempt to prevent a stampede and combat the companies' claims of how many had returned to work, the leaders of the dye workers called a meeting of all strikers from Weidmann's and Simon and Auger's plants for July 14. Only two workers came.[47]

The communal solidarity and discipline of the Italian dyers' helpers, so effective at the height of the strike, was not well suited to a situation in which unanimity had already broken down. Unlike a weaver, a dyers' helper who was starving was unlikely to say so at a shop meeting or to argue for ending the strike by compromising on the original aim. He was more likely to avoid the meeting and go back to work on his own, without being part of a decision and without taking back anything with which to bargain with his employer. Accustomed to meeting, as they worked, in large shops, the dyers' helpers used meetings as expressions of solidarity rather than as forums for debate; the vote taken was intended more as a show of strength than as a barometer of opinion. On July 16 some 300 dyers' helpers met and voted unanimously to stay out; two days later, at an open air meeting, several hundred dyers' helpers and finishers repeated the exercise. Meanwhile, more and more dyers' helpers returned to work. On July 17, in a desperate attempt to help, a group of thirty women strikers picketed Weidmann, confronted strikebreakers, and were chased by the police, who caught and arrested eight of them. By Monday, July 21, 900 employees were working at the Weidmann plant, and National Silk was practically full. The dye houses had begun to turn away anyone who had been particularly active in the strike and—as one ex-Weidmann worker bitterly complained—to refuse work even to some of those who had merely stayed out rather than become strikebreakers. A strike meeting called for July 23 for the purpose of allowing the dyers' helpers to decide whether to continue the strike or officially call it off was adjourned without a vote because of the lack of attendance. Alone among the major groups on strike, the dye workers went back in total disarray, without receiving concessions. The backbone of the strike had been broken.[48]

By contrast, the ribbon weavers retreated in orderly fashion. In the crisis of July their discipline was reinforced by their long democratic traditions. They were used to debating issues at length, listening to heretical views, exploring terms of a possible compromise, and using a secret ballot to achieve a realistic sense of the group. Always deliberate, they could not be stampeded by either the manufacturers or the IWW speakers. At the beginning of the strike they had met again and again, late into the night, before deciding to join the broad-silk weavers and dyers' helpers. Now, on July 7, 2,000 of them met in Helvetia Hall, carefully compiling delegates' reports of how many were working in each shop and how many were still on strike, and printing the results in alphabetical order in the Paterson *Evening News*: "Dexter and Lambert—At work, none; on strike, 42. Frank and Dugan, Market St.—At work, none; on strike, 87. Frank and Dugan, R.R. Ave.—At work, 35; on strike, 173. Graef Hat Band—At work, 8; on strike, 52."[49] This was the way to combat rumors. On July 11, July 14, and July 18 the ribbon weavers repeated this process, publishing the latest figures in the newspaper. As the dyers' strike disintegrated in the second and third week of July, the ribbon weavers fell back on their traditional level of struggle, in the shop. In the June referendum, alone of the three major groups, they had shown a majority in favor of a shop-by-shop settlement. At their July 18 meeting, after listening to a delegate from the Smith and Kaufman ribbon shop in New York describe the recent nine-hour settlement there, the Paterson ribbon weavers voted to abandon both the general strike and the demand for the eight-hour day and to seek instead a nine-hour settlement on a shop-by-shop basis.[50]

The broad-silk weavers were already returning to work, with vague promises from the manufacturers to discuss grievances and a more solid pledge to abolish the three- and four-loom system. On Monday, July 21, the ribbon weavers met and resolved to fight alone if necessary for a nine-hour day and a restoration of at least 80 percent of the 1894 scale for piece wages. They resolved that weavers who were granted concessions and returned to work would be assessed a percentage of their wages to help support the strike against those shops that still rejected the demands. But on Wednesday the Relief Committee closed the store and the three restaurants, explaining that money coming in from outside had suddenly dried up; instead of $800 to $900 a day, less than $100 was now being received. Strike leaders observed that the New York papers had given wide publicity to the breaks in the strike during the second and third weeks of July, causing New Yorkers to believe that the strike was over and that there was no longer any point in making contributions. "These breaks received such wide publicity that aid stopped coming in," explained Flynn.[51] On Friday, July 25, at their regular meeting, the ribbon weavers decided to return to work on Monday because they could not continue the strike without organized relief. Even on Monday, however, between 6,000 and 7,000 silk workers were still on strike, of whom about 4,000 were ribbon weavers. During the week more weavers went back, but eleven ribbon shops (including Dexter and Lambert, and Frank and Dugan) continued to hold out a little longer for the nine-hour day. The ribbon weavers had lost, but they had not been routed.[52]

Officially, the strike was still on because no one in authority had the heart to call it off, until Lessig finally did so at a meeting at Water Street on August 2. The last time it showed signs of real life, however, was at the meeting of the Central Strike Committee on July 29. The meeting accomplished little; the shop delegates were both unable to breathe life into the strike and unwilling to admit that it was dead. Counting shop by shop, the delegates were able to conclude that a total of twenty-one firms had conceded a reduction in hours from ten to nine. But the real achievement of the meeting, the extraordinary thing about it, was the fact of its taking place at all, a week after the strike had completely collapsed. With more than two-thirds of the strikers back at work and many others blacklisted or still out of town, over 300 delegates—almost the whole committee—met for more than four hours.[53] Even in defeat, the Paterson activists of 1913 showed, one last time, what they had learned about democratic organization.

Nevertheless, the atmosphere of the last days was grim. The strike had interrupted the daily routine for five months but had not finally succeeded in transforming it. At its height the strike seemed almost to defy common sense. Now common sense reasserted itself. An eighteen-year-old picket who was arrested on July 21 refused to give her name in court.[54] Pickets who had been arrested during the first four months had gone to jail singing, secure in their belief not only in the rightness of their cause but also in their eventual triumph. In defeat, the strikers knew the manufacturers would have the power to blacklist all those who had been arrested, and the eighteen-year-old—who was brave enough to picket—was afraid of the future. At its height the strike had reached out to New York, culminating in the triumphant performance of the Pageant. Now, in desperation, Haywood and Flynn went to New York, trying to counter the impression that the strike was dead and to get support flowing again to the Relief Committee. Renting the Fifth Avenue Hippodrome at 105th Street and charging ten cents admission, Haywood and Flynn spoke, respectively, on July 21 and July 22, while motion pictures were shown to attract an audience and the Paterson chorus sang "the same selections as were a feature of the great pageant at Madison Square Garden recently."[55] This faint echo of the Pageant could produce no miracles, however, and the Relief Committee was forced to close.

At its height, the strike bloomed in Haledon. But attendance at Haledon was down in July. The biggest meeting of the month, on Sunday, July 20, numbered only 5,000 to 10,000 and up to the last moment the Paterson *Evening News* was uncertain whether Sheriff Radcliff would allow it to take place, since Haledon was now effectively "under the supervision and charge of the sheriff" and his special deputies.[56] During the following week Mayor Brueckmann was indicted, and either he or (more probably) the Haledon councilmen acting in his absence simply canceled the meeting for the next Sunday, July 27. Finally, on August 3, the inspiring tradition of Sunday in Haledon petered out with a small meeting held among the pines of the Cedar Cliff woods rather than in the regular place; Pietro Botto, responding to the defeat, had refused to allow the silk workers or the IWW to use his house.[57] In a strike characterized by solidarity, self-interest had reasserted itself everywhere, as individuals and groups sought to protect their own futures as best they could.

CLASS STRUGGLE AFTER 1913

Pietro Botto could not protect his family from the effects of his involvement in the strike. His daughter Adele, who was nineteen, was fired when she tried to go back to her job as a warper in a ribbon mill. As a skilled worker, she had no difficulty finding work elsewhere, but her new employer gave her a warning when he found out that she was Pietro's daughter. To be on the safe side, her younger sister Eva denied that she was a member of the famous Botto family when she returned to the mills.[58]

Fragmented, the once-unified silk workers could not protect their own. The manufacturers had endured, and now they distributed the reward of work to some and the punishment of the blacklist to others. "In many cases the manufacturers are discriminating against those weavers in their own shops who have taken the most active part in the strike and who have been leaders at the shop meetings," observed the Paterson *Evening News*. "The word is being quietly passed that all of these are 'trouble makers,' and it would be just as well if they were not put back to work."[59] After five months of intimate struggle, each manufacturer knew who had been picketing outside his mill every day, who from his shop had been arrested, who had urged other members of the shop to hold out for the full demands. They became his targets. In a typical example, fifteen teenage girls who had picketed the Miesch mill regularly and who held out to the end finally reported for work on July 28; they were given their tools and told they were discharged.[60] To blacklist the troublemakers from his own shop, the manufacturer added their names to an alphabetical list circulated throughout the city. About 2,000 men and women were blacklisted in this way—activists who for five months had effectively controlled their own lives and now paid the price. "Our most aggressive brothers were blacklisted or out of work during the year," acknowledged Local 152 in the summer of 1914.[61] Trying to escape, some weavers changed their names, and "some have gone to other cities; but the bosses' blacklist has always followed them," concluded a strike sympathizer who conducted his own investigation in 1915.[62]

Blacklisting was not a new weapon in Paterson. The strikers knew from previous strikes that they would face the blacklist if they lost and had originally asked the IWW to send outside speakers to Paterson because only outsiders could speak without fear of losing their jobs. What was new after the 1913 strike was the unity, forged in the struggle, of the large manufacturers. In the fall the temporary combination of the three manufacturers' associations (ribbon, broad-silk, and dyeing) was made permanent. Samuel McCollom, who had presided over the manufacturers' victory and had been gratefully presented with a gold watch, a silver service, and a burglarproof steel chest, was elected president of the permanent organization.[63] Fear, which had brought the manufacturers together in 1913, continued to unite them after the strike, and their new unity made the blacklist more effective. Designed as an instrument of class domination, the blacklist required the manufacturer to subordinate his individual right to hire whomever he wished to the more fundamental right of his class to be free from interference by labor organizations. When one small manufacturer hired a blacklisted skilled worker, the large firms gave him twenty-four hours to fire the worker, and told him that if he refused he would be unable to get his silk dyed anywhere in Paterson.[64] Frightened by the strike experience, Paterson's silk manufacturers sufficiently overcame their individualism to combine forces against the common enemy, in the hope of preventing a recurrence of 1913.

Circumstances nevertheless forced the manufacturers to employ the blacklist with a certain flexibility. Because their supply of skilled weavers remained limited, they would sometimes hire known activists during busy spring and fall seasons; then, "as soon as the depression comes in again they get rid of those men."[65] The blacklist was also more critical in some branches of the industry than in others. Difficult to enforce in broad silk, where the number of tiny shops kept multiplying after the strike, it was more useful against the ribbon weavers, who were concentrated in larger shops and who had emerged from the strike in the best fighting shape.[66] Edward Zuersher, who had been a leader in the shop meetings of the Colonial Ribbon Company during the strike, told the Industrial Relations Commission about the way the blacklist was enforced by ribbon manufacturers. When Zuersher and the other weavers from his shop reported for work as a group at the end of the strike, most of the others were rehired, but although "there were looms standing with warps in them" waiting for weavers, he was told that there was no work for him.

> I then sought employment in other mills, and whenever I mentioned the firm's name who I worked for last I was told to leave my name and address and they would send for me, but none of them ever sent for me. I worked in a mill called the Craft Hat Band—started at 1 o'clock in the afternoon and at half past 4 was discharged. I immediately asked the reason for my discharge and the foreman told me that he had instructions from the office. . . .
>
> I then went to another firm and asked for a position. They asked me whom I worked for last, and I mentioned Fisher, as he was more popularly known by that name than by the firm name. Well, he said, "I can't hire anybody from his place. I don't want him coming up here raising a racket here."[67]

Having outlasted the strikers, the mill owners were determined to reassert control of their industry and reap the rewards of their considerable sacrifices. Yet their victory proved more qualified than they had hoped. The strike had not only hurt them financially; it had also shaken their confidence. The solidarity and discipline of their employees in 1913 frightened them. For the rest of the decade, they tried to avoid major confrontations with the silk workers and to prevent conflicts in single shops from turning—as the conflict in the Doherty mill had done—into an industrywide struggle. Their new permanent organization established a committee on industrial conditions, "to keep in touch with the movements of labor and be called upon to settle disputes in individual plants before trouble develops to an extent likely to threaten the city's good and welfare."[68] As always, the manufacturers automatically identified their own good with the city's good, but their arrogance was tempered now by caution.

In 1916 and again in 1919 the manufacturers as a group made significant concessions to the silk workers on the length of the work day rather than risk a general strike. In the 1919 dispute the owners' representative asked the federal government's War Labor Board to impose a compromise; if the board failed to act, he said, it would "simply mean 1913 over again."[69] During this period of moderation, which lasted until 1920, manufacturers curbed their distaste for unions. In 1914, they actually helped sponsor a new Paterson union, called the Brotherhood of American Silk Workers, with the express purpose of preventing strikes by settling conflicts through arbitration. After the Brotherhood proved stillborn, the manufacturers returned to an idea they had first tried in 1913: from 1916 to 1919 they worked closely with the AFL textile union; on both sides, the aim of the collaboration was to head off more radical labor organizations and to mute class conflict.[70]

The manufacturers showed new flexibility regarding the touchy issues of work hours and union organization because they were convinced that they could not withstand another victory like that of 1913. On the four-loom issue, which had proved the most explosive of all, they proceeded with uncharacteristic restraint, increasing the loom assignments where they could but pulling back as soon as there was trouble. In 1919, two-loom assignments were still standard in Paterson—and only in Paterson. Everywhere else, broad-silk weavers worked four looms. From the point of view of the 1913 strikers, defeating the stretch-out was their most lasting achievement. "The thing in 1913 that we really acted upon and won," said a Paterson weaver who came of age in the years after the strike, "was the two-loom system."[71] From the point of view of the manufacturers, the lesson of 1913 was that four looms should not be introduced in a piecemeal and disorganized fashion. "Radical changes of this kind which so directly affect and stir the antagonism of labor are seldom brought about by one or two mills leading and assuming all the burden," observed the *American Silk Journal*.[72] In the future the manufacturers would try to walk in step with each other, even if it meant going more slowly.

In addition to the strategy of avoiding confrontation, the manufacturers developed two strategies aimed at transforming the structure of the silk industry in Paterson and making a recurrence of 1913 impossible. One of these was to get out of Paterson. "Because of having experienced the stubborn resistance by workers against the three and four loom system, as well as longer hours," the large Paterson manufacturers increasingly began "to move parts, or all, of their business to other states," explained the historian of the industry. In the 1880s and 1890s they had moved the throwing mills to Pennsylvania; in the early twentieth century they had moved much of the plain silks. "The 1913 strike, however, accelerated this movement and the manufacturers began to move not only the manufacturing of plain staple goods, but also relatively high grade fabrics to Pennsylvania, where labor was easier to control."[73] Unable to control labor in Paterson, the large manufacturers ran away from the city, making it the haven of the small shop. Before 1913, the Paterson silk industry had been characterized by medium-sized shops. Within a decade after 1913, Paterson—and only Paterson, among the silk centers—became dominated by the small shop. Big new silk mills continued to open, but not in Paterson, the Doherty mill turned out to be the last one built in the area. As the larger companies moved out, small family weaving shops moved into the abandoned buildings. By 1920 there were nearly 150 family shops in Paterson, and others were sprouting up. Relying on the strategy which had enabled them to win the strike, the large Paterson manufacturers sent more and more of their capital to the comparative safety of Pennsylvania.[74]

Some large companies kept their capital in Paterson, but removed it from the process of production. They became "converters," supplying material to the family shops and purchasing the woven silk from them. Philip McLewin has argued convincingly that Paterson broad-silk manufacturers welcomed the rise of the family shops after 1913 and used them as a way of escaping from labor conflict. During the wartime boom in the silk industry that lasted from 1915 to 1919, the large mill owners put out extra work to the family shops on a commission basis rather than expand their own work force. After the boom ended, many large Paterson manufacturers closed down their production and sent all their work to the family shops. By abandoning manufacturing, they effectively gave their own employees the choice of being unemployed or of doing commission weaving for them in a family shop. For the broad-silk weavers, the family shop was usually a step down. In debt for the purchase of their equipment, owing rent for their space in the mill buildings, and totally dependent on the converter for their income, the family shops had to work as many looms as they could and as many hours as they could, simply to break even. By the same token, the former broad-silk manufacturer improved his position. As a converter, he got the weavers to exploit themselves for his benefit in ways he had never been able to exploit them directly.[75]

Like the strategies of moderation and migration, the strategy of putting out work to the family shop was shaped by fear of the Paterson silk workers. But whereas moderation represented only a temporary phase in the class struggle, the combination of emigration to Pennsylvania with utilization of the family shop in Paterson seemed to offer a permanent solution. In 1936 the New York *Times* noted that many large manufacturers who were "impatient under pressure from organized labor" had moved to other states "where labor would trouble them less" than in Paterson. "Other large operators who remained behind in Paterson, however, recognized in the 'family loom' an escape from organized labor and other irksome regulations. They sold their looms to workers on the installment plan, or they turned them over to machinery exchanges which did it. The larger operators become brokers or converters, with no more responsibility for labor conditions."[76]

The silk weavers, however, challenging the owners' control of the shop and the industry, matched the strategic moves of the manufacturers with moves of their own. Even at their moment of greatest defeat in 1913, they had forced their employers to bend. Many firms had offered concessions at the end of July in order to entice their weavers back to work: the broad-silk manufacturers had agreed to abolish the three- and four-loom system; most ribbon manufacturers had agreed to wage increases of 5 to 20 percent and some to a nine-hour day. More impressive than these concessions, which were commonly made at the end of a strike and just as commonly unmade after things settled down, was the determination of many weavers to enforce the agreements. Teresa Cobianci, weaving again for Bamford, felt hopeful and determined. The publicity during the strike had put Bamford on the defensive: the firm had granted everyone a wage increase, and Teresa was making 25 percent more than when she went out on strike. Bamford also put safety guards on dangerous machinery, installed fire alarms, and promised to end the contract system when the current contracts expired. "Nor do they holler at us so," Teresa added. When asked by her interviewers whether any of this would last, she realistically replied, "I don't know. If it don't, we strike again."[77] Over the next months, years, and decades the Paterson silk workers would strike again. Their hopes would never be as high as they were in 1913 or their unity as great, and the manufacturers' new strategies would make struggle more difficult. But by refusing to be beaten, the weavers continued to slow the deterioration of their position.

The ribbon weavers, in particular, fought back in the months after the 1913 defeat. At one mill where management insisted on keeping a longtime employee who had crossed the picket line, the ribbon weavers went back out on strike. At another ribbon mill, a nonunion man who had refused to join Local 152 of the IWW was forced to do so by a shop strike. One man who had served the winning side as a special deputy found that he was punished rather than rewarded. Returning to his job as a loomfixer at the mill where he had worked for fifteen years, he was greeted by a walkout of his fellow workers, who stayed out until he was fired; he was then fired at several other mills because everyone else simply refused to work with him. During the year, ribbon weavers at several Paterson mills successfully required everyone in the shop to join Local 152 as a condition of employment. In the spring, perhaps misreading the manufacturers' 1913 victory, a new foreman at the United Ribbon Mill attempted to impose a speed-up. The ribbon weavers struck, demanding that the foreman be dismissed; after two weeks the manufacturer fired the foreman, and the strike ended.[78]

Despite the defeat of 1913, the ribbon weavers continued to contest the manufacturers' control of the shop. Against the blacklist they put the closed shop; against the denial of work to known activists they put the denial of work to those whom they regarded as class traitors. They were in the best position among the silk workers to wage these battles for shop control because they had maintained their discipline and organization. In one mill—eight months after the defeat—ribbon weavers walked off the job at four o'clock, formulated demands for higher wages, returned in the morning while their committee presented the demands, and walked out again at four o'clock when the demands were not met—until finally the manufacturer gave in.[79]

In effect, the ribbon weavers returned to earlier forms of struggle. In the years before 1913 their shop strikes and Socialist politics had been their primary means of challenging the power of the manufacturers. When they realized in the summer of 1913 that their solidarity with the broad-silk weavers and dyers' helpers could not break the deadlock, the ribbon weavers began again to express interest both in shop settlements and in the impending mayoral election. Their longtime leader, Louis Magnet, was even considered for a while as a possible Socialist candidate; Quinlan, who had suggested him for public office and who was temporarily out of jail, worked closely with ribbon weavers during the campaign. Propelled by the votes of male weavers who were citizens, the Socialist candidate outpolled the Democrat in November and finished second to the Republican (a banker) with 5,155 votes. The Socialists' total was more than three times greater than their previous high in Paterson. In Haledon, Socialists for the first time captured the Borough Council, as they swept into office.[80] In their combined struggles for shop control and political control during 1913–14, the ribbon weavers showed that they had not been crushed by the defeat.

Despite their efforts, however, they could not escape the consequences of defeat. After the strike, once in the fall and once in the spring, militant ribbon weavers mounted campaigns for the nine-hour day, threatening to unleash a new general strike. Both campaigns failed. Fearing another long strike as much as the mill owners did, the broad-silk weavers and dyers' helpers refused to walk out. In the fall even Flynn, Tresca, and Quinlan, as well as the local IWW leaders, failed to move the broad-silk weavers and dyers' helpers; the ribbon weavers, facing isolation, decided not to go out themselves. One ribbon manufacturer, who had conceded the nine-hour day when a general strike appeared imminent, quickly restored the ten-hour day. In the spring, sixty-five employees of one ribbon mill who were striking for the nine-hour day were forced to do it alone when militant ribbon weavers and Local 152 were again unable to persuade the silk workers to strike en masse. After seven months the shop strike was finally broken, and only eight of the original sixty-five strikers were rehired.[81]

The failure of the nine-hour campaign revealed a stalemate in Paterson's class struggle. One year after the 1913 strike, the weavers and dyers' helpers were working ten hours and the broad-silk weavers were tending two looms, as they had before the strike. The manufacturers had not won an increase in loom assignments, and the silk workers had not won a decrease in the hours of work. Each side was afraid of a repetition of 1913 and reluctant to press its demands aggressively. Exhausted by the five-month struggle, the manufacturers and the silk workers settled for the status quo, postponing the achievement of their primary objectives to a later date.

Widespread unemployment among weavers in 1914–15, caused by the usual cyclical downturn and exacerbated by the dislocation in the silk trade resulting from the outbreak of World War I, gave the mill owners a chance: they took back any gains in wages or hours that workers had made in 1913 and began to raise the loom assignments. By 1916, however, the increased demand generated by the war in Europe created an upswing in many American industries, including silk; in Paterson, as throughout the country, workers took advantage of the resulting decrease in unemployment to renew their demands. With militant ribbon weavers again in the lead, the silk workers met together and threatened to strike for the nine-hour day. This time the ribbon manufacturers, treating the threat seriously, convinced the broad-silk manufacturers to join them in granting the reduction. For the next three years, through 1919, the Paterson silk industry continued to thrive, and the silk workers remained on the offensive until finally, in 1919—after a wave of shop strikes—the Paterson broad-silk and ribbon weavers won the eight-hour day.[82]

THE LONG DEFEAT

Despite their gains, the silk workers were unable to solve their structural problems, and when hard times came again, they were not in a position to protect what they had won. They had not succeeded in getting a union to organize in Pennsylvania. The AFL union, claiming credit for the nine-hour settlement in 1916, promised to lead a nine-hour campaign in the Pennsylvania silk centers, and many Paterson weavers immediately offered to help pay for it—but nothing came of it.[83] The Pennsylvania plants, still unorganized, remained a powerful weapon in the hands of the manufacturers.

In Paterson the silk workers were weakened by the reappearance of organizational divisions along craft and nationality lines. As David Goldberg has shown, German and English ribbon weavers tended to remain in the IWW longer than anyone else; then in 1919, after trying and rejecting the AFL, the Paterson ribbon weavers created a radically democratic union unaffiliated with any national union and narrowly focused on shop organization. By contrast, in the years after 1913, many Jewish broad-silk weavers gravitated back toward

the Socialist Labor Party union and then, in 1919, flocked to the new Amalgamated Textile Workers of America, an industrial union with an aggressively
socialist and international outlook. It was as if the old IWW had split in two,
the ribbon weavers continuing the IWW's emphasis on workers' control of the
union and the workplace, and the broad-silk weavers pursuing the IWW's
emphasis on industrial unionism and anti-capitalist philosophy.

The Italian dyers' helpers fell between these two competing unions. Left
out in the cold after 1913 as Local 152 of the IWW adopted the ribbon weavers' strategy of short shop strikes—little strikes could not beat Weidmann
or National Silk—the workers at the city's big dye houses soon became as
isolated as they had been in 1902 and 1912. As an industrial union, the
Amalgamated Textile Workers tried to reach out to the dryers' helpers in 1919
but found itself handicapped by a lack of Italian organizers. When the dyers'
helpers went on strike in 1919 for eight hours and a raise, they received little
aid from the weavers and were easily defeated by Weidmann and National
Silk.[84] Unable to prevent fragmentation or to promote organization in Pennsylvania, even in their period of aggressive activity, Paterson's silk workers were
vulnerable to the manufacturers' new offensive of 1920–21.

After 1913 the silk workers were as militant as ever, but they lacked any
organizational means of giving full expression to their idealism and class
consciousness. Split into rival unions, the broad-silk weavers and ribbon
weavers became divided from each other and from the dyers' helpers. Having
learned to trust each other in 1913, they learned again to mistrust each other.
The AFL and the Social Labor Party always appealed to one section of the
Paterson workers as opposed to others. Only the IWW in 1913 had appealed
simultaneously to Italian dyers' helpers and Jewish broad-silk weavers and
English-speaking ribbon weavers, reinforcing the lessons of solidarity that
the silk workers had drawn from their own experience. The techniques of
democratic control, perfected in Lawrence, helped the silk workers to run their
own strike; the deliberate encouragement given both to women and to
immigrants fostered the emergence of leadership from below; the forms of
mass participation—picketing, singing, booing, and above all the Pageant
—heightened the strikers' sense of their own power. In 1913 the IWW had
helped the silk workers to discover their own unity. After 1913, the IWW
became one more faction in the Paterson labor movement.

From the disappointing aftermath in Lawrence, where the blacklist and
plant runaways had been used against the victorious strikers, the national IWW
had learned the importance of following through after the conclusion of a
textile strike.[85] In Paterson it maintained a continuous presence in the months
and years after the 1913 strike and with the help of Koettgen, its specialist in
silk organizing, developed a new two-part strategy in response to the experience of defeat. "To strike often but never very long is better than these long
drawn out hunger strikes," wrote Koettgen in the winter of 1913–14.[86] Part of
the new strategy was to encourage and support the short shop strikes and job

actions favored by the ribbon weavers, who by the winter of 1913 already made up the bulk of Local 152's membership. The other and, in the long run, more important part was to organize against the runaways in Pennsylvania. "Districts have been pitted against districts," Koettgen noted later in the winter. "For instance Pennsylvania has been pitted against Paterson." This was a more fundamental lesson of the 1913 strike: the Paterson silk workers could not win, regardless of how well they were organized, unless the Pennsylvania silk workers were also organized. The general strike of 1913 had not been general enough. "The I.W.W. has a strong foothold among the silk workers in New Jersey, New York, Connecticut and some parts of Pennsylvania. We must extend this, especially in Pennsylvania."[87] During the winter of 1913–14 the IWW held two conferences of silk workers from New Jersey, New York, and Connecticut. At the second conference a secretary was elected to promote communications between the different regions, with headquarters in Paterson, and plans were discussed by the delegates for sending organizers into Pennsylvania.[88] These plans were crucial: either the solidarity of 1913 would be extended to include the coal miners' daughters in Pennsylvania—a long and difficult but not impossible task—or solidarity in Paterson would eventually decline. Either the experience of 1913 would lead to a successful strategy for organizing in Pennsylvania, or the hopes of 1913 would fade. The Paterson silk workers could not combat the runaway shops in Pennsylvania by themselves; they needed help. When the IWW failed to carry through on its plans for Pennsylvania, it hurt itself and them badly.

Two years after the strike, in June 1915, a writer for *Solidarity* returned to Paterson. Everywhere he found signs of decline. Disillusioned with the results, many silk workers now believed that the IWW-led strike had been "an absolute failure." Only a very small group of silk workers were still active in Local 152. How had the bosses undone the accomplishments of the strike? the writer asked. The small group of IWW loyalists explained the effective combination of the runaway shop and the blacklist: "Shop organization was broken down, by opening up new shops, 'annexes', elsewhere, laying off their active spirits, discharging leaders, and thereby discouraging the rest." As for the IWW's own promised offensive against the annexes in Pennsylvania, all the writer for *Solidarity* could cite was some local success in Easton, across the Delaware from New Jersey.[89] In fact, by 1915 the IWW was suffering from a double depression. In Paterson and elsewhere, as the writer noted, the economic depression made resistance difficult for the moment. But the IWW itself had become permanently depressed in the East as a result of the infighting after the 1913 defeat.[90] Its own energies sapped by fratricidal battles, the national IWW was in no position to promote organization in Pennsylvania or to help bring the silk workers together in Paterson.

The Paterson labor movement recovered in 1916, pushing back the four-loom system and instituting the nine-hour day, but the IWW did not recover. Despite the renewal of militant strike activity by workers in Paterson and elsewhere, the decline of the IWW continued throughout the East. Local 152 had claimed 468 members just before the 1913 strike and 2,000 members six months after the strike. By 1916 it had become one small faction among several, pushing its own line and attacking rival unions.[91] At its best, the IWW had been part of the process leading to a wider solidarity among silk workers. Now, it became part of the process of fragmentation. Though Tresca and especially Flynn returned again and again to Paterson—promoting the nine-hour campaign late in 1913, holding meetings of the unemployed in 1914, challenging the ban on outside speakers and attempting to reverse the decline of Local 152 in 1915—the national organization they represented was no longer capable of sustained organizing in the East. By 1916 the IWW was itself too sick to be able to keep its promises in Pennsylvania or in Paterson. "That hurt me," said a 1913 striker, "because I felt for certain they would take over, and be our union."[92] With no organization capable of extending their unity to Pennsylvania in the years after 1913, Paterson's silk workers joined competing organizations along ethnic, craft, and ideological lines, and lost their unity with one another.

The solidarity of the manufacturers survived the 1913 strike; the solidarity of the silk workers did not; and the fragmentation of the silk workers' movement encouraged the employers to counterattack. Spurred by the depression of 1920–21 and the national open shop drive, the Paterson Silk Manufacturer's Association began its own drive against unions and against the two-loom system. The Amalgamated Textile Workers folded, hurt as much by attacks from IWW Local 152 as by the open-shop drive of the manufacturers. But the weavers did not fold. In 1922 a large ribbon mill that tried to abolish the eight-hour day was beaten by a fourteen-week strike. As one militant weaver later explained, "We had to win the eight-hour day again, over and over."[93]

In 1924 the broad-silk weavers struck en masse for two looms and the eight-hour day, winning agreements with the large manufacturers that were, however, immediately undercut by the ubiquitous family shops. Superficially, the 1924 strike resembled the 1913 strike. The goals in 1924 were, again, two looms and eight hours. Koettgen and especially Lessig played leading roles; Turn Hall was closed, and outside speakers banned. New York radicals and intellectuals came to help the strikers and challenge the ban on outside speakers. Judge Minturn, sitting now on the Court of Appeals, was one of a panel of three judges who overturned the conviction of Roger Baldwin, which was based on the same 1796 statute limiting free assembly that had been invoked against Lessig and Haywood in 1913, when Minturn had dismissed the case.

But the differences between the two strikes were far more important. First of all, the 1924 strike was purely defensive; there was no hope after 1919 of winning new ground. Second, the structural weaknesses of the weavers were revealed in 1924 by their inability to close the family shops or prevent them from doing work for the mills that were closed by the strike. Third, craft and ethnic tensions persisted among the weavers in 1924, despite the apparent unity; after the Amalgamated folded, Jewish broad-silk weavers had joined the union founded by the ribbon weavers but were excluded from leadership positions in both the union and the strike by the German and English ribbon weavers. Finally, the Socialists and Communists who supported the strikers in 1924, in contrast to the Socialists and Wobblies of 1913, seemed more determined to hurt each other than to help the strikers. Polish Jews, who as a community had supported the 1913 strike through the Workmen's Circle, were becoming permanently divided over the question of the family shops and, even more, over the question of Communism. A veteran of the Jewish labor movement in Paterson in the 1920s to 1940s recalls that "the bitter feelings between the Socialists and Communists among the Paterson Jews were deeper and stronger than the bad feelings between the workers and family-shop bosses in the Workmen's Circle."[94] In the years after 1924 all these weaknesses of the Paterson labor movement—the purely defensive nature of the struggle, the inability to cope with the family shop, the recurring division between ethnic groups, and the ideological division between Socialists and Communists— became endemic.

Damaged by their divisions, the silk workers continued to resist the employers' offensive; it was checked but not halted by the 1924 strike. In 1928 the weavers struck again. On the eve of the Great Depression, with the significant exception of the family-shop weavers, Paterson's weavers were still clinging to the eight-hour day and the forty-four-hour week. Their counterparts in Pennsylvania were working fifty-four hours.[95] Though unable to prevent an increase in loom assignments, the Paterson weavers had not struggled entirely in vain.

But the Depression swept all their gains. By 1938 those weavers fortunate enough to find work at all were generally tending six looms. Wages had collapsed as production fell. Family-shop weavers, like the English handloom weavers a century earlier, begged for commission work and took it at any price. In desperation, some family shops turned to weaving synthetics, especially rayon, which further undermined the market for silk. Though Paterson's silk industry had been expanding more slowly than the Pennsylvania industry since the turn of the century, in absolute terms it had continued to grow, reaching its peak employment in 1919 and its greatest number of looms in 1926. But in the 1930s, with the exception of Jacquard weaving, the industry was dying. And still the silk workers fought back. The dye workers struck in 1933 and 1934 under (and against) the National Recovery Administration (NRA) and finally won a contract with a minimum wage and an eight-hour day. Appropriately, the 1933 dyers' strike began at the Weidmann plant, and the shop chairmen and delegates in the 1934 strike met at the Sons of Italy hall—the old traditions of struggle persisted. Weavers went on strike in 1931 (particularly against the Henry Doherty company) and in 1933, with the strike spreading into Pennsylvania for the first time since 1913. In 1937 another general silk strike, backed now by the CIO, won union recognition and collective bargaining for the weavers (Carrie Golzio was on the executive board of the union by then). More remarkable, the small employers themselves went on strike. Organizing against all odds, in the best Paterson tradition, the family-shop commission weavers struck for one week in 1936 against the converters, demanding and receiving a one cent per yard increase. Even in their new guise as converters, the Paterson silk manufacturers could not entirely escape the class struggle.[96]

Within Paterson labor history the 1913 strike appears as the largest and most dramatic of a series of silk strikes stretching back to the 1870s and forward to the 1930s. As a battle in the Paterson labor wars the 1913 strike was not decisive. The manufacturers won, but not by a knockout. Like the silk workers the manufacturers emerged scarred from 1913 and eager to avoid a rematch. They had not succeeded in establishing the four-loom system; indeed, they did not succeed in doing so until after their employees had won the eight-hour day. The 1913 strike is important in Paterson history because it pitted the two sides against each other when each was at the peak of its strength and confidence. It showed what the Paterson silk workers and the IWW could do and what they could not yet do: they could not yet shut down the manufacturers in Pennsylvania.

There is no way of knowing what would have happened if the IWW had not fallen apart nationally, especially in the East. Could Koettgen and his colleagues have built viable local organizations in Pennsylvania, to serve as flash points when the next conflagration occurred? Or was it already too late for the Paterson silk workers? Historians cannot go very far on the roads not taken. All we can say—and it is a paradox—is that the loss of the Paterson strike of 1913 became a major turning point for the silk workers only because it became a major turning point for the IWW.

CHAPTER EIGHT

Defeat Becomes Disaster

The IWW had come to Paterson with high hopes. Following their almost incredible success in Lawrence, the IWW leaders expected another victory in Paterson. When the unexpected happened, they were badly hurt and never able to regain the initiative in organizing industrial workers. All histories of the IWW agree that the organization suffered, that its invasion of the East was turned back at Paterson. What is not made clear is the mechanism by which a lost battle became a lost war. Why did defeat in Paterson prove fatal for the IWW in the East?

By the end of July 1913 the silk workers had given up and returned to work. For years afterward Local 152 of the IWW tried to transform the defeat into the basis for a future victory. But long before Local 152 itself finally gave up, the IWW as a national organization had to deal somehow with the fact of its defeat in Paterson. Its critics forced it to do so. With the loss of the strike, a terrific barrage of criticism came at the IWW from all sides—from the established press, from the Socialists, from the AFL, from the anarchists. This chapter analyzes the IWW's response to the loss and the criticism and shows how that response turned a limited defeat into a disaster.

The IWW knew that its enemies would take advantage of its defeat. In November 1913 *Solidarity* remarked, without surprise, that "the capitalists and labor fakirs of the A.F. of L. and other minor organizations have devoted considerable time and money to what they are pleased to call the disastrous Paterson strike."[1] *Solidarity* had already reprinted, but had not taken the trouble to refute, a report in the New York *Journal of Commerce* on the annual convention of the AFL's national textile union, held in Massachusetts earlier in the fall. According to that report, "the most important development during the past year, as regards the textile labor situation in the United States, has been the apparent decadence of the Industrial Workers of the World. In the ranks of the old-line unions the feeling is that the defeat of the IWW at Paterson, N.J., in the big silk strike, and at Hopedale, Massachusetts, in the Draper Company strike, has robbed the socialist organization of all the prestige that it got out of its successes at Lawrence."[2] Predictions by capitalists and trade unionists of the IWW's imminent decline were themselves predictable. If this sort of criticism hurt at all, it was only because it portrayed the Wobblies no longer as dangerous revolutionaries but rather as losers. This was a less flattering charge.

But the attacks that hurt the most came from the IWW's erstwhile friends, the Socialists and anarchists. In June, with the outcome of the Paterson strike still in doubt, the IWW had been stung by a critical editorial in the Socialist New York *Call*, which had previously strongly supported the Paterson strike. The *Call* did not attack the strike as such; rather, it tried to puncture IWW claims that strikes were the revolution. The editorial pointed out structural similarities between the Paterson strike and strikes led elsewhere by the AFL (which, of course, did not agree: in July, Gompers wrote that the IWW was bound to lose in Paterson because it conducted a strike as if it were a revolution.)[3] The *Call*'s editor intended the piece as an argument for political action. In his view, all economic struggles were necessarily limited and reformist, regardless of who conducted them. But to *Solidarity*, the *Call*'s editorial, coming while the strike was "in a critical stage and requiring every bit of financial and moral support," was a bullet fired by the Socialists "into the backs of the striking Paterson workers."[4]

The collapse of the strike greatly intensified and embittered the conflict between the Socialists and the IWW. When in the strike's terrible final days, Socialist Jacob Panken published his attack on the IWW in the *Call*, Joseph Ettor of the IWW burst out: "At a time when all forces, enemies of the working class, are exulting and feasting riotously over the 'defeat' of the I.W.W. in Paterson, it is but fitting for you, an attorney at law, whose service as legal advisor for corporations and unions is highly paid, to join in the chorus." Ettor put "defeat" in quotation marks because he refused to admit that the strike had really been lost: "The Paterson struggle is not over." Counterattacking, he blamed the New York Socialists for not helping enough with relief and for promoting the shop-by-shop settlement: "The crime against the Paterson workers was not committed in Paterson but in New York on the lower East side." He also blamed the AFL for having promoted craft unionism in Paterson for years, at the expense of working-class solidarity.[5] In Ettor's article, written in August, the pattern of IWW response to criticism of the Paterson strike was already taking shape: simultaneously to blame defeat on Socialists and the AFL and to deny that it was a defeat.

During the fall the attacks and counterattacks between the IWW and the Socialists escalated. In September, at the IWW's annual convention in

Chicago, Ettor and the rest of the General Executive Board officially condemned the *Call*, proclaiming that "the annals of the labor movement in America furnish no more glaring example of the betrayal of the workers than the conduct of the Socialist Party Press in attacking the I.W.W. at the critical period of the Paterson strike and the trial of the Little Falls' Strikers."[6] Despite all their differences, the moderate Socialists and the IWW had not previously waged all-out war in the East. The practical task they had shared of helping the Paterson strikers win (Panken, for example, had spoken at meetings in New York with Bill Haywood and other Wobbly leaders to raise funds for relief, as well as at meetings in Paterson)[7] had muted their hostility in New York and New Jersey and actually brought them somewhat closer together. Failure to win drove them apart. For months during the strike many Socialists had withheld criticism of the IWW in order not to jeopardize the strike. Now, as if to make up for their restraint, they attacked violently.[8]

And the IWW leaders, at this moment, were extremely vulnerable. They had come to Paterson so confidently, invested so many of their organization's resources in the strike, claimed so many times that victory was near, called for so many sacrifices by the nearly 50,000 silk strikers in Paterson and elsewhere, and placed so much importance on general strikes as the means of bringing about revolutionary change that even without any outside criticism the leaders would have been badly shaken by the outcome. For them, even more than for their left-wing critics, the defeat was depressing. In October, Algenon Lee, another New York Socialist, announced that "the I.W.W. has no future. It has reached its climax and decline in Paterson and will soon disappear." Justus Ebert, who had been so confident of the IWW's future after its Lawrence victory, quoted Lee in *Solidarity* and said he was right: the IWW was, "in many respects, a lamentable failure"; Paterson had given it "a black eye." But an organization that had come through several previous crises in its career should, he thought, despite its undeniable "signs of decadence," be able to come through the crisis of Paterson as well.[9]

Defeat in Paterson, combined with the IWW's resulting loss of prestige, shook the faith of the IWW in itself. A guest editorial in *Solidarity*, late in August, announced that in "making Industrial Unionism fit the every-day life of the workers we have failed miserably." The author took comfort, however, in the continued numerical growth of the IWW, despite its mistakes.[10] By the following spring, the IWW was faced by declining numbers as well, especially in textiles. "Whatever may be in store for it in the future," wrote Ettor, in an uncharacteristically somber vein, the IWW had served "its purpose in developing necessary elements of future labor struggles."[11]

Ettor was responding to yet another critic. Tom Mann, British syndicalist leader and a hero to many members of the IWW, had visited the United States in the summer of 1913 and had spoken in Paterson early in August as part of his tour of North America. Then he had gone home and written articles criticizing the IWW's strategy of competing with existing trade unions, concluding that it should work within the AFL. Not only Ettor but Haywood, too, tried to refute him. Haywood, in particular, sounded defensive, almost petulant.[12] In a different context, criticism by Mann would not have been so threatening. Over the years the IWW had come to define itself largely negatively. It was not the AFL and, as it had discovered, it was not the Socialist Labor Party or even the Socialist Party; it was also not the anarchists or even the syndicalists. It had grown and become itself, not in spite of conflicts but through them. Mann's emphasis on the difference between British syndicalism and American industrial unionism need not have been destructive. But Mann had been to Paterson in the immediate aftermath of defeat. Because his criticism appeared to the Wobblies as part of the wave of attacks upon them after Paterson, it served to heighten their defensiveness, their feeling of isolation, and their loss of self-confidence.

Perhaps, as Ebert suggested, the IWW could have worked through the experience of defeat in Paterson, and learned from it. But the overwhelming criticism the Wobblies met, especially from former friends and allies, gave them no time or space in which to assimilate that experience and to grow as a result. "May the Lord deliver us from our friends," cried a Wobbly in September 1913. Writing in response to an anarchist piece titled, "The Paterson Fiasco," he bemoaned the fact that "since the ending of the Paterson strike" the IWW's allies had joined its declared enemies in "analyzing, dissecting, weighing and with unanimous accord finding the IWW wanting."[13]

The organization was not entirely alone during this time; it did get some help from its friends. *The Masses* stood behind it through the strike and—more important—throughout the long crisis after the strike. The anarchists, for example, accused the IWW of not having been revolutionary enough in Paterson and, specifically, of disarming the strikers by urging them not to fight back against the police. "Of course they all criticize: for the socialists we were too radical, for the anarchists we were too conservative," complained Flynn bitterly.[14] But *The Masses* didn't criticize. Instead, it responded to the anarchists in the September issue with a cartoon by John Sloan, showing an extremely well-dressed lady lounging on her sofa as she remarked to a gentleman friend: "Why don't those strikers do something—let a few of them get shot, and it'll look as if they meant business." The cartoon was titled "The Extreme Left."[15]

Such loyal expressions of support for the IWW, however, became almost inaudible in the din raised by its critics. One of the loudest voices raised against it after Paterson was that of Margaret Sanger. Earlier, she had been active with both the IWW and the anarchists, but the Paterson defeat pushed her to choose. In an anarchist publication early in January 1914, she developed the usual anarchist argument against the IWW's policy of nonviolence in Paterson: the strikers "avoided many clashes with the police which might have brought out the militia, thereby intensifying the situation by burdening the taxpayer so that pressure be [*sic*] brought upon the bosses and an earlier settlement made." What genuine "revolutionary momentum" had existed in Paterson, she asserted, had been due to the small anarchist element there. She added that the IWW should have fought an all-out battle for free speech during the strike, that it should have actively promoted the use of sabotage, that it should not have allowed the strike to become such a long one, and that it should have shunned all support from Socialists, particularly the Socialists of nearby Haledon.[16]

Having been an IWW organizer, Sanger knew how to wound the IWW. Her criticisms put the organization on the defensive because, in every case, she was condemning its conduct of the strike in terms of old Wobbly values and attitudes. Fighting for free speech, avoiding long-drawn-out strikes, mistrusting Socialists, and encouraging self-defense by workingmen were all part of the IWW tradition, especially as it had developed in the West. In coming East and engaging in industrial strikes, the IWW had begun to evolve in new directions. Defeat in Paterson cut short these changes, and the Wobblies lost the chance to find their way in the industrial East.

Put on the defensive, they could not let go of the 1913 strike. Explaining why Flynn was back in Paterson in August, Haywood said that "she is a national organizer of an organization that doesn't know when it is licked. Though the press, both the capitalist press and the socialist press, claims that the IWW is defeated, we want to announce that the strike has just begun."[17] Sometimes, however, it is better to know when you are licked. "Remember this strike is not over," said Koettgen to the silk workers as they returned to work at the end of July.[18] "The strike was no failure," he insisted in his report at the annual IWW convention in September.[19] "The I.W.W. has full control of the situation" in Paterson, maintained the General Executive Board at the convention.[20] Such denials had a political purpose: they strengthened the industrially oriented eastern leadership of the IWW and protected it where it was most vulnerable—in the apparent failure of its industrial policy—to the challenge of the western Wobblies. But the denials of defeat continued beyond the convention and beyond any conceivable practical purpose. Eleven months after the end of the strike, Lessig amazed the lawyer for the Senate's Industrial Relations Commission.

THOMPSON: Did the strike end?
LESSIG: It did not.
THOMPSON: Is it still on?
LESSIG: Well, the—
THOMPSON (interrupting): Has the strike ended?
LESSIG: Well, the strike, to my mind, has not ended yet.
THOMPSON: It has not?
LESSIG: No, sir; simply deferred.[21]

Six months after the end of the strike, Elizabeth Gurley Flynn and Patrick Quinlan each refused to admit that the battle for Paterson had really been lost.

In two articles in the left-wing Socialist press, Quinlan claimed that the strike had achieved significant economic gains. In his estimation, an even more hopeful sign for the future was the support given to Socialist candidates by the silk workers in the November elections.[22] Flynn, on the contrary, in her speech at the New York Civic Club Forum, maintained that the really hopeful thing about the strike was that the workers emerged from the experience with a "trust in themselves and a distrust for everybody else," including a distrust for Socialist politicians. Flynn admitted that the strike had achieved none of its original economic goals, but she argued that this failure was more than offset by the gain in class consciousness that resulted from the process of the strike itself.[23] The contradictory claims made by Flynn and Quinlan about the outcome had in common only their desperate need to deny the reality of defeat.

Both Flynn and Quinlan clearly felt put on the defensive by the attacks launched against the IWW by its erstwhile allies. "When the strike was over the Socialist papers of the country were inundated with a flood of discussion on the merits, demerits, methods and tactics of the I.W.W.," complained Quinlan.[24] Flynn's speech can be taken as a semi-official response of the strike leadership to its critics. "The reason why I undertake to give this talk at this moment," she explained, "is that the flood of criticism is unabated, becoming more vicious all the time, drifting continually from the actual facts, and involving as a matter of course the policies and strike tactics of the I.W.W."[25] She tried, pathetically, to refute each of Sanger's points as well as those of other critics—pathetically, because the damage had already been done, not only by Sanger but by all the Socialists and anarchists who saw in the defeat of the IWW in Paterson a moral illustration of the consequences of its sins; pathetically, too, because her response, like that of Quinlan, Ettor, and the other IWW leaders who could not accept the fact of defeat, only made matters worse. Flynn identified too strongly with the strike to discuss it or its critics objectively. As she admitted, "it is rather difficult for me to separate myself from my feelings about the Paterson strike, to speak dispassionately."[26] In fact, she was outraged by the critics. Refuting the anarchists' favorite charge against the strike leaders, she made the same point that *The Masses* had made, but she could muster none of the magazine's humor. "I know of one man in particular who wrote an article . . . about how 'the blood of the workers should dye the streets in the city of Paterson in protest' but he didn't come to Paterson to let his blood dye the streets, as the baptism of violence. In fact we never saw him in the city of Paterson from the first day of the strike to the last."[27] Flynn took criticism of the strike personally. The criticisms were especially painful because—although she could not afford publicly to admit it—she too wondered what had gone wrong. Like the IWW as a whole, Flynn had put her best energy and effort into the strike, and she was tormented by the question of responsibility for its collapse.

BLAME

From the moment defeat became certain, in July, the question was "why?" Speaking to the remnant of strikers during the last terrible week, denying that they had been completely defeated, Flynn framed the question of "why?" in terms of "who?" "If any persons are to blame for the strike being lost it is those who threw up the sponge at the last moment when victory was at the door and went back to work. We had the strike won two weeks ago when there were breaks in the ranks. Those breaks received such wide publicity that aid stopped coming in." And again, for emphasis: "There is no one to blame but your fellow workers who deserted you."[28] Six months later, speaking at the Civic Club, she was more specific. The traitors were the ribbon weavers, whose willingness to settle shop by shop had caused the strike to falter just when it was on the verge of victory.[29] Yet at the moment Flynn publicly attacked the ribbon weavers, blaming them for the defeat, they were the most active group of silk workers in Paterson and constituted the bulk of the membership of IWW Local 152.[30] Unable to accept having lost the battle, the IWW organizers began to hurt their chances of winning the war.

The IWW would follow to the end the inconsistent pattern, first sketched by Flynn and Ettor, of denying that it had been defeated at Paterson while simultaneously blaming the loss on class traitors. Someone had snatched away the victory. Was it the Central Strike Committee, the ribbon weavers, the Socialists, the New York intellectuals, or perhaps certain elements in the IWW leadership itself? Gradually, despite itself, the IWW began to join the chorus of criticism—began, that is, to blame itself for the defeat. What did we do wrong, asked its leaders, and—more ominously—who did it? Sanger named Tresca and Boyd as alone deserving praise, the former for acting like an anarchist and the latter for advocating sabotage, and singled out Quinlan for special blame because of his ties to the Socialists. By the time Sanger wrote and Flynn tried to refute her, the IWW had begun the bloody process of looking for the individuals who were to blame.

An alternative direction did exist. In August, Quinlan had blamed only hunger, which had gotten "the best of the strikers as it does of everybody"; Killenbeck had similarly attributed defeat to "a foe which it is impossible to overcome—hunger."[31] *The Masses* made the same point. A humorous column ironically listed July's main events, beginning with "Commerce Court passes away amid widespread self control" and ending with "Self-appointed Committee meets in New York to decide on a mayor and endorse popular government." The July 20 entry stood out because of its complete lack of irony: "Paterson silk manufacturers starve workers into surrender."[32] In other words, the manufacturers had simply been stronger. This sane view found expression within the IWW itself. In August the Italian IWW paper, *Il Proletario*, published an analysis by Giovanni Di Gregorio that took a clearheaded approach to the lessons of the defeat: "The Paterson strike, I think, teaches one lesson, that is, that there is no 'cocksure' method yet devised or devisable under the present system by which a strike can be won, when the workers are confronted by capitalists of unlimited wealth and viciousness."[33]

The alternative to recrimination, then, lay in the recognition that no organization could expect to win every battle in the class struggle. In this sense, the single most helpful reading of the defeat—one that focused not on the supposed weakness of the strikers and IWW but on the strength and endurance of the manufacturers—was offered by the New York *Call*. The strikers were "beaten by sheer hunger, and nothing else" it asserted. The manufacturers had one advantage: "Through their investments in the industry elsewhere, or through their ability to send their most pressing work to be made up by other manufacturers, they seem to have been able to fill part of their orders. The strike, as far as Paterson is concerned, was complete. It was not a general strike in the silk industry. . . . While it dragged along locally and was fought with almost unexampled solidarity, at the same time in other sections the mills were running full blast."[34]

Had the IWW adopted this sort of analysis, it would have spurred the organization of silk workers in Pennsylvania. But emphasizing the superior power of the manufacturers ran counter to the IWW's preferred way of seeing itself. "The capitalists could not defeat the workers, not they!" insisted an earlier IWW pamphlet titled *Why Strikes Are Lost: How to Win*. Reviewing AFL strike defeats, the pamphlet blamed the loss of strikes solely on bad leadership.[35] The Lawrence victory strengthened the IWW's assumption that defeats in strikes were a result of poor leadership. The Wobbly organizers in Paterson were unable to see the defeat as one inflicted by a (temporarily) stronger enemy partly because they had always tended to assume that in strikes the leadership was responsible for the outcome. Instead of learning from their defeat, they began to inflict it on each other.

"We cannot permit ourselves to waste our energies in petty, insignificant, personal sham battles," pleaded Mathilda Rabinowitz, who early in 1913 had helped lead the IWW to victory in Little Falls. "Let us not divide against ourselves." And as if to counter the tendency toward internal dissension, Rabinowitz praised "the great battle in Paterson, which the capitalist press hastened to proclaim a complete defeat for the I.W.W. and even our socialist friends ridiculed and misrepresented."[36] "What we need is not a destructive campaign of internal wrangling," warned another writer in the same issue of *Solidarity*. "Think it over, and call a halt."[37]

In the end, the IWW was unable to call a halt. Desperately, it clung to its image—which it had cultivated in its battle with the AFL and which the media had magnified since Lawrence—as *the* organization that had mastered the revolutionary theory and practice of strikes. In the process of maintaining its image, the IWW lost whatever chance it had for an honest internal discussion of the experience of defeat. Reluctantly but inevitably, given its rejection of the alternative of recognizing the superior strength of the enemy in 1913, it proceeded to hunt for an internal enemy or enemies.

GETTING PERSONAL

It was the Paterson strike leaders who felt particularly responsible, and particularly vulnerable to criticism of the strike. After defeat, they turned on each other. There was no big purge, no single great split along ideological lines. The IWW remained too open for that. The disintegration took place quietly and slowly. To see the traumatic effect of Paterson, to recreate the pattern of disintegration, one must look closely at the ties between strike leaders, including Haywood, Flynn, Tresca, Quinlan, Koettgen, Lessig, John Steiger (a leader of the silk strikers in New York after the strike spread there), and Boyd, the New Yorker arrested for preaching sabotage to the strikers in Paterson.

Boyd, alone of this group, was not a strike organizer. Born in England, a New York Socialist who had joined the IWW at the time of the Lawrence strike, he had come out to Paterson on March 31 to talk at the regular mass meeting. His speeches that morning and the next day caused a sensation in the local press; he had spoken disrespectfully about the American flag and advised the strikers, in explicit detail, how to commit sabotage when they returned to the mills. The Strike Committee announced that Boyd was no longer welcome to speak at mass meetings. The local authorities indicted him. The New York Socialists condemned him. After the strike, Koettgen held him partly responsible for the defeat; without mentioning Boyd by name, Koettgen denounced IWW speakers who "advocate extreme sabotage in an industry with which they are not familiar," thereby creating disunity among the strikers.[38] Years later, in her autobiography, Flynn suggested that Boyd may have been a provocateur in Paterson, and at least one historian has followed her lead.[39] But at the time, Flynn defended Boyd, convinced the committee to restore his right to speak from the strike platform, and went on to write an aggressive pamphlet for the IWW in which she advocated sabotage as an important weapon in the class struggle.[40] Clearly, Flynn did not think Boyd was a provocateur when she first heard him speak. Her later charges against him were second thoughts, part of the pattern of IWW response to defeat.

There were countercharges as well. Steiger, who published his version of the great strike in 1914, reported a conversation with Boyd and his wife in which Mrs. Boyd blamed Flynn and Haywood for pressuring her husband into making the inflammatory speeches, against his will.[41] And in 1915, in an attempt to gain a shorter sentence, Boyd did repudiate the IWW. But Steiger's account cannot be taken at face value. As Harry Kemp emphasized in *More Miles*, the Paterson strike leaders consistently discouraged all talk in public that might justify repression of the strike, especially talk about sabotage.[42] The charges of the Boyds and/or Steiger against Flynn and Haywood, like the later charges of Flynn against Boyd, tell less about the strike itself than about how they all felt about losing it.

Steiger himself is an extreme example of the falling-out between strike leaders, so extreme that historians of the IWW have generally ignored him. The book he published in Paterson in 1914, at his own expense, was a forerunner of the lurid I-was-a-Red genre. In his *Memoirs of a Silk Striker*, Steiger accused his former IWW comrades of every bad motive and form of bad faith, and announced his conversion to the ways of capitalistic progress. His accusations are indeed worthless as history of the strike, and historians have rightly dismissed them. But as part of the history of the disintegration of the IWW leadership, his account is revealing. Steiger joined the Wobblies during the early days of the Paterson strike, at the height of IWW power and popularity in the East. He helped lead his fellow New York silk workers out on strike at a time when the spreading strike seemed about to shut down the entire silk industry in the East. He played a major role in raising money in New York for the relief of the Paterson strikers, and without his fund-raising efforts among New York workers, the Pageant might not have taken place. Yet in the waning days of the strike he was charged by other IWW leaders with dishonesty in handling funds and with betrayal of IWW strike principles.[43] After the strike was lost, he came to Paterson to work in the mills and to help finish off the remnants of IWW influence there. His 1914 book, with its view of the IWW as a cynical moneymaking conspiracy for exploiting honest working men, was intended to defend his reputation and bury the IWW. Later in the year Steiger became one of the incorporators and trustees of the Brotherhood of American Silk Workers, with support from the Paterson silk manufacturers.[44] Although he had served briefly in the IWW, Steiger had never been committed to its principle of class struggle. Attracted to it when it seemed the wave of the future, he rejected it totally when it failed.

Other conflicts began late in the strike. The local IWW organizers, Koettgen and Lessig, had originally sent to the national office for help and would undoubtedly have remained appreciative of the leadership provided by Flynn and Haywood if the strike strategy of the national leaders had resulted in victory. When Lessig, impotently raging against the power of the Paterson manufacturers and their allies in local government, threatened in May to "put this city in darkness,"[45] his threat—duly publicized by the Paterson press—undercut Flynn's careful effort to build support for the strike among Paterson's small businessmen. By June, Flynn and Lessig were openly fighting over the sending away of the young men. In her autobiography Flynn attacked Lessig's integrity, accusing him of having been a company agent in a later strike.[46]

Haywood, for his part, criticized both Lessig and Koettgen in the final days of the Paterson strike. According to Steiger, Haywood said that both had acted irresponsibly in agreeing to settle the strike and, dismissing Koettgen as Lessig's puppet, accused Lessig of getting "cold feet" as a result of the indictment against him in Paterson.[47] Steiger's testimony must always be treated cautiously. But here it is confirmed by Ettor, who wrote that Koettgen and Lessig had gone to New York late in July to participate in a Socialist scheme to settle the Paterson strike shop by shop, behind the backs of the national IWW organizers.[48] After the strike, Koettgen and Lessig continued to do textile organizing for the IWW. But the accounts of Steiger and Ettor, in conjunction with Flynn's later charge, suggest that the working relationship between the local and national strike leaders was undermined by the frustrating experience of being unable to achieve victory together.

Unity among the four organizers sent to Paterson by the IWW was also destroyed by defeat and by the withering criticism that followed. Quinlan was the first to split away. His desperate attempt to break the strike deadlock by proposing a rent strike, like Lessig's threat to darken Paterson, conflicted with Flynn's effort to develop middle-class support. In June it was already rumored in the local press that Quinlan was on bad terms with Flynn and Haywood. By July he was arguing in the *Call* for political action as a necessary supplement to strikes—an argument correctly perceived by the magazine *Current Opinion* as being "against the views of many of his own colleagues."[49] His defense and appeals on the charge of inciting to riot were paid for by the Socialist *Appeal to Reason* rather than by the IWW. Quinlan had worked for the Socialists for five years before he began working with the Wobblies in 1912. When the strike was lost and the split between the two organizations became irrevocable, Quinlan had to choose, and he chose the Socialists. Temporarily released from prison during the last week in July, he went directly to a Socialist pre-election rally in Paterson. Criticized in *Solidarity* for allying himself with the Socialists and for interfering in the IWW's collection of defense funds—"he has proven himself to be either a damn fool, or . . . a traitor to the working class"[50]— Quinlan refused to follow Steiger's and Boyd's route of publicly denouncing the IWW, though doing so might well have shortened his sentence. But upon his release from prison in 1916, he formally repudiated the IWW,[51] thereby completing a split that had begun during the frustrating deadlock of the strike.

The experience of being unable to win the strike tore apart the men and women who felt most responsible for its outcome. The only exceptions were Flynn and Tresca, who had been lovers since they met in Lawrence in 1912. Their connection survived the strike, and despite their later political differences (Tresca turned back to anarchism, where he had started, while Flynn drifted very slowly toward Communism) they remained together well into the 1920s. Alone among the major organizers of the strike, Flynn and Tresca managed not to take defeat out on each other. Their relationship was strong enough to withstand the long experience of defeat at Paterson.

Their mutual friendship with Haywood, however, became a casualty of the defeat. In Lawrence both Flynn and Tresca had become close to Big Bill and had looked up to him. Haywood, in turn, praised them both in his autobiography for their work in Lawrence but failed even to mention them in connection with Paterson, where their contribution had been much greater. By the time Haywood was writing his life story, in 1926, his conflict with Flynn had become well known. In that year, in an interview with the *American Mercury*, Flynn elaborated an earlier charge that Haywood's flight to Russia in 1920 was a betrayal of the IWW and a cause of its collapse.[52] Some historians have kept her version of these events alive, but a recent study of the IWW revives Haywood's charge of treason against Flynn for opting out of the big Chicago trial of the IWW in 1918.[53]

Thus the conflict between Flynn and Haywood continues. Not only are there two existing and opposing versions of their conflict from 1918 to 1920, when the United States government was crushing what was left of the IWW, but there are also opposing versions of their conflict in 1916, when the IWW was enjoying a temporary upswing in the West and Midwest. Flynn's supporters criticize Haywood for having tried to control the 1916 strike in the Mesabi Range of South Dakota from IWW headquarters in Chicago, and defend her for circumventing that control and for allowing some strikers to plead guilty to manslaughter in return for the release of Tresca and other IWW organizers.[54] The case against Flynn blames her for letting personal considerations (that is, her love for Tresca) blind her to the necessity of placing the good of the arrested strikers first.[55] After Haywood officially reprimanded Flynn in 1916, she stopped organizing for the IWW; when she wrote to President Wilson in 1918, asking to have her case severed from that of Haywood and the other Chicago defendants, she cited the "violent disagreements" within the IWW in 1916 that had virtually ended her activity in the organization.[56]

Historians have tended to become entrapped in the Haywood-Flynn controversy. But more important than the question of who was right or wrong is the question of why there were so many charges and countercharges. When did the conflict between Flynn and Haywood start, and what does it tell us about the IWW? Joseph Conlin, in his study of Haywood, provides a clue. By 1916, Conlin writes, "Haywood had so structured the IWW's procedures that he disciplined his friends Elizabeth Gurley Flynn and Carlo Tresca for decisions made in a Mesabi Range strike, decisions that earlier would have been grist for cordial argument."[57] This new structure was made possible by the IWW's national convention of 1913. One response of Haywood and his supporters to the defeat at Paterson, and to the criticism that followed it, was to press harder within the IWW for greater central office control over the organizer in the field. The 1913 convention was not the first or the last time the issue of hierarchical discipline was debated in the IWW, but as James Osborne shows in his study of the Paterson strike, it was the first time the issue was decisively resolved, in a way that would last until the 1920s.[58] And as Osborne also points out, the debate over structure took place in a particular context: "The strike in Paterson had ended some six weeks previously, but the almost incessant discussion and criticism arising from it was still ringing in the ears of most I.W.W. delegates."[59]

The final split between Haywood and Flynn in 1916 can in this way be traced back to the defeat they shared in 1913. Were they indeed "friends" until 1916, as Conlin implies? By the summer of 1914 they were already on opposite sides of a bruising struggle over tactics in the IWW, with Flynn arguing for an aggressive stance—including unemployment organizing and the possibility of violence—and Haywood and Ettor urging a more minimal strategy "until we gather sufficient strength," as Ettor put it.[60]

In fact, the "ill-feeling" between Flynn and Haywood, as Conlin himself indicates elsewhere, began in 1913 over the Paterson Pageant.[61] Haywood, with Reed and Dodge, created the idea for the Pageant and gave it shape; it was his biggest effort to break the deadlock of the strike. For the rest of his life he considered the Pageant as perhaps his greatest accomplishment.[62] Flynn and Tresca seem at first to have opposed the idea,[63] only to be won over (or beaten down) by the enthusiasm of Haywood and the silk strikers. After the strike, Flynn repeatedly blamed the Pageant for the defeat. But to blame the Pageant was to blame Haywood, the strike leader most responsible for it. Before 1913 Flynn and Haywood liked and respected each other and enjoyed working together. But their relationship, like those between most of the strike leaders, did not survive the battle for Paterson. Concretely, personally, the double defeat at the hands of the silk manufacturers and of their own critics tore the strike leaders apart, leaving them in no position to deal with the actual issues raised by the strike.

Responding to Sanger and other critics who had questioned the wisdom of leading such a long-drawn-out strike, Flynn argued in her speech at the Civic Club that the Paterson strike leaders could not have proposed the alternative of a short strike without alienating the silk workers. "We would simply have duplicated what every grafting, corrupt leader has done in Paterson and the United States—to tell them 'go back to work, your strike is lost.'" Then, in a rare acknowledgment of personal motivation, Flynn admitted that there was a deeper reason:

> For us to advocate a short strike . . . would have been directly contrary to our own feelings. We felt that the strike was going to be won. And it may seem to you a very foolish piece of optimism when I say that I believed the Paterson strike was going to be won up to the Sunday before the Paterson strike was lost. We didn't tell the people to stay out on a long strike knowing in our hearts that they were losing. We couldn't have talked to them if we felt that way. But every one of us was confident they were going to win that strike. And you all were. Throughout the United States the people were.[64]

The pressures that drove Flynn and Haywood and the other strike leaders apart were not only a result of losing the strike, or even of the subsequent criticism. One of the worst pressures came from remembering how they had expected to win—and with the whole country watching.

In June, Flynn had told the strikers that "all over the country workers are watching."[65] Newspapers and magazines had discovered the Paterson strike in

May and made it a test case for the IWW and its brand of industrial union-ism.[66] The IWW accepted these terms: victory at Paterson, Flynn argued repeatedly from May to July, would bring a national eight-hour day and would determine the success of the IWW as a national labor organization.[67] " 'This is the life or death of the workers' organization of the United States,' she fairly shouted at the great crowd that thronged the green in Haledon."[68] Though his rhetoric was slightly more restrained, Haywood shared her view of the impor-tance of the strike; so did *Solidarity*, which abandoned restraint by claiming, in capitals, that "THE STRIKE MUST BE WON. IT WILL MEAN A CENTURY OF ADVANCEMENT FOR THE WORKING CLASS."[69] The IWW's inflated sense of the consequences of the strike served as prophecy. With the whole country watching, the Wobblies blamed each other for defeat, even accused each other of treason, rather than admit that the enemy had beaten them.

Nine months after the strike, Max Eastman offered in *The Masses* a psychological explanation of the infighting on the left. His analysis was provoked by diatribes against other feminists in Sanger's new magazine, the *Rebel Woman*, but it applied more generally to the aftermath of Paterson, of which Sanger's magazine was a part.

> I think the phenomenon might be described, in Freudian language, as a trans-
> ference of hate from the original object to another object from which one can
> get a more satisfactory response! The entrenchments of custom and capital and
> privilege are so impregnable to our attacks—they ignore us and we have no
> satisfaction, and so we turn upon our own weaker sisters and brothers who
> will recoil and fight back, and give us an exhaust for our emotions.[70]

It was in Paterson that Flynn and Haywood, Tresca and Quinlan, Lessig and Koettgen, Boyd and Steiger and Sanger felt just how impregnable were the entrenchments of capital to their attacks. Eastman's model of the redirection of hate fit not only what Ettor had called "this seemingly fratricidal war between Wobblies and Socialists,"[71] and the renewal of fighting between Wobblies and anarchists, but also the outbreak of infighting within the IWW. Shaken in the hope of a succession of big strikes culminating in revolution, the strike leaders took their disappointment out on each other. Brought together in the process of victory in Lawrence, they were torn apart by the defeat in Paterson.

WORKERS' CONTROL?

The IWW, having expanded after Lawrence, contracted after Paterson. The organization made its greatest gains in the year from August 1912 to August 1913, leading more strikes, founding more locals, and taking in more members than in any previous twelve-month period. In the latter part of 1913 it began to decline, most precipitously in the East, where it had made its greatest gains.[72] Few new locals were organized to replace those that ceased to function. In 1914 the annual convention lasted four days instead of the usual two weeks. In

1915 there was no convention. The economic depression was partly responsible for the decline, but so was the IWW's own internal depression. Looking back after the 1914 convention, *Solidarity* recognized that "we have been hit hard, both from within and from the outside, during the past year."[73]

During 1915–16 the IWW was able in the West and Midwest to take advantage of the expansion of lumber and agricultural production caused by the European war. But once the United States entered the war, the government no longer tolerated interference in production, and the massive 1917–18 repression directed against the IWW ended its effective life as a movement. In both numbers and spirit, the year between Lawrence and Paterson remained the high-water mark of the IWW. "Strife and dissension, which has [*sic*] so hampered the constructive work of the organization in the past, has quite naturally been eliminated by the growth of the organization," wrote IWW organizer James Cannon in November 1912. As the IWW grew in numbers after Lawrence, Cannon explained, its activity and self-confidence also grew, and so did its internal harmony.[74] The converse, however, was just as true. Discouragement after Paterson led, as we have seen, to new strife and dissension, especially within the strike leadership.

Expanding after its Lawrence victory, the IWW had absorbed Socialists like Quinlan and Boyd and anarchists like Tresca.[75] In effect, such recruits represented the IWW's working alliances with both left-wing Socialists and anarchists. The Paterson defeat shattered those alliances. Boyd, Quinlan, Tresca, and Steiger left the organization in the aftermath of the strike, leaving behind Wobbly principles as well and returning to some version of their own earlier ideas. Steiger, who joined last, left first; Tresca, whose connections with the organization were the most complex, was the last to break away. But for all four, it was as if their careers in the IWW had been aborted by the defeat at Paterson. In that sense they embodied the IWW's own aborted career in the East.

In contrast to these four relative newcomers, Haywood and Flynn had been committed Wobblies for all or almost all of the organization's life; they had nowhere else to go. Even after Flynn ceased her IWW activity, she remained loyal for years, possibly for decades.[76] And Haywood, as he was dying in Soviet Russia, expressed the opinion that "the I.W.W. has fought more political battles for the working class than any other labor organization or political party in America."[77] But their roles within the IWW and their whole concept of organization changed significantly after Paterson. Flynn never again led a strike. Despite the remarkable practical abilities she had demonstrated in Paterson, she returned to the role she had played in Lawrence—as a fund raiser in support of strikes (led by men) rather than as a strike leader herself. At the same time, her public posture grew increasingly defensive and hostile.[78] Haywood, too, retreated from the IWW battle lines after Paterson, but he did so at first by moving upstairs. The administrative positions he assumed after 1913, first as general organizer and then as secretary-treasurer, were intended, as Flynn guessed, to provide him with some respite from the strain of class struggle.[79] Physically, Haywood was broken by Paterson. In October, a letter to *Solidarity* from his friend Jessie Ashley notified the membership that "William D. Haywood is seriously ill in New York City. He is suffering from a complete breakdown as a result of the Paterson strike."[80] He had lost eighty pounds during the strike and never fully recovered his health.[81]

As the two most prominent and powerful leaders, Flynn and Haywood were under the greatest pressure during and after the strike. The pressure hurt them both, destroyed their friendship, and changed them. Neither of them had the strength or desire to attend the 1913 convention of the IWW, and neither was ever the same again. In their remaining years with the organization, Flynn and Haywood each came to embody an aspect of its new emphasis on hierarchical control—an emphasis that should be seen as part of the IWW's contraction after Paterson.

Haywood's contribution to the new concern with control is the more obvious one. He and his supporters built up the centralized disciplinary power within the organization, which he wielded against Flynn in 1916. "Increasingly after 1913," according to Conlin, "he thought primarily in terms of forging an I.W.W. like the old Western Federation of Miners, a union as highly organized and disciplined as the corporation it combatted."[82] Haywood's reorganization meant that a local organizer like Koettgen—who was best positioned to follow up on the Paterson strike and who emphasized the importance of organizing in Pennsylvania—would have less initiative and probably less influence on strategy. (In 1913, coal miners in the AFL gave considerable support to the IWW silk strike in Hazleton, especially before Golden's intervention. In 1916, 5,000 to 10,000 Pennsylvania coal miners actually joined an IWW strike led by Joseph Ettor—yet his efforts were hampered by the IWW's weakness and even more by Haywood's rigidly centralized structure.[83])

But Flynn's contribution to the new direction is the more interesting one. In her Civic Club speech against the critics she asked, "What lessons has the Paterson strike given to the I.W.W.?" and answered, "One of the lessons it has given to me is that when the I.W.W. assumes responsibility of a strike the I.W.W. should control the strike absolutely through a union strike committee."[84] This emphasis on control was new for Flynn, part of her response to the crushing double defeat. If the organization were to be held accountable and castigated for losing, at least it should be in a position, she felt, to call the shots during the strike. Haywood wanted the headquarters of the IWW to have control over the organizers in the field; Flynn wanted the organizers to have control over the workers on strike. The difference between them, in this instance, is less crucial than the fact that both were retreating from the IWW's traditional emphasis on control from below.

It is not easy to evaluate this increasing emphasis on control from above. Many observers today, as in 1914, confuse hierarchy with organization and therefore assume that the IWW's attempts to tighten up after 1913 represented progress, however belated, in practical organization. Such observers have pointed to the inability of the IWW not only to win in Paterson but to hold its gains after it had won in Lawrence; they believe that more effective control over both its organizers and, through them, over the textile workers might have prevented these losses. Over the years this explanation of the IWW's decline in the East, offered alike by Wobbly and academic historians, has come to seem familiar and attractive.[85] The exciting but unrealistic IWW was punished for its lack of hierarchical organization by its inability to take hold in the East.

Against this plausible view, two suggestions are offered here. The first is that the IWW's famous inability, after a strike was over, to hold the workers it had organized during the strike was only normal. Other organizations, with very different purposes and methods, met with the same results.

> In spite of its promising beginning, the union . . . had a short life. With the immediate objects of their strike attained, the members lost interest in their organization and within a short time the union disbanded. The lack of organization led to a new deterioration of labor standards and to a new revolt, another strike, and a revival of the union, followed by an inevitable decline and eventual dissolution.

This is Morris Hillquit, a leading Socialist critic of the IWW, describing the attempts of Jewish trade unionists to organize a bakers' union in New York City between 1890 and 1910. "Such also was the history of the Knee Pants Makers' Union and of practically all other Jewish trade unions organized since the advent of the United Hebrew Trades," Hillquit added. And he explained that "in practically all cases the unions were short-lived. They came and went and had to be reorganized every few years. In the minds of the Jewish workers of that period, unions were associated with strikes and were little more than instruments of strikes. . . . It took twenty years of patient and persistent work to educate the Jewish workers to a realization of the value of trade unions in peace as well as in war."[86]

Whether the Wobblies would have succeeded in permanently organizing the textile workers and other Eastern industrial workers if they too had had fifteen or twenty years, we have no way of knowing. The IWW failed to hold its organizational gains after a strike primarily because the workers it recruited, like most immigrant workers, viewed unions as instruments of strikes. AFL organizers complained that immigrant weavers and dyers' helpers in Paterson supported unions only when there was a strike: "They have had maybe 20 or 25 organizations in the last 20 years," said a local AFL leader in 1914, "but the trouble has been to get them to see the necessity of organization. . . . They can see it at the time of the strike, but to keep up the organization to protect their trade they can not see it." This enemy of the IWW regarded the loss of Wobbly membership in Paterson—"they had about 9,000 and now they have about 1,300"—as entirely normal.[87] Historians have not been so kind. By blaming the IWW's decline in Lawrence and Paterson on its openness, historians are perhaps repeating the post-1913 mistakes of Flynn and Haywood. The loss of that openness may be the greatest loss.

The second suggestion offered here is that the IWW enjoyed its greatest successes when it gave the greatest scope not only to the initiative of its organizers on the spot but also to the initiative of the people they organized. Lawrence is again the crucial case. If Paterson was a double defeat for the IWW, Lawrence was a double victory: the strike itself was unprecedented, and so was the one-day general strike on behalf of Ettor and Giovannitti that took place six months afterward. Ettor and Giovannitti, from jail, opposed going ahead with the protest strike; letters from them were read to a mass meeting, in various languages, by Flynn, Tresca, and other leaders; Local 20 of the IWW endorsed their advice. But a number of workers were not satisfied. They went to the jail and asked Ettor and Giovannitti if the letters were genuine. Still not satisfied, "the workers thereupon proceeded to act on their own account; they ignored advice, they set aside the action of the Central Committee . . . and proceeded with determination—the industrial democracy reasserted itself once more, the general strike took place." In this contemporary account by Justus Ebert, it is clear that at its height the IWW often did not lead but allowed itself to be led. In the protest strike "the rank and file prevailed; and the I.W.W. wisely stood behind them both locally and nationally; so that a united front against the common enemy was the final outcome."[88]

From 1909, and especially from 1912 to 1913, the IWW was on the cutting edge of social change in the East. After 1913 it lagged behind militant workers. It ceased growing in the East not in 1911—when the question first was raised—but in 1914, when the organization became hardened, overstructured, and unable to generate new responses to working-class needs. "Paradoxically, the greater the scope and intensity of the struggles in the Northeast grew, the more exclusively the IWW's attention became riveted on timber and agriculture workers of the South and West," writes David Montgomery.[89] The great upsurge of eastern industrial workers in 1919—including the workers of Paterson and Lawrence—took new forms and left the IWW behind.

The tightening-up that was evident at all levels of the organization after 1913 was part of the IWW's response to defeat in Paterson. Beaten by the manufacturers, the Wobblies tried harder to control the movement toward industrial organization. Confronted with overwhelming criticism, they finally blamed each other. Unable to accept their defeat, they desperately denied that it *was* a defeat—and turned it into a disaster. The high hopes with which Flynn, Haywood and others had come from Lawrence did not survive the experience of Paterson. Unable to assimilate that experience, the IWW leaders continued to suffer it, and as a result their movement suffered. The massive federal repression of 1917–19 did not kill the IWW; in the East, at least, it merely finished off a movement that was already dying—in part from self-inflicted wounds.

View from the Bridge

With the Paterson strike the creative force of the American left reached its fullest expression—then it was checked and ultimately reversed. The hopes that the silk workers, Wobblies, and intellectuals brought to the strike, their respect for each other, and their ability to develop democratic, nonviolent forms of struggle were valuable to the left, and they were valuable in ways that become even clearer in retrospect. This conclusion places the strike in the context of the subsequent history of the left, in which many of the qualities of 1913 were lost. Something happened in Paterson. Our difficulty in recognizing that something happened is a measure of how much we have lost.

THE DECLINE OF THE LEFT

The rapid decline of the American left after 1917 has often been attributed to the combined effects of wartime repression at home and successful revolution abroad. Not satisfied with this explanation, some historians have asked why the left in 1917 was already so weak and vulnerable. They have looked for prewar causes of the postwar breakup of the left and have located them in the split between the Socialist Party and the IWW. For these historians, the decisive event was the 1912 Socialist National Convention's resolution against sabotage, which was aimed at the IWW in general and Haywood in particular.[1] But resolutions become effective only through persons. It is true that Haywood was the national symbol of cooperation between the Socialist Party's left wing and the IWW and that Haywood was recalled from the National Executive Committee of the Socialist Party early in 1913, in accordance with the resolution of 1912. But the recall of Haywood did not end IWW-Socialist cooperation. On the contrary, local cooperation between them flourished in 1913. In Rhode Island, Socialists agitated in support of IWW-led textile strikes, enabling the predominantly Italian-speaking work force to gain significant support in the English-speaking community for the first time.[2] In Little Falls, Socialists from Schenectady began the organizing work and then turned leadership of the strike over to the IWW.[3] Citing Little Falls, Akron, and Pittsburgh in a review of new scholarship on local IWW struggles, David Goldberg concluded that "historians have been overly preoccupied by disagreements on the national level between the Socialist Party and the I.W.W. whereas on the local level both groups continued to work closely together."[4]

The silk strikes in Paterson, New York City, and Pennsylvania are the most powerful example of continuing cooperation between Socialists and Wobblies in 1913. Here, as elsewhere, the case of Pennsylvania is crucial. Because the IWW was not yet established in the coal towns, it relied heavily on the Pennsylvania Socialists. Whereas Socialists in Paterson and New York played vital support roles, in Pennsylvania they were the sea in which the IWW swam. Pennsylvania Socialists introduced the IWW organizers to local contacts and resources, provided them with a base among local silk workers, and gave them halls in which to speak.[5] This aid seemed, in 1913, only a foretaste of what would be possible in the future. In 1912 a longtime Socialist had been elected president of the Pennsylvania AFL; in May 1913, under his leadership, the state convention of the AFL endorsed industrial unionism and pledged support to the Paterson strike. As an officer of John Golden's own United Textile Workers explained, "I do not care if they do belong to the I.W.W.; they are fighting the capitalist class and we ought to be with them."[6] The growing strength of Pennsylvania Socialists inside and outside the AFL, and their willingness to help the IWW organize, augured well for the future.

Despite the referendum against sabotage and the recall of Haywood, Socialist cooperation with the IWW appeared more promising in 1913 than ever before. At the height of the Paterson strike, Alexander Scott, the Socialist editor, celebrated the "tremendous power" of the IWW and the Socialist Party "when united to fight a common enemy. No force is powerful enough to overcome them."[7] Later in the strike another Socialist contrasted the gains that his party was making among workers in Passaic County with its continuing lack of working-class support in neighboring Essex County; he attributed the difference to "the Passaic County Comrades, who placed themselves, their paper and all their resources at the disposal of the struggling proletariat."[8] After the November elections, Quinlan and other Socialists were able to point to the tremendous growth of the party not only in Paterson but in Haledon as proof of the wisdom of participating in the Paterson strike.[9]

Even those Socialists who opposed the IWW and supported the anti-sabotage resolution and the Haywood recall were initially carried beyond their official position by the drama of the strike. On the third day of the strike, the New York *Call*, an organ of anti-IWW opinion, enthusiastically reported on its front page the final tally of the national referendum that completed Haywood's recall. Immediately adjacent was a much larger and even more enthusiastic article announcing the entrance of the Socialists into the IWW-led fight.[10] The irony was not lost on *Solidarity*, which noted that "Killingbeck, secretary, New Jersey, S.P., is compelled to break into an I.W.W. strike on the very day the Haywood recall was announced by the national Socialist Party"—compelled, in *Solidarity's* view, by the IWW's growing success in organizing industrial workers. "Under the circumstance the I.W.W. can afford to ignore the Haywood recall."[11] Haywood himself ignored the recall, insofar as he continued to consider himself a Socialist Party member and continued to maintain that political action at the polls could complement direct action at the point of production.[12] And Flynn, sounding remarkably like Upton Sinclair, chided silk workers in Paterson for having helped elect the "same old" politicians and parties, thereby giving the police a free hand.[13] For their part, Flynn, Haywood, Tresca, Koettgen, and Lessig were "compelled" during the strike to accept their growing dependence on the Socialist haven of Haledon. The practical advantages of cooperation to both organizations outweighed all considerations of doctrinal purity.

In the spring of 1913 no one knew that the Socialist Party and the IWW were on the verge of an irrevocable split. It was only in the last desperate days that Panken and other moderate New York Socialists, who had helped build the bridge to Paterson, began to criticize the IWW's handling of the strike, leading to Flynn's brutal counterattack on them. It was only then that Quinlan began to feel that he had to choose between the IWW and the Socialists. And it was not even then but only after two years of fratricidal warfare that Haywood finally stopped calling the IWW "socialist" and began correcting those who continued to do so.[14] At that point, and only at that point, did the split with the IWW that the Socialist Party had decreed in 1912 become effective in the industrial East.

As Joseph Conlin has argued, the decline of both the Socialists and the IWW stems from the split between them; separately, they were much weaker than when they had been partially connected.[15] Even separately, however, each organization seemed too vital to become reduced, in less than a decade, to the position of a helpless sect. Chapter Eight explained the decline of the IWW in the industrial East as a result of its inability to come to grips with defeat in Paterson. The decline of the Socialist Party has been examined in greatest detail by James Weinstein. Dismissing the IWW as unimportant to American socialism, Weinstein adopts the conventional emphasis on the Russian Revolution as the cause of the splintering of the American Socialist Party in 1919. He notes, however, that the Socialist majority that went Communist in 1919 included many "experienced radicals, with roots in both the Socialist movement and the IWW. They were overcome by the siren call of the Third International, but they retained some consciousness of the relative strength of the IWW and AFL, and they were aware of the difficulties facing a revolutionary movement in the United States."[16] These radicals turned to the Soviet Union because their "roots in the IWW" had gone rotten. For many left-wing Socialists, Paterson was the beginning of their recognition of the weakness of the IWW. Paul Buhle observes that "the result of the Wobblies' failure was central to the whole future of the Socialist Party. So long as the Lawrence strike and the unrest of immigrant workers pointed toward an immediate realignment of class forces, the IWW and pro-IWW members of the Socialist movement could hail the opening of an industrial orientation *within* political Socialism."[17] In other words, left-wing Socialists were overcome by the siren call from abroad because they no longer had faith in the revolutionary movement in America.

The Paterson defeat hurt the Socialist Party by precipitating the mutually destructive split with the IWW and by discouraging left-wing Socialists from the struggle toward an American socialism. Conlin makes a similar point about the IWW itself. The Wobblies who were drawn to Soviet Communism "were chiefly from the eastern wing. The reason for the development is obvious enough—the Communists had accomplished something."[18] An American left that had led a succession of major industrial strikes could have met the Bolsheviks on more equal terms. Indeed, in Seattle, where their prewar history was entirely different, IWW members emerged from wartime repression to participate in the general strike of 1919; in conjunction with other radicals, they creatively borrowed from the Soviets instead of slavishly imitating them.[19]

John Reed and Elizabeth Gurley Flynn, the youngest and most energetic leaders of their respective groups in Paterson, both died in the Soviet Union. So did Bill Haywood. Reed and Flynn had gone there on political visits, as representatives of American Communism, whereas Haywood had gone to avoid prison in the United States. Nonetheless, the Russian deaths of the three Paterson activists—Reed in 1920, Haywood in 1928, and Flynn in 1964—suggest a pattern of flight. Tresca turned back to his native Italy for the focus of his radical activities, America becoming again his place of exile.[20] After Paterson, those who had thrown themselves into the strike began to lose faith in America. In Lawrence the IWW had initiated the different nationalities into America. After the defeat of 1913 the great vision of an international American community receded. For Tresca, Haywood, Flynn, Reed, and many others, the disintegration of that American dream did not begin in 1917 when the United States entered the war, or even in 1914 when war began and the Second International failed to oppose it, but in 1913—at Paterson.

Rose Pastor Stokes had heard the strikers speak for themselves in Paterson at a Pageant rehearsal; after the defeat she tried to speak for them. In a poem she called "Paterson," published in *The Masses* in November, Stokes claimed to express the "bitter hopes" and "bruised hearts" of the silk workers.

> Beware!
> You dream that we are weaving what you will?
> Take care!
> Our fingers do not cease:
> We've starved—and lost; but we are weavers still,
> And Hunger's in the mill![21]

The bruises, the bitterness, and the impotent threat of "Beware" belonged less to the Paterson weavers than to their supporters in New York. Art Shields, the crime reporter, spoke more directly and honestly for these New Yorkers when he acknowledged, much later, that "this defeat was a sad lesson to me. I had been so impressed by the strikers' magnificent solidarity that I thought they were invincible."[22] Young New Yorkers like Shields and Stokes had been moved by solidarity in Haledon and Paterson; the possibility of democratic revolution had seemed very real. The sad lesson for them was that the world was more resistant to change from below than they had imagined.

Stokes and Shields, like many others, would eventually place their hope in Soviet Communism. Back in Paterson two and a half years after the defeat, Reed said to the silk workers: "If the Germans or Japanese should land in this country and invade Paterson, you would be better off if you joined the invaders."[23] Once Flynn had insisted in Paterson that "the IWW represents the ideal spirit of America." In 1916, asked by *The Masses* whether she believed in patriotism, she replied that the rich "owned" America and "I would be ashamed to be patriotic in such a country."[24]

Before 1917, before the Soviet Revolution, many of the most dedicated American radicals had begun to make their choice. For them, the later flight to Russia (a physical flight for some, an emotional flight for many more) was not as decisive as they themselves would try to pretend. Russia was not their first love, nor would it be the first to break their hearts.

EITHER/OR

More than most Socialists, Village writers and artists had given themselves to the strike and the bridge, and were consequently more vulnerable to the disappointment of defeat. In the years after 1913, as the IWW declined and the bridge collapsed, Village radicals confronted a series of devastating choices: either America or Russia, either art or revolution, either the personal or the political. The moment of 1913 had passed, and the sense of connection and convergence gave way to the perception of the necessity for choosing.

Dodge's salon had nurtured the relationships between Wobblies and Villagers during 1913. By late 1914, with the IWW in full decline, Dodge had ended her "evenings"; in 1915, sensitive as always to cultural currents, she turned her back on politics for good. However, in March 1914, seven months after the defeat, New York reporters who pushed their way into Dodge's salon were surprised by what they saw. "Mr. Haywood and others got up and moved to the center of the room, whereupon became visible one of the red I.W.W. banners used last year in the Paterson pageant in Madison Square Garden."[25] Clinging to the symbols of their collaboration with workers—to the pageant, and to Haywood himself—Village intellectuals tried to hang onto the bridge.

The Masses, too, had built the bridge and tried to sustain it. Soon after the end of the strike the magazine received an appeal from silk workers in Paterson. Mired in "the backwash of a strike, the period of dead interest and spent enthusiasm," they asked people to send money for the defense of Haywood, Flynn, Tresca, Quinlan, Lessig, and Boyd. *The Masses* printed this appeal in full, and Eastman added a bitter editorial of his own. After the silk workers' sacrifice, he said, when they "might enjoy the little gain that was made," they were being forced to fight against legal persecution "until the last cent of the wage increase that was won is extracted from them. Meanwhile—Progressivism! Social Reform! New Democracy! Uplift! My God what mockeries!"[26] Unable to mock, Eastman and his friends began to lose their balance, even as they kept the bridge open.

Within a year the bridge itself was cracking. In Provincetown in August 1914, a group of Villagers and Wobblies enacted a parody of their former faith. Reacting to the outbreak of war in Europe, a group that included Eastman, Hapgood, Vorse, and Joe O'Carroll of the IWW went to a meeting called by Boyd, who was out on bail. The purpose of the meeting was to draw up an antiwar message that would somehow be sent to the working classes of the world. That night Boyd tried to telegraph a message to European heads of state; then he appeared at Vorse's house, waving a gun; at dawn, still acting out and still drawing a response, he organized an orgiastic nude bathing party.[27] In Paterson he had been notorious for trying to force a solution; a year later he was now more desperate and hysterical, but he was no longer alone. For the Villagers who had helped build the bridge, the outbreak of war confirmed the lesson of Paterson: despite the best efforts of the left, the world was out of control.

Later in 1914, Vorse and Flynn tried to limit the damage to the bridge. No longer trusting to spontaneity, as Vorse explained, they "carefully prepared" a big meeting to raise money for imprisoned strike leaders. Renting Carnegie Hall for the meeting, Vorse managed to sell boxes to wealthy people, and she and Flynn lined up a typical mix of speakers, including Eastman on Ludlow, Colorado; Giovannitti on Lawrence; and Haywood. But they made two mistakes: they asked Haywood to speak first, and they asked him to speak on Paterson. He "threw the whole meeting into an uproar. Raising his great fist, he shook it at the audience." Early in 1914, speaking on Paterson to New Yorkers, Flynn also had attacked the audience. But whereas she had painstakingly prepared an analysis distributing blame for the defeat, Haywood abandoned his assigned topic and—in "an extemporaneous speech that had bubbled out of his emotion"—threatened to call a general strike if the United States joined the war.[28] Like Flynn, Eastman, and Sanger, Haywood could not discuss Paterson calmly; as a result, he undermined the careful efforts of Vorse and Flynn to use the bridge. The time of buoyant faith and growing solidarity was over, and the time of impotent rage had begun.

By March 1916 the bridge itself had long since collapsed, carrying with it the possibility of artists collaborating with workers, and the editors of *The Masses* felt compelled to choose between art and politics. On behalf of art,

John Sloan led the attack on Eastman's editorial direction; on behalf of socialism, Art Young led the counterattack on Sloan. Having failed to overthrow Eastman, Sloan and three of the other artists resigned. Later, Eastman recognized that "it was a quarrel, essentially between art and propaganda, poetry and practical effort—between the very two interests whose satisfaction within the same covers had made the magazine unique."[29] Conflicts that had once been experienced as creative tensions had by 1916 become destructive divisions between people, and within people. Today we may "understand" these divisions too quickly; we may assume that art and politics cannot mix, that bohemian rebellion and working-class revolution must be enemies. But Sloan and Eastman, who were good friends, appear to have been bewildered by their inability to contain the quarrel. In later years each would be attracted to Soviet Communism, become disillusioned with it, and drift toward mainstream, Cold War politics—with Eastman, now the more political of the two, going much further in both the pro- and anti-Communist directions. Neither would ever again do work that was as exciting as the work each had done when they were together at *The Masses*.[30]

The Communist Party did not create the split on the left between art and politics but, rather, institutionalized it. *The Masses* died in 1917, killed by wartime repression. Its successor, the *Liberator*, remained under Eastman's direction until 1922, when the Communist Party took it over and created two separate groups of associate editors: "political editors," who were mostly Communists; and "art editors," mostly left over from *The Masses* or early *Liberator* days. "The realm of art, presumably less serious, was left for the artists," one of the two new chief editors reported. He recognized that Reed, Eastman, Giovannitti, and others had written for *The Masses* "on the assumption that nothing human was alien to them"; they had written as poets *and* as radicals. "Under the aegis of the Party this tradition was of necessity ended."[31] Those artists in the 1920s who accepted the Communist position on the subordination of art to politics and those who, making the opposite choice, proclaimed art to be an end in itself were equally the victims of the perceived necessity to choose. Whether one looked to Moscow for inspiration or to Paris, the range of options had narrowed.

Some radical intellectuals embraced the choice passionately; others resisted the necessity for choice as best they could. Robert Minor, a talented cartoonist for *The Masses* after 1913, carried the new tendency of artistic self-denial to an extreme. Selflessly serving the party, he did what was asked in every area but one: after 1926 he refused to draw cartoons, despite entreaties from his comrades. As Minor saw it, he could live either as an artist or as a revolutionary.[32] John Dos Passos rejected this either/or. Writing in 1928 in the *New Masses*, which succeeded the *Liberator*, he called for a theater of radicals and of workers, a theater that would "deal with things that mattered to a large and largely workers' audience." Fifteen years after the Pageant, Dos Passos hoped to cut across the boundaries between theater and politics, intellectuals and workers, higher culture and popular culture. "The main difficulty in getting such an organization under way," he acknowledged, "is that the whole drift of American cultural life is against it. . . . It may be that the task is an impossible one."[33] What had become impossible was the shared vision that workers and intellectuals could come together to fight for their freedom.

Reed and Sanger, Haywood and Hapgood, Vorse and Eastman, and even Dodge and Flynn had once been excited by the new currents in personal and political life. In the moment of 1913 the idea of free love and the idea of workers' control had seemed two aspects of a single revolt. Opening themselves to the new currents, Dodge's salon and *The Masses* had made the Village a center of radical hope. Afterward, the survivors, guided by habit more than by hope, carried on.

In 1926, in a Village speakeasy, Flynn and E. E. Cummings debated the alternatives. Flynn was still an activist and not yet a Communist; she was also on the verge of the emotional and physical breakdown that would take her out of politics for a decade. (A clue to her breakdown and to the new cultural climate is provided by her friend Vorse's admiring description of her, also in 1926: "She does not think of herself at all. It's as though she considered Elizabeth Flynn merely as a tool for accomplishing certain pieces of work.") In their argument, Flynn and Cummings shared the assumption that the personal and the political were opposing realms. "Flynn," said Cummings, "what in hell makes you a radical?"

> FLYNN: The world is a lousy place. It's full of poverty, misery, ignorance, war. The mass of people live like hell. We could have a decent world for everybody. Is there anything better than to fight for that?
> CUMMINGS: Flynn, you're a savior, a rabble rouser, a pulpit thumper. You're kidding yourself. Men don't want to be saved. They want to have a good time.
> FLYNN: There are various ways of having a good time. Mine is as good as yours and more useful.
> CUMMINGS: Men want love and liquor.
> FLYNN: Men need security, freedom, creative labor.
> CUMMINGS: Bah! Have a scotch on me.[34]

Missing from the debate, on either side, was a belief that working men and women could save themselves.

The view from the bridge illuminates what was lost when the vision of revolution from below receded. The defeat of the Paterson strike and the decline of the IWW damaged the left in ways from which it has not yet recovered. Hidden beneath the surface of brittle realism affected by Flynn, Cummings, and many others, the damage may be traced in the lives of those individuals—on both the Paterson and New York sides of the bridge—who had the most to lose.

WHAT WAS LOST

Among New Yorkers, Sanger and Reed represent poles of response to the collapse of the strike, the IWW, and the bridge. Sanger had been swept away and transformed by the Lawrence strike, but her experience of Paterson was very different. "I was thoroughly despondent after the Paterson debacle, and had a sickening feeling that there was to be no end; it seemed to me the whole question of strikes for higher wages was based on man's economic need of supporting his family, and that this was a shallow principle upon which to found a new civilization." Before Paterson, Sanger had seen birth control as part of the working-class struggle for socialism. After Paterson, she moved away from radicalism and became a single-issue reformer: "The pageant," she said, "was a fitting conclusion to one period of my life."[35]

Sanger's attack on the conduct of the strike, published in January 1914, did not immediately end her association with the IWW. Her new magazine, the *Rebel Woman*, endorsed the IWW and was in turn circulated through IWW locals. But by the end of 1914, on a trip to England, she was persuaded by Havelock Ellis and others to focus exclusively on the issue of birth control and to drop her emphasis on class struggle. Thereafter, the changes in her associations and ideology accelerated, and by 1917 she had severed her remaining radical connections. Birth control became respectable and triumphed. Sanger triumphed with it. What must be remembered is that this success was conditioned by her "sickening feeling" of defeat in Paterson. Or, as her grandson put it, "It was only when she encountered failure in her I.W.W. work that she was to turn to birth control."[36] In 1918 she would write that "all our problems are the result of overbreeding among the working class"; birth control would solve "our" problems by limiting the number of poor people.[37] Originally, Sanger, Flynn, and the other early advocates had thought of birth control as a way to improve the lives of working women in the present and as a step toward working-class power in the future. Under Sanger's forceful leadership the movement was divorced from the movement for workers' control and became a means of controlling the working class.

Recently, historians have rediscovered the radical possibilities of the early birth control agitation. To Mari Jo Buhle, the decline of that early agitation badly hurt the socialist movement and the women's movement by depriving them of an issue that reached into women's personal lives.[38] Linda Gordon explains that the early advocates "did not want to limit their pregnancies; they wanted to change the world."[39] Meredith Tax emphasizes the role played by the IWW as a bridge between economic struggles and women's needs: "By bringing these two realms together, the IWW added a new dimension to both the labor movement and the movement for women's liberation."[40]

At once socialist and feminist, these perspectives suggest that not only Sanger but America lost something when birth control became respectable. Unlike later birth-control advocates, who were middle-class reformers, the

IWW could speak to immigrants and other workers in terms of their experience and values. Flynn, Haywood, and Sanger had urged Paterson's immigrant women to take direct action to limit the size of their families instead of passively submitting to nature and their husbands. In 1914 Sanger flooded Paterson and other centers of IWW activity with her popular, provocative pamphlet, *Family Limitation*, which offered practical techniques and a class perspective.[41] But the vision of what Flynn called "a different world for men and women" did not survive the decline of the IWW. In Paterson, no working-class organization ever again appealed so deeply to immigrant women or so effectively combined issues of shop control and quality of life. As the larger program of 1913 became fragmented and Sanger's middle-class reformers took possession of birth control, immigrant women were left out. A generation later, in 1936, female silk workers in Paterson moved to reclaim the issue for themselves. They asked a woman from Sanger's American Birth Control League to advise them how to set up a clinic in Paterson. Speaking professionally, the visitor warned them to proceed quietly and avoid publicity. An immigrant woman stood up to disagree, explaining in broken English that the Paterson women wanted publicity, expected opposition, and were prepared to fight, because "we want to reach the women like myself."[42] In 1913 the IWW had reached women like her.

The collapse of the IWW as a bridge between the classes partly shaped the course of Sanger's career. It also shaped Reed's career. But whereas Sanger had helped to build the bridge in Lawrence and to dismantle it after Paterson, Reed was not involved in the Lawrence strike. For him, Paterson was—and remained—the crucial experience. It was in Paterson that he first experienced the possibility of connecting with working people, and it was in Paterson that he helped make that possibility real. Reed never accepted the collapse of the bridge and worked for the rest of his life to recreate it as best he could.

Reed was in Italy with Dodge when the strike was broken. "For God's sake, write and tell me whether the Paterson strike is finished or not," he begged Lippman in September. "No one will write me—and the *Globe*, which we have taken all summer, never said a word about it. I've written everyone to ask—but they pay no attention."[43] This silence was all Reed experienced of the terrible last month of the strike. He, personally, was not defeated at Paterson. What hurt him more were the disastrous decline of the IWW and the narrowed possibilities that were the long-range consequence of that decline.

"I quit my job to work on the Pageant," he explained in 1917, "and when it was all over I went to pieces nervously, and friends took me abroad for the summer. The strike was starved and lost . . . and the leaders, too, broke down under the long strain of the fight. The I.W.W. itself seemed smashed—indeed it has never recovered its old prestige." The collapse of the IWW stunned Reed and deprived him of a sense of purpose: "For six months I did almost nothing." Then he went to Mexico, and with Pancho Villa's rebels "I found myself again." After Paterson, he was able to connect with working-class movements only outside of the United States. In early 1917, after the IWW's decline had begun to seem permanent and after America's entrance into the war, he admitted that "I am not sure any more that the working class is capable of revolution, peaceful or otherwise."[44]

Then came the Soviet Revolution. In Russia as in Mexico, he immersed himself in the movement of workers in revolt, writing the story of his experience and theirs, in accounts that became justly famous. As much as possible in these accounts he followed the method of the Paterson Pageant, allowing the words and actions of working people to speak for themselves. But he was never again able, after Paterson, to connect his own activity with that of workers in such a way that they appeared as co-creators.

Within the United States, Reed became one of the founders of a revolutionary communist party. From the point of view of his biographer Granville Hicks in 1936—a Communist point of view—Reed's life appears as triumphant growth from poetic rebel and political adventurer to mature revolutionary.[45] Robert Rosenstone's recent biography, *The Romantic Revolutionary,* is written from a point of view closer to Reed's own in 1913. Rosenstone takes Reed's bohemian aspirations seriously, his commitment to art *and* politics, to personal *and* social liberation, to playfulness *and* socialism. From this perspective Reed's life appears, from about 1915, as a series of narrowings.[46] He became increasingly famous, admired, respected—and for real accomplishments. He wrote *Ten Days that Shook the World* and saw his political commitments through to the end. Except for his early death, Reed's life was a success story, at least as much as Sanger's. Nonetheless, with the collapse of the bridge from the Village to Paterson, from bohemians to the working class, Reed had to choose not only between different worlds but between different parts of himself. That was his tragedy, and it is a continuing one.

The limits of Reed's and Sanger's careers were set by the IWW's defeat in Paterson. What the IWW represented to Reed, Sanger, and other Village radicals was the possibility of a revolution that was liberating for them as well as for working people. Sooner or later, they had to renounce that possibility. The choices they made are less important, for us, than their need to make a choice, a need imposed on them by the IWW's defeat in Paterson and its loss of vitality in the East.

In Paterson, too, people were eventually forced to choose. When reporter Mel Most tried to interview 1913 survivors and their children for a story in a local paper in 1973, he met with widespread resistance. One neighbor of the Botto family in Haledon "was terrified she would be mentioned in this story."[47] In the popular memory the 1913 strike had become associated with the decline of Paterson, with violence, and with un-American radicalism. The democratic and nonviolent nature of the strike, and the communal support it received from the Workmen's Circle and the Sons of Italy, had been transformed into the opposite, as if a band of outside agitators had terrorized the city. The fact that 9,000 Patersonians joined the IWW union in 1913 had become a taboo topic, especially among their descendants.[48]

Despised as "wops" and "sheenies," the Italians and Jews had marched together in 1913, proudly wearing the American flag in their lapels and red almost everywhere else. Then came World War I, the Soviet Revolution, and the Red Scare, with the accompanying outburst of anti-immigrant feeling and the fatal identification of "radical" with "un-American." In September 1917, as part of a massive attempt to crush the organization nationally, IWW headquarters in Paterson were raided by the federal government. A weaver, arrested in the aftermath and released on bail, was asked what he had done to cause his arrest. "The only thing that I see [is] that I stuck by the members of my class, and was always prepared to get better working conditions."[49] A Paterson girl who was active in Local 152 during and after the war remembers that "if you said IWW, it was the same as if you were saying you were some kind of criminal." The collective loss of memory probably dates from this period. "For years there were many people who would not let you know they had been IWW's. They would deny it simply out of fear."[50] In 1924, emboldened by the national atmosphere of sharpened hostility toward immigrants and radicals, the mayor of Paterson announced that the records of the 1924 strikers were being examined to determine who could be deported as foreign agitators; his leadership was praised by the Ku Klux Klan.[51]

By then, red meant Russian, foreign, un-American. The immigrant silk workers' vision of a cooperative America, an America where different peoples would together come into their own, faded more rapidly than their industry. Once, the IWW had articulated that vision. Weakened by internal dissension after Paterson and smashed by federal repression during the war, the IWW no longer represented an alternative. In the 1919 strike the remnant of the IWW in Paterson hurt the newer and more vital socialist union with anti-intellectual attacks on its leadership.[52] The radical bridge between the classes was gone.

Now, there was only one American dream, the dream of individual success. In Haledon, Mayor Brueckmann had been reelected in 1914 and 1916. As a Socialist and even more as a German, he became suspect during the war. Changing his colors, he ran for mayor as a Progressive in 1925 and 1927, winning the latter race before being finally defeated by a Republican in a contest for tax collector. After that, he retreated into his family and into making money, though in his heart he remained a Socialist.[53]

In 1928 the *New Masses* published two poems by a young Paterson weaver whose mother, father, and grandfather were also weavers. One was called "Paterson":

> O Paterson, my home, my town, Paterson,
> With your Syrians, Polaks, Italians and Jews,
> All hating each other and living apart,
> With your dismal streets and stinking river—
>
> Some of us dreamed once to make you over. . . .

The other poem reached back to the time when that dream was real:

> Gold and green and crimson
> Are the flowers I am weaving
> On the Jacquard looms.
> Beautiful, beautiful!
> They remind me now
> Of a summer meadow in Haledon. . . .[54]

In the Haledon of Pietro Botto and Mayor Brueckmann it had seemed possible for different nationalities to overcome separation and make the world over. Now, the dream was crushed, though people struggled on.

For decades, most aging immigrant weavers and even their children remained class conscious. A picket line was still a picket line, and a scab was still a scab. But separated from their own earlier idealism and vision, they tended to fear and look down on the new immigrants to Paterson.[55] In Haledon the Piedmontese generally became conservative and tried to forget their radical origins. More upwardly mobile, most Jews eventually left Paterson behind and moved into middle-class suburbs; in terms of their parents' hopes in 1913, their private victories were, in part, a social defeat.

Immigrant women may have lost the most. Meredith Tax describes those of Lawrence after 1912:

> As far as we can tell, the women of Lawrence sank back into household obscurity, child-bearing, and endless labor in the mills when the strike was over. They had been able to rise when their whole class rose: in the crisis enough pressure was lifted from the backs of working mothers to give them room to think and move. But when their class went under in defeat, they were the more submerged, for the struggle for equality within the working-class movement could only succeed when the whole class was in motion.[56]

The same was true of the immigrant women of Paterson. In 1913 young Italian and Jewish women had seized the chance to become historical actors. Changed by their participation in the strike, encouraged by Flynn not only to support their men but in many ways to take the lead, they returned to roles that had grown much too small for them.

Hannah Silverman was only seventeen when the strike ended. She was almost certainly blacklisted, and it is not clear how she spent the next nine years, but in 1922 she married a thirty-nine-year-old immigrant Jew who had been living in Boston and was new to Paterson. She became a housewife and had two children. The family struggled economically; in 1935, they moved from Paterson to Brooklyn, where her husband tried to make a living from a candy store. After he went bankrupt, they were dependent on relief for several years. Eventually, her husband acquired a new store in Paterson, and Hannah worked eighteen hours a day in the store and at home. At ease in the working-class neighborhood in which she lived, she voted Democratic. There was little sign of her radical youth except for her continued indifference to religion. Her siblings reflected the class division in the Jewish community. Her older sister married a mill owner who moved his business out of state to escape Paterson's labor movement. Her younger brother was a silk worker who complained in family gatherings about "slave wages" and denounced the bosses. Hannah was always particularly kind to him. Without scope for her own abilities as speaker and organizer, she lived out her life with quiet integrity. Once, in the 1940s, a niece who knew of her past called her the black sheep of the family, and Hannah would not speak to her for months. Though she and her husband frequently made mention of Flynn, Haywood, and the IWW, and he sometimes teased her about her strike activities, she never spoke of her own role in front of the children. When she died in 1960, they had no idea their mother had been a leader of the 1913 strike.[57]

The emergence of young women as leaders of the strike remains perhaps its most telling symbol. The best fictional account of the Paterson strike by a participant tells of a previously unknown young woman who rose to speak for the first time at the daily mass meeting of strikers. Pointing to the need for organizing relief, she explained: "If we're going to run the earth let's begin at home." Seated again, almost embarrassed to have spoken, she listened with excitement as others took up her suggestion. "And the girl who had roused the discussion, her nervousness forgotten now, rose up again and again with so many quick, eager suggestions, that when the first relief station was opened that evening she was one of those placed in charge."[58]

Published in 1915, Ernest Poole's novel *The Harbor*, though set in New York, actually drew heavily on his Paterson experience in 1913.[59] It captures the dynamic of an IWW strike, the emergence of women as rank-and-file leaders, the nonviolence, the overcoming of separations between nationalities, the democratic control of strike activities, the vision of a world run by workers. The narrator, an uncommitted New York writer, is gradually transformed by his strike experience. At an outdoor meeting of 30,000 he listens to speeches by an IWW organizer, by a young radical intellectual, and by the once nervous young woman, and he watches the strikers in the crowd. "It was not their poverty now but their boundless fresh vitality that took hold of me so hard. I had read many radical books of late. . . . But now the crowd through its leaders had laid hold upon the thoughts in these books, had made them its own, and so given them life."[60]

Poole's novel is the only one to capture the excitement of men and women from Paterson and New York who were together changing the world and changing themselves. Virtually all other participant accounts, whether fictional or nonfictional, impose later disappointments and splits on 1913. Poole's advantage was that he was writing in 1913 and 1914, before the complete collapse of the IWW or the bridge. By the time Kemp and Eastman published their Paterson fictions—*More Miles* (1926), and *Venture* (1927)—the hopes of 1913 could not be recreated even by those who had once shared them. Unlike Poole, both had come to assume that intellectuals were unwelcome in a working-class struggle, that poetry had no place in politics. In Eastman's Paterson a wise old Russian revolutionary is on hand to describe the Bolshevik "science of revolution" and to contrast it with the immaturity of the IWW and the intellectuals; in Kemp's Paterson the silk workers appear as a frighteningly inhuman force.[61] Making opposite choices, Eastman and Kemp both read the necessity to choose back into their stories of 1913.

In a similar fashion, the memoirs written by Paterson strike participants invariably flatten out their earlier experience. It is as if some aspects became too painful to remember. Flynn's autobiography portrays her personal life as unimportant in the story of labor's struggle; Dodge's autobiography reinterprets her worldly involvements as mere substitutes for inadequate love relationships.[62] In these accounts and others like them, the hope and playfulness of 1913 have been lost in memory as well.

Writing at the height of the new left of the 1960s, Christopher Lasch argued that "those who wish to change America must now pick up the thread of radical thought and action where it was broken, not in the thirties and forties, but in an even more distant period."[63] In line with Lasch's challenge, one purpose of this book is to go back to Paterson so that we can get over it and move on. The tragedy is not that the moment of 1913 passed; the tragedy is that 1913 became an ending instead of a beginning. The sense of a growing self in a growing world soon gave way to the desperate pursuit of objectivity, of will, intellect, and the correct policy for forcing the world to change—or to the equally desperate cultivation of self, of art-for-art's sake, and of subjectivity bravely asserted against a fixed and hostile world. The Pageant is proof that it was not always so. In telling the story of the strike and the Pageant, this book aims at becoming, itself, a kind of bridge between 1913 and now.

In 1918 in Chicago, reporting on the federal trial that would decimate the IWW, John Reed recalled happier times when the IWW was an American labor movement that sang, and when IWW halls were frequently the intellectual centers of small towns. As the trial began, he noted that the prosecutor tested the fitness of prospective jurors with such questions as "Don't you think that the owner of an industry ought to have more say-so in the management of it than all his employees put together?" and "Can you conceive of a system of society in which the workers own and manage industry themselves?"[64] More than half a century later, reviewing five new studies of the IWW, William Preston returned to the 1918 trial and suggested that even today the Wobblies were not getting a fair hearing; by condemning them to irrelevance, most histories of the Wobblies were re-enacting their earlier suppression.[65] Taking a clue from Preston, we might reverse the prosecutor's test and say that those of us who can conceive of a society managed by working people are best fitted to judge the IWW, the Village intellectuals, and the Paterson silk workers; to learn from what they accomplished together in 1913; and to continue what they began.

NOTES

INTRODUCTION

1. David Montgomery, *Workers' Control in America: Studies in the History of Work, Technology, and Labor Struggles* (Cambridge, 1967), 93–95; Meredith Tax, *The Rising of the Women: Feminist Solidarity and Class Conflict, 1880–1917* (New York, 1980), 14; Paul Buhle, "Italian-American Radicals and Labor in Rhode Island, 1905–1930," *Radical History Review*, no. 17 (Spring 1978), 121, 130–33. (All information in the Introduction not attributed to specific sources is cited in later chapters.)

2. Carrie Golzio, interview with author, Haledon, N.J., 13 June 1983.

3. New York *Times*, 17 March 1912, p. VI. Note that the IWW's claim of a steel strike victory in McKees Rocks, Pennsylvania in 1909 has been contested by recent scholarship. More important, the IWW was not famous or feared in the East in 1909. See John Ingham, "A Strike in the Progressive Era: McKees Rocks, 1909," *Pennsylvania Magazine of History and Biography* 90 (July 1966): 366, 371, 374–75.

4. William D. Haywood, *The General Strike*, 16 March 1911, pamphlet in IWW Collection, Box 162, Archives of Labor History, Wayne State University, Detroit.

5. Quoted in James Montgomery, "The Lawrence Strike and the Literacy Test," *New Review* 1 (22 March 1913): 378. See the summary of conservative reaction in Robert Justin Goldstein, *Political Repression in Modern America: From 1870 to the Present* (Cambridge, Mass., 1978), 82.

6. Leslie H. Marcy and Frederick Sumner Boyd, "One Big Union Wins," *International Socialist Review* 12 (April 1912): 613, 630; "Now Is the Time to Unite," *International Socialist Review* 13 (January 1913): 561. On the eighty articles, see Lillian Symes and Travers Clement, *Rebel America* (New York, 1934), 272. On left-wing Socialists' enthusiasm for Lawrence and post-Lawrence optimism, see Ira Kipnis, *The American Socialist Movement, 1897–1912* (New York, 1952), 392.

7. "After the Battle," *Survey* 38 (6 April 1912): 1–2. See also Paul F. Brissenden, *The I.W.W.: A Study of American Syndicalism*, 2d ed. (1919; New York, 1957), 293.

8. Haywood speech at Cooper Union, quoted in William D. Haywood, *Bill Hay-*

wood's Book: The Autobiography of William D. Haywood (New York, 1929), 255. For the effect of Lawrence on Haywood, see Joseph R. Conlin, *Big Bill Haywood and The Radical Union Movement* (Syracuse, N.Y., 1969), 137.

9. "Is the I.W.W. European?" *Solidarity*, 14 September 1912, p. 2.

10. Elizabeth Gurley Flynn, *The Rebel Girl: An Autobiography* (New York, 1973), 134–35.

11. Justus Ebert, "The I.W.W. in Jersey," *Solidarity*, 13 April 1912, p. 1.

12. On IWW flexibility, see Brissenden, *The I.W.W.*, 260. On IWW membership in 1913, see Louis Levine, "The Development of Syndicalism in America," *Political Science Quarterly* 28 (September 1913): 478; Levine too stresses the IWW's pragmatism (p. 472).

13. Mary Heaton Vorse, *A Footnote to Folly: Reminiscences of Mary Heaton Vorse* (New York, 1935), 13–14; by "us" Vorse meant herself and Joseph O'Brien, whom she married.

14. Margaret Sanger, *Margaret Sanger: An Autobiography* (1938; rpt., New York, 1971), 82; Alexander Campbell Sanger, "Margaret Sanger: The Early Years, 1910–1917" (senior thesis, Princeton University, 1969), 29.

15. "Knowledge and Revolution," *The Masses* 4 (December 1912): 5. *The Masses* moved to the Village in May: "A Word from *The Masses*," New York *Call*, 27 May 1913, p. 6.

16. John Sloan, *John Sloan's New York Scene: From the Diaries, Notes, and Correspondence, 1906–1913*, ed. Bruce St. John (New York, 1965), 627, 633.

17. Sloan, *New York Scene*, 475 (original emphasis). For a similar statement, see Art Young, interview by Grace Potter, in *The Masses* 1 (January 1911): 11. On Sloan's (and Young's) candidacies in 1913, see Don D. Walker, "American Art on the Left, 1911–1950," *Western Humanities Review* 8 (Autumn 1954): 330. In 1912 it was Young who suggested Eastman as new editor for *The Masses* and Sloan who recruited him; Dolly became the business manager: Lloyd Goodrich, *John Sloan* (New York, 1952), 41–43.

18. *The Masses* 4 (July 1913): 6.

19. Mary Heaton Vorse, letter to Arthur M. Colton, 7 February 1913, in Vorse Collection, Box 54, Archives of Labor History.

20. Bernardine Kielty Scherman, *Girl from Fitchburg* (New York, 1964), 63. Kielty was a young unmarried woman living in the Village in 1913. On the central importance of women in both the immigrant and bohemian revolts, see Linda Gordon, *Woman's Body, Woman's Right: A Social History of Birth Control in America* (Middlesex, England, 1977), 197–99.

21. Max Eastman, *Enjoyment of Living* (New York, 1948), 399.

22. Vorse, *Footnote to Folly*, 42.

23. Paterson *Evening News*, 22 May 1913, p. 9; *Solidarity*, 31 May 1913, p. 4.

24. Flynn, *Rebel Girl*, 145.

25. Ibid., 152, 147.

26. *Solidarity*, 2 August 1913, p. 2. On the IWW's sense of universal revolt, see also *Solidarity*, 17 May 1913, p. 4.

27. Arturo Giovannitti, introduction to Emile Pouget, *Sabotage* (Chicago, 1913), 15. For a contemporary sketch of the poetic tendencies of Giovannitti, Flynn, Haywood, and Tresca, see "The Irrespressible I.W.W.," *Current Opinion* 55 (August 1913): 80.

28. Helen Keller, letter to John Macy, 19 November 1912, in *International Social-*

ist Review 13 (January 1913): 518. For her defense of Haywood, see Helen Keller, letter to the editor, New York *Call*, 4 January 1913, reprinted in *Out of the Dark* (New York, 1913), 46–47. See also Van Wyck Brooks, *Helen Keller: Sketch for a Portrait* (New York, 1956), 86.

29. Randolph Bourne, *Youth and Life* (New York, 1913; rpt., Freeport, N.Y., 1967), 308. Some of these essays appeared in magazines one or two years earlier.

30. Walter Lippmann, *A Preface to Politics* (1913; rpt., Ann Arbor, Mich., 1962), 73, 208–10.

31. Upton Sinclair, *American Outpost: A Book of Reminiscences* (Pasadena, Calif., 1932), 261, 185.

32. Hutchins Hapgood, "Art and Unrest," New York *Globe and Commercial Advertiser* (hereafter New York *Globe*), quoted in *Camera Work*, April–July 1913, p. 43.

33. Mabel Dodge Luhan, *Movers and Shakers*, vol. 3 of *Intimate Memories* (New York, 1936), 39.

34. Sanger, *Autobiography*, 68, 75–79.

35. Eastman, *Enjoyment of Living*, 433–34.

36. John Reed, *The Day in Bohemia; Or, Life among the Artists* (New York, 1913), 42. Reed published the poem in January.

CHAPTER ONE

1. Paterson *Evening News*, 25 February 1913, p. 10.

2. *Appeal to Reason*, 16 August 1913, p. 2; Quinlan wrote the article. See also New York *Call*, 26 February 1913, p. 1, and 9 May 1913, p. 1; Paterson *Evening News*, 9 May 1913, p. 11; *Solidarity*, 11 December 1915, p. 4; Elizabeth Gurley Flynn, *The Rebel Girl: An Autobiography* (New York, 1973), 155.

3. The State v. Patrick Quinlan, Passaic Quarter Sessions, Paterson, N.J., stenographic minutes (12, 13, 14 May 1913), 353 (in the possession of E. A. Smyk, Passaic County historian); New York *Call*, 14 May 1913, p. 1. I have combined these two versions, which differ very slightly. On Quinlan's arrest, conviction, and sentencing, see Eugene Tobin, "Direct Action and Conscience: The 1913 Paterson Strike as an Example of the Relationship between Labor Radicals and Liberals," *Labor History* 20 (Winter 1979): 77–78, 81–85. Note that at the pre-strike meeting the previous evening, Quinlan had warned the silk workers not to provoke the police: New York *Call*, 25 February 1913, p. 1.

4. New York *Times*, 26 February 1913, p. 22; New York *Call*, 26 February 1913, p. 1. On Kaplan's later return to Paterson, see Paterson *Evening News*, 3 March 1913, p. 7. On Bimson's first refusal, in 1912, to permit out-of-town speakers, see Philip Newman, "The First I.W.W. Invasion of New Jersey," in *Proceedings of the New Jersey Historical Society* 58 (October 1940): 268–83.

5. New York *Call*, 26 February 1913, p. 1.

6. John Fitch, "The I.W.W., an Outlaw Organization," *Survey* 30 (7 June 1913): 355. For a summary of local testimony blaming the strike on the IWW, see Morris William Garber, "The Silk Industry of Paterson, New Jersey, 1840–1913: Technology and the Origins, Development, and Changes in an Industry" (doctoral diss., Rutgers University, 1968), 254–56.

7. U.S. Commission on Industrial Relations, *Industrial Relations, Final Report*,

vol. 3, 64th Cong., 1st sess., 1916, S. Doc. 415, 2565 (hereafter cited as *Report of C.I.R.*).

8. Ibid., 2554–55. Mayor McBride was not related to Captain McBride.

9. *Solidarity*, 19 April 1913, p. 2. I have eliminated the editorial comments of Frank Pease from the dialogue.

10. Leo Mannheimer, "Darkest New Jersey," *Independent* 74 (29 May 1913): 1190.

11. *Report of C.I.R.*, 2555.

12. Melvyn Dubofsky, *We Shall Be All: A History of the Industrial Workers of the World* (Chicago, 1969), 271, 272, 274; Philip S. Foner, *The Industrial Workers of the World, 1905–1917*, vol. 4 of *History of the Labor Movement in the United States* (New York, 1965), 356, 357; Joseph R. Conlin, *Big Bill Haywood and the Radical Union Movement* (Syracuse, N.Y., 1969), 147; Joyce L. Kornbluh, ed., *Rebel Voices: An I.W.W. Anthology* (Ann Arbor, Mich., 1964), 199; Nancy Fogelson, "They Paved the Streets with Silk: Paterson, New Jersey, Silk Workers, 1913–1924," *New Jersey History* 97 (Autumn 1979): 137.

13. E.g., Dubofsky's chapter on Paterson mentions only one other silk strike, in 1912; Foner gives only one sentence to the history of Paterson's labor movement. See Dubofsky, *We Shall Be All*, 268; Foner, *Industrial Workers of the World*, 353.

14. James D. Osborne, "Italian Immigrants and the Working Class in Paterson: The Strike of 1913 in Ethnic Perspective," in *New Jersey's Ethnic Heritage*, ed. Paul A. Stellhorn (Trenton, N.J., 1978), 20, 30; James D. Osborne, "Industrialization and the Politics of Disorder: Paterson Silk Workers, 1880–1913" (doctoral diss., University of Warwick, England, 1979), 323 and passim. An older work, similarly useful on the continuities in the Paterson labor movement, is James E. Wood, "History of Labor in the Broad-Silk Industry of Paterson, New Jersey, 1879–1940" (doctoral diss., University of California, Berkeley, 1941), 73–315. Note that David J. Goldberg, in a book review of Joseph Conlin, ed., *At the Point of Production: The Local History of the I.W.W.* (Westport, Conn., 1981), in *International Labor and Working Class History*, no. 23 (Spring 1983): 106, criticizes Osborne for ignoring the solidarity of old and new immigrants in IWW Local 152.

15. Ewald Koettgen, "Making Silk," *International Socialist Review*, no. 14 (March 1914): 552–53; Schichiro Matsui, *The History of the Silk Industry in the United States* (New York, 1930), 154; Garber, "The Silk Industry of Paterson," 166, 172; Osborne, "Industrialization and the Politics of Disorder," 43–44.

16. Quoted in Osborne, "Industrialization and the Politics of Disorder," 58.

17. Quoted in ibid., 58; see also 59.

18. Matsui, *History of the Silk Industry*, 154; Garber, "The Silk Industry of Paterson," 185; National Industrial Conference Board, *Hours of Work as Related to Output and Health of Workers: Silk Manufacturing*, Research Report 16 (Boston, 1919), 19. On the persistence of hand-loom weaving into the twentieth century, in America and esp. in Lyons, France, see Richard Dobson Margrave, "The Emigration of Silk Workers from England to the United States of America in the Nineteenth Century, with Special Reference to Coventry, Macclesfield, Paterson, New Jersey, and South Manchester, Connecticut" (doctoral diss., London School of Economics and Political Science, 1981), 319–21; *American Silk Journal* 32 (August 1913): 61–62.

19. William Strange, quoted in Garber, "The Silk Industry of Paterson," 228.

20. Margrave, "The Emigration of Silk Workers," 150–51, 157–58, 162, 234, 187–90.

21. *Silk*, November 1907, quoted in U.S. Senate, *The Silk Industry*, vol. 4 of *Report on Condition of Woman and Child Wage-Earners in the United States*, 61st Cong., 2d sess., 1911, S. Doc. 645, 23.

22. Catalogue advertising at auction the Ashley and Bailey Mills, quoted in *The Masses* 5 (December 1913): 19.

23. James Chittick, *Silk Manufacturing and Its Problems* (New York, 1913), 227.

24. Horace B. Cheney, quoted in National Industrial Conference Board, *Hours of Work*, 20.

25. *Report of C.I.R.*, 2604.

26. Matsui, *History of the Silk Industry*, 204, 206; National Industrial Conference Board, *Hours of Work*, 4; on the delicacy of silk and the relatively large amount of handwork required in weaving it, see also pp. 3–4, 9, 19. On piece work and time work among ribbon weavers, see U.S. Senate, *Silk Industry*, 166.

27. Matsui, *History of the Silk Industry*, 148, 188, 206; *Report of C.I.R.*, 2604, 2589; *Solidarity*, 1 April 1913, p. 1; Wood, "History of Labor in the Broad-Silk Industry," 137; Herbert Gutman, "Class, Status, and Community Power in Nineteenth-Century American Industrial Cities: Paterson, New Jersey—A Case Study," in *Work, Culture, and Society in Industrializing America: Essays in American Working-Class and Social History* (New York, 1976), 242–46. See also Margrave, "The Emigration of Silk Workers," 301–2.

28. Wood, "History of Labor in the Broad-Silk Industry," 156–69; New York *Call*, 3 March 1913, p. 2.

29. Frederick Molt, New York *Call*, 3 March 1913, p. 2.

30. Quoted in Osborne, "Italian Immigrants," 11–12; see also p. 17 on the role of aldermen in late nineteenth-century Paterson. In 1913 an ex-alderman was a striker: The State v. Patrick Quinlan, 497.

31. Florence L. Sanville, "Silk Workers in Pennsylvania and New Jersey," *Survey* 28 (18 May 1912): 312; see also p. 308 on a successful strike in Pennsylvania in 1907. On the growth of the Pennsylvania silk industry, see Margrave, "The Emigration of Silk Workers," 335; National Industrial Conference Board, *Hours of Work*, 2.

32. Charles Homer, quoted in Garber, "The Silk Industry of Paterson," 228. On the reasons for the flight to Pennsylvania, with emphasis on the militance of Paterson's silk weavers, see Margrave, "The Emigration of Silk Workers," 329–30, 333; Osborne, "Industrialization and the Politics of Disorder," 159–63. Note that even the Child Labor Law (1883) of New Jersey—cited by Margrave as one motive for the exodus to Pennsylvania—was partly the result of labor's power in New Jersey.

33. Ruth Tierney, "The Decline of the Silk Industry in Paterson, New Jersey" (master's thesis, Cornell University, 1938), 18.

34. *Solidarity*, 19 April 1913, p. 1; *Report of C.I.R.*, 2427; Koettgen, "Making Silk," 553.

35. *Solidarity*, 19 April 1913, p. 1; *Report of C.I.R.*, 2596.

36. *Report of C.I.R.*, 2492. The same view of progress, in an even more extreme form, was expressed by silk manufacturer Henry Doherty; see *Report of C.I.R.*, 2434. In fact, however, the percentage of women working in the silk industry declined slightly from 1875 to 1910: Delight W. Dodyk, "Women's Work in the Paterson, New Jersey, Silk Industry during the Nineteenth and Early Twentieth Centuries" (paper delivered 31 October 1979 at a conference sponsored by the Great Falls Development Corporation, Paterson), 23.

37. Elizabeth Gurley Flynn, "The Truth about the Paterson Strike," in Joyce L.

Kornbluh, ed., *Rebel Voices: An I.W.W. Anthology* (Ann Arbor, Mich., 1964), 216.

38. *Report of C.I.R.*, 2573. See also Fitch, "The I.W.W.," 361.

39. *Report of C.I.R.*, 2595.

40. Ibid., 2573.

41. Ibid.

42. Alan Dawley, *Class and Community: The Industrial Revolution in Lynn* (Cambridge, Mass., 1976), 228–29.

43. The independence of the skilled ribbon weavers eventually proved troublesome even to Flynn; after the strike she blamed their Socialism and supposed conservatism for the defeat: Flynn, "The Truth about the Paterson Strike," 223–24. Because historians have been overly impressed with Flynn's version and have tended to lump the English-speaking male ribbon weavers together with the small number of loomfixers and twisters and warpers who had belonged to AFL craft unions for years and who opposed the strike, they have missed the key role played by the skilled ribbon weavers. See Osborne, "Industrialization and the Politics of Disorder," 300–2; Dubofsky, *We Shall Be All*, 271, 281; Graham Adams, Jr., *Age of Industrial Violence, 1910–1915: The Activities and Findings of the United States Commission on Industrial Relations* (New York, 1966), 246. Actually, the *least* skilled workers in Paterson's silk industry—the hard-silk workers—were the most difficult of the large groups to involve in the strike. See Paterson *Evening News*, 18 April 1913, p. 1; *American Silk Journal* 32 (May 1913): 31.

44. Ben Stanton, interview with author, Paterson, N.J., 25 September 1981.

45. Matsui, *History of the Silk Industry*, 193; National Industrial Conference Board, *Hours of Work*, 11, 19.

46. *Solidarity*, 3 May 1913, p. 2, "A Paterson Dyers' Story," written by Scully Bell.

47. *Report of C.I.R.*, 2444–45; *Solidarity*, 19 April 1913, p. 4, and 3 May 1913, p. 2; Koettgen, "Making Silk," 554.

48. *Report of C.I.R.*, 2427, 2595, 2604; Matsui, *History of the Silk Industry*, 201–2; *Outlook* 104 (7 June 1913): 285–86. Note that even the weavers of plain broad silks were making about $13 per week in 1913, according to the strikers themselves. See Paterson strike leaflet, *Hungry Babies! Hungry Mothers! Hungry Men!* in the IWW Collection, Box 3, Wagner Archives, Tamiment Library, New York University.

49. Rudolph J. Vecoli, *The People of New Jersey* (Princeton, N.J., 1965), 191; Osborne, "Italian Immigrants," 23; James D. Osborne, "The Paterson Strike of 1913: Immigrant Silk Workers and the I.W.W. Response to the Problem of Stable Unionism" (master's thesis, University of Warwick, 1973), 26; Matsui, *History of the Silk Industry*, 187; U.S. Senate, *Silk Goods Manufacturing and Dyeing*, pt. 5 of *Reports of the Immigration Commission: Immigrants in Industry*, 61st Cong., 2d sess., 1911, S. Doc. 633, 117, 124.

50. Carlo C. Altarelli, "History and Present Conditions of the Italian Colony of Paterson, N.J." (master's thesis, Columbia University, 1911), 20; see also pp. 2–3.

51. Carrie Golzio, interview with author, Haledon, N.J., 13 June 1983.

52. Martin Mooney, "The Industrial Workers of the World and the Immigrants of Paterson and Passaic, New Jersey: 1907–1913" (master's thesis, Seton Hall University, 1969), 36. On the drift away from Catholicism by Italian immigrants in American cities in this period, see Robert F. Foerster, *The Italian Emigration of Our Times* (Cambridge, Mass., 1919), 397–98.

53. Altarelli, "History of the Italian Colony," 21–22. On the Italian population, see U.S. Senate, *Silk Goods Manufacturing*, 19.

54. Altarelli, "History of the Italian Colony," 21, 24–25.

55. Vecoli, *The People of New Jersey*, 191; Altarelli, "History of the Italian Colony," 8.

56. Quoted in Wood, "History of Labor in the Broad-Silk Industry," 158; see also p. 154.

57. Ibid., 181–89; Osborne, "Industrialization and the Politics of Disorder," 230. By 1902 most dyers' helpers were Italian: Vecoli, *The People of New Jersey*, 193–94.

58. Osborne, "Industrialization and the Politics of Disorder," 115, 129–30, 135, 251–53, 276; Margrave, "The Emigration of Silk Workers," 238. The old chief's suspension was temporary; he returned to his post for a few years (until Bimson became permanent chief), but his suspension signaled a new era in police-community relations.

59. Osborne, "Italian Immigrants," 19, 28–29. By 1913 there was also one Jewish policeman, who translated strike speeches made in Yiddish: The State v. Patrick Quinlan, 168–69. Like the two Italians, he was reluctant to make arrests; sometimes he only pretended to club people (thanks to Dave Welsh). On the reluctance of the Italian detectives, see *Report of C.I.R.*, 2568. On the business-sponsored reform of local government in 1907, see Helena Flam, "Democracy in Debt: Credit and Politics in Paterson, N.J., 1890–1930," *Journal of Social History* 18 (Spring 1985): 445–47; James D. Osborne, "Paterson Immigrant Strikers and the War of 1913," in Conlin, *At the Point of Production*, 71; William B. Killingbeck, "Commission Government for Paterson," New York *Call*, 25 April 1913, p. 6. On anti-anarchist hysteria, which had reached a new height in the United States by 1908, see Robert Justin Goldstein, *Political Repression in Modern America: From 1870 to the Present* (Cambridge, Mass., 1978), 78–79.

60. Paterson *Evening News*, 28 April 1913, p. 7. On the Sons of Italy, see E. L. Biagi, *The Purple Aster: A History of the Order, Sons of Italy* (New York, 1961), 15, 19, 131–32; Paterson *Evening News*, 3 March 1913, p. 7.

61. Altarelli, "History of the Italian Colony," 10.

62. Paterson *Evening News*, 19 May 1913, p. 1.

63. See, e.g., *The United States of America vs. William D. Haywood, et al.*, indictment on sections 6, 19, and 37 of the Criminal Code of the United States and section 4 of the Espionage Act of 15 June 1917 (Chicago, n.d.), 11751–52.

64. *Report of C.I.R.*, 2569.

65. Ibid., 2551.

66. Max Eastman, "Profiles: Troublemaker—I," *New Yorker* 10 (15 September 1934): 31. See also Paterson *Evening News*, 23 April 1913, p. 10.

67. Thanks to John Herbst.

68. U.S. Senate, *Silk Goods Manufacturing*, 32–33.

69. Joseph Hoffspiegel, interview with author, Clifton, N.J., 17 December 1981.

70. Golzio interview.

71. Quoted by Nora Levin, *Jewish Socialist Movements, 1871–1917: While Messiah Tarried* (London, 1978), 40. On the Jews, see also Vecoli, *The People of New Jersey*, 193; on the northern Italians, see Osborne, "Industrialization and the Politics of Disorder," 177, 178, and "Italian Immigrants," 26, 28.

72. William Gerstein, interview with author, Wayne, N.J., 24 March 1983 (William is Max's son). On the Workmen's Circle in Paterson, including the quotation on

Socialist traditions, see Joe Krause, untitled manuscript, 3 December 1982 (in Charles Goldman Judaica Library, YM/YWHA, Wayne, N.J.), 2, 4. On the Workman's Circle generally, see Melech Epstein, *Jewish Labor in U.S.A.: An Industrial, Political, and Cultural History of the Jewish Labor Movement* (New York, 1950), 1:299–311.

73. See, e.g., Helen Meadow, interview by Rita Isaacs and Jerry Nathans, 17 and 24 August 1982 (on tape in Charles Goldman Judaica Library). Meadow's father, a weaver in Lodz, became an activist in the Workmen's Circle and a striker in 1913. On Lodz, see Levin, *Jewish Socialist Movements*, 323; I. J. Singer, *The Brothers Ashkenazi*, trans. Joseph Singer (New York, 1980), esp. 207, 252; the novel was originally published in Yiddish in 1937.

74. Abe Greene, interview by Randy Freeman and Bernice Lindenberg, 18 December 1979 (on tape in Charles Goldman Judaica Library), it was the "big shul" that fired Rabbi Mannheimer. See also U.S. Senate, *Silk Goods Manufacturing*, 19; Wood, "History of Labor in the Broad-Silk Industry," 76; Mooney, "The Industrial Workers of the World," 37–38; Edward S. Shapiro, "The Jews of New Jersey," in *The New Jersey Ethnic Experience*, ed. Barbara Cunningham (Union City, N.J., 1977), 306.

75. U.S. Senate, *Silk Goods Manufacturing*, 19.

76. Paterson *Evening News*, 7 July 1913, p. 1.

77. Horace B. Cheney, "What 86 Years Have Taught Us about Selecting Labor," *Monthly Labor Review*, no. 18 (1925): 934, 933.

78. Meadow interview.

79. *Report of C.I.R.*, 2594. For examples of Italian-Jewish alliances in other cities during this period, see David Montgomery, *Workers' Control in America: Studies in the History of Work, Technology, and Labor Struggles* (Cambridge, 1979), 100; John H. M. Laslett, *Labor and the Left: A Study of Socialist and Radical Influences in the American Labor Movement, 1881–1924* (New York, 1970), 109–12.

80. W. L. Kinkead, letter to the editor, *Survey* 30 (31 May 1913): 315.

81. Samuel McCollom, letter to George C. Low, quoted in *Solidarity*, 11 April 1914, p. 1. McCollom was president of the Paterson Silk Manufacturers Association.

82. Quoted by Garber, "The Silk Industry of Paterson," 238. On the struggles over the increase from one loom to two, see Wood, "History of Labor in the Broad-Silk Industry," 141.

83. "Statement of the General Strike Committee," Paterson *Evening News*, 29 May 1913, pp. 1, 9.

84. On the prominent role of the Jewish weavers in the 1912 strike and their citywide relief committee, see *Solidarity*, 29 June 1912, p. 2; *Report of C.I.R.*, 2467. On Local 25 of the Socialist Labor Party, which led the 1912 strike, see also *Solidarity*, 6 April 1912, p. 4.

85. *Report of C.I.R.*, 2429, 2469; National Industrial Conference Board, *Hours of Work*, 14.

86. *Report of C.I.R.*, 2454, 2471. Thomas Morgan, the local AFL leader who had negotiated the introduction of four looms with Doherty, explained the process and the strike in almost identical terms (pp. 2416–17).

87. Mary Brown Sumner, "Strike of New Jersey Silk Workers," *Survey* 30 (19 April 1913): 81. The broad-silk weavers in Paterson averaged nearly $5.00 more per week than broad-silk weavers in Pennsylvania—$11.88 in Paterson in 1911, and only $6.93 in Pennsylvania: Matsui, *History of the Silk Industry*, 201.

88. Tobin, "Direct Action and Conscience," 84. Joseph Mangor was the shop

chairman. On the four-loom weavers in the strike at the Doherty mill in January 1913, see Wood, "History of Labor in the Broad-Silk Industry," 244. For examples of historians who have contrasted the strikers' short-range goals and the IWW's long-range goals, see Dubofsky, *We Shall Be All*, 284–85; Robert H. Zieger, "Robin Hood in the Silk City: The I.W.W. and the Paterson Silk Strike of 1913," *Proceedings of the New Jersey Historical Society* 84 (1966): 182–95.

89. New York *Times*, 26 February 1913, p. 22. The *Times* version of the strike call is highly condensed; for the full version, see *Solidarity*, 1 March 1913, p. 4.

90. "Statement of the General Strike Committee," published in Paterson *Evening News*, 21 April 1913, p. 1; and New York *Call*, 22 April 1913, p. 2.

91. *Solidarity*, 3 May 1913, p. 1. The dye worker was Scully Bell. On 1902, see Wood, "History of Labor in the Broad-Silk Industry," 187–88.

92. Joseph P. McDonell, quoted by Garber, "The Silk Industry of Paterson," 243. On McDonell, see Gutman, "Class, Status, and the Gilded Age Radical: A Reconsideration," in *Work, Culture and Society*, 260–92.

93. Garber, "The Silk Industry of Paterson," 244. Note that the demand for the eight hour day was first raised by Paterson weavers in the 1860s! See Margrave, "The Emigration of Silk Weavers," 203.

94. *Solidarity*, 16 November 1912, p. 2. See also Flynn, "The Truth about the Paterson Strike," 216; Paterson *Evening News*, 26 July 1913, p. 1.

95. New York *Call*, 26 February 1913, p. 1. See also *Report of C.I.R.*, 2573, 2592; Paterson *Evening News*, 21 July 1913, p. 1.

96. The State v. Patrick Quinlan, 38.

97. New York *Call*, 1 March 1913, p. 1.

98. Paterson *Evening News*, 1 March 1913, p. 1. See also Wood, "History of Labor in the Broad-Silk Industry," 245.

99. New York *Call*, 5 March 1913, p. 1; Paterson *Evening News*, 13 March 1913, p. 10, and 28 April 1913, p. 7; Garber, "The Silk Industry of Paterson," 259.

100. New York *Times*, 26 February 1913, p. 22.

101. New York *Call*, 27 February 1913, pp. 1–2.

102. Paterson *Evening News*, 27 February 1913, p. 12; New York *Call*, 28 February 1913, p. 1.

103. *Report of C.I.R.*, 2523; New York *Call*, 1 March 1913, p. 1. Passaic County Socialists were attracted to the IWW after becoming disillusioned with Socialist Labor Party management of the 1912 Paterson and Passaic strikes. See *Solidarity*, 20 April 1912, p. 3, and 10 May 1912, p. 4; Michael H. Ebner, "The Passaic Strike of 1912 and the Two I.W.W.'s," *Labor History* 11 (Autumn 1970), 452–66.

104. New York *Call*, 1 March 1913, p. 1; Paterson *Evening News*, 12 March 1913, p. 9. See also *C.I.R.*, 2524.

105. New York *Call*, 19 March 1913, p. 2. See also *Solidarity*, 19 April 1913, p. 1.

106. New York *Call*, 4 March 1913, p. 2. On Bimson's surrender, see also *Solidarity*, 15 March 1913, p. 1.

107. *Report of C.I.R.*, 2573. On the meetings of the ribbon weavers that resulted in their decision to strike, see Paterson *Evening News*, 3 March 1913, p. 7, and 5 March 1913, p. 9; New York *Call*, 5 March 1913, p. 1.

108. *Solidarity*, 15 March 1913, p. 4.

109. New York *Call*, 5 March 1913, p. 6. See also Frederick Sumner Boyd, "The

General Strike in the Silk Industry," in *The Pageant of the Paterson Strike*, ed. Brooks McNamara (New York, 1913), 6; John Black, "Paterson's Chief of Police—He Favors Strikes," New York *Call*, 11 March 1913, p. 6.

110. Paterson *Evening News*, 26 April 1913, p. 9. Also *Report of C.I.R.*, 2453, 2466, 2469, 2470; William D. Haywood, "The Rip in the Silk Industry," *International Socialist Review* 13 (May 1913): 784. During the strike Lessig would sometimes speak in English and then in German. See, e.g., Paterson *Evening News*, 12 July 1913, p. 1.

111. Art Shields, *My Shaping-up Years: The Early Life of Labor's Great Reporter* (New York, 1983), 162. See also *Report of C.I.R.*, 2455; *Solidarity*, 13 April 1912, p. 1.

112. Paterson *Evening News*, 29 July 1913, p. 1.

113. *Solidarity*, 18 January 1913, p. 4.

114. Patrick Quinlan, "The Paterson Strike and After," *New Review* 2 (January 1914): 287; *Solidarity*, 8 March 1913, p. 4, and 15 March 1913, p. 11; Wood, "History of Labor in the Broad-Silk Industry," 244. On the makeup of the Central Strike Committee, see Flynn, "The Truth about the Paterson Strike," 216.

115. *Report of C.I.R.*, 2598, and on Zuersher, pp. 2596, 2602, 2604; Garber, "The Silk Industry of Paterson," 255 n.57.

116. *Solidarity*, 19 April 1913, p. 1.

117. Paterson *Evening News*, 8 March 1913, p. 9. Haywood left on 12 March, returning to Paterson on March 17; see ibid., 11 March 1913, p. 9, and 12 March 1913, p. 1; New York *Call*, 18 March 1913, p. 1; Peter Carlson, *Roughneck: The Life and Times of Big Bill Haywood* (New York, 1983), 201, 204, 205. On the Akron strike, which lasted from 11 February to 25 March 1913, see Roy T. Wortman, "The I.W.W. and the Akron Rubber Strike of 1913," in Conlin, *At the Point of Production*, 49–60.

CHAPTER TWO

1. *Solidarity*, 8 March 1913, p. 4. The article was written on February 28.

2. New York *Call*, 5 March 1913, p. 1.

3. Paterson *Evening News*, 14 March 1913, p. 15.

4. *Solidarity*, 22 March 1913, p. 1. On the hard-silk workers, loomfixers and twisters, and mill-supply workers, see Paterson *Evening News*, 13 March 1913, p. 7; 5 March 1913, p. 9; 6 March 1913, p. 12; 14 March 1913, p. 15. On the numbers at the end of the second week, see Paterson *Evening News*, 8 March 1913, p. 1.

5. *Solidarity*, 8 March 1913, p. 4.

6. Franklin Allen, quoted in James D. Osborne, "Industrialization and the Politics of Disorder: Paterson Silk Workers, 1880–1913" (doctoral diss., University of Warwick, 1979), 163.

7. *Proceedings of the Eighth I.W.W. Convention*, September 15–29, 1913, stenographic report (Cleveland, n.d.), 81.

8. Elizabeth Gurley Flynn, "The Truth about the Paterson Strike," in Joyce L. Kornbluh, ed., *Rebel Voices: An I.W.W. Anthology* (Ann Arbor, Mich., 1964), 216.

9. New York *Call*, 6 March 1913, p. 2; Paterson *Evening News*, 10 March 1913, p. 1.

10. Robert J. Wheeler, "The Allentown Silk Dyers' Strike," *International Socialist Review* 13 (April 1913): 820–21.

11. Patrick M. Lynch, "Pennsylvania Anthracite: A Forgotten IWW Venture, 1906–1916" (master's thesis, Bloomsburg State College, Pa., 1974), 110–31, 139;

Proceedings of the Eighth I.W.W. Convention, 38–39. On Hazleton, see also New York *Call*, 29 March 1913, p. 6; *Solidarity*, 1 March 1913, p. 4, and 19 April 1913, p. 3; Paterson *Evening News*, 8 April 1913, p. 9, and 21 April 1913, p. 1.

12. James D. Osborne, "The Paterson Strike of 1913: Immigrant Silk Workers and the I.W.W. Response to the Problem of Stable Unionism" (master's thesis, University of Warwick, England, 1973), 76–81. On the strikers' limited success in Pennsylvania, see Paterson *Evening News*, 14 March 1973, p. 1, and 4 June 1913, p. 1; New York *Call*, 6 March 1913, p. 2; *American Silk Journal* 32 (May 1913): 31, and 32 (April 1913): 43. On the negative effect on silk production in Pennsylvania of the Paterson dyers' strike, see *American Silk Journal* 32 (May 1913): 31, and 32 (October 1913): 43; *New Review* 1 (June 1913): 545. On the ability of manufacturers to move their mills out of Paterson to Pennsylvania during the strike, see Paterson *Evening News*, 19 March 1913, p. 12; 26 April 1913, p. 9; 5 May 1913, p. 10; also *Solidarity*, 11 April 1914, p. 1; Joseph Hoffspiegel, interview with author, Clifton, N.J., 17 December 1981.

13. New York *Call*, 12 March 1913, p. 2; 18 March 1913, p. 1; 22 March 1913, p. 2; 27 March 1913, p. 3; 1 April 1913, p. 2; also Paterson *Evening News*, 14 March 1913, p. 15; 31 March 1913, p. 9; 9 April 1913, p. 1; *Solidarity*, 29 March 1913, p. 1; *Proceedings of the Eighth I.W.W. Convention*, 39; Frederick Sumner Boyd, "The General Strike in the Silk Industry," *The Pageant of the Paterson Strike*, ed. Brooks McNamara (New York, 1913), 8.

14. New York *Call*, 20 March 1913, p. 1; 27 March 1913, p. 3; 3 May 1913, p. 2; 5 May 1913, p. 1; also Paterson *Evening News*, 6 March 1913, p. 12; *Solidarity*, 29 March 1913, p. 1; 10 May 1913, p. 1; 31 May 1913, p. 4.

15. Paterson *Evening News*, 25 April 1913, p. 13; 27 May 1913, p. 2; 14 June 1913, p. 1; also *Solidarity*, 10 May 1913, p. 1.

16. William D. Haywood, "The Rip in the Silk Industry," *International Socialist Review* 13 (May 1913): 783–84.

17. Boyd, "The General Strike in the Silk Industry," 3.

18. New York *Call*, 14 March 1913, p. 1, and 8 March 1913, p. 1; *Solidarity*, 15 March 1913, p. 4; Paterson *Evening News*, 14 March 1913, p. 15; 14 March 1913, p. 12; 21 March 1913, p. 18.

19. New York *Call*, 14 March 1913, p. 1.

20. *Solidarity*, 15 March 1913, p. 4; Paterson *Evening News*, 3 March 1913, p. 7; New York *Call*, 5 March 1913, p. 1; New York *Times*, 11 March 1913, p. 22.

21. New York *Call*, 13 March 1913, p. 1; 14 March 1913, p. 4; 15 March 1913, p. 4.

22. Paterson *Evening News*, 11 March 1913, p. 9.

23. Bertold Brecht, "Thoughts concerning the Duration of Exile," in *Selected Poems*, trans. H. R. Hays (New York, 1947), 167.

24. New York *Call*, 4 March 1913, p. 2; 5 March 1913, p. 1; 13 March 1913, p. 1; also letter of Wilbur Dutchess to the *Sunday Record* (New Jersey), 31 January 1982. By the second month, with sixty "special detectives" added to Bimson's force to work nights, police officers no longer had to be on duty around the clock: *Report of C.I.R.*, 2558, 2664.

25. Paterson *Evening News*, 18 March 1913, pp. 1, 9.

26. *Proceedings of the Eighth I.W.W. Convention*, 36; *Solidarity*, 7 June 1913, p. 4; Paterson *Evening News*, 21 April 1913, p. 10; Kornbluh, *Rebel Voices*, 199–200; F. G. R. Gordon, "A Labor Man's Story of the Paterson Strike," *National Civic Feder-*

ation Review 4 (1 December 1913): 16; Rose Villano, interview with author, Paterson, N.J., 25 September 1985. On the restaurants for single men, see Dominic Mignone, in *Solidarity Forever: An Oral History of the IWW*, ed. Stewart Bird, Dan Georgakas, and Deborah Shaffer (Chicago, 1985), 82.

27. Paterson *Evening News*, 4 April 1913, p. 9; New York *Call*, 19 March 1913, p. 3; Scott Exhibit, No. 1, in *Report of C.I.R.*, 263; Helen Meadow, interview by Rita Isaacs and Jerry Nathans, 24 August 1982 (on tape in Charles Goldman Judaica Library, YM/YWHA, Wayne, N.J.); Joe Krause, untitled manuscript, 3 December 1982 (Charles Goldman Judaica Library), 7; William Gerstein, interview with author, Wayne, N.J., 24 March 1983.

28. Paterson *Evening News*, 31 March 1913, p. 9; 9 April 1913, p. 9; 18 April 1913, p. 11; 21 April 1913, p. 10; 25 April 1913, p. 13; 29 April 1913, p. 10; also New York *Call*, 24 June 1913, p. 4; Mel Most, "The 1913 Silk Strike Terror: The Hoax That Killed Silk City," *Sunday Record Magazine*, 30 September 1973, p. 12; Carrie Golzio, interview with author, Haledon, N.J., 13 June 1983; *Solidarity*, 21 June 1913, p. 1; Mignone, in Bird et al., *Solidarity Forever*, 82. Purity Cooperative gave a total of $750 in cash during the first three months: Paterson *Evening News*, 2 June 1913, p. 9.

29. See, e.g., New York *Call*, 28 April 1913, p. 2.

30. Paterson *Evening News*, 7 March 1913, p. 12, and 8 July 1913, p. 5; New York *Call*, 7 March 1913, p. 1, and 18 March 1913, p. 1; Gregory Mason, "Industrial War in Paterson," *Outlook* 104 (7 June 1913): 287; James D. Osborne, "Italian Immigrants and the Working Class in Paterson: The Strike of 1913 in Ethnic Perspective," in *New Jersey's Ethnic Heritage*, ed. Paul A. Stellhorn (Trenton, N.J., 1978), 28; Osborne, "Industrialization and the Politics of Disorder," 208; New York *Globe*, 24 May 1913, p. 2; *Report of C.I.R.*, 2631; Flynn, "The Truth about the Paterson Strike," 221.

31. Joseph Hoffspiegel, interview with author, Clifton, N.J., 17 December 1981. See also *Solidarity*, 31 May 1913, p. 1; *Proceedings of the Eighth I.W.W. Convention*, 39.

32. Paterson *Evening News*, 11 March 1913, p. 10; 18 March 1913, pp. 3, 10; 8 April 1913, p. 1; also *Solidarity*, 7 June 1913, p. 4; Kornbluh, *Rebel Voices*, 200; Sophie Cohen, interview with author, Youngsville, N.Y., 27 December 1981; Osborne, "Italian Immigrants," 16; Osborne, "Industrialization and the Politics of Disorder," 296; New York *Globe*, 4 June 1913, p. 4.

33. Paterson *Evening News*, 19 March 1913, p. 12; 1 April 1913, p. 11; 2 April 1913, p. 1; 25 April 1913, p. 13; 26 April 1913, p. 9; 3 June 1913, p. 1; 12 June 1913, p. 1; also *Report of C.I.R.*, 2446, 2458; Hoffspiegel interview.

34. Paterson *Evening News*, 31 March 1913, p. 9; see also 19 March 1913, p. 10.

35. Ibid., 25 April 1913, p. 13 and 9 June 1913, p. 1; New York *Call*, 10 June 1913, p. 1.

36. Minnie Keller, interview with author, Paterson, N.J., 18 June 1982.

37. Alexander Scott, "What the Reds Are Doing in Paterson," *International Socialist Review* 13 (June 1913): 854.

38. But note that in the 1912 strike, too, Bimson had ordered the mass arrest of pickets: Philip Newman, "The First I.W.W. Invasion of New Jersey," *Proceedings of the New Jersey Historical Society* 58 (October 1940): 279.

39. *Proceedings of the Eighth I.W.W. Convention*, 39. See also Villano interview.

40. Testimony of Thomas Morgan, *Report of C.I.R.*, 2421; see also pp. 2462, 2541; Scott, "What the Reds Are Doing in Paterson," 854; Osborne, "Italian Immigrants," 18–19; Villano interview.

41. Villano interview.

42. William D. Haywood, "On the Paterson Picket Line," *International Socialist Review* 13 (June 1913): 848.

43. John Reed, "Sheriff Radcliff's Hotel: What One Man Saw in a County Jail," *Metropolitan* 38 (September 1913), 14. See also Patrick Quinlan, "A Modern Bastile," *Appeal to Reason*, 26 August 1913, p. 2; Adolph Lessig, "A Poet in Jail," *Solidarity*, 19 April 1913, p. 3; *Report of C.I.R.*, 2527, 2528; New York *Call*, 23 May 1913, p. 1; Haywood, "On the Paterson Picket Line," 848.

44. *Proceedings of the Eighth I.W.W. Convention*, 39.

45. On the restraint of the pickets, see Paterson *Evening News*, 27 May 1913; *Report of C.I.R.*, 2420; New York *Call*, 5 May 1913, p. 1; John Fitch, "The I.W.W., an Outlaw Organization," *Survey* 30 (7 June 1913): 358. On the restraint of the police, see *Report of C.I.R.*, 2421, 2543, 2594; Osborne, "Italian Immigrants," 29–30; Paterson *Evening News*, 5 May 1913, p. 9. On the prejudice of the police toward the Italian and Jewish strikers, see *Report of C.I.R.*, 2463, 2565, 2594; and Osborne, "Industrialization and the Politics of Disorder," 312–13.

46. See, e.g., New York *Call*, 6 March 1913, p. 2, and 17 May 1913, p. 2; Paterson *Evening News*, 17 April 1913, p. 9; 18 April 1913, p. 11; 11 June 1913, p. 1; also Newark *News*, 26 April 1913; Alfred Cappio, "Paterson Silk Strike of 1913," July 1975 (manuscript in Paterson Public Library), 8; Golzio interview; *Report of C.I.R.*, 2420, 2594; Mignone, in Bird et al., *Solidarity Forever*, 82–83.

47. Most, "The 1913 Silk Strike Terror," 7, 9, and passim. Recently, James Osborne has revived the notion of the violence of the strikers. Osborne's thesis is that they relied heavily on tactics of disorder because they were not well organized. In support, Osborne lumps jeers and hoots together with stones and bombs ("Italian Immigrants," 21) and uncritically accepts the word of Prosecutor Dunn and the biased local press on supposed strike violence—including attempts to derail locomotives, though children doing it for a lark were later caught. Osborne rejects the testimony of manufacturers that silk workers were "afraid of being called scabs," asserting without evidence that violence was more effective in preventing strikebreaking; he attributes the universal testimony of outside observers on the peacefulness of the strikers to tricky IWW publicity, overlooking the fact that many observers (e.g., Gregory Mason, Rabbi Leo Mannheimer, John Fitch) knew the local scene too well to be fooled by publicity ("Industrialization and the Politics of Disorder," 285, 302, 329–30).

48. New York *Call*, 26 February 1913, p. 1; Paterson *Evening News*, 28 March 1913, p. 11, and 8 May 1913, p. 1; Flynn, "The Truth about the Paterson Strike," 218.

49. *Report of C.I.R.*, 2459, 2458.

50. Flynn, "The Truth about the Paterson Strike," 217.

51. New York *Call*, 31 March 1913, p. 1; 1 April 1913, p. 2; 4 April 1913, p. 1; 7 April 1913, p. 1; also Paterson *Evening News*, 31 March 1913, p. 9; 4 April 1913, p. 1; 5 April 1913, pp. 1, 7; 7 April 1913, p. 1; also New York *Globe*, 2 April 1913, p. 10; Phillips Russell, "The Arrest of Haywood and Lessig," *International Socialist Review* 13 (May 1913): 789–92.

52. Paterson *Evening News*, 26 April 1913, p. 9; Newark *News*, 26 April 1913.

53. Patrick Quinlan, "Silk, Starvation, and Solidarity," *Appeal to Reason*, 16 August 1913, p. 2.

54. *Solidarity*, 13 April 1912, p. 1.

55. Paterson *Evening News*, 19 March 1913, p. 12; 1 April 1913, p. 11; 4 April 1913, p. 1; 14 March 1913, p. 15; also The State v. Patrick Quinlan, Passaic Quarter

Sessions, Paterson, N.J. stenographic minutes (12, 13, 14 May 1913), 229, 306, 336; New York *Call*, 26 March 1913, p. 2.

56. Paterson *Evening News*, 14 March 1913, p. 15; 19 March 1913, p. 12; 4 April 1913, p. 1; also New York *Call*, 5 April 1913, p. 1.

57. *Report of C.I.R.*, 2598; see also 2602.

58. Paterson *Evening News*, 10 March 1913, p. 7.

59. Philip S. Foner, *Women and the American Labor Movement: From Colonial Times to the Eve of World War I* (New York, 1979), 404.

60. Elizabeth Gurley Flynn, *The Rebel Girl: An Autobiography* (New York, 1973), 62, 64, 82–83, 131; Paterson *Evening News*, 10 March 1913, p. 7, and 22 May 1913, p. 5; The State v. Patrick Quinlan, 331; Flynn, *Rebel Girl*, 83; Rosalyn Fraad Baxandall, "Elizabeth Gurley Flynn: The Early Years," *Radical America* 9, no. 1 (1975): 102; New York *Call*, 10 March 1913.

61. Paterson *Evening News*, 18 March 1913, p. 9, and 13 March 1913, p. 10; see also 26 April 1913, p. 9.

62. Ibid., 11 March 1913, p. 1. See also Flynn, *Rebel Girl*, 155.

63. Paterson *Evening News*, 13 March 1913, p. 10.

64. Ibid., 19 March 1913, p. 12.

65. André Tridon, "Haywood," *New Review* 1 (May 1913): 504. See also Paterson *Evening News*, 28 March 1913, p. 11. Haywood had use of only one eye, as a result of a childhood accident; hence the reference to Cyclops.

66. Paterson *Evening News*, 9 May 1913, p. 1; see also 28 April 1913, p. 7.

67. *Solidarity*, 31 May 1913, p. 1.

68. On the Pageant in Madison Square Garden, see Chapter Six.

69. *Solidarity*, 31 May 1913, p. 1. See also *Solidarity*, 29 March 1913, p. 1; New York *Call*, 18 March 1913, p. 1.

70. Cohen interview.

71. New York *Call*, 10 March 1913, p. 1. On the IWW's tradition of using songs, see Gibbs Smith, *Joe Hill* (Salt Lake City, Utah, 1969), 18–19, 23–24.

72. Cohen interview.

73. Paterson *Evening News*, 5 April 1913, p. 1; see also 22 March 1913, p. 7.

74. John Reed, "War in Paterson," in *Echoes of Revolt: The Masses, 1911–1917*, ed. William L. O'Neill (Chicago, 1966), 146.

75. Cohen interview.

76. Paterson *Evening News*, 24 March 1913, p. 1.

77. Ibid., 11 March 1913, p. 10.

78. Ibid., 17 April 1913, p. 9.

79. *Solidarity*, 31 May 1913, p. 1. On the number of arrests, see *Report of C.I.R.*, 2572, 2595.

80. Paterson *Evening News*, 4 April 1913, p. 9; New York *Call*, 5 April 1913, p. 1.

81. *Report of C.I.R.*, 2591–92.

82. Testimony of Moses Strauss, *Report of C.I.R.*, 2492, 2489.

83. Paterson *Evening News*, 18 March 1913, p. 1, and 12 June 1913, p. 7. Note that in a 1901 ribbon weavers' strike, many women at the Dale mill were strikebreakers: Delight W. Dodyk, "Women's Work in the Paterson Silk Mills: A Study in Women's Industrial Experience in the Early Twentieth Century," in *Women in New Jersey History*, ed. Mary R. Murrin (Trenton, N.J., 1985), 19.

84. Florence Lucas Sanville, "Women in the Pennsylvania Silk Mills," *Harper's Monthly Magazine* 120 (April 1910): 661; Florence L. Sanville, "Silk Workers in Pennsylvania and New Jersey," *Survey* 28 (18 May 1912): 307–12; Schichiro Matsui, *The History of the Silk Industry in the United States* (New York, 1930), 202; Paterson *Evening News*, 1 April 1913, p. 10; *American Silk Journal* 32 (April 1913): 59; Dodyk, "Women's Work in the Paterson Silk Mills," 12, 16; U.S. Senate, *The Silk Industry*, vol. 4 of *Report of Condition of Woman and Child Wage-Earners in the United States*, 61st Cong., 2d sess., 1911, S. Doc. 645, 49, 59, and table 29, 574–79.

85. William D. Haywood, *Bill Haywood's Book: The Autobiography of William D. Haywood* (New York, 1929), 265. See also letter from Wilbur Dutchess to *The Record*.

86. Haywood, "On the Paterson Picket Line," 850–51.

87. Golzio interview.

88. Adele Giardino, interview by Robert Kirkman, Haledon, N.J., 24 March 1981.

89. The State v. Patrick Quinlan, 276.

90. Elizabeth Gurley Flynn, "Contract Slavery in the Paterson Silk Mills," in McNamara, *Pageant of the Paterson Strike*, 29.

91 Villano interview.

92. Paterson *Evening News*, 17 April 1913, p. 9.

93. Ibid., 18 March 1913, p. 9.

94. Ibid., 26 April 1913, p. 9; New York *Call*, 26 April 1913, p. 1, and 4 June 1913, p. 1.

95. New York *Call*, 22 May 1913, p. 3; Paterson *Evening News*, 21 May 1913, p. 11; *Solidarity*, 31 May 1913, p. 4; New York *Times*, 22 May 1913, p. 4.

96. New York *Call*, 23 May 1913, p. 3.

97. Paterson *Evening News*, 23 May 1913, p. 1; *Report of C.I.R.*, 2533; New York *Call*, 2 June 1913, p. 1, and 4 June 1913, p. 2.

98. New York *Call*, 5 June 1913, p. 1, and 6 June 1913, p. 1.

99. Paterson *Evening News*, 6 June 1913, and 5 June 1913, p. 7; New York *Call*, 6 June 1913, p. 1; *Report of C.I.R.*, 2526, 2533; Paterson *Evening News*, 7 June 1913; Elizabeth Gurley Flynn, "The I.W.W. Call to Women," *Solidarity*, 31 July 1915, p. 9.

100. Giardino interview. As the daughter of Pietro Botto, whose house was used for the meetings in Haledon, Giardino had frequent opportunities to meet Flynn informally.

101. Foner, *Women and the American Labor Movement*, 450 (this song had been popular in Lawrence, too: Kornbluh, *Rebel Voices*, 180). On Flynn's popularity with young women, see, e.g., Paterson *Evening News*, 8 April 1913, p. 9. On Haywood's participation, see *Report of C.I.R.*, 2455.

102. Letter from "a silk worker" to the editor, Paterson *Evening News*, 22 April 1913, p. 5. See also the slightly fictionalized first-person account by Mathilda Rabinowitz Robbins, "Maida Lynn" (manuscript in M. Robbins Collection, Box 1, Archives of Labor History, Wayne State University, Detroit), 1–2; Baxandall, "Elizabeth Gurley Flynn," 104–5; Sophie Cohen, interview by Deborah Shaffer and Stewart Bird, 17 December 1977 (typescript, Program on Women and Work, University of Michigan/ Wayne State University), pts. 1, 7.

103. Paterson *Evening News*, 6 March 1913, p. 12, and 7 March 1913, p. 12; New York *Call*, 6 March 1913, p. 2.

104. See, e.g., New York *Call*, 4 March 1913, p. 2; Paterson *Evening News*, 5 March 1913, p. 9.

105. Paterson *Evening News*, 11 March 1913, p. 9. (The New York *Call*, 11 March 1913, p. 1, said Helvetia Hall.)

106. The State v. Patrick Quinlan, 478. On the Tuesday meetings, see, e.g., Paterson *Evening News*, 31 March 1913 p. 9; 23 April 1913, p. 10; 7 May 1913, p. 1. Occasionally, women's meetings were held on other week nights.

107. Flynn, *Rebel Girl*, 53.

108. Irma Lombardi, in Bird et al., *Solidarity Forever*, 71; Newark *News*, 31 March 1909; Flynn, *Rebel Girl*, 165–66.

109. Quoted in Meredith Tax, *The Rising of the Woman: Feminist Solidarity and Class Conflict, 1880–1917* (New York, 1980), 155. See also Mari Jo Buhle, *Women and American Socialism, 1870–1920* (Urbana, Ill., 1981), 202; and Foner, *Women and the American Labor Movement*, 404–7. Within IWW locals—perhaps even within the Paterson local—Flynn tried to help women become officers. See Elizabeth Gurley Flynn, "Problems in Organizing Women," *Solidarity*, 15 July 1916, p. 3.

110. Paterson *Evening News*, 9 April 1913, p. 1.

111. Ibid., 22 April 1913, p. 10, and 23 April 1913, p. 10.

112. Paterson *Evening News*, 11 April 1913, p. 10; 28 April 1913, p. 7; 13 May 1913, p. 10; also Flynn, "Contract Slavery in the Paterson Mills," 30; Tax, *The Rising of the Women*, 162.

113. Flynn, "The I.W.W. Call to Women," 9.

114. Paterson *Evening News*, 5 March 1913, p. 9. The traditional male leadership in Paterson seems to have monopolized the twenty-member Executive Committee during the strike: see Dodyk, "Women's Work in the Paterson Silk Mills," 24.

115. Flynn, *Rebel Girl*, 166. On the date of the meeting, see New York *Call*, 18 March 1913, p. 1; Paterson *Evening News*, 18 March 1913, p. 9. In 1923 Tresca was arrested for disseminating birth control information in his Italian-language newspaper, *Il Martello*: American Civil Liberties Union, *Foreign Dictators of American Rights: The Tresca and Karolyi Cases* (New York, 1925), 4–6. Note that in 1913 Haywood probably said "family limitation" rather than "birth control," since the latter phrase did not come into usage until Margaret Sanger coined it in 1915. See Linda Gordon, *Woman's Body, Woman's Right: A Social History of Birth Control in America* (Middlesex, England, 1977), 206, 220.

116. Haywood, "On the Paterson Picket Line," 850.

117. Tax, *The Rising of the Women*, 287. On birth control and contradictions in the IWW's attitude toward women, see also pp. 126–34, 160–63; Foner, *Women and the American Labor Movement*, 398–99, 402, 406–7, 457. On the general recognition within the IWW of the militance of women in Lawrence and in the garment strikes, see *Women and the American Labor Movement*, 438; *Solidarity*, 15 March 1913, p. 2.

118. Quoted in *The Masses* 4 (June 1913): 5.

119. Flynn, "Contract Slavery in the Paterson Mills," 29–30; "I Make Cheap Silk," ed. Inis Weed and Louise Carey, *The Masses* 5 (November 1913): 7; *Solidarity*, 22 March 1913, p. 1; New York *Times*, 4 April 1913, p. 10; Osborne, "Industrialization and the Politics of Disorder," 69.

120. Cappio, *Paterson Silk Strike*, 8.

121. Flynn, "Contract Slavery in the Paterson Mills," 29.

122. Ibid.

123. Emilia Perrone, interview by Robert Kirkman, Haledon, N.J., 11 May 1981; Paterson *Evening News*, 18 March 1977, p. 10. On child labor in Paterson, see Hay-

wood, "The Rip in the Silk Industry," 786; Martin Mooney, "The Industrial Workers of the World and the Immigrants of Paterson and Passaic, New Jersey: 1907–1913" (master's thesis, Seton Hall University, 1969), 13–14.

124. Weed and Carey, "I Make Cheap Silk," 7.

125. Flynn, "Contract Slavery in the Paterson Mills," 30; Weed and Carey, "I Make Cheap Silk," 7.

126. New York *Call*, 22 March 1913, p. 2.

127. Weed and Carey, "I Make Cheap Silk," 7.

128. New York *Call*, 4 March 1913, p. 2. On Little Falls, see Robert E. Snyder, "Women, Wobblies and Workers' Rights: The 1912 Textile Strike in Little Falls, New York," *New York History* 60 (January 1979): 34, 52–53.

129. See Chapter Seven.

130. *To the Silk Workers of Paterson* (leaflet in IWW Collection, Box 3, Wagner Archives, Tamiment Library, New York University). On the membership of Local 152, see *Proceedings of the Eighth IWW Convention*, 68; *Report of C.I.R.*, 2457; Paterson *Evening News*, 29 July 1913, p. 1.

131. Ewald Koettgen, *One Big Union in the Textile Industry* (Cleveland, Ohio, 1914), 10. This pamphlet was first published as an article in *Solidarity*, 3 January 1914.

132. William D. Haywood, speech given in New York, 16 March 1911 (in IWW Collection, Box 162, Archives of Labor History, Wayne State University, Detroit), 15, 17.

133. On memories of Goldfield, see Paul F. Brissenden, *The I.W.W.: A Study of American Syndicalism*, 2d ed. (New York, 1957), 200–201; for the overly optimistic view of the organization in Lawrence which prevailed in Wobbly circles during the Paterson strike, see Phillips Russell, "Cells of the New Society," *International Socialist Review* 13 (April 1913): 725–26.

134. Paterson *Evening News*, 12 May 1913, p. 10. Plunkett, who was middle class, had dropped out of Cornell University in 1912. In Paterson he joined in a threat to plunge Paterson into darkness; the following year, he took part in a disastrous anarchist bomb plot in New York: Paul Avrich, *The Modern School Movement: Anarchism and Education in the United States* (Princeton, N.J., 1980), 185, 332. See also *Solidarity*, 15 March 1913, p. 4; New York *Times*, 18 May 1913, p. II-2; Wheeler, "The Allentown Silk Dyers' Strike," 820.

135. New York *Call*, 10 March 1913, p. 1.

136. Flynn did articulate familiar themes of the labor movement. See, e.g., Paterson *Evening News*, 28 May 1913, p. 7, and 9 March 1913, p. 12.

137. Flynn, *Rebel Girl*, 171.

138. The State v. Patrick Quinlan, 421; Paterson *Evening News*, 14 May 1913, p. 12. On the two anarchists, see Paterson *Evening News*, 9 May 1913, p. 1.

139. "Haywood's Battle in Paterson," *Literary Digest* 46 (10 May 1913): 1044. For another version of the same speech, see Paterson *Evening News*, 29 April 1913, p. 10. Also see Paul Buhle, "Italian-American Radicals and Labor in Rhode Island, 1905–1930," *Radical History Review*, no. 17 (Spring 1978): 134. On Tresca's blood-for-blood speech, see Paterson *Evening News*, 23 April 1913, p. 1; New York *Call*, 23 April 1913, p. 2.

140. Haywood, quoted in New York *Call*, 31 May 1913, p. 3; Koettgen, in *Proceedings of the Eighth IWW Convention*, 39. For examples of shop control in Paterson ribbon mills in 1913–14, see Chapter Seven. On the primacy of the shop commit-

tees during the strike, see *Report of C.I.R.*, 2527. On the Central Strike Committee, see *Report of C.I.R.*, 2457; New York *Call*, 8 March 1913, p. 1; Osborne, "Industrialization and the Politics of Disorder," 326–27. The committee included many silk workers who did not belong to Local 152. For workers' control in practice, after an IWW strike victory in 1913, see Patrick Lynch, "Pittsburgh, the I.W.W., and the Stogie Workers," in *At the Point of Production: The Local History of the I.W.W.*, ed. Joseph R. Conlin (Westport, Conn., 1981), 90.

141. Koettgen, *One Big Union*, 13.

142. Paterson *Evening News*, 10 April 1913, p. 4. On sabotage and on Lessig's proposal, see Paterson *Evening News*, 2 April 1913, p. 1; 3 April 1913, p. 1; 20 May 1913, p. 9.

143. Elizabeth Gurley Flynn, "The Value of Propaganda Leagues," *Solidarity*, 19 September 1914, p. 2.

144. See B. H. Williams, "The Trend toward Industrial Freedom," *American Journal of Sociology* 20 (March 1915): 627–28.

145. Fitch, "The I.W.W.," 362.

146. Irma Lombardi, in "The Great Paterson Silk Strike of 1913," a slide show produced by Philip J. McLewin, Ramapo, N.J.; in Bird et al., *Solidarity Forever*, 73; and in *The Wobblies*, a film directed by Stewart Bird and Deborah Shaffer, 1980 (16 mm, 89 min., distributed by First Run Features, New York).

147. Sophie Cohen, quoted by Mel Most, "Going Back: Silk Striker Sophie Returns to Paterson," *Sunday Record* (New Jersey), 30 September 1973, p. 20.

CHAPTER THREE

1. New York *Daily Trade Record*, quoted in Paterson *Evening News*, 13 March 1913, p. 10.

2. Paterson *Evening News*, 23 April 1913, p. 1, and 25 April 1913, p. 13; New York *Call*, 8 March 1913, p. 1, and 30 April 1913, p. 1; James D. Osborne, "Industrialization and the Politics of Disorder: Paterson Silk Workers, 1880–1913" (doctoral diss., University of Warwick, England, 1979), 104; *American Silk Journal* 32 (August 1913): 43.

3. Paterson *Evening News*, 22 March 1913, p. 7.

4. New York *Call*, 15 April 1913, p. 1; see also 3 May 1913, p. 2.

5. Paterson *Evening News*, 8 May 1913, p. 1; New York *Call*, 2 May 1913, p. 2. See also New York *Call*, 26 March 1913, p. 2; and 8 April 1913, p. 1; Paterson *Evening News*, 21 May 1913, p. 1.

6. New York *Call*, 10 April 1913, p. 6; 9 May 1913, p. 6; 26 July 1913, p. 6; *Report of C.I.R.*, 2526; William D. Haywood, "The Rip in the Silk Industry," *International Socialist Review* 13 (May 1913): 785—but Haywood understood that "the big capitalists have never tried to enter the silk trade." So did Flynn: Elizabeth Gurley Flynn, "The Truth about the Paterson Strike," in *Rebel Voices: An IWW Anthology*, ed. Joyce L. Kornbluh (Ann Arbor, Mich., 1964), 216.

7. "Who has Paterson by the Throat?" (IWW Papers, Box 3, Tamiment Library, New York University); also *Solidarity*, 7 June 1913, p. 1, and New York *Call*, 19 June 1913, p. 6, where it was signed by Justus Ebert. Patrick Quinlan, in a July article, followed the same line and used the same research: New York *Call*, 4 July 1913, p. 2. Also reflecting the belief in an international capitalist conspiracy was the rumor that the

strikers would "show jap bosses in IWW pageant": New York *Call*, 5 June 1913, p. 1.

8. "Who has Paterson by the Throat?"

9. Paterson *Evening News*, 14 March 1913, p. 15; James Chittick, *Silk Manufacturing and Its Problems* (New York, 1913), 191. On the earlier difficulties of the manufacturers in winning acceptance, see Herbert G. Gutman, "Class, Status, and Community Power in Nineteenth-Century American Industrial Cities: Paterson, New Jersey: A Case Study," in *Work, Culture, and Society in Industrializing America: Essays in American Working-Class and Social History* (New York, 1976), 256–58.

10. Richard D. Margrave, "The Emigration of Silk Workers from England to the United States of America in the Nineteenth Century" (doctoral diss., University of London, 1981), 166–68, 228–29, 340, 346, 349; Flavia Alaya, *Silk and Sandstone: The Story of Catholina Lambert and His Castle* (Paterson, N.J., 1984), 3–19; Edward M. Graf, *Catholina Lambert: A Biographical Sketch* (Paterson, N.J., 1970), 1–2; Morris W. Garber, "The Silk Industry of Paterson, New Jersey, 1840–1913: Technology and the Origins, Development, and Changes in an Industry" (doctoral diss., Rutgers University, 1968), 216.

11. James E. Wood, "History of Labor in the Broad-Silk Industry of Paterson, New Jersey, 1872–1940" (doctoral diss., University of California, 1941), 150.

12. Ramsay Peugnet, "Six Months' Review of Trade," *American Silk Journal* 32 (October 1913): 43. Peugnet was secretary of the Silk Association of America.

13. John Fitch, "The I.W.W., an Outlaw Organization," *Survey* 30 (7 June 1913): 361. See also *Report of C.I.R.*, 2491–92.

14. Garber, "The Silk Industry of Paterson," 218–19. These figures do not include the dye houses. See also *American Silk Journal* 32 (February 1913): 70.

15. Wilson B. Killingbeck, in New York *Call*, 9 May 1913, p. 1. On the small-mill preference for plain work, see W. L. Kinkead, letter to the editor, *Survey* 30 (31 May 1913): 315.

16. See, e.g., *American Silk Journal* 32 (June 1913): 69; Paterson *Evening News*, 9 April 1913, p. 1.

17. Patrick A. Striano, interview with author, West Paterson, N.J., 5 June 1983; Philip B. Scranton, "An Exceedingly Irregular Business: Structure and Process in the Paterson Silk Industry, 1885–1910," in *Silk City: Studies of the Paterson Silk Industry, 1860–1940*, ed. Philip B. Scranton (Newark, N.J., 1985), 53. On the character of the manufacturers, see Garber, "The Silk Industry of Paterson," 221–25; Nancy Fogelson, "They Paved the Streets with Silk: Paterson, New Jersey, Silk Workers, 1913–1924," *New Jersey History* 97 (Autumn 1979): 139.

18. F. G. R. Gordon, "A Labor Man's Story of the Paterson Strike," *National Civic Federation Review* 4 (1 December 1913): 16; New York *Call*, 15 March 1913, p. 4; Paterson *Evening News*, 25 April 1913, p. 1; *American Silk Journal* 32 (October 1913): 60.

19. Gregory Mason, "Industrial War in Paterson," *Outlook* 104 (7 June 1913): 285; New York *Globe*, 21 May 1913, p. 4. See also *American Silk Journal* 32 (July 1913): 64.

20. Philip Newman, "The First IWW Invasion of New Jersey," *Proceedings of the New Jersey Historical Society* 58 (October 1940): 279.

21. *Report of C.I.R.*, 2580. See also *Solidarity*, 21 June 1913, p. 1.

22. Paterson *Evening News*, 19 March 1913, p. 12; New York *Call*, 17 May 1913, p. 2, and 20 May 1913, p. 2; New York *Globe*, 19 May 1913, p. 1, and 20 May 1913, p. 1. Eventually, the arrested pickets were released, partly on the basis of Price's testi-

mony; see New York *Call*, 26 June 1913, p. 1. For the effect of the strikers' no-individual-settlement policy on the manufacturers, see Philip S. Foner, *The Industrial Workers of the World, 1905–1917*, vol. 4 of *History of the Labor Movement in the United States* (New York, 1965), 369.

23. Paterson *Evening News*, 6 March 1913, p. 12.

24. Graf, *Catholina Lambert*, 3; Alaya, *Silk and Sandstone*, 21–22; Garber, "The Silk Industry of Paterson," 216. Ashley and Bailey also went bankrupt: *American Silk Journal* 32 (November 1913): 60.

25. James Weinstein, *The Corporate Ideal in the Liberal State, 1910–1918* (Boston, 1968), 4. See also New York *Call*, 10 April 1913, p. 6, and 23 May 1913, p. 3; *Report of C.I.R.*, 2580.

26. Haywood, "The Rip in the Silk Industry," 785. Fixing prices, however, would not have been as simple as Haywood made it sound, because uncontrollable fluctuations in the demand for silk were tied to changes in fashion. On the extreme competitiveness of the silk industry, see B. Edmund David, "The Silk Trade Conditions," *American Silk Journal* 32 (May 1913): 63.

27. New York *Call*, 18 July 1913, p. 1. See also U.S. Senate, *The Silk Industry*, vol. 4 of *Report of Condition of Woman and Child Wage-Earners in the United States*, 61st Cong., 2d sess., 1911, S. Doc. 645, 325.

28. Albert H. Heusser, ed., *The History of the Silk Dyeing Industry in the United States* (Paterson, N.J., 1927), 208–22. Griggs remained after 1909 as an officer of the reorganized corporation.

29. Heusser, *History of the Silk Dyeing Industry*, 257, 259.

30. Paterson *Morning Call*, 24 June 1902, quoted in Wood, "History of Labor," 181.

31. *Report of C.I.R.*, 2562. On the O'Brien men, see also New York *Call*, 11 June 1913, p. 6.

32. Paterson *Evening News*, 21 April 1913, p. 10. On the shooting, see also p. 1; and James D. Osborne, "Paterson: Immigrant Strikers and the War of 1913," in *At the Point of Production: The Local History of the I.W.W.*, ed. Joseph R. Conlin (Westport, Conn., 1981), 65–66; *Report of C.I.R.*, 2525.

33. Irma Lombardi, in *Solidarity Forever: An Oral History of the IWW*, ed. Stewart Bird, Dan Georgakas, and Deborah Shaffer (Chicago, 1985), 72: Paterson *Evening News*, 18 April 1913, p. 1. On the conflict in the dyeing industry, see also Wood, "History of Labor," 180; Paterson *Evening News*, 14 May 1913, p. 1, and 31 May 1913, p. 1; *Solidarity*, 8 March 1913, p. 4, and 31 May 1913, p. 4.

34. Paterson *Evening News*, 18 April 1913, p. 11; New York *Call*, 19 April 1913, p. 1. See also *Report of C.I.R.*, 2528, 2567; Frederick Sumner Boyd, "The General Strike in the Silk Industry," in *The Pageant of the Paterson Strike*, ed. Brooks McNamara (New York, 1913), 5; New York *Call*, 18 April 1913, p. 1.

35. Quoted by Henry Marelli, *Report of C.I.R.*, 2537. Marelli had written Minturn's words down at the time, after the third grand jury in a row failed to indict Cutherton.

36. P. F. Gill and R. S. Brennan, quoted in Osborne, "Industrialization and the Politics of Disorder," 310; on the relationship between the mill owners and the police, see also pp. 269, 286; *Report of C.I.R.*, 2524; New York *Call*, 27 May 1913, p. 1.

37. *Report of C.I.R.*, 2463. On Carroll, see also Michael B. Ebner, "Mrs. Miller and 'The Paterson Show': A 1911 Defeat for Racial Discrimination," *New Jersey*

History 86 (Summer 1968): 88–92; Osborne, "Industrialization and the Politics of Disorder," 310–11.

38. Quoted in Osborne, "Industrialization and the Politics of Disorder," 312.

39. Paterson *Evening News*, 1 April 1913, pp. 10–11; New York *Call*, 2 April 1913, p. 1. See also New York *Call*, 29 March 1913, p. 1; Paterson *Evening News*, 27 May 1913, p. 1; Richard A. Noble, "The Relation of the Middle Classes and Local Government of Paterson, New Jersey, to the Labor Movement in the Paterson Silk Industry, 1872–1913" (senior thesis, Princeton University, 1973), 84–85.

40. Paterson *Evening News*, 23 April 1913, p. 10. See also New York *Call*, 23 April 1913, p. 2.

41. *Report of C.I.R.*, 2494, 2512–14. On the silk manufacturers' lack of interest in Taylorism, see Daniel Nelson, *Managers and Workers: Origins of the New Factory System in the United States, 1880–1920* (Madison, Wis., 1975), 71; Chittick, *Silk Manufacturing*, 411–14. On the timing of workers in the dye shops, see *Solidarity*, 19 April 1913, p. 4.

42. Newark *Star*, quoted in Alexander Scott, "What the Reds Are Doing in Paterson," *International Socialist Review* 13 (June 1913): 855; and in *Solidarity*, 29 March 1913, p. 1. On flag day, see *Solidarity*, 19 July 1913, p. 3; New York *Call*, 18 March 1913, p. 1. On Haywood's "red flag" speech, see, e.g., New York *Times*, 11 March 1913, p. 22; New York *Call*, 11 March 1913, p. 1. On McKees Rocks, see John Ingham, "A Strike in the Progressive Era: McKees Rocks, 1909," *Pennsylvania Magazine of History and Biography* 90 (July 1966): 371. On Lawrence, see Elizabeth Gurley Flynn, *The Rebel Girl: An Autobiography* (New York, 1973), 151.

43. Paterson *Evening News*, 17 March 1913, p. 9. For a similar vision of America, see Paterson *Evening News*, 3 April 1913, p. 9.

44. Haywood, "The Rip in the Silk Industry," 786.

45. New York *Call*, 25 March 1913, p. 3.

46. New York *Call*, 17 March 1913, p. 1.

47. Mark Karson, *American Labor Unions and Politics, 1910–1918* (Carbondale, Ill., 1958), 244, 253–54.

48. Wilson B. Killingbeck, "From Paterson to Hazleton," New York *Call*, 29 March 1913, p. 6. On the collusion of the United Textile Workers with the president of the Pennsylvania Silk Association in the Hazleton strike, see Patrick M. Lynch, "Pennsylvania Anthracite: A Forgotten IWW Venture, 1906–1916" (master's thesis, Bloomsburg State College, Penna., 1974), 140–42. On Golden at Skowhegan, see New York *Call*, 21 April 1913, p. 1; New York *Times*, 17 March 1912, p. V-2.

49. Paterson *Evening News*, 21 April 1913, p. 10.

50. New York *Call*, 3 March 1913, p. 6. On Golden in Lawrence, see also Meredith Tax, *The Rising of the Women: Feminist Solidarity and Class Conflict, 1880–1917* (New York, 1980), 265–66; Joe Hill, "John Golden and the Lawrence Strike," in Kornbluh, *Rebel Voices*, 181.

51. "Haywood's Battle in Paterson," *Literary Digest* 46 (10 May 1913): 1043.

52. Paterson *Evening News*, 21 April 1913, p. 10.

53. Quoted in Weinstein, *The Corporate Ideal*, 14. See also Samuel Gompers, "Destruction the Avowed Purpose of I.W.W.," *American Federationist* 20 (July 1913): 536; Henry Streifler, "Textile Workers Organizing," *American Federationist* 19 (June 1912): 474.

54. Paterson *Evening News*, 21 April 1913, p. 4; 25 April 1913, p. 1; 28 April

1913, p. 7; also Mason, "Industrial War in Paterson," 284. See also "Haywood's Battle in Paterson," 1044; Wood, "History of Labor," 203–4; Paul Buhle, "Italian-American Radicals and Labor in Rhode Island, 1905–1930," *Radical History Review*, no. 17 (Spring 1978): 136; Paterson *Evening News*, 9 June 1913, p. 1.

55. *American Silk Journal* 32 (May 1913): 31.
56. Boyd, "The General Strike in the Silk Industry," 7.
57. See Fitch, "The I.W.W.," 362; Melvyn Dubofsky, *We Shall Be All: A History of the Industrial Workers of the World* (Chicago, 1969), 271; Robert A. Zieger, "Robin Hood in the Silk City," *Proceedings of the New Jersey Historical Society* 84 (1966): 191.
58. Gordon, "A Labor Man's Story," 16.
59. Wood, "History of Labor," 228.
60. Leo Troy, *Organized Labor in New Jersey* (Princeton, N.J., 1965), 81–82.
61. U.S. Senate, *Silk Industry*, 311.
62. Wood, "History of Labor," 215, 217.
63. Ibid., 222.
64. Ibid., 228.
65. Ewald Koettgen in *Solidarity*, 23 December 1911, p. 4. See also Paterson *Evening News*, 21 April 1913, p. 10.
66. *Solidarity*, 23 December 1911, p. 4.
67. *Report of C.I.R.*, 2422, 2430.
68. Ibid., 2612–13. Starr had helped to start the Warpers' Association in the early 1890s. On Starr, see also Wood, "History of Labor in the Broad-Silk Industry," 296. On the AFL's attitude, see also Osborne, "Industrialization and the Politics of Disorder," 94–97, 99–100.
69. *Report of C.I.R.*, 2423.
70. Paterson *Evening News*, 24 February 1913, p. 7 (the newspaper paraphrased the loomfixers and twisters).
71. Ibid., 19 March 1913, p. 9. On the loomfixers and warpers during the strike, see New York *Call*, 21 April 1913, p. 1, and 7 May 1913, p. 2; "General Strike Call," *Solidarity*, 1 March 1913, p. 4; Paterson *Evening News*, 31 March 1913, p. 9, and 15 May 1913, p. 9.
72. E. B. White, quoted in Wilson B. Killingbeck, "The Paterson Strike Breakers," New York *Call*, 7 May 1913, p. 6. See also Gordon, "A Labor Man's Story," 16. But some members of Paterson's Central Labor Council opposed Golden's intervention: "Haywood's Battle in Paterson," 1044.
73. Paterson *Evening News*, 19 April 1913, p. 4.
74. *Solidarity*, 3 May 1913, p. 1.
75. New York *Call*, 22 April 1913, p. 1.
76. Paterson *Evening News*, 19 April 1913, p. 1. See also *Report of C.I.R.*, 2467.
77. New York *Call*, 22 April 1913, p. 4. See also *Solidarity*, 3 May 1913, p. 4; Scott, "What the Reds are Doing," 855–56; William D. Haywood, "On the Paterson Picket Line," *International Socialist Review* 13 (June 1913): 849–50; Boyd, "The General Strike in the Silk Industry," 7–8; Flynn, *Rebel Girl*, 167; New York *Globe*, 22 April 1913, 8. Some of these accounts put the number allowed back much lower. For the AFL version, see Gordon, "A Labor Man's Story," 16.
78. Wood, "History of Labor in the Broad-Silk Industry," 187–88.
79. New York *Call*, 9 May 1913, p. 2.

80. Paterson *Evening News*, 18 April 1913, p. 11.

81. Ibid.; also 21 April 1913, p. 10, and 25 April 1913, p. 13.

82. See, e.g., *Solidarity*, 7 June 1913, p. 4; New York *Call*, 24 April 1913, p. 2; 7 May 1913, p. 2; 5 April 1913, p. 1; also Paterson *Evening News*, 17 April 1913, p. 9. Gordon, "A Labor Man's Story," 17, probably exaggerated the extent of contributions to the strikers by the AFL unions.

83. New York *Call*, 21 April 1913, p. 1.

84. Paterson *Evening News*, 2 April 1913, p. 1, reproduced the general strike call in its entirety.

85. New York *Call*, 3 April 1913, p. 1; Paterson *Evening News*, 4 April 1913, p. 1; New York *Herald*, 18 May 1913, cited in full in *Solidarity*, 24 May 1913, p. 1. See also *Report of C.I.R.*, 2419, 2618.

86. Gutman, "Class, Status, and Community Power," 257; Paterson *Guardian*, 27 February 1913, quoted in James D. Osborne, "Italian Immigrants and the Working Class in Paterson: The Strike of 1913 in Ethnic Perspective," in *New Jersey's Ethnic Heritage*, ed. Paul A. Stellhorn (Trenton, N.J., 1978), 27.

87. The State v. Patrick Quinlan, Passaic Quarter Sessions, Paterson, N.J., stenographic minutes (12, 13, 14 May 1913), 400–402.

88. Paterson *Evening News*, 20 May 1913, p. 9; New York *Call*, 21 May 1913, p. 2.

89. Paterson *Evening News*, 4 April 1913, p. 1.

90. Mel Most, "The 1913 Silk Strike Terror: The Hoax That Killed Silk City," *Sunday Record* (New Jersey), 30 September 1973, p. 13.

91. Paterson *Evening News*, 9 May 1913, p. 11, and 11 June 1913, p. 1. See also New York *Call*, 9 May 1913, p. 1; *Solidarity*, 17 May 1913, p. 1; Fred Harwood's interview with Henry Doherty, Rose Pastor Stokes Collection, XIX:22 (Tamiment Library, New York University).

92. New York *Call*, 13 March 1913, p. 1; Paterson *Evening News*, 11 March 1913, p. 1.

93. *Report of C.I.R.*, 2578. See also Fred Harwood's interview with Father Andrew Stein, Rose Pastor Stokes Collection.

94. Paterson *Evening News*, 4 April 1913, p. 9; New York *Call*, 4 April 1913, pp. 1–2.

95. Editorial, New York *Call*, 11 April 1913, p. 6.

96. On Stein and the high school meeting, see New York *Call*, 9 April 1913, p. 1; 10 April 1913, p. 1; 11 April 1913, p. 1; also Fitch, "The I.W.W.," 356–57; "City Officials Adopt Repressive Measures," *Survey* 30 (19 April 1913): 83; *Solidarity*, 19 April 1913, p. 2. Flynn and Haywood at this time rejected the whole idea of third-party intervention and therefore opposed participating in the aldermen's meeting: see Paterson *Evening News*, 9 April 1913, p. 1.

97. On Mannheimer's dismissal, see New York *Times*, 19 April 1913, p. 9; *Solidarity*, 19 July 1913, p. 3; Graham Adams, Jr., *Age of Industrial Violence, 1910–1915: The Activities and Findings of the United States Commission on Industrial Relations* (New York, 1966), 93. He was dismissed four days after the armory meeting. On his continued efforts to mediate, see, e.g., New York *Call*, 28 May 1913, p. 1, and 15 June 1913, p. 1; Leo Mannheimer, "Darkest New Jersey," *Independent* 74 (29 May 1913), 1190–92.

98. *Report of C.I.R.*, 2577.

99. Fred Harwood's interview with W. C. Snodgrass, Rose Pastor Stokes Collection.

100. *Report of C.I.R.*, 2578.

101. Paterson *Evening News*, 10 April 1913, p. 10; also New York *Call*, 10 April 1913, p. 2. Like many weavers, Gallaway seems to have changed his mind later about the possibility of a shop-by-shop settlement: Paterson *Evening News*, 17 May 1913, p. 7.

102. Paterson *Evening News*, 5 May 1913, pp. 9–10; see also 3 May 1913, p. 9. For other strike appearances by Gallaway, see Paterson *Evening News*, 14 April 1913, p. 7; New York *Call*, 15 April 1913, p. 1, and 29 May 1913, p. 1. On the strikers' feelings toward Gallaway, see also Carrie Golzio, interview with author, Haledon, N.J., 13 June 1983; Dominic Mignone, in Bird et al., *Solidarity Forever*, 82–83.

103. Flynn, *Rebel Girl*, 166.

104. Paterson *Evening News*, 14 April 1913, p. 1.

105. New York *Call*, 26 May 1913, p. 1. See also Paterson *Evening News*, 23 May 1913, p. 4.

106. Inis Weed and Louise Carey, eds., "I Make Cheap Silk," *The Masses* 5 (November 1913): 7.

107. Fitch, "The I.W.W.," 357; Alfred Cappio, "Paterson Silk Strike of 1913," 1975 (manuscript in Paterson Public Library), 5.

108. Paterson *Evening News*, 19 June 1913, pp. 1, 7.

109. Quoted in Flynn, *Rebel Girl*, 159.

110. Fitch, "The I.W.W.," 261. See also Wood, "History of Labor," 269; *Report of C.I.R.*, 2527.

111. Paterson *Evening News*, 14 March 1913, p. 15; Flynn, *Rebel Girl*, 159; see also p. 133; *Solidarity*, 21 June 1913, p. 1.

112. Paterson *Evening News*, 14 March 1913, p. 15; see also Flynn, *Rebel Girl*, 159.

113. Elizabeth Gurley Flynn, "Facts and Figures," in McNamara, *Pageant of the Paterson Strike*, 21. This article was first published in *Solidarity*, 19 April 1913, p. 1.

114. Most, "The 1913 Silk Strike Terror," 13; "The End of the Paterson Strike," *Outlook* 104 (9 August 1913): 780; New York *Call*, 5 April 1913, p. 1.

115. Paterson *Evening News*, 26 May, 1913, p. 7.

116. Ibid., 12 June 1913, p. 7.

117. New York *Call*, 8 July 1913, p. 1; also Paterson *Evening News*, 11 June 1913, p. 1. The petition is quoted in full in Morris B. Grossman, letter to the editor, Paterson *Evening News*, 10 July 1913, p. 2. In June, Hapgood, John Fitch, Rabbi Mannheimer, and a number of nationally known Progressive reformers had called for a federal probe. See New York *Call*, 5 June 1913, p. 1, and 6 June 1913, p. 2. On the Jewish merchants, see also New York *Call*, 13 June 1913, p. 1.

118. See Osborne, "Industrialization and the Politics of Disorder," 120–21.

119. Paterson *Evening News*, 9 April 1913, p. 9; Patrick Quinlan, "The Paterson Strike," *Solidarity*, 15 March 1913, p. 1; Patrick Quinlan, "Impressions, Triumphs, and Attitudes," *Solidarity*, 19 April 1913, p. 2; Patrick Quinlan, "The Paterson Strike and After," *New Review* 2 (January 1914): 29–30. See also Paterson *Evening News*, 9 June 1913, p. 7, and 28 June 1913, p. 7; New York *Call*, 16 June 1913, p. 1; *Solidarity*, 21 June 1913, p. 1.

120. Alexander Scott, letter to New York *Call*, 14 July 1913, p. 5.

121. Note that although Flynn had earlier opposed state intervention, by May both Haywood and the strikers were calling for federal intervention and the manufacturers were opposing it. Paterson *Evening News*, 19 March 1913, p. 12; 19 May 1913, p. 1; 27 May 1913, p. 10.

122. W. K. Kinkead, letter to *Survey* 30 (31 May 1913): 315–16.

123. *Report of C.I.R.*, 2541.

124. See John Higham, *Strangers in the Land: Patterns of American Nativism, 1860–1925* (New Brunswick, N.J., 1955), 160, 176; Osborne, "Italian Immigrants," 27 and passim; Caroline Golab, "Comment," in Stellhorn, *New Jersey's Ethnic Heritage*, 63.

125. Philip S. Foner, *Fellow Workers and Friends: IWW Free-Speech Fights as Told by Participants* (Westport, Conn., 1981), 163, 166–73. The quotation is from p. 172; "traitor" is capitalized in the original account, which is by Youmans.

126. T. J. Cooper, letter to the editor, Paterson *Evening News*, 21 July 1913, p. 8.

127. Morris S. Grossman, letter to the editor, Paterson *Evening News*, 10 July 1913, p. 2.

128. See, e.g., editorial, Paterson *Evening News*, 22 March 1913, p. 1; on Haines's financial contributions, see also editorial of 19 June 1913, p. 4.

129. Editorial, Paterson *Evening News*, 22 March 1913, p. 9. See also New York *Call*, 26 February 1913, p. 2.

130. *Report of C.I.R.*, 2538.

131. Paterson *Evening News*, 21 March 1913, p. 1, and 9 April 1913, p. 1. See also New York *Call*, 10 April 1913, p. 1.

132. *Report of C.I.R.*, 2527.

133. Editorials, Paterson *Evening News*, 19 May 1913, pp. 1, 9; 20 May 1913, p. 4; 21 May 1913, p. 1.

134. Editorials, Paterson *Evening News*, 9 June 1913, p. 4; 10 June 1913, p. 7. On the three- and four-loom system, see editorial, Paterson *Evening News*, 24 May 1913, p. 7. Haines's reasoning about Pennsylvania competition was spurious because many Pennsylvania mills were annexes of Paterson companies and because they specialized in cheaper grades of silk.

135. Paterson *Evening News*, 5 May 1913, p. 10; Mannheimer, "Darkest New Jersey," 1192.

136. *Solidarity*, 19 April 1913, p. 2. Henry Doherty showed that he understood this point when he offered his employees the opportunity to run his mill—provided they would guarantee him 5 percent profit, repudiate the IWW, and work ten hours on four looms: see New York *Times*, 18 May 1913, p. VIII-10; New York *Call*, 13 May 1913, p. 2; William D. Haywood, *Bill Haywood's Book: The Autobiography of William D. Haywood* (New York, 1929), 268.

137. Guthroe Barton, *Three Parts Scotch: An Informal Autobiography* (Indianapolis, Ind., 1946), 65.

138. Fitch, "The I.W.W.," 357. The article was written in late May.

139. Ibid.

140. Testimony of John W. Ferguson, *Report of C.I.R.*, 2580.

141. Paterson *Press*, 29 March 1913, quoted in Fitch, "The I.W.W.," 358.

142. Paterson *Press*, 23 April 1913, p. 1, and 24 April 1913, p. 1, both quoted in *Report of C.I.R.*, 2583, 2584; Fitch, "The I.W.W.," 357; *Survey*, 32 (27 June 1914), 340.

143. Paterson *Evening News*, 7 May 1913, p. 10; Fitch, "The I.W.W.," 357; *Solidarity*, 10 May 1913, p. 4. The doctor was Walter B. Johnson; the minister was David Hamilton. Later, the AFL, too, justified appeals to vigilante justice against the IWW; see Gordon, "A Labor Man's Story," 17.

144. New York *Call*, 23 April 1913, p. 2.

145. Testimony of Henry Marelli, *Report of C.I.R.*, 2539. None of the four IWW organizers was ever convicted by a foreign jury.

146. Paterson *Evening News*, 21 May 1913, p. 1.

147. Paterson *Evening News*, 5 April 1913, p. 7.

148. New York *Call*, 11 June 1913, p. 2.

149. Paterson *Evening News*, 25 April 1913, p. 13; the speaker was Charles Plunkett.

150. Ibid., 26 April 1913, p. 9; the striker was Emil Cox.

151. Ibid.

152. Eugene M. Tobin, "Direct Action and Conscience: The 1913 Paterson Strike as an Example of the Relationship between Labor Radicals and Liberals," *Labor History* 20 (Winter 1979), 78. On the beginning of the trial, see Newark *News*, 7 May 1913; on the decrease in picketing, New York *Call*, 8 May 1913, p. 2. See also Mason, "Industrial War in Paterson," 287; New York *Times*, 15 May 1913, p. 2.

153. New York *Times*, 15 May 1913, p. 1.

154. New York *Call*, 15 May 1913, p. 1, and 16 May 1913, p. 1; New York *Times*, 15 May 1913, p. 1; Fitch, "The I.W.W.," 358; Paterson *Evening News*, 15 May 1913, p. 9; *Solidarity*, 24 May 1913, p. 4.

155. Paterson *Evening News*, 19 May 1913, p. 10; New York *Call*, 20 May 1913, pp. 1–2; *Report of C.I.R.*, 2566; Boyd, "The General Strike in the Silk Industry," 4; New York *Globe*, 15 May 1913, p. 1. On Turner, see also New York *Call*, 8 May 1913, p. 2; and on the purpose of sending police to strikers' meetings, 15 May 1913, p. 2.

156. New York *Call*, 21 May 1913, p. 1; *Report of C.I.R.*, 2567, 2610; New York *Times*, 25 May 1913, p. II-1; Paterson *Evening News*, 20 May 1913, and 3 June 1913, p. 7. See also The State v. Patrick Quinlan, 268; Flynn, "The Truth about the Paterson Strike," 218–19; Flynn, *Rebel Girl*, 159; New York *Call*, 26 April 1913, p. 1; 20 May 1913, p. 1; 21 May 1913, p. 1; also Osborne, "Industrialization and the Politics of Disorder," 206–7; Fitch, "The I.W.W.," 358; Paterson *Evening News*, 23 May 1913, p. 14; 24 May 1913, p. 1; 6 June 1913, p. 13.

157. New York *Call*, 26 May 1913, p. 1; 27 May 1913, p. 1; 30 May 1913, p. 1; 11 June 1913, p. 6; also Paterson *Evening News*, 26 May 1913, p. 7; *Solidarity*, 31 May 1913, p. 1. On the experiments with the time of meetings, see, e.g., Paterson *Evening News*, 22 May 1913, p. 9; New York *Call*, 3 June 1913, p. 1. For emphasis on signs of breaks, see Paterson *Evening News*, 28 May 1913, p. 1; 29 May 1913, p. 4; 11 June 1913, p. 1. Note that the only paper devoted to the strikers all along, Scott's *Weekly Issue*, was subject to continued interference by police; news dealers were warned against selling "that Goddamned sheet," and strikers could be arrested merely for having a copy: *Report of C.I.R.*, 2524, 2527.

158. New York *Globe*, 16 May 1913, p. 2 (on the circus), and 19 May 1913, p. 1.

159. *Solidarity*, 14 June 1913, p. 4, and 21 June 1913, p. 1; *Report of C.I.R.*, 2525; Paterson *Evening News*, 20 May 1913, p. 9; 21 May 1913, p. 1; 22 May 1913, p. 9; also New York *Call*, 7 June 1913, p. 2. The third IWW speaker singled out by the Executive Committee was Plunkett.

160. "On One Meal a Day!" *International Socialist Review* 13 (June 1913): 851. The visitor was not identified.

161. Mason, "Industrial War in Paterson," 283.

162. *Solidarity*, 10 May 1913, p. 1; Paterson *Evening News*, 29 May 1913, p. 1; New York *Times*, 25 May 1913, p. II-4. "Deadlock" was frequently used by this time to describe the strike situation. For a slightly earlier example, see Paterson *Evening News*, 26 April 1913, p. 9; for a slightly later one, 12 June 1913, p. 1.

163. New York *Globe*, 21 May 1913, p. 4.

164. Ibid., 23 May 1913, p. 6. See also James Osborne, "The Paterson Strike of 1913: Immigrant Silk Workers and the I.W.W. Response to the Problem of Stable Unionism" (master's thesis, University of Warwick, England, 1973), 69–74.

CHAPTER FOUR

1. Justin Kaplan, *Lincoln Steffens: A Biography* (New York, 1974), 203, applies the phrase (invented by Tom Wolfe) to the attitude of the Village intellectuals toward Wobblies and anarchists; he uses Mabel Dodge's salon as an example. Peter Carlson, *Roughneck: The Life and Times of Big Bill Haywood* (New York, 1983), 212, also uses the phrase to characterize Dodge's salon.

2. Paterson *Evening News*, 4 June 1913, p. 4. On the arrests of the farmers, see Paterson *Evening News*, 22 March 1913, p. 1, and 5 April 1913, p. 1. For the editorial on the Zapatistas, see "Zapata as an Ally of Capitalism," *Solidarity*, 23 May 1914, p. 2 (but note a more sensitive current of interpretation, within the IWW, of the Zapatista movement, in *Solidarity*, 6 September 1913, p. 1, and 6 December 1913, p. 1). For the IWW's dismissal of American farmers as belonging to the "cockroach class" or the "petty 'bushwar,'" even when they voted Socialist, see *Solidarity*, 10 April 1915, p. 2, and 10 July 1915, p. 1. On the IWW's anti-intellectualism, see below, n. 35.

3. John Reed, "Almost Thirty," *The New Republic Anthology: 1915–1935*, ed. Groff Conklin (New York, 1935), 70.

4. Max Eastman, *Enjoyment of Living* (New York, 1948), 387.

5. *The Masses* 5 (January 1914): 5; see also 4 (January 1913): 18–19.

6. Max Eastman, *Love and Revolution*, 126, quoted in James Burkhart Gilbert, *Writers and Partisans: A History of Literary Radicalism in America* (New York, 1968), 25.

7. On *The Masses* after the decline of the IWW, see Conclusion.

8. Mari Jo Buhle, *Women and American Socialism, 1870–1920* (Urbana, Ill., 1981), 262.

9. *The Masses* 4 (June 1913): 5; see also 4 (July 1913): 6.

10. Ibid., 4 (June 1913): 5. Pankhurst was the militant leader of the British suffrage movement.

11. Ibid., 4 (January 1913): 5.

12. For Heterodoxy members and *The Masses*, see Judith Schwarz, *Radical Feminists of Heterodoxy: Greenwich Village 1912–1940* (Lebanon, N.H., 1982), ii–iii, 30. For the IWW defense of *The Masses* during the legal troubles with the Associated Press, see *Solidarity*, 21 March 1914, p. 2. On the close relationship between the IWW and *The Masses*, see *Solidarity*, 2 August 1913, p. 2; 6 March 1915, p. 3 ("Get the Masses for March . . ."); 31 July 1915, p. 9; also Paul F. Brissenden, *The I.W.W.: A Study of American Syndicalism*, 2d ed. (New York, 1957), 404; Harry Kemp, *More Miles: An Autobiographical Novel* (New York, 1926), 357. For examples of articles and

cartoons reprinted from *The Masses*, see *Solidarity*, 17 January 1913, p. 3; 7 June 1913, p. 1; 8 November 1913, p. 3; 27 March 1915, p. 3. For examples of articles in *The Masses* by Haywood and Flynn, see William D. Haywood, "Insurance against Agitation," *The Masses* 5 (February 1914): 22; and Flynn's contribution to the symposium "Do You Believe in Patriotism," *The Masses* 7 (March 1916): 12.

13. Art Young, *Art Young: His Life and Times* (New York, 1939), 439–40, 444–45. For examples of Young cartoons reprinted by the IWW, see Justus Ebert, *The Trial of a New Society* (Cleveland, Ohio, 1913), opposite Contents; *Solidarity*, 7 June 1913, p. 1.

14. Gilbert, *Writers and Partisans*, 26, 28. On *The Masses* as the only magazine being sold in the Garden, see Paterson *Evening News*, 9 June 1913, p. 7. Only one newspaper was sold: the *Weekly Issue*.

15. Young, *His Life and Times*, 450–51, 453.

16. *The Masses* 4 (December 1912): 15. On Young's blossoming at *The Masses*, see Albert Parry, *Garretts and Pretenders: A History of Bohemianism in America* (New York, 1960), 300.

17. *The Masses* 5 (November 1913): 5. For a similar conflict between Brisbane and Young, see New York *Evening Journal*, 21 March 1913.

18. Lloyd Goodrich, *John Sloan* (New York, 1952), 44. See also Richard Fitzgerald, *Art and Politics: Cartoonists of The Masses and Liberator* (Westport, Conn., 1973), 151.

19. *New Review*, 1 (4 January 1913): 5. See also Eastman, *Enjoyment of Living*, 544–45, and Leslie Fishbein, *Rebels in Bohemia: The Radicals of the Masses, 1911–1917* (Chapel Hill, N.C., 1982), 21.

20. Mabel Dodge Luhan, *Movers and Shakers*, vol. 3 of *Intimate Memories* (New York, 1936), 86–87.

21. For Young's and Sloan's cartoons, see *The Masses* 4 (June 1913): 15, and 4 (July 1913): 17. For Carrol's notice and Haywood's comment, see 4 (August 1913): 16; and Eastman, *Enjoyment of Living*, 445. Reed was first listed as "contributing editor" in March and as "managing editor" in October 1913.

22. Gilbert, *Writers and Partisans*, 29. See also William O'Neill, ed., *Echoes of Revolt: THE MASSES, 1911–1917* (Chicago, 1966), 21.

23. Max Eastman, "The Anarchist Almanac," *The Masses* 5 (March 1914), in O'Neill, *Echoes of Revolt*, 48.

24. Eastman, *Enjoyment of Living*, 402, 409.

25. Ibid., 409.

26. Paul Avrich, *The Modern School Movement: Anarchism and Education in the United States* (Princeton, N.J., 1980), 79–80, 118, 130–33, 140, 147–49, 155, 372 n.75. On the Ferrer Center, see also Bernardine Kielty Scherman, *Girl from Fitchburg* (New York, 1964), 69.

27. Even this material is limited by the lack of precise dates; we often don't know whether a particular discussion took place before May 1913 or after it. But because the discussions were dramatic, participants have left invaluable detailed records of them.

28. Lincoln Steffens, *The Autobiography of Lincoln Steffens* (New York, 1931), 655. Dodge herself credited Steffens with the idea for the evenings: Dodge Luhan, *Movers and Shakers*, 81.

29. Margaret Sanger, *Margaret Sanger: An Autobiography* (New York, 1971), 73. On Sanger's uncertainties about her own abilities, see pp. 70, 76. On the beginning date

for the "evenings," see Lois Palken Rudnick, *Mabel Dodge Luhan: New Woman, New Worlds* (Albuquerque, N.M., 1984), 74.

30. Sanger, *Autobiography*, 35.

31. Dodge Luhan, *Movers and Shakers*, 88–90. Dodge noted that Walter Lippman tried to draw Haywood out, to no avail.

32. For Dodge's view of Walling as a moderate, see *Movers and Shakers*, 286. Walling in 1913 was in fact a revolutionary socialist: see William English Walling, "Class Struggle within the Working Class," *The Masses* 4 (January 1913), in O'Neill, *Echoes of Revolt*, 49–50, which anticipates the formation of a bridge between militant workers and radical intellectuals.

33. *Bill Haywood's Book: The Autobiography of William D. Haywood* (New York, 1929), 11–12, 16–17, 26–28, 103–7, 145, etc.

34. Mary Heaton Vorse, Columbia Oral History Collection, quoted in Meredith Tax, *The Rising of the Women: Feminist Solidarity and Class Conflict, 1880–1917* (New York, 1980), 250. See also Dodge Luhan, *Movers and Shakers*, 59, 87; Ernest Poole, *The Bridge: My Own Story* (New York, 1940), 198–99.

35. The IWW's *Industrial Union Bulletin* (10 October 1908, p. 1), published De Leon's defense under the heading "The Intellectual against the Worker," and Vincent St. John's attack under "The Worker against the Intellectual." See also *Solidarity*, 20 April 1912, p. 1; Joseph Biscay, "What Marx Would Say," *Solidarity*, 19 March 1910, p. 1; Austin Lewis, *Militant Proletariat* (Chicago, 1911), 35; André Tridon, *The New Unionism* (New York, 1913), chap. 4 ("The New Unionism and the Intellectuals"), esp. 59. For a similar AFL view, see Samuel Gompers, "They Don't Suit the Intellectuals," *American Federationist* 20 (February 1913): 128–32.

36. Haywood felt bad about having been defeated in debate in January 1912 by Morris Hillquit, a moderate socialist, at Cooper Union in New York. See *Bill Haywood's Book*, 229, and André Tridon, "Haywood," *New Review* 1 (May 1913): 505.

37. *Bill Haywood's Book*, 198; see also pp. 14–15, 18, 19–20, 23, 79.

38. William D. Haywood's "The General Strike" (transcript of 16 May 1911 speech at Cooper Union), 19, in IWW Collection, Box 162, Archives of Labor History, Wayne State University, Detroit.

39. See William D. Haywood, "Blanket Stiff Philosophy," *International Socialist Review* 13 (September 1913): 258; "Testimony of William D. Haywood before the Industrial Relations Commission," 31–32, in IWW Collection, Tamiment Library, New York University.

40. Hutchins Hapgood, *A Victorian in the Modern World* (New York, 1939), 293.

41. Quoted in ibid., 293–94, 295. See also Phillips Russell, "Cells of the New Society," *International Socialist Review* 13 (April 1913): 726.

42. Tridon, "Haywood," 505–6.

43. Melvyn Dubofsky, *We Shall Be All: A History of the Industrial Workers of the World* (Chicago, 1969), 280.

44. Frank P. Walsh, "My Impressions of the Witnesses and their Testimony," *Solidarity*, 31 June 1915, p. 6. Contrast the less perceptive description of Haywood by Carlo Tresca, "With Big Bill Haywood on the Battlefields of Labor," in *Rebel Voices: An I.W.W. Anthology*, ed. Joyce L. Kornbluh (Ann Arbor, Mich., 1964), 209.

45. Dodge Luhan, *Movers and Shakers*, 90.

46. Max Eastman, *Venture* (New York, 1927), 210–11. Note, however, Eastman's

warning that his account contained "some flourishes": Eastman, *Enjoyment of Living*, 523. See also Kemp, *More Miles*, 352–53.

47. Dodge Luhan, *Movers and Shakers*, 90–91. For a confrontation between Haywood and Sloan that had a similar result, see John Sloan, *John Sloan's New York Scene: From the Diaries, Notes, and Correspondence, 1906–1913*, ed. Bruce St. John (New York, 1965), 607–8.

48. Young, *His Life and Times*, 435. Rauh, an actress and sculptor who also had a law degree, was married to Eastman.

49. Schwarz, *Heterodoxy*, 15–16.

50. Ibid., 14–15; see also pp. i, 9–10, 13, 21, 81. The member was Inez Irwin.

51. Elizabeth Gurley Flynn, *The Rebel Girl: An Autobiography* (New York, 1973), 80–81, 115, 279. Schwarz, *Heterodoxy*, 31, implies a 1915 date for Flynn's joining, but Schwarz's chronology is shaky: she puts the Paterson Pageant in 1915, too. Flynn herself mentioned Sanger's address to Heterodoxy, which was in 1914. See Flynn, *Rebel Girl*, 279; Schwarz, *Heterodoxy*, 165. According to Rosalyn Fraad Baxendall, who saw Flynn's papers before the Communist Party withdrew them from public scrutiny, Flynn received postcards informing her of Heterodoxy meetings from 1912; a diary entry by Flynn in 1913 listed a Heterodoxy meeting date (Baxendall, phone conversation with author, 11 July 1984).

52. Nancy Schrom Dye, *As Equals and as Sisters: Feminism, the Labor Movement, and the Women's Trade Union League of New York* (Columbia, Mo., 1980), 4, 6, 105–6, 109, 112–13, 122–23; Tax, *The Rising of the Women*, 227–28, 266–68. On Rauh, see Dye, *As Equals and as Sisters*, 135, 144; note (p. 69) that one unsuccessful WTUL project was an attempt to organize female ribbon weavers in New York.

53. Buhle, *Women and American Socialism*, 289; see also Tax, *Rising of the Women*, 195, 231.

54. Marie Jenney Howe, "An Anti-Suffrage Monologue," in Schwarz, *Heterodoxy*, 97–101.

55. Schwarz, *Heterodoxy*, 25. The trade unionist was Rose Schneiderman. On the involvement of some Heterodoxy members in WTUL-supported strikes, see pp. 27–28. On the role of Village radicals in expanding Heterodoxy's definition of feminism beyond suffrage, see Tax, *The Rising of the Women*, 198; Schwarz, *Heterodoxy*, 23; and June Sochen, *The New Woman in Greenwich Village, 1910–1920* (New York, 1972), 11. On Flynn's uniqueness, see Sochen, *The New Woman*, 23–24, 143; June Sochen, *Movers and Shakers: American Women Thinkers and Activists* (New York, 1974), 87.

56. Flynn, *Rebel Girl*, 280.

57. Ibid., 29–30; see also Tax, *The Rising of the Women*, 142–43.

58. Flynn, *Rebel Girl*, 53; also pp. 55–59, 63–65.

59. Quoted in Schwarz, *Heterodoxy*, 1.

60. Flynn, *Rebel Girl*, 280.

61. Ibid., 113.

62. Quoted in Tax, *The Rising of the Women*, 146. For Tresca's conservative views on motherhood, see Mary Heaton Vorse, *A Footnote to Folly: Reminiscences of Mary Heaton Vorse* (New York, 1935), 55; on being a mother and a radical, see also pp. 61, 403; *Rebel Girl*, 7; Sanger, *Autobiography*, 76.

63. Schwarz, *Heterodoxy*, 16–17. As a young single mother and revolutionary, Flynn also received support—including financial support—from Emma Goldman: see

Goldman, *Living my Life* (New York, 1931), 1:488–89. On motherhood in the Village, see Floyd Dell, *Intellectual Vagabondage: An Apology to the Intelligentsia* (New York, 1927), 171; Sochen, *The New Woman*, 134.

64. Flynn, "Problems in Organizing Women," *Solidarity*, 15 July 1916, p. 3. On the Wobblies and their wives, see also Rosalyn Fraad Baxandall, "Elizabeth Gurley Flynn: The Early Years," *Radical America* 9, no. 1 (1975): 100.

65. Flynn, "Men and Women," 1915 manuscript, quoted in Tax, *The Rising of the Women*, 140. For Rabinowitz's criticism, see Mathilda Rabinowitz Robbins, "Maida Lynn," (in M. Robbins Collection, Box 1, Archives of Labor History), 4–5. See also Tax, *The Rising of the Women*, 144; Flynn, "The I.W.W. Call to Women," *Solidarity*, 31 July 1915, p. 9.

66. Flynn, *Rebel Girl*, 280; Tax, *The Rising of the Women*, 153. Note that one other IWW member, Jessie Ashley, was an outspoken feminist. But Ashley was middle class and never regarded as a real Wobbly. See Sanger, *Autobiography*, 71; Vorse, *Footnote to Folly*, 57; Flynn, "The Value of Propaganda Leagues," *Solidarity*, 19 September 1914, p. 2; *Proceedings of the Eighth IWW Convention, September 15 to 29, 1913*, stenographic report (Cleveland, Ohio, n.d.), 76.

67. Flynn, "Problems in Organizing Women."

68. Flynn, "Women and Unionism," *Solidarity*, 27 May 1911, p. 4. Other radical women had similar attitudes. See Buhle, *Women and American Socialism*, 228; Helen Keller, "To An English Woman-Suffragist," in Philip S. Foner, ed., *Helen Keller: Her Socialist Years* (New York, 1967), 31–33.

69. Paterson *Evening News*, 12 June 1913, p. 7.

70. On Flynn's women's meetings in Paterson, see Chapter Two.

71. Flynn, "The I.W.W. Call to Women," *Solidarity*, 31 July 1915, p. 9. On the position of the IWW, and of Flynn, toward feminism and suffrage, see Tax, *The Rising of the Women*, 126–34, 178–83; Philip S. Foner, *Women and the American Labor Movement: From Colonial Times to the Eve of World War I* (New York, 1979), 405; *Industrial Worker*, 21 March 1912, p. 2; *Solidarity*, 10 May 1913, p. 4. For a critique of the IWW attitude toward the women's movement, see Katherine Hill, letter to the editor, *Solidarity*, 17 May 1913, p. 4.

72. Hutchins Hapgood, "Men and Ideas," New York *Globe*, 14 April 1913, p. 8. For Haywood's reference to women's rights in his Cooper Union speech (21 December 1911), see Haywood, "Socialism the Hope of the Working Class," *International Socialist Review* 12 (February 1912): 466–67.

73. Haywood, "On the Paterson Picket Line," *International Socialist Review* 13 (June 1912): 850 (the article was written May 12).

74. See, e.g., Elizabeth Gurley Flynn, "Memories of the Industrial Workers of the World (IWW)," talk given at Northern Illinois University, 8 November 1962 (transcript, in American Institute of Marxist Studies, New York, 1977), 10.

75. Note that originally, in 1906, Flynn's own acceptance into the IWW was problematic because she was not a wage worker: *Rebel Girl*, 77. On her physical and emotional breakdown, see Baxandall, "Elizabeth Gurley Flynn," 110–11. On her ambivalence toward Village intellectuals, see Helen C. Camp, "Gurley: A Biography of Elizabeth Gurley Flynn, 1890–1964" (doctoral diss., Columbia University, 1980), 113–14.

76. Note that at the time of the Paterson strike, the Liberal Club had not yet moved to the Village (it did so later in 1913) or caught its rebellious spirit.

CHAPTER FIVE

1. Upton Sinclair, *American Outpost: A Book of Reminiscences* (Pasadena, Calif., 1932), 262.

2. Letter from Wilbur Daniel Steele to Mary Heaton Vorse, n.d., in Vorse Collection, Box 54, Archives of Labor History, Wayne State University, Detroit.

3. Elizabeth Gurley Flynn, quoted in Paterson *Evening News*, 19 March 1913, p. 10; see also 11 March 1913, p. 1, and 14 May 1913, p. 1; Mary Sumner Brown, "Broad Silk Weavers of Paterson," *Survey* 27 (16 March 1912): 1932–33.

4. Max Eastman, *Enjoyment of Poetry* (New York, 1913), 169.

5. Paterson *Evening News*, 1 May 1913, p. 1; Alfred Cappio, "Paterson Silk Strike of 1913," July 1975 (manuscript in Paterson Public Library), 11.

6. Hutchins Hapgood, "A Day at Paterson," New York *Globe*, 22 April 1913, p. 8.

7. See, e.g., Albert Parry, *Garretts and Pretenders: A History of Bohemianism in America* (New York, 1960), 304; Leslie Fishbein, *Rebels in Bohemia: The Radicals of the Masses, 1911–1917* (Chapel Hill, N.C., 1982); and even Henry May, *The End of American Innocence: A Study of the First Years of Our Own Time, 1912–1917* (New York, 1964), 317.

8. E.g., the weekly *New Review* did not mention the strike until April 12. See also James M. Reilly, letter to New York *Call*, 3 June 1913, p. 6.

9. *Solidarity*, 19 April 1913, pp. 1, 2, 4. *Solidarity* had been moving its offices during the previous weeks and had missed two issues.

10. New York *Call*, 21 April 1913, p. 6.

11. Ibid., 3 April 1913, p. 2. On April 1, Koettgen and Magnet had spoken to a smaller audience at New York's Labor Temple: New York *Call*, 2 April 1913, p. 2.

12. New York *Globe*, 2 April 1913, p. 10. For Ashley's title as secretary, see New York *Call*, 1 April 1913, p. 3; "Monster Mass Meeting," leaflet in IWW Collection, Tamiment Library, New York University.

13. Paterson *Evening News*, 4 April 1913, p. 2. See also New York *Times*, 4 April 1913, p. 10; New York *Call*, 4 April 1913, p. 2.

14. *Solidarity*, 10 May 1913, p. 4. The ex-member of Parliament was Victor Grayson. For other April publicity and fund-raising events, see, e.g., New York *Call*, 7 April 1913, p. 1; 6 April 1913, p. 5; 18 April 1913, p. 5; 28 April 1913, p. 2; also *Solidarity*, 3 May 1913, p. 1.

15. Hutchins Hapgood, "Men and Ideas," New York *Globe*, 14 April 1913, p. 8. Note that in California in 1913, the IWW did turn to Women's Clubs for financial support: Joseph R. Conlin, *Bread and Roses Too: Studies of the Wobblies* (Westport, Conn., 1969), 79. (In Paterson in 1913 there were suffrage meetings, and a local men's group for women's suffrage was formed—but the IWW and strikers appear to have made no effort to contact the suffragists.) On the link Hapgood found between modern art and the IWW, see also Paul Avrich, *The Modern School Movement: Anarchism and Education in the United States* (Princeton, N.J., 1980), 138.

16. New York *Times*, 2 July 1913, p. 18.

17. *Bill Haywood's Book: The Autobiography of William D. Haywood* (New York, 1929), 262. On the booing, see also *Report of C.I.R.*, 2546. On the contrast between the new picketing and the old, see Meredith Tax, *The Rising of the Women: Feminist Solidarity and Class Conflict, 1880–1917* (New York, 1980), 247–48; Phillips Russell, "Strike Tactics," *New Review*, 1 (29 March 1913): 405–7; Mary E. Marcy, "The New York Garment Workers," *International Socialist Review* 13 (February 1913): 586.

18. Testimony of John W. Ferguson, *Report of C.I.R.*, 2580. On the importance of preventing Paterson from becoming another Lawrence, see also New York *Call*, 27 February 1913, p. 6.

19. New York *Call*, 14 March 1913, p. 4.

20. William D. Haywood, "On the Paterson Picket Line," *International Socialist Review* 13 (June 1913): 849; William Morris Feigenbaum, "Paterson and Lawrence (Some Inside Facts)," New York *Call*, 3 May 1913, p. 6.

21. Paterson *Evening News*, 5 March 1913, p. 9; New York *Call*, 27 February 1913, p. 1, and 29 March 1913, p. 1; Haywood, "On the Paterson Picket Line," 851; *Solidarity*, 17 May 1913, p. 1. See also Paterson *Evening News*, 4 April 1913, p. 9, and 12 May 1913, p. 10.

22. Elizabeth Gurley Flynn, "The Truth about the Paterson Strike," in *Rebel Voices: An I.W.W. Anthology*, ed. Joyce L. Kornbluh (Ann Arbor, Mich., 1964), 219. For Flynn's recognition of the role of Pennsylvania, see pp. 216–17, 224.

23. Russell, "Strike Tactics," 407. Note that the Little Falls strike was seen by the IWW as "a miniature repetition of the great Lawrence strike": Haywood, *Bill Haywood's Book*, 257. Also see untitled manuscript on Little Falls (M. Robbins Collection, Box 2, Archives of Labor History), 2.

24. Elizabeth Gurley Flynn, *The Rebel Girl: An Autobiography* (New York, 1973), 155.

25. Paterson *Evening News*, 1 April 1913, p. 11.

26. Ibid., 4 April 1913, p. 9, and 4 April 1913, p. 1 (the *Evening News* was quoting Flynn and paraphrasing the IWW speakers). See also New York *Call*, 16 May 1913, p. 2. On Haywood's support for a federal investigation *because* it worked in Lawrence, see Paterson *Evening News*, 14 April 1913, p. 7. On the small businessmen, compare Flynn's notes for a Paterson speech with the same points she made in Lawrence: *Rebel Girl*, 159, 133.

27. For the IWW's chronic dissatisfaction with the amount of picketing, see, e.g., Paterson *Evening News*, 28 April 1913, p. 7.

28. Paterson *Evening News*, 13 March 1913, p. 10.

29. Ibid., 17 April 1913, p. 9. The same article cites Haywood's April 14 announcement.

30. Ibid., 18 April 1913, p. 1; see also 21 April 1913, p. 10. The possibility of sending the children away was mentioned by the IWW as early as March: New York *Call*, 20 March 1913, p. 1.

31. On the attempt to recruit Italian children, see New York *Call*, 25 April 1913, p. 2; Paterson *Evening News*, 5 May 1913, p. 9. On the demand exceeding the supply, see *Solidarity*, 7 June 1913, p. 4; Paterson *Evening News*, 9 May 1913, p. 11. On parental fear and parental pride, see Newark *News*, 30 April 1913, and Minnie Keller, interview with author, Paterson, N.J., 18 June 1982.

32. New York *Call*, 28 April 1913, p. 1; Paterson *Evening News*, 1 May 1913, p. 1, and 6 May 1913, p. 11. The Ferrer School, which had taken children from Lawrence, also took children from Paterson: Avrich, *The Modern School Movement*, 90. Applications in New York were sent to Sanger: New York *Call*, 25 April 1913, p. 2. On Sanger, Ashley, and Sloan in Paterson, see New York *Call*, 22 April 1913, p. 2; Paterson *Evening News*, 1 May 1913, p. 1, and 6 May 1913, p. 11.

33. New York *Call*, 2 May 1913, p. 1; Paterson *Evening News*, 1 May 1913, p. 1. On the excitement of the trip, see the *Record* (New Jersey), 26 September 1983, p. A6.

34. Ann Janowitz Korn, quoted in Paterson *Evening News*, 27 September 1983, p. 2.

35. Ella Taub Dorfman, interview by Ruth Schwartz, 16 July 1983, on tape in Charles Goldman Judaica Library, YM/YWHA, Wayne, N.J.

36. Dave Welsh, quoted in Paterson *Evening News*, 27 September 1983, p. 3, and the *Record*, 26 September 1983, p. A6. See also interview with Dave Welsh, 1 August 1983 (on tape in Charles Goldman Judaica Library).

37. Charles Taub, quoted in Paterson *Evening News*, 27 September 1983, p. 3, and the *Record*, 26 September 1983, p. A6.

38. Hutchins Hapgood, *A Victorian in the Modern World* (New York, 1939), 356.

39. Paterson *Evening News*, 27 June 1913, p. 1. By the end of May, 427 children were already in New York, and 116 were in Elizabeth, according to the Paterson *Evening News*, 31 May 1913, p. 1; somewhat lower figures were given by *Solidarity*, 7 June 1913, p. 4. Note that when New York families went away on summer vacation, children were sometimes placed with families who had to be paid to keep them, thereby draining the relief fund: New York *Call*, 23 June 1913, p. 2.

40. See, e.g., New York *Call*, 24 April 1913, p. 1; 25 April 1913, p. 2; 23 May 1913, p. 6.

41. "Haywood's Battle in Paterson," *Literary Digest* 46 (10 May 1913): 1044. On McBride's offer, see also New York *Call*, 28 April 1913, p. 1. A committee of five striking mothers, with Carrie Golzio as their spokesperson, led the first group of eighty-five children and their parents to City Hall in the hope of exposing the insincerity of the mayor's offer: New York *Call*, 1 May 1913, p. 1; Carrie Golzio, interview with author, Haledon, N.J., 13 June 1983; Paterson *Morning Call*, 1 May 1913—where Golzio is cited as Gold. (Thanks to Delight Dodyk.) On Little Falls, see Robert Snyder, "Women, Wobblies, and Workers' Rights: The 1912 Textile Strike in Little Falls, New York," *New York History* 60 (January 1979): 52.

42. Hutchins Hapgood, "The Poet's Arrest," New York *Globe*, 7 May 1913, p. 10.

43. Hapgood, "The Poet's Arrest," 10; Robert A. Rosenstone, *Romantic Revolutionary: A Biography of John Reed* (New York, 1975), 119. In jail, Reed sometimes said he was gathering material for a story (New York *Globe*, 28 April 1913, p. 1) or for "an epic," according to Eddy Hunt (Rosenstone, *Romantic Revolutionary*, 126).

44. New York *Times*, 28 April 1913, p. 2. For what he saw on Ellison Street, see John Reed, "War in Paterson," *The Masses* 4 (June 1913), in *Echoes of Revolt: THE MASSES, 1911–1917*, ed. William O'Neill (Chicago, 1966), 143. For his own version of his arrest, which is similar to that in the *Times*, see Reed, "War in Paterson," 144; and John Reed, "Sheriff Radcliff's Hotel: What One Man Saw in a County Jail," *Metropolitan* 38 (September 1913): 14. Other accounts give a different reason for Reed's arrest: see New York *Globe*, 1 April 1913, p. 1; Max Eastman, "Jack Reed—A Memoir," in *The Complete Poetry of John Reed*, ed. Jack Alan Robbins (Washington, D.C., 1983), 71–72; Max Eastman, *Heroes I Have Known* (New York, 1942), 210–11; *Report of C.I.R.*, 2560. What seems clear is that when confronted with a choice of jail or backing down, Reed chose jail. On the pickets' use of stoops to avoid arrest, see James D. Osborne, "Italian Immigrants and the Working Class in Paterson: The Strike of 1913 in Ethnic Perspective," in *New Jersey's Ethnic Heritage*, ed. Paul A. Stellhorn (Trenton, N.J., 1978), 18; James D. Osborne, "Industrialization and the Politics of Disorder: Paterson Silk Workers, 1880–1913" (doctoral diss., University of Warwick, England, 1979), 133.

45. New York *Call*, 30 April 1913, p. 6. For the interview, see New York *Globe*, 28 April 1913, p. 1. See also New York *Times*, 29 April 1913, p. 1; and Rosenstone, *Romantic Revolutionary*, 120, 397 (on the New York *Evening Sun*).

46. New York *Call*, 30 April 1913, p. 6; Patrick Quinlan, "Silk, Starvation, and Solidarity," *Appeal to Reason*, 16 August 1913, p. 2.

47. Margaret Sanger, *Margaret Sanger: An Autobiography* (New York, 1971), 70.

48. Paterson *Evening News*, 19 May 1913, p. 10.

49. *Report of C.I.R.*, 2560.

50. John Reed, *The Day in Bohemia; Or, Life among the Artists* (New York, 1913), 15–16. The poem was privately printed in January 1913.

51. Letter from John Reed to Eddy Hunt, n.d., quoted in Rosenstone, *Romantic Revolutionary*, 121.

52. Reed, "War in Paterson," 147. For echoes of his earlier attitude, see 145.

53. New York *Call*, 7 May 1913, p. 1; 8 May 1913, p. 2; 9 May 1913, p. 2; also *Solidarity*, 24 May 1913, p. 1.

54. John Reed, letter to the Editor, 12 May 1913, in New York *Globe*, 13 May 1913, p. 10. Reed listed several addresses to which readers could bring goods.

55. Reed, "War in Paterson," 143.

56. Franklin Pierce Adams, quoted in Granville Hicks, *John Reed: The Making of a Revolutionary* (New York, 1936), 101; John Reed, letter to Robert Andrew, 17 October 1912, quoted in Rosenstone, *Romantic Revolutionary*, 98.

57. Paterson *Evening News*, 19 May 1913, p. 10; Haywood, *Bill Haywood's Book*, 262. On Reed's embarassment and on Lippmann, Dodge, and Jones, see Hicks, *John Reed*, 100.

58. Paterson *Evening News*, 19 May 1913, p. 10; Hutchins Hapgood, "See No Sign of Strike's Loss," New York *Globe*, in Mabel Dodge Luhan, *Movers and Shakers*, vol. 3 of *Intimate Memories* (New York, 1936), 202.

59. John Reed, "Almost Thirty," in *The New Republic Anthology: 1915–1935*, ed. Groff Conklin (New York, 1936), 70. On Reed's openness to and readiness for Paterson, see Rosenstone, *Romantic Revolutionary*, 123.

60. Moses Rischin, introduction to Hutchins Hapgood, *The Spirit of the Ghetto* (Cambridge, Mass., 1967), ix–xx, xxxiii–xxxv. For a purely psychological (and hostile) view of Hapgood's search for alternative sources of value, see Robert E. Humphrey, *Children of Fantasy: The First Rebels of Greenwich Village* (New York, 1978), 54–81.

61. Hapgood, "Men and Ideas."

62. Hapgood, "A Day at Paterson."

63. Ibid.

64. Hapgood, "Facts and Feelings," New York *Globe*, 24 April 1913, p. 8.

65. Hapgood, "See No Sign of Strike's Loss," 203. As the title suggests, Hapgood stressed that firsthand experience of the strike dispelled all press-inspired rumors of its demise.

66. Ibid., 202.

67. New York *Globe*, 21 May 1913, p. 4.

68. Hapgood, "Creative Liberty," New York *Globe*, 7 June 1913, p. 7.

69. Hapgood, "The Socialists and the Social Movement," New York *Globe*, 2 June 1913, p. 8. For a similar point, see E.L., letter to the editor, New York *Globe*, 5 June 1913, p. 5.

70. One of Tridon's photographs of Haywood with silk strikers is in Phillips Russell, "The Arrest of Haywood and Lessig," *International Socialist Review* 13 (May 1913): 792.

71. André Tridon, "Haywood," *New Review* 1 (May 1913): 502 (original emphasis); Tridon estimates Haywood's height, p. 503. Haywood's actual height is given by Peter Carlson, *Roughneck: The Life and Times of Big Bill Haywood* (New York, 1983), 16.

72. Tridon, "Haywood," 506.

73. André Tridon, *The New Unionism* (New York, 1913), 2. Tridon was more directly tied to European syndicalism than to the IWW. See David Montgomery, *Worker's Control in America: Studies in the History of Work, Technology, and Labor Struggles* (London, 1979), 91.

74. Dodge Luhan, *Movers and Shakers*, 187.

75. Mathilda Rabinowitz Robbins, "My Story," (M. Robbins Collection, Box 2, Archives of Labor History), 56; note that Rabinowitz was also critical of Flynn. On Sanger's confusion about Haywood and violence, see Sanger, *Autobiography*, 158; she blamed Haywood's policy of nonviolence for the defeat of the strike.

76. Mary Heaton Vorse, "Elizabeth Gurley Flynn" (typescript in Vorse Collection, Box 19, Archives of Labor History), 4.

77. Sanger, *Autobiography*, 85: "I only walked on. . . ." For a modern version that falls prey to her own, see David M. Kennedy, *Birth Control in America: The Career of Margaret Sanger* (New Haven, Conn., 1970), 11.

78. Patrick M. Lynch, "Pennsylvania Anthracite: A Forgotten IWW Venture, 1906–1916" (master's thesis, Bloomsburg State College, Bloomsburg, Penna., 1974), 131–32; Alexander Campbell Sanger, "Margaret Sanger: The Early Years, 1910–1917" (senior thesis, 1969), 47; Paterson *Evening News*, 9 April 1913, p. 7; New York *Call*, 9 April 1913, p. 1; *Solidarity*, 19 April 1913, p. 3. See also Haywood, *Bill Haywood's Book*, 268.

79. A. Sanger, "Margaret Sanger," 48; Lynch, "Pennsylvania Anthracite," 135.

80. Margaret Sanger, "Hazleton Strikers Repudiate A.F. of L.," *Solidarity*, 19 April 1913, p. 3. On this article's lack of realism, see Lynch, "Pennsylvania Anthracite," 132–33.

81. New York *Call*, 22 April 1913, p. 2; A. Sanger, "Margaret Sanger," 49.

82. New York *Call*, 10 June 1913, p. 4. The title of the book, like that of the articles, was *What Every Girl Should Know*. On the role of IWW women in the national birth control network, see Tax, *Rising of the Women*, 157–58. On the IWW and birth control, see also Caroline Nelson, "Neo-Malthusianism: The Control of Child Bearing," *International Socialist Review* 14 (October 1913): 230; Elizabeth Gurley Flynn, "Problems in Organizing Women," *Solidarity*, 15 July 1916, p. 3; Tax, *Rising of the Women*, 155–56. Sometimes Flynn and the IWW regarded birth control as a type of sabotage: see Elizabeth Gurley Flynn, *Sabotage* (Cleveland, Ohio, 1914), 28–29; Arturo Giovannitti, introduction to Emile Pouget, *Sabotage* (Chicago, 1913), 17–18.

83. Harold Hersey, "Margaret Sanger: The Biography of the Birth Control Pioneer" (unpublished manuscript, 1938, in Rare Book Collection, New York Public Library), 108–10. Hersey interviewed Tresca and apparently corresponded with Mrs. Boyd. See also Delight W. Dodyk, "Women's Work in the Paterson Silk Mills: A Study in Women's Industrial Experiences in the Early Twentieth Century," in *Women in New Jersey History*, ed. Mary R. Murrin (Trenton, N.J., 1985), 22.

84. New York *Call*, 8 June 1913, p. 2. See also Rosenstone, *Romantic Revolutionary*, 127; Kornbluh, *Rebel Voices*, 201.

85. Harry Kemp, *More Miles: An Autobiographical Novel* (New York, 1926), 401, 403–4, 405–6, 408 (Sanger is called Lilla Matthewson; Boyd is Sam Flood). Note that Kemp is worthless on the silk workers, interesting but unreliable on the IWW speakers, and good on the Villagers.

86. Looking back, Sanger emphasized class differences *within* the left in 1913: *Autobiography*, 71–74.

87. Florence Lucas Sanville, "A Woman in the Pennsylvania Silk Mills," *Harpers' Monthly Magazine* 120 (April 1910): 652.

88. Ibid., 660.

89. Kemp, *More Miles*, 399 (Rodman is called Godman). On Rodman in Paterson, see also Rosenstone, *Romantic Revolutionary*, 125. On the efforts of New Yorkers in the relief stations, see Max Eastman, *Venture* (New York, 1927), 232.

90. Carl Van Vechten, *Peter Whiffle* (New York, 1923), 124 (Dodge is "Edith Dale"). On Dodge in Paterson, see also Hicks, *Reed*, 100.

91. *Report of C.I.R.*, 2524.

92. Hapgood, "A Day at Paterson," 8. Hapgood, visiting Paterson for the first time on April 21, left before the armory meeting. Sanger was in Paterson that day, too, but doesn't fit Hapgood's description. Whoever it was, Hapgood must have talked to her late Monday or early Tuesday in order to get her account in the Tuesday *Globe*—and he regularly visited Dodge in the morning: see Dodge Luhan, *Movers and Shakers*, 200.

93. Inis Weed and Louise Carey, eds., "I Make Cheap Silk," *The Masses* 5 (November 1913), 7. Published in November, most of the interview was conducted during the strike.

94. On Ashley in Paterson as a legal advisor, see New York *Call*, 8 May 1913, p. 2. On Ashley in Hazleton, see Lynch, "Pennsylvania Anthracite," 133; Haywood, *Bill Haywood's Book*, 268.

95. Paterson *Evening News*, 5 June 1913, p. 7. Keller spoke in Passaic in April, but there is no indication that she mentioned the strike. See Paterson *Evening News*, 8 April 1913, p. 11.

96. On Schloss, see New York *Call*, 1 March 1913, p. 1; *Solidarity*, 15 March 1913, p. 4. Her Little Falls activities are described in Snyder, "Women, Wobblies, and Workers' Rights," 42–48. On Malkiel, see Paterson *Evening News*, 28 March 1913, p. 11; New York *Call*, 29 March 1913, p. 1, and 2 April 1913, p. 1. On Thompson, see Paterson *Evening News*, 6 March 1913, p. 12. On Goldstein, see Paterson *Evening News*, 7 July 1913, p. 9.

97. Paterson *Evening News*, 25 April 1913, p. 13; New York *Call*, 25 April 1913, p. 2.

98. On Panken, Paterson *Evening News*, 19 March 1913, p. 12; New York *Call*, 21 March 1913, p. 2; 4 April 1913, p. 2; 16 April 1913, p. 5. On former Assemblyman James Reed and former Mayor Emil Seidel, see New York *Call*, 23 April 1913, p. 2; Paterson *Evening News*, 5 April 1913, p. 7.

99. Ernest Poole, *The Bridge: My Own Story* (New York, 1940), 198. See also Sinclair, *American Outpost*, 262; Rosenstone, *Romantic Revolutionary*, 125.

100. New York *Times*, 19 May 1913, p. 1; Paterson *Evening News*, 19 May 1913, p. 9; New York *Call*, 19 May 1913, p. 1; Upton Sinclair, *The Brass Check* (Pasadena, Calif., 1928), 123.

101. Paterson *Evening News*, 20 May 1913, p. 10, and 17 April 1913, p. 9. On the "ill feeling" created by Harrison's speech, see also John Fitch, "The I.W.W., an Outlaw Organization," *Survey* 30 (7 June 1913): 360.

102. Paterson *Evening News*, 22 May 1913, p. 5. During the strike, Koettgen explained to a visitor that there were no blacks among the strikers because "the silk bosses . . . won't hire Black men and women. The IWW welcomes Black workers": Art Shields, *My Shaping-up Years: The Early Life of Labor's Great Reporter* (New York, 1983), 162. The IWW at this time was organizing blacks and whites together, in the Louisiana woods as well as on the Philadelphia docks.

103. Paterson *Evening News*, 28 April 1913, p. 7. On the minister's other appearances before the strikers or on their behalf, see New York *Call*, 1 March 1913, p. 1; 7 April 1913, p. 1; 19 May 1913, p. 1; 30 May 1913, p. 1; also *Solidarity*, 15 March 1913, p. 4; Paterson *Evening News*, 8 April 1913, p. 9; New York *Times*, 19 May 1913, p. 2.

105. On the Manhattan and Brooklyn connections, see letter from Sam Handelman, John Harrison, Z. Lefkovitch, H. Margolis, and L. Rosen to *Jewish Daily Forward*, 8 August 1909, and letter from Patricia Lievow to Sylvia Firshein, 4 March 1984, both in Charles Goldman Judaica Library; also George Shea, interview with author, 23 May 1983, New York. On the pledge of support to the strike on its very first day by the Passaic County Socialist Party, see New York *Call*, 26 February 1913, p. 2.

106. New York *Call*, 7 March 1913, p. 1. Speakers from New Jersey were also requested.

107. See Chapter Four. On the Ferrer School and Paterson children, see New York *Call*, 2 May 1913, p. 1, and 17 May 1913, p. 1; New York *Globe*, 1 May 1913, p. 1. In 1915 a Ferrer Sunday School opened in a Paterson storefront, which was sometimes used for IWW meetings in later strikes: Avrich, *Modern School Movement*, 47, 666; Sophie Cohen, interview by Deborah Shaffer and Stewart Bird, 17 December 1977 (typescript, Program on Women and Work, University of Michigan/Wayne State University), pt. 1, 19. On the role in the 1913 strike of the old Yiddish anarchist Saul Yanofsky, see New York *Call*, 31 May 1913, p. 2.

108. On Leroy Scott, e.g., see Rosenstone, *Romantic Revolutionary*, 125; Sinclair, *American Outpost*, 262; and Chapter Six, n. 34.

109. Walter Lippmann, "The I.W.W. — Insurrection or Revolution," *New Review*, 1 (August 1913): 701, 702, 705. Lippmann made the identical point just *before* Paterson; see his *A Preface to Politics* (1913; Ann Arbor, Mich., 1962), 183.

110. Daniel S. McCorkle, letter to New York *Globe*, 24 May 1913, p. 6.

111. Shields, *My Shaping-Up Years*, 159–64.

112. George Middleton, *These Things Are Mine: The Autobiography of a Journeyman Playwright* (New York, 1947), 114.

113. Paterson *Evening News*, 26 April 1913, p. 1. On his ambivalence about speaking, see also Kemp, *More Miles*, 404–7.

114. Kemp, *More Miles*, 399, 400.

115. Max Eastman, *Enjoyment of Living* (New York, 1948), 447, 445–46.

116. Ibid., 445–47.

117. Ibid., 447–48; Eastman, *Venture*, 232.

118. Hapgood, "See No Sign of Strike's Loss," 202.

119. Eastman, *Enjoyment of Living*, 446. He was referring to speaking in Paterson in 1913 and in Colorado in 1914.

120. *The Masses* 4 (June 1913): 6.

121. "A Key Word," *The Masses* 4 (August 1913): 6.

122. Ibid., "Abracadabra." Mary Heaton Vorse similarly concluded that the wartime hatred and persecution of the IWW had nothing to do with its supposed violence but had everything to do with its genuine commitment to workers' control; see her *Footnote to Folly: Reminiscences of Mary Heaton Vorse* (New York, 1935), 159–60.

123. "Abracadabra," *The Masses* 4 (August 1913): 6; Eastman, *Enjoyment of Living*, 447.

124. Richard Perin, "Go to Haledon," New York *Call*, 17 May 1913, p. 6; this column was reprinted in *Solidarity*, 24 May 1913, p. 2.

125. Helen Meadow, interview by Rita Isaacs and Jerry Nathans, 17 August 1982, and 24 August 1982, on tape in the Charles Goldman Judaica Library.

126. Alexander Scott, "What the Reds Are Doing in Paterson," *International Socialist Review* 13 (June 1913): 854. Note that Haledon's Borough Council, which was not Socialist and which generally opposed Brueckmann, agreed to allow the strikers to meet in Haledon: New York *Call*, 3 March 1913, p. 1.

127. Paterson *Evening News*, 20 May 1913, p. 10; *Report of C.I.R.*, 2526.

128. *Report of C.I.R.*, 2567. The Socialist deputies were "husky strikers" who resided in Haledon: Paterson *Evening News*, 30 June 1913, p. 10.

129. See, e.g., Russell, "The Arrest of Haywood and Lessig," 789. On Haledon as a streetcar suburb, see John Herbst, *A Slice of the Earth* (Haledon, N.J., 1982), 38–43, originally published as an article in *New Jersey History* 99 (Spring/Summer 1981).

130. New York *Call*, 10 March 1913, p. 1, and 18 March 1913, p. 6; *Solidarity*, 15 March 1913, p. 3.

131. See New York *Times*, 24 May 1913, p. 6; *Solidarity*, 31 May 1913, p. 4; and Chapter Seven.

132. New York *Call*, 3 March 1913, p. 1.

133. Paterson *Evening News*, 3 March 1913, p. 7. See also New York *Call*, 3 March 1913, p. 1, and 4 April 1913, p. 2; *Solidarity*, 15 March 1913, p. 4. For the even bigger March 9 meeting, see New York *Call*, 4 April 1913, p. 1.

134. Paterson *Evening News*, 3 March 1913, p. 7.

135. Paterson *Evening News*, 4 April 1913, p. 9. The first Sunday meeting at the Botto house was on April 6: New York *Call*, 7 April 1913, p. 1. On the beginning of the singing, see New York *Call*, 10 March 1913, p. 1; and on the first big picnic day in Haledon, 5 May 1913, p. 1.

136. Flynn, *Rebel Girl*, 165. On the hill, woods, and house, see also New York *Call*, 7 April 1913, p. 1; *Solidarity*, 24 May 1913, p. 4. On Pietro Botto, a weaver from Piedmont, and his family, see Bunny Kuiken and Sylvia Bochese, interview by Robert Kirkman, Haledon, N.J., 19 March 1981; Herbst, *A Slice of the Earth*, 37, 44.

137. William Haywood, "The Rip in the Silk Industry," *International Socialist Review* 13 (May 1913): 788. On the translating and shushing, Carl Zigrosser, "Sunday at Haledon," New York *Call*, 11 June 1913, p. 6 (which spelled his name "Gigrosser").

138. Paterson *Evening News*, 4 April 1913, p. 9. On the disappointment of the police, see also New York *Call*, 7 April 1913, p. 2. On the collections at Haledon, see *Solidarity*, 7 June 1913, p. 4; Paterson *Evening News*, 19 May 1913, p. 9.

139. New York *Call*, 4 April 1913, p. 1.

140. New York *Times*, 19 May 1913, p. 1, which put the crowd at "more than 20,000." *Solidarity*, 24 May 1913, p. 4, called it the largest meeting yet.

141. *Solidarity*, 31 May 1913, p. 1; New York *Call*, 26 May 1913, p. 1; New York *Times*, 26 May 1913, p. 2. Note that May 18 constituted the strikers' answer to Quinlan's conviction, and May 25 their answer to the closing of the halls.

142. New York *Call*, 25 May 1913, p. 1.

143. Paterson *Evening News*, 9 April 1913, p. 1; Flynn, "The Truth about the Paterson Strike," 219.

144. Shields, *My Shaping-Up Years*, 160.

145. Perin, "Go to Haledon."

146. Zigrosser, "Sunday at Haledon."

147. Hapgood, "See No Sign of Strike's Loss," 202, 203. On the respect shown by the strikers for Maria Botto's lawn, see also *Report of C.I.R.*, 2526.

148. Eastman, *Enjoyment of Living*, 447; Poole, *The Bridge*, 198.

149. Testimony of Scott, *Report of C.I.R.*, 2526.

150. Perin, "Go to Haledon."

151. On the continuing round of meetings in New York, see, e.g., New York *Times*, 12 May 1913, p. 2, and 17 May 1913, p. II-8; Paterson *Evening News* 23 May 1913, p. 4; *Solidarity*, 24 May 1913, p. 1; New York *Call*, 21 May 1913, p. 2, and 30 May 1913, p. 1. On the diminishing returns from these repeated meetings, see, e.g., New York *Call*, 1 June 1913, p. 1. On more imaginative "benefits" (including one featuring movies of the strike!), see New York *Call*, 28 May 1913, p. 4; 29 May 1913, pp. 1, 4; 3 June 1913, p. 1; 4 June 1913, p. 4. (On film as a means of Socialist propaganda, see Julius Hopp, letter to the editor, New York *Call*, 26 June 1913, p. 5.)

CHAPTER SIX

1. Raymond Williams, *Modern Tragedy* (Stanford, Calif., 1966), 20.

2. See, e.g., Graham Adams, Jr., *Age of Industrial Violence, 1910 to 1915: The Activities and Findings of the United States Commission on Industrial Relations* (New York, 1966), 96–97; Philip S. Foner, *The Industrial Workers of the World, 1905–1917*, vol. 4 of *History of the Labor Movement in the United States* (New York, 1965), 366–67; Daniel Aaron, *Writers on the Left* (New York, 1961), 35; Granville Hicks, *John Reed: The Making of a Revolutionary* (New York, 1936), 103–4.

3. See, e.g., James D. Osborne, "The Paterson Strike of 1913: Immigrant Silk Workers and the I.W.W. Response to the Problem of Stable Unionism" (master's thesis, University of Warwick, England 1973), 61–63; Melvyn Dubofsky, *We Shall Be All: A History of the Industrial Workers of the World* (Chicago, 1969), 279–81; Joseph R. Conlin, *Big Bill Haywood and the Radical Union Movement* (Syracuse, N.Y., 1969), 142; Robert A. Rosenstone, *Romantic Revolutionary: A Biography of John Reed* (New York, 1975), 131; Robert E. Humphrey, *Children of Fantasy: The First Rebels of Greenwich Village* (New York, 1978), 21–22.

4. *Solidarity*, 28 December 1912, p. 4.

5. Foner, *Industrial Workers of the World*, 324, 340–41. See also Lillian Symes and Travers Clement, *Rebel America* (New York, 1934), 272.

6. New York *Times*, 25 May 1913, p. II-4.

7. *Solidarity*, 31 May 1913, p. 1. For an example of the editorial stance of New York newspapers, see New York *Times*, 30 May 1913, p. 6. On the complaints of the left about the way the newspapers in New York treated the strike, see Haywood, quoted

in New York *Times*, 25 May 1913, p. II-4; New York *Call*, 23 May 1913, p. 6. On the difficulty in getting newspaper publicity for an IWW strike in Pittsburgh in 1913, see Patrick Lynch, "Pittsburgh, the I.W.W. and the Stogie Workers," in *At the Point of Production: The Local History of the I.W.W.*, ed. Joseph R. Conlin (Westport, Conn., 1981), 86.

8. Paterson *Evening News*, 16 May 1913, p. 1.

9. New York *Times*, 13 May 1913, p. 20.

10. Ibid., 18 May 1913, p. II-1.

11. Letter from William Varney to New York *Globe*, 16 May 1913, p. 10, and 15 May 1913, p. 8; New York *Times*, 15 May 1913, p. 2. Another Paterson striker had already been arrested in April for soliciting in New York for the relief fund. Paterson *Evening News*, 25 June 1913, p. 5. On fund raising for the Paterson strike in Newark, Chicago, Detroit, Pittsburgh, Philadelphia, Schenectady, Rome (New York), Boston, Lowell, Lawrence, and Baltimore, see New York *Call*, 10 May 1913, p. 3, and 15 May 1913, p. 2; *Solidarity*, 19 April 1913, p. 4, and 28 June 1913, p. 4; Paterson *Evening News*, 3 May 1913, p. 1; 5 May 1913, p. 10; 22 May 1913, p. 9; 10 June 1913, p. 1; also New York *Globe*, 1 May 1913, p. 1; New York *Times*, 28 April 1913, p. 2.

12. William D. Haywood, *Bill Haywood's Book: The Autobiography of William D. Haywood* (New York, 1929), 262. On the details of the meeting, see Hutchins Hapgood, "The Poet's Arrest," New York *Globe*, 7 May 1913, p. 10.

13. William D. Haywood, "The Rip in the Silk Industry," *International Socialist Review* 13 (May 1913), 784 (this article was written in mid-April).

14. Hutchins Hapgood, *A Victorian in the Modern World* (New York, 1939), 350.

15. Mabel Dodge Luhan, *Movers and Shakers*, vol. 3 of *Intimate Memories* (New York, 1936), 188.

16. New York *Times*, 22 May 1913, p. 4.

17. Harry Kemp, *More Miles: An Autobiographical Novel* (New York, 1926), 403 (Reed is Halton Mann in the book).

18. Paterson *Evening News*, 9 June 1913, p. 7.

19. Ibid., 24 June 1913, p. 1. On the relief fund in the weeks after the Pageant, see below, Chapter Seven.

20. Compare, e.g., Paterson *Evening News*, 19 May 1913, p. 1, and 7 June 1913, p. 7.

21. New York *Globe*, 21 May 1913, p. 4.

22. For examples of the early reports of huge profits, see New York *Times*, 8 June 1913, p. II-2; New York *Press*, 8 June 1913, p. 1. For a protest against the subsequent condemnation of the IWW by the press, see Jessie Ashley, letter in Paterson *Evening News*, 14 June 1913, p. 2.

23. *Solidarity*, 7 June 1913, p. 4.

24. "Paterson Pageant Financial Statement," issued by the Pageant Executive Committee and printed in full in New York *Call*, 26 June 1913, p. 5. The Executive Committee consisted of Haywood, Dodge, Reed, Ashley, Boyd, and Sanger.

25. Ibid. See Phillips Russell, "The World's Greatest Labor Play," *International Socialist Review* 14 (July 1913): 8. Russell's article was written before the financial loss became known.

26. Paterson *Evening News*, 16 May 1913, p. 11.

27. New York *Times*, 19 May 1913, p. 2.

28. Paterson *Evening News*, 19 May 1913, p. 10. On Reed's cheerleading background, see John Reed, "Almost Thirty," in *The New Republic Anthology: 1915–1935*, ed. Groff Conklin (New York, 1936): 65. See also Upton Sinclair, *American Outpost: A Book of Reminiscences* (Pasadena, Calif., 1932), 263.

29. Hicks, *John Reed*, 101.

30. Ibid., 101–2. On Reed's relationship to the strikers, see also Susan Glaspell, *Road to the Temple* (New York, 1927), 250.

31. New York *Call*, 6 June 1913, p. 2.

32. Ibid., 7 June 1913, p. 1 (Rose Pastor Stokes wrote the article). Another striker in the Pageant made the same point: Carrie Golzio, interview with author, Haledon, N.J., 13 June 1983.

33. Hutchins Hapgood, "The Strikers' Pageant," New York *Globe*, 9 June 1913, p. 6.

34. Paterson *Evening News*, 3 June 1913, p. 5. On playing the police, see also New York *Call*, 29 May 1913, p. 1, and 7 June 1913, p. 1.

35. New York *Globe*, 6 June 1913, p. 5.

36. New York *Call*, 21 May 1913, p. 2.

37. New York *Globe*, 7 June 1913, p. 1; Paterson *Evening News*, 7 June 1913, p. 1, 7; New York *Call*, 8 June 1913, p. 2. On the hungry strikers and lunch, see Sinclair, *American Outpost*, 263.

38. Linda Nochlin, "The Paterson Strike Pageant of 1913," *Art in America* 52 (May–June 1974), 67. On the organic relation between the strike and the Pageant, see also Hapgood, *A Victorian in the Modern World*, 351.

39. "Paterson Pageant Financial Statement."

40. Rosenstone, *Romantic Revolutionary*, 127; New York *Globe*, 6 June 1913, p. 5; Paterson *Evening News*, 27 May 1913, p. 1.

41. Sinclair, *American Outpost*, 263.

42. *Bill Haywood's Book*, 263. In addition to doing the scenery, staging, and publicity, New Yorkers built the great stage and runway, raised the money, rented a hall (at first they had wanted the Hippodrome), arranged for the special train that brought the performers to New York and for the big red "IWW" that lit up vertically above the Garden and over New York (too late for the police to start the legal machinery to turn it off). They even begged red carnations from floral shops throughout the city for the funeral scene. See Dodge Luhan, *Movers and Shakers*, 203–4.

43. Hapgood, *A Victorian in the Modern World*, 351. See also Adams, *Age of Industrial Violence*, 95.

44. Percy MacKaye, *The Civic Theatre in Relation to the Redemption of Leisure* (New York, 1912), 18–19. On MacKaye, Reed, and the Pageant, see Hicks, *Reed*, 101.

45. W.L.S., "The Civic Theater," *New Review* 1 (15 March 1913): 351.

46. Nochlin, "The Paterson Strike Pageant," 68. On the extent to which the Pageant's creators succeeded in transforming pageantry, see also "The Paterson Strike Pageant," *Independent* 74 (19 June 1913): 1406.

47. Rose Pastor Stokes, "Tonight's Red Pageant at Garden," New York *Call*, 7 June 1913, p. 1.

48. Dodge Luhan, *Movers and Shakers*, 204.

49. Paterson *Evening News*, 9 June 1913, p. 7; New York *Press*, 8 June 1913, p. 1; New York *Call*, 9 June 1913, p. 6.

50. Grace Potter, "Max Eastman's Two Books," *New Review* 1 (September 1913): 795. On Potter, see Judith Schwarz, *Radical Feminists of Heterodoxy: Greenwich Village, 1912–1940* (Lebanon, N.H., 1982), 10, 43, 51, 91. The big silk mill in the backdrop was said to represent the Doherty plant: New York *Call*, 8 June 1913, p. 1.

51. "The Paterson Strike Pageant," 1406.

52. *Solidarity*, 14 June 1913, p. 3.

53. Russell, "The World's Greatest Labor Play," 9.

54. Quoted in Dodge Luhan, *Movers and Shakers*, 206.

55. New York *Press*, 8 June 1913, p. 1.

56. *Solidarity*, 14 June 1913, p. 3.

57. Paterson *Evening News*, 9 June 1913, p. 4. Haines had attended the Pageant.

58. New York *Times*, 8 June 1913, p. II-2; Paterson *Evening News*, 9 June 1913, p. 7. For the inclusion of Silverman among those arrested in this scene, see New York *Press*, 8 June 1913, p. 3.

59. *Solidarity*, 14 June 1913, p. 3.

60. Paterson *Evening News*, 9 June 1913, p. 7.

61. New York *Tribune*, quoted in *Current Opinion* 55 (July 1913): 32.

62. Dodge Luhan, *Movers and Shakers*, 204.

63. Russell, "The World's Greatest Labor Play," 9; New York *Press*, 8 June 1913, p. 3.

64. Paterson *Evening News*, 9 June 1913, p. 7.

65. *The Pageant of the Paterson Strike*, ed. Brooks McNamara (New York, 1913), 16.

66. "The Paterson Strike Pageant," 1407.

67. *Bill Haywood's Book*, 264. See also Dodge Luhan, *Movers and Shakers*, 209.

68. McNamara, *The Pageant of the Paterson Strike*, 17.

69. New York *Tribune*, quoted in *Current Opinion* 55 (July 1913): 32.

70. Paterson *Evening News*, 9 June 1913, p. 4. On the earlier opposition of the *Evening News*, see 27 May 1913, p. 1.

71. New York *Times*, quoted in *Current Opinion* 55 (July 1913): 32.

72. Russell, "The World's Greatest Labor Play," 8.

73. "The Paterson Strike Pageant," 1407.

74. "Pageant of the Paterson Strike," *Survey*, July 1913, quoted in *Rebel Voices: An I.W.W. Anthology*, ed. Joyce L. Kornbluh (Ann Arbor, Mich., 1964), 214. On "the self-directing ability of the workers," see also New York *Call*, 9 June 1913, p. 6.

75. *Current Opinion* 55 (July 1913): 32.

76. *Mother Earth* 8 (June 1913): 102.

77. Ibid., 8 (May 1913): 74.

78. *Social War*, quoted in *Solidarity*, 13 September 1913, p. 2.

79. Samuel Gompers, "The I.W.W. Strikes," *American Federationist* 20 (August 1913): 623–24.

80. Dodge Luhan, *Movers and Shakers*, 210.

81. Paterson *Evening News*, 9 June 1913, p. 7.

82. Mary Heaton Vorse, *A Footnote to Folly: Reminiscences of Mary Heaton Vorse* (New York, 1935), 53. Note that Tresca originally opposed the Pageant plan on the grounds that it could not be done: Hicks, *Reed*, 101.

83. John H. Steiger, *Memoirs of a Silk Striker* (Paterson, N.J., 1914), 114.

84. Elizabeth Gurley Flynn, "The Truth about the Paterson Strike," in Kornbluh, *Rebel Voices*, 221–22.

85. Elizabeth Gurley Flynn, *The Rebel Girl: An Autobiography* (New York, 1973), 169.

86. See Paterson *Evening News*, 25 April 1913, pp. 1, 13; 28 April 1913, p. 7; 1 May 1913, p. 9; 5 May 1913, p. 9; 6 May 1913, p. 1 (the May 1 and 5 reports cited complaints by Flynn herself of insufficient picketing); Flynn also warned against the possibility that the court trials would detract from picketing: 8 May 1913, p. 10. On the difference of opinion between the weavers and the IWW leaders on the amount of picketing necessary, see Chapter Seven. On the number of pickets arrested in June, see New Jersey Bureau of Statistics of Labor and Industries, *Thirty-Sixth Annual Report* (Trenton, 1914), 224–26. For examples of substantial picketing after the Pageant, see New York *Call*, 10 June 1913, p. 1; Paterson *Evening News*, 11 June 1913, p. 1.

87. Flynn, "The Truth about the Paterson Strike," 222.

88. Paterson *Evening News*, 18 June 1913, p. 8. See also 24 June 1913, p. 9. On the lingering hopes for a profit, see 14 June 1913, p. 7.

89. Flynn, "The Truth about the Paterson Strike," 222. According to Flynn, $150 came to Paterson from the Pageant (p. 221). According to the Pageant Executive Committee, $348.00 was paid to the Paterson strikers from the collection (taken at the Garden, and also during the parade to the Garden) and an identical amount to the New York strikers. As Flynn said, the scale of the Pageant made it impossible to make a profit from a single performance. The Executive Committee's figures show that the cost of renting the Garden was $1,000; scenery, $600; erection of the special stage, $600; the train and other transportation for the Paterson strikers, $681.28; theatrical license, $250; advertising in the New York *Call* alone, $275; program printing, $252—and so on—whereas ticket receipts totaled only $3,550.61 (or an average of less than twenty-five cents for each of the approximately 15,000 spectators): "Paterson Pageant Financial Statement."

90. "Paterson Pageant Financial Statement."

91. Paterson *Evening News*, 6 June 1913, p. 9.

92. Flynn, "The Truth about the Paterson Strike," 217.

93. *Solidarity*, 21 June 1913, p. 1.

94. See, e.g., André Tridon, "Haywood," *New Review* 1 (May 1913): 502–6; H.S., "Let Us Recall the Recall," *New Review* 1 (April 1913): 450–51. Haywood was himself an editor of and regular contributor to the *International Socialist Review*.

95. Conlin, *Big Bill Haywood*, 141.

96. Ralph Chaplin, *Wobbly: The Rough and Tumble Story of an American Radical* (Chicago, 1948), 140.

97. *Solidarity*, 14 June 1913, p. 1; the reporter was Justus Ebert.

98. Paterson *Evening News*, 24 June 1913, p. 9; at this point, New York strikers were hoping to find a place for another performance of the Pageant: 27 June 1913, p. 1.

99. *Proceedings of the Eighth I.W.W. Convention, September 15 to 29, 1913*, stenographic report (Cleveland, Ohio, n.d.), 39.

100. *Solidarity*, 28 June 1915, p. 4; the article was by Robin Dunbar.

101. Randolph Bourne, quoted in Arthur F. Wertheim, *The New York Little Renaissance: Iconoclasm, Modernism, and Nationalism in American Culture, 1908–1917* (New York, 1976), 56.

102. Bernardine Kielty Scherman, *Girl from Fitchburg* (New York, 1964), 71, 72.

103. Hapgood, "The Strikers' Pageant," New York *Globe*, 9 June 1913, p. 6.

104. Robert Rosenstone, letter to the author, 28 February 1984; Irwin Marcus, letter to the author, 1 June 1981.

105. Hicks, *Reed*, 213–14.

106. Glaspell, *Road to the Temple*, 250.

107. Letter from Wilbur Daniel Steele to Mary Heaton Vorse, 14 June 1913, in Vorse Collection, Box 54, Archives of Labor History, Wayne State University, Detroit.

108. Aaron, *Writers on the Left*, 35. More recently, studies of the radical intellectuals have echoed the consensus, which has become so strong that evidence is no longer necessary: see Arthur Wertheim, *The New York Little Renaissance*, 56; Humphrey, *Children of Fantasy*, 22; Leslie Fishbein, *Rebels in Bohemia: The Radicals of the Masses, 1911–1917* (Chapel Hill, N.C., 1982), 186.

109. Dubofsky, *We Shall Be All*, 280–81, 508 n.34. See also the other major study of the IWW: Foner, *Industrial Workers of the World*, 367.

110. Osborne, "The Paterson Strike of 1913," 61–63. These points, and the reference to Flynn, are repeated in James D. Osborne, "Industrialization and the Politics of Disorder: Paterson Silk Workers, 1880–1913" (doctoral diss., University of Warwick, England, 1979), 332–35. In his most recent version he abandons all attempts at balance: James D. Osborne, "Paterson: Immigrant Strikers and the War of 1913," in Conlin, *At the Point of Production*, 74.

111. Rosenstone, *Romantic Revolutionary*, 131. After reading an earlier version of this chapter, Rosenstone generously wrote to me (28 February 1984) explaining that by following the "common wisdom of the Pageant," including Flynn's speech and autobiography, he unfortunately came to take a position that was contrary not only to Reed's view but to his own hopes about art and radical change.

112. Conlin, *Big Bill Haywood*, 131.

113. Ibid., 142. Conlin's version of the Pageant's failure has become less qualified as the consensus on the Pageant has gathered momentum; see Conlin, *At the Point of Production*, 13. The newest biography of Haywood follows Flynn on the Pageant; see Peter Carlson, *Roughneck: The Life and Times of Big Bill Haywood* (New York, 1983), 220, 336.

114. Nochlin, "The Paterson Strike Pageant," 67. See also the appreciation in Harry Goldman and Mel Gordon, "Worker's Theatre in America: A Survey, 1913–1978," *Journal of American Culture* 1 (Spring 1978): 39.

115. Hapgood, *Victorian in the Modern World*, 351–52.

116. Williams, *Modern Tragedy*, 371.

CHAPTER SEVEN

1. Paterson *Evening News*, 28 June 1913, p. 1.

2. Ibid., p. 7, and 30 June 1913, p. 10. This was the letter *The Masses* printed.

3. New York *Call*, 21 June 1913, p. 1.

4. Ibid., 14 June 1913, p. 1. The technical charge against Hagerdorn and the thirty-six others was "unlawful assemblage."

5. Paterson *Evening News*, 18 July 1913, p. 1.

6. Ibid., 15 July 1913, p. 1.

7. Ibid., 20 June 1913, p. 1, and 26 July 1913, p. 1.

8. New York *Call*, 14 June 1913, p. 1, and 18 June 1913, p. 6; Paterson *Evening News*, 14 June 1913, p. 7, and 25 July 1913, p. 16. The strikers, by contrast, were prevented from extending their reach in New Jersey by the Lodi chief of police. On Hannah Silverman, Carlo Tresca, and the chief, see Paterson *Evening News*, 19 June 1913, p. 1.

9. On Brueckmann, see New York *Call*, 21 July 1913, p. 1; 22 July 1913, p. 1; 25 July 1913, p. 1; also Paterson *Evening News*, 21 July 1913, p. 9; 22 July 1913, p. 1; 24 July 1913, p. 1. On Boyd, see *Report of C.I.R.*, 2542. On Scott, see New York *Call*, 12 June 1913, p. 6, and 19 June 1913, p. 6; Paterson *Evening News*, 5 June 1913, p. 4, and 6 July 1913, p. 2; *Report of C.I.R.*, 2520–22, 2527–28; "A Possible Paterson," *Outlook* 104 (14 June 1913): 319–20. Scott's conviction was reversed—ten months later—by the Supreme Court of New Jersey; see "Alexander Scott Freed," *International Socialist Review* 14 (June 1914): 763.

10. New York *Call*, 11 June 1913, p. 6.

11. Paterson *Evening News*, 16 June 1913, p. 9.

12. Ibid., 19 June 1913, p. 7.

13. "Hunger Wolf Menaces 25,000 Strikers at Paterson: Help Is Needed at Once," New York *Call*, 20 June 1913, p. 1.

14. *Hungry Babies! Hungry Mothers! Hungry Men!* (leaflet in IWW Collection, Box 3, Tamiment Library, New York University).

15. Paterson *Evening News*, 8 June 1913, p. 5.

16. New York *Call*, 10 June 1913, p. 2.

17. Paterson *Evening News*, 21 June 1913, p. 7.

18. New York *Call*, 25 June 1913, p. 1; 26 June 1913, p. 1; 18 July 1913, p. 4; also Paterson *Evening News*, 24 June 1913, p. 9, and 25 June 1913, p. 5; New York *Times* 26 June 1913, p. 1.

19. The $1,000 a day needed, specified by the Relief Committee, was reported in Paterson *Evening News*, 19 June 1913, p. 8; the total of almost $60,000 raised during the strike divided by the number of days the committee was in existence produces the $500 figure. For the $60,000 total, see Elizabeth Gurley Flynn, "The Truth about the Paterson Strike," in *Rebel Voices: An IWW Anthology*, ed. Joyce L. Kornbluh (Ann Arbor, Mich., 1964), 221; Fred Thompson, *The I.W.W.: Its First Fifty Years* (Chicago, 1955), 61; *Solidarity*, 4 June 1914, p. 2. The Paterson *Evening News*, 23 July 1913, p. 1, reported "over $50,000." By July about 2,000 families were getting bread and potatoes at strike headquarters daily: New York *Call*, 12 July 1913, p. 1.

20. New York *Call*, 15 July 1913, p. 6.

21. Paterson *Evening News*, 17 June 1913, p. 1, and 26 June 1913, p. 8.

22. On the fairness of the committee and its reputation of being able to stretch a dollar, see ibid., 26 June 1913, p. 1; *Solidarity*, 2 August 1913, p. 4.

23. Paterson *Evening News*, 24 June 1913, p. 1, and 12 July 1913, p. 1, reported a growing relief fund; so did Lessig and the Central Strike Committee: 24 June 1913, p. 9, and 5 July 1913, p. 1. But a *Solidarity* report dated 29 June said that contributions had fallen off in the previous two weeks: *Solidarity* 5 July 1913, p. 1. These conflicting versions may reflect the fact that *Solidarity* was appealing to the public for funds, whereas Lessig was trying to reassure the strikers. In July, before the final crisis, support had been coming in at the (substantial but inadequate) rate of $2,000 per week: "End of Paterson Strike," *Outlook* 104 (9 August 1913): 780.

24. Peter W. Kirschbaum, secretary of the Relief Committee, letter to Brooklyn Defense Conference, in Paterson *Evening News*, 8 July 1913, p. 5.

25. Paterson *Evening News*, 19 June 1913, p. 8.

26. Ibid., 17 June 1913, p. 1; 19 June 1913, pp. 1, 8, and 24 June 1913, p. 9; New York *Call*, 18 June 1913, p. 6. The *Call*'s total of only 1,500 departures appears to be erroneous; by July 18, 1,500 ribbon weavers alone had left Paterson: Paterson *Evening News*, 18 July 1913, p. 11. Lessig had noted the exodus of strikers as a positive development in May, when smaller numbers had begun to leave: Paterson *Evening News*, 15 May 1913, p. 1.

27. Paterson *Evening News*, 19 June 1913, p. 8.

28. Ibid., 19 June 1913, p. 8; 23 June 1913, p. 1; 24 June 1913, p. 9.

29. Ibid., 17 June 1913, p. 1; 18 June 1913, p. 8; 20 June 1913, p. 1; 23 June 1913, p. 7; 24 June 1913, p. 9; 26 June 1913, p. 9; 28 June 1913, p. 1; 30 June 1913, p. 1; also New York *Call*, 21 June 1913, p. 1, and 23 June 1913, p. 1.

30. On the ribbon weavers' vote, see Paterson *Evening News*, 27 June 1913, p. 1; On Strauss of Frank and Dugan, see 18 June 1913, p. 1, and 23 June 1913, p. 1. Two weeks later, at Frank and Dugan's Railroad Avenue Mill, 173 were on strike and 35 were working: 7 July 1913, p. 1. Just prior to the shop-by-shop controversy, fewer than 1,000 silk workers were back at work, and many of these were not weavers: 14 June 1913, p. 1. On the pride of many weavers, which made them reluctant to accept strike relief, see 24 June 1913, p. 1. The IWW tradition of contempt for skilled workers went back to the founding 1905 convention, where Haywood articulated it: William D. Haywood, *Bill Haywood's Book: The Autobiography of William D. Haywood* (New York, 1929), 187. In 1914, Flynn applied IWW concepts of work directly to silk workers and showed that she still did not understand their pride; see Elizabeth Gurley Flynn, *Sabotage* (Cleveland, Ohio, 1914), 27. Note that shop-by-shop settlements have been typical of craft unions, whereas industrial unions have usually held out for general settlements. But in Pittsburgh in 1913, an IWW union of stogie workers settled shop by shop—and won: Patrick Lynch, "Pittsburgh, the I.W.W., and the Stogie Workers," in *At the Point of Production: The Local History of the I.W.W.*, ed. Joseph R. Conlin (Westport, Conn., 1981), 88–89.

31. Paterson *Evening News*, 9 June 1913, p. 1.

32. New York *Call*, 17 June 1913, p. 3; Paterson *Evening News*, 13 June 1913, p. 1; 14 June 1913, p. 1; 27 June 1913, p. 1; 7 July 1913, p. 1.

33. New York *Call*, 26 June 1913, p. 1; Paterson *Evening News*, 11 June 1913, p. 1; 14 June 1913, p. 7; 16 June 1913, p. 1; 21 June 1913, p. 1; 23 June 1913, p. 1; 26 June 1913, p. 9; 28 June 1913, p. 7.

34. See, e.g., Paterson *Evening News*, 13 June 1913, p. 1; *Solidarity*, 21 June 1913, p. 1. On the vote and what it meant, see Paterson *Evening News*, 28 June 1913, p. 1; *Solidarity*, 5 July 1913, p. 1.

35. New York *Call*, 2 July 1913, p. 1.

36. Ibid. On the help that Ashley and Heterodoxy members gave Flynn when she fought for the right to speak in Paterson in 1915, was retried and acquitted, see Newark *News*, 12 November 1915, p. 4, and 1 December 1915, p. 12; "Elizabeth Flynn's Contest with Paterson," *Survey* 35 (11 December 1915): 283; "Free Speech in Paterson," *Outlook* 3 (24 November 1915): 692–93; Elizabeth Gurley Flynn, *The Rebel Girl: An Autobiography* (New York, 1973), 172.

37. Paterson *Evening News*, 1 July 1913, p. 1.

38. New York *Times*, 2 July 1913, p. 18.

39. Ibid., 4 July 1913, p. 14.

40. Paterson *Evening News*, 30 June 1913, p. 1, and 30 July 1913, p. 1; New York

Call, 2 July 1913, pp. 1, 2; New York *Times*, 3 July 1913, p. 18, and 4 July 1913, p. 14. The judge was Abram Klenert, who tried many of the Paterson cases.

41. Art Shields, *My Shaping-up Years: The Early Life of Labor's Great Reporter* (New York, 1982), 164; Dominic Mignone in *Solidarity Forever: An Oral History of the IWW*, ed. Stewart Bird, Dan Georgakas, and Deborah Shaffer (Chicago, 1985), 83.

42. *American Silk Journal* 32 (May 1913): 24.

43. Ibid., 63, and 32 (July 1913): 47.

44. Ibid., 32 (January 1913): 57.

45. New York *Globe*, 21 May 1913, p. 4; Flynn, "The Truth about the Paterson Strike," 216–17. On the movement of plants during the strike, see *American Silk Journal* 32 (June 1913): 66, 68, 71, and 32 (July 1913): 64; New York *Times*, 27 March 1913, p. 13, and 19 April 1913, p. 9.

46. Patrick Quinlan, "The Paterson Strike and After," *New Review* 2 (January 1914): 29.

47. Paterson *Evening News*, 1 July 1913, p. 1; 7 July 1913, p. 1; 10 July 1913, p. 1; 12 July 1913, p. 7; 14 July 1913, p. 1; 15 July 1913, p. 1.

48. Ibid., 16 July 1913, p. 7; 18 July 1913, p. 1; 21 July 1913, p. 1; 24 July 1913, p. 1; 29 July 1913, p. 7. Note that the hard-silk workers, who were also unskilled, broke before the dye workers: Paterson *Evening News*, 11 July 1913, p. 1. Note also that women had been conspicuous on the picket line during the summer and conspicuous among those returning to work; see New York *Call*, 23 June 1913, p. 4; Paterson *Evening News*, 7 July 1913, p. 1.

49. Paterson *Evening News*, 7 July 1913, p. 1. For examples of the use in July of secret ballots in ribbon shops, see 21 July 1913, p. 1, and 23 July 1913, p. 10.

50. Ibid., 11 July 1913, p. 1; 14 July 1913, p. 1; 18 July 1913, pp. 1, 11.

51. Flynn, quoted in "The End of the Paterson Strike," 780. On the strike leaders' emphasis on the role of New York papers in publicizing the breaks and hurting strike support, see also New York *Call*, 18 July 1913, p. 1. On the vague promises to the broad-silk weavers, see, e.g., Paterson *Evening News*, 7 July 1913, p. 1; Henry Doherty announced that his weavers were returning to four looms: 21 July 1913, p. 1. Note that as late as July 24, in contrast to the dyers' helpers, the broad-silk weavers could still get 2,000 strikers to a meeting: 24 July 1913, p. 1. On the ribbon weavers' decision to fight alone, and their subsequent decision to return because of the collapse of relief, see 21 July 1913, p. 1, and 23 July 1913, p. 1. Flynn later blamed the ribbon weavers for destroying solidarity by deciding to settle shop by shop; see Flynn, "The Truth about the Paterson Strike," 224.

52. Paterson *Evening News*, 25 July 1913, p. 1; 28 July 1913, p. 1; 31 July 1913, p. 1; 1 August 1913, p. 1; also New York *Call*, 24 July 1913, p. 1; 25 July 1913, p. 1; 26 July 1913, p. 3. In New York those ribbon weavers who had not been granted the nine-hour day continued their strike into August: New York *Call*, 2 August 1913, p. 2.

53. Paterson *Evening News*, 29 July 1913, p. 1, and 2 August 1913, p. 1.

54. New York *Call*, 22 July 1913, p. 2.

55. Ibid., 18 July 1913, p. 4, and 22 July 1913, p. 2.

56. Paterson *Evening News*, 19 July 1913, p. 1, and 21 July 1913, p. 9; New York *Call*, 21 July 1913, p. 1. The IWW later claimed that 15,000 attended the Haledon meeting: *Solidarity*, 12 September 1914, p. 1.

57. Paterson *Evening News*, 4 August 1913, p. 9.

58. Adele Giardino, interview by Robert Kirkman, Haledon, N.J., 24 March 1981; Bunny Kuiken and Sylvia Bochese, interview by Robert Kirkman, Haledon, N.J., 19

March 1981; author's conversations with John Herbst. Giardino is Pietro Botto's daughter, Kuiken and Bochese are granddaughters; Herbst was the first director of the Botto House/American Labor Museum.

59. Paterson *Evening News*, 28 July 1913, p. 1.

60. Ibid.

61. *Solidarity*, 14 July 1914, p. 2. On the Miesch mill, see Paterson *Evening News*, 28 July 1913, p. 1; for the blacklisted figure, see "Work of the I.W.W. in Paterson," *Literary Digest* 47 (9 August 1913): 197.

62. Fred Harwood, Report to Rose Pastor Stokes (Rose Pastor Stokes Collection XIX:22, Tamiment Library), 1. See also Dominic Mignone in Bird et al., *Solidarity Forever*, 83; the blacklist followed Mignone from Paterson to Massachusetts.

63. *American Silk Journal* 32 (October 1913): 60, and 32 (November 1913): 54.

64. Harwood Report, 2. By 1915 the skilled silk worker had become a laborer in the construction industry.

65. Testimony of Edward Zuersher, *Report of C.I.R.*, 2589.

66. Paterson *Evening News*, 30 July 1913, p. 1; David J. Goldberg, "The Battle for Labor Supremacy in Paterson, 1916–22," in *Silk City: Studies of the Paterson Silk Industry, 1860–1940*, ed. Philip B. Scranton (Newark, N.J., 1985), 110–11.

67. *Report of C.I.R.*, 2589. In New York, too, the most active ribbon weavers faced a blacklist: New York *Call*, 2 August 1913, p. 2.

68. *American Silk Journal* 32 (November 1913): 54.

69. Mandeville, quoted in James E. Wood, "History of Labor in the Broad-Silk Industry of Paterson, N.J., 1879–1940," (doctoral diss., University of California, Berkeley, 1941), 296. On 1916 and 1919, see Goldberg, "The Battle for Labor Supremacy," 112, 115.

70. Goldberg, "The Battle for Labor Supremacy," 111, 113–15.

71. Sophie Cohen, interview by Deborah Shaffer and Stewart Bird, 17 December 1977 (typescript, Program on Women and Work, University of Michigan/Wayne State University), pt. 1, 9. On the success of Paterson's broad-silk weavers in fending off four looms, see National Industrial Conference Board, *Hours of Work as Related to Output and Health of Workers: Silk Manufacturing* (Boston, 1919), 9.

72. *American Silk Journal* 32 (April 1913): 24.

73. Schichiro Matsui, *The History of the Silk Industry in the United States* (New York, 1928), 218.

74. Morris W. Garber, "The Silk Industry of Paterson New Jersey, 1840–1913: Technology and the Origins, Development, and Changes in an Industry," (doctoral diss., Rutgers University, 1968), 263–64; Wood, "History of Labor in the Broad-Silk Industry," 44–46; Philip J. McLewin, "Labor Conflict and Technological Change: The Family Shop in Paterson," in Scranton, *Silk City*, 136, 139. Some Paterson mill owners began to consider moving farther away, to the South, "to get away from disturbing elements which exist in the north": *American Silk Journal* 32 (December 1913): 54.

75. McLewin, "Labor Conflict and Technological Change," 136–39, 142–44, 146–51. On the commission system and the family shop, see also Wood, "History of Labor in the Broad-Silk Industry," 38; Ruth Tierney, "The Decline of the Silk Industry in Paterson, New Jersey" (master's thesis, Cornell University, 1938), 23. Note that the situation many Jewish broad-silk weavers faced in Paterson in the 1920s and 1930s was similar to that in Bialystok, from which they or their parents had fled before World War I. On Bialystok's middlemen and small shops, see Nora Levin, *Jewish Socialist Movements, 1871–1917: While Messiah Tarried* (London, 1978), 39.

76. New York *Times*, 12 April 1936, p. II-1, quoted in McLewin, "Labor Conflict and Technological Change," 143.

77. "I Make Cheap Silk," ed. Inis Weed and Louise Carey, *The Masses* 5 (November 1913): 7. When the silk workers' movement faltered in 1913–14, Bamford was able to break its promises; in June 1914 it was still using the contract system; see *Report of C.I.R.*, 2596. On the wage increase at the end of the 1913 strike, see *American Silk Journal* 32 (August 1913): 21.

78. *Solidarity*, 16 August 1913, p. 1; 31 January 1914, p. 1; 11 April 1914, p. 4; *Proceedings of the Eighth IWW Convention, September 15 to 29, 1913*, stenographic report (Cleveland, Ohio, n.d.), 74; Wood, "History of Labor in the Broad-Silk Industry," 270; *American Silk Journal* 32 (December 1913): 24; Patrick Quinlan, "The Paterson Strike and After," *New Review* 2 (January 1914): 30.

79. *Solidarity*, 21 March 1914, p. 1.

80. Quinlan, "The Paterson Strike and After," 31; Patrick Quinlan, "Glorious Paterson," *International Socialist Review* 14 (December 1913): 356. In Haledon, Republicans had previously controlled the council and had made things difficult for Mayor Brueckmann: George Shea, interview with author, New York City, 23 May 1983 (Shea is Brueckmann's grandson). On Magnet, see Paterson *Evening News*, 11 April 1913, p. 9; Flynn, "The Truth about the Paterson Strike," 223; *Report of C.I.R.*, 2575–76.

81. New York *Call*, 29 November 1913, pp. 1, 3, and 2 December 1913, p. 1; Martin C. Mooney, "The Industrial Workers of the World and the Immigrants of Paterson and Passaic, New Jersey, 1907–1913" (master's thesis, Seton Hall University, 1969), 88–89; James D. Osborne, "The Paterson Strike of 1913: Immigrant Silk Workers and the I.W.W. Response to the Problem of Stable Unionism" (master's thesis, University of Warwick, England, 1973), 133–34; Wood, "History of Labor in the Broad-Silk Industry," 270–71; John H. Steiger, *Memoirs of a Silk Striker* (Paterson, N.J., 1914), 106; *Solidarity*, 11 April 1914, p. 4. On the solidarity of the manufacturers when faced with the ribbon weavers' demand for a nine-hour day, see Paterson *Evening News*, 22 July 1913, p. 1; *American Silk Journal* 32 (December 1913): 24.

82. Goldberg, "The Battle for Labor Supremacy," 112–21; note (p. 114) that the Workmen's Circle and the Sons of Italy supported the struggle for the eight-hour day in 1918–19.

83. Ibid., 112.

84. Ibid., 109, 118–27. On the defeat of the dye workers in 1919, see also Tierney, "Decline of the Silk Industry in Paterson," 79–80. Note that the ups and downs of the Paterson labor movement in 1915–21 were closely related to the cycles of both the silk industry and the American labor movement; see David Montgomery, *Workers' Control in America: Studies in the History of Work, Technology, and Labor Struggles* (London, 1979), 94–95; Wood, "History of Labor in the Broad-Silk Industry," 312, 374–77.

85. Meredith Tax, *The Rising of the Women: Feminist Solidarity and Class Conflict, 1880–1917* (New York, 1980), 274. On what the IWW learned from the aftermath in Lawrence, see also Flynn, *Rebel Girl*, 171, and Goldberg, "The Battle for Labor Supremacy," 110–11.

86. Ewald Koettgen, *One Big Union in the Textile Industry* (Cleveland, Ohio, 1914), 13 (first published as an article in *Solidarity*, 3 January 1914, p. 6). Note that even before 1913 the IWW preferred short strikes.

87. *Solidarity*, 28 February 1914, p. 4.

88. Ibid., 31 January 1914, pp. 1, 4, and 28 February 1914, p. 4.

89. Ibid., 19 June 1915, pp. 1, 4; see also 12 September 1914, p. 1.

90. See Chapter Eight.

91. Wood, "History of Labor in the Broad-Silk Industry," 271; Goldberg, "The Battle for Labor Supremacy," 109, 118–27; Paterson *Evening News*, 29 July 1913, p. 1; *Solidarity*, 31 January 1914, p. 1. See also *Report of C.I.R.*, 2457.

92. Irma Lombardi, in Bird et al., *Solidarity Forever*, 73. On the return of Flynn and Tresca to Paterson and their continued attention to that city, see *Solidarity* 12 September 1914, p. 1; 16 January 1915, p. 4; 6 February 1915, p. 1; 15 July 1916, p. 1; also Mooney, "The Industrial Workers of the World," 88–89; Osborne, "The Paterson Strike of 1913," 133–34; *Report of C.I.R.*, 2607; Flynn, *Rebel Girl*, 171–73; "Elizabeth Flynn's Contest with Paterson," *Survey* 35 (December 1915): 283; "Free Speech in Paterson," *Outlook* 3 (24 November 1915): 692–93.

93. Sophie Cohen, interview with author, Youngsville, N.Y., 27 December 1981. See also Carrie Golzio, interview with author, Haledon, N.J., 13 June 1983. On the 1922 strike and the open-shop drive, see Goldberg, "The Battle for Labor Supremacy," 126–28.

94. Joe Krause, untitled manuscript (3 December 1982), 6, in Charles Goldman Judaica Library, YM/YWHA, Wayne, N.J. On the 1924 strike, see Nancy Fogelson, "They Paved the Streets with Silk: Paterson, New Jersey, Silk Workers, 1913–1924," *New Jersey History* 97 (Autumn 1979): 142–46; McLewin, "Labor Conflict and Technological Change," 144–45; Martha Glaser, "Paterson 1924: The ACLU and Labor," *New Jersey History* 94 (Winter 1976): 162, 166, 170–71; Shields, *My Shaping-up Years*, 164; Goldberg, "The Battle for Labor Supremacy," 128. On the continuation of the Socialist-Communist split into the 1950s, see Robert Snyder, "The Paterson Jewish Folk Chorus: Politics, Ethnicity, and Musical Culture," *American Jewish History* 74 (September 1984): 39.

95. Matsui, *History of the Silk Industry*, 198.

96. Tierney, "Decline of the Silk Industry in Paterson," 48, 83–91; McLewin, "Labor Conflict and Technological Change," 152–53, 156 n.53; Wood, "History of Labor in the Broad-Silk Industry," 2–5, 30, 67; Golzio interview; Margo Anderson Conk, *The United States Census and Labor Force Change: A History of Occupation Statistics, 1870–1940* (Ann Arbor, Mich., 1980), 98 (on the comparison with England); Herman Wolf, *After 141 Years: What Dye Workers Have Won in Two Successful Strikes* (Paterson, N.J., 1935), 3–15, 26–34. Thanks to Sol Stetin for the information about the Sons of Italy hall; according to Stetin, Carlo Tresca spoke at the Paterson dyers' local several times in 1933. On the role played by rayon after 1926, see Wood, "History of Labor in the Broad-Silk Industry," 7; Tierney, "Decline of the Silk Industry in Paterson," 47. It is a symbol of the change that *American Silk Journal* was absorbed by the rayon textile monthly in 1938.

CHAPTER EIGHT

1. *Solidarity*, 29 November 1913, p. 1. For an example of the AFL's glee, see F. G. R. Gordon, "A Labor Man's Story of the Paterson Strike," *National Civic Federation Review* 4 (1 December 1913): 16–17.

2. *Solidarity*, 18 October 1913, p. 4.

3. New York *Call*, 15 June 1913, p. 8; Samuel Gompers, "The 'I.W.W. Strikes,'" *American Federationist* 20 (August 1913): 623.

4. *Solidarity*, 23 June 1913, p. 4.

5. Ibid., 9 August 1913, p. 2. Ettor had led the Lawrence strike, was a member of the IWW's General Executive Board, and had been in Paterson frequently toward the end of the 1913 strike. For Panken, see Jacob Panken, "The I.W.W. and Paterson, New York *Call*, 26 July 1913, p. 6.

6. *Proceedings of the Eighth IWW Convention, September 15 to 29, 1913*, stenographic report (Cleveland, Ohio, n.d.), 34.

7. New York *Call*, 7 July 1913, p. 1; see also Chapter Five.

8. On the restraint of Socialists, see Panken, "The I.W.W. and Paterson"; *Solidarity*, 5 July 1913, p. 1. On the attacks after the strike, see Philip S. Foner, *The Industrial Workers of the World, 1905–1917*, vol. 4 of *History of the Labor Movement in the United States* (New York, 1965), 411.

9. *Solidarity*, 18 October 1913, p. 2. On Ebert after Lawrence, see Justus Ebert, *The Trial of A New Society* (Cleveland, Ohio, 1913).

10. *Solidarity*, 23 August 1913, p. 2; the editorial was signed L.C.R.

11. Joseph Ettor, "I.W.W. *versus* A.F. of L.," *New Review*, 2 (May 1914): 282.

12. William D. Haywood, "An Appeal for Industrial Solidarity," *International Socialist Review* 14 (March 1914): 544–46.

13. *Solidarity*, 13 September 1913, p. 2.

14. Elizabeth Gurley Flynn, "The Truth about the Paterson Strike," in Joyce L. Kornbluh, ed., *Rebel Voices: An I.W.W. Anthology* (Ann Arbor, Mich., 1964), 217.

15. *The Masses* 4 (September 1913): 4.

16. Margaret H. Sanger, "The Paterson Strike," in Hippolyte Havel, ed., *The Revolutionary Almanac* (New York, 1914), 47–49.

17. *Solidarity*, 9 August 1913, p. 1. See also New York *Call*, 4 August 1913, p. 2.

18. Paterson *Evening News*, 26 July 1913, p. 1. See also *Solidarity*, 16 August 1913, p. 1.

19. *Proceedings of the Eighth IWW Convention*, 38.

20. Ibid., 36.

21. *Report of C.I.R.*, 2464–65; *Solidarity*, 13 December 1913, p. 1.

22. Patrick Quinlan, "Glorious Paterson," *International Socialist Review* 14 (December 1913): 356–57; Patrick Quinlan, "The Paterson Strike and After," *New Review* 2 (January 1914): 30–31.

23. Flynn, "The Truth about the Paterson Strike," 226.

24. Quinlan, "Glorious Paterson," 29.

25. Flynn, "The Truth about the Paterson Strike," 215.

26. Ibid.

27. Ibid., 218.

28. Paterson *Evening News*, 23 July 1913, p. 1; New York *Call*, 24 July 1913, p. 1.

29. Flynn, "The Truth about the Paterson Strike," 223–24.

30. See Chapter Seven; James D. Osborne, "The Paterson Strike of 1913: Immigrant Silk Workers and the I.W.W. Response to the Problem of Stable Unionism" (master's thesis, University of Warwick, England, 1973), 128. For the contrary view of the shop-by-shop settlement held by a Wobbly who was a ribbon weaver, see *Report of C.I.R.*, 2603.

31. Patrick Quinlan, "Silk, Starvation, and Solidarity," *Appeal to Reason*, 16 August 1913, p. 2; William B. Killingbeck, quoted in *Solidarity*, 2 August 1913, p. 4.

32. Howard Brubaker, "Midsummer Madness," *The Masses* 4 (September 1913): 11.

33. Reprinted in *Solidarity*, 30 August 1913, p. 2.

34. "The Paterson Fight," New York *Call*, 21 July 1913, p. 6.

35. W. E. Trautmann, *Why Strikes Are Lost: How to Win* (Newcastle, Pa., n.d.), 15, 17–18.

36. *Solidarity*, 22 November 1913, p. 2.

37. Ibid., 4.

38. *Proceedings of the Eighth IWW Convention*, 38. On Koettgen's attitude toward Boyd's advocacy of sabotage, see also William B. Killingbeck, "Hutchins Hapgood and the Socialists," New York *Call*, 10 June 1913, p. 6. On what Boyd said on March 31 and April 1, see Paterson *Evening News*, 24 June 1913, p. 7.

39. Elizabeth Gurley Flynn, *The Rebel Girl: An Autobiography* (New York, 1973), 162; Joseph R. Conlin, *Bread and Roses Too: Studies of the Wobblies* (Westport, Conn., 1969), 108.

40. Elizabeth Gurley Flynn, *Sabotage* (Cleveland, Ohio, 1916). This pamphlet was apparently written in 1914.

41. John H. Steiger, *Memoirs of a Silk Striker* (Paterson, N.J., 1914), 94.

42. Harry Kemp, *More Miles: An Autobiographical Novel* (New York, 1926), 406–8. See also *Solidarity*, 13 September 1913, p. 2. On Boyd's 1915 appeal for clemency, see "Paterson Strike Leaders in Jersey Prison," *Survey* 34 (3 April 1915): 3. Note that Paterson weavers had quietly employed sabotage for many years without naming it; they needed no instruction from an outsider like Boyd. See *Report of C.I.R.*, 2600–2601; Flynn, *Sabotage*, 24. See also Herbert G. Gutman, *Work, Culture, and Society in Industrializing America: Essays in American Working-Class and Social History* (New York, 1976), 58; James D. Osborne, "Industrialization and the Politics of Disorder: Paterson Silk Workers, 1880–1913" (doctoral diss., University of Warwick, England, 1979), 63–64. The Wobblies used advocacy of sabotage to demonstrate that they had broken with bourgeois proprieties, thereby separating themselves from middle-class Socialists; see *Industrial Worker*, 14 March 1912, p. 2; Flynn, *Sabotage*, 15–16, 22; Newark *News*, 29 December 1913. During the Paterson strike however, practical cooperation with the Socialists was more important than scoring rhetorical points; the IWW maintained only that sabotage by the workers was no worse than sabotage by the bosses, who adulterated the silk before dyeing it. See *Solidarity*, 19 April 1913, p. 2, and 3 May 1913, p. 1; Paterson *Evening News*, 26 June 1913, p. 9; William D. Haywood, "The Rip in the Silk Industry," *International Socialist Review* 13 (May 1913): 786; *The Masses* 4 (June 1913): 5; Ewald Koettgen, "Making Silk," *International Socialist Review* 14 (March 1914): 553–54; William D. Haywood, *Bill Haywood's Book: The Autobiography of William D. Haywood* (New York, 1929), 261–62.

43. Steiger, *Memoirs of a Silk Striker*, 41–42, 82. On Steiger's fund raising for the Pageant, see Paterson *Evening News*, 24 June 1913, p. 1.

44. Paterson *Evening News*, reprinted in *Solidarity*, 26 December 1914, p. 1.

45. Paterson *Evening News*, 16 May 1913, p. 11.

46. Flynn, *Rebel Girl*, 166. See also Osborne, "The Paterson Strike of 1913," 67, 70–71; Harbor Allen, "The Flynn," *American Mercury* 9 (December 1926): 431 (Allen's article was based almost solely on interviews with Flynn). Lessig was "tried"

by silk workers in a later strike, probably 1924. See Sophie Cohen, interview with author, Youngsville, N.Y., 27 December 1981; Nancy Fogelson, "They Paved the Streets with Silk: Paterson, New Jersey, Silk Workers, 1913–1924," *New Jersey History* 97 (Autumn 1979): 144.

47. Steiger, *Memoirs of a Silk Striker*, 72.

48. *Solidarity*, 9 August 1913, p. 2. See also Flynn, "The Truth about the Paterson Strike," 224.

49. "The Social War in New Jersey," *Current Opinion* 55 (August 1913): 81. On Quinlan vs. Haywood, see, e.g., Paterson *Evening News*, 19 June 1913, p. 1, and 21 June 1913, p. 2.

50. *Solidarity*, 27 December 1913, p. 1. At the height of the strike, *Solidarity*, 14 June 1913, p. 3, had praised Quinlan.

51. Eugene M. Tobin, "Direct Action and Conscience: The 1913 Paterson Strike as Example of the Relationship between Labor Radicals and Liberals," *Labor History* 20 (Winter 1979): 87.

52. Allen, "The Flynn," 433.

53. Melvyn Dubofsky, *We Shall Be All: A History of the Industrial Workers of the World* (Chicago, 1969), 426–28. Dubofsky criticizes historians Philip Taft and Patrick Renshaw for following Flynn's version. Mary Heaton Vorse, *A Footnote to Folly: Reminiscences of Mary Heaton Vorse* (New York, 1935), 157, also followed Flynn.

54. Foner, *Industrial Workers of the World*, 514–15; Vorse, *Footnote to Folly*, 146.

55. *Bill Haywood's Book*, 292. Fred Thompson, *The I.W.W.: Its First Fifty Years, 1905–1955* (Chicago, 1955), 103, follows Haywood.

56. Letter from Elizabeth Gurley Flynn to Woodrow Wilson, 10 January 1918, p. 3; a copy of this letter is in the Tamiment Library, New York University. Note that Flynn did not actually terminate her membership in the IWW until 1937; see Rosalyn Fraad Baxandall, "Elizabeth Gurley Flynn: The Early Years," *Radical America* 9, no. 1 (1975): 113, 115 n.42. Dubofsky explains that by 1916 Haywood's centralization had pushed Flynn into a minor role: *We Shall Be All*, 332–33, 345.

57. Joseph R. Conlin, *Big Bill Haywood and the Radical Union Movement* (Syracuse, N.Y., 1969), 173.

58. Osborne, "The Paterson Strike of 1913," 111–14.

59. Ibid., 96.

60. *Solidarity*, 25 July 1914, p. 1; see also 18 July 1914, p. 1; *Industrial Worker*, 28 February 1948, p. 4; Foner, *Industrial Workers of the World*, 164.

61. Conlin, *Big Bill Haywood*, 142.

62. Ralph Chaplin, *Wobbly: The Rough and Tumble Story of an American Radical* (Chicago, 1948), 140; *Bill Haywood's Book*, 261–64.

63. On Tresca's opposition to the initial Pageant plan, see Granville Hicks, *John Reed: The Making of a Revolutionary* (New York, 1937), 101.

64. Flynn, "The Truth about the Paterson Strike," 220.

65. Paterson *Evening News*, 16 June 1913, p. 9.

66. For a summary of the press's view of the stakes at Paterson, see "Work of the I.W.W. in Paterson," *Literary Digest* 47 (August 1913): 197–98.

67. See, e.g., Paterson *Evening News*, 17 May 1913, p. 7; 19 May 1913, p. 9; 2 July 1913, p. 9; also Newark *News*, 27 June 1913; *Solidarity*, 31 May 1913, p. 4.

68. New York *Times*, 26 May 1913, p. 2.

69. *Solidarity*, 17 May 1913, p. 1. On Haywood, see, e.g., Paterson *Evening News*, 6 May 1913, p. 11, and 1 July 1913, p. 13; on the view of the IWW leaders generally, see Gregory Mason, "Industrial War in Paterson," *Outlook* 104 (7 June 1913): 285.

70. Max Eastman, "The Rebel Woman," *The Masses* 5 (May 1914), reprinted in William L. O'Neill, ed., *Echoes of Revolt: The Masses, 1911–1917* (Chicago, 1966), 206.

71. *Solidarity*, 9 August 1913, p. 2.

72. Paul F. Brissenden, *The I.W.W.: A Study of American Syndicalism*, 2d ed. (New York, 1957) 283, 332–33; Dubofsky, *We Shall Be All*, 259–60.

73. *Solidarity*, 24 October 1914, p. 2.

74. J. P. Cannon, "The Seventh I.W.W. Convention," *International Socialist Review* 12 (November 1912): 424.

75. Note that Tresca and Quinlan were so identified with other organizations that western Wobblies questioned whether they were even members of the IWW at the time of the Paterson strike: *Proceedings of the Eighth IWW Convention*, 71.

76. See Flynn's letters to Mary Heaton Vorse, esp. 1929–34 (Vorse Collection, Boxes 59–62, Archives of Labor History, Wayne State University, Detroit).

77. *Bill Haywood's Book*, 222.

78. On the distinction between Flynn's roles in Lawrence and in Paterson, see Mary Heaton Vorse, "Elizabeth Gurley Flynn" (manuscript in Vorse Collection, Box 19, Archives of Labor History), 5. For her hostility, see Flynn, "The Truth about the Paterson Strike"; Flynn, *Sabotage*; *Solidarity*, 18 July 1914, pp. 1, 4, and 4 October 1913, p. 4.

79. Elizabeth Gurley Flynn, *Debs, Haywood, Ruthenberg* (New York, 1939), 26–27; Flynn, *Rebel Girl*, 204.

80. *Solidarity*, 25 October 1913, p. 1. See also *Solidarity*, 20 September 1913, p. 1; *Bill Haywood's Book*, 272; Peter Carlson, *Roughneck: The Life and Times of Big Bill Haywood* (New York, 1983), 222. Note that Flynn as well as Haywood collapsed physically just before the strike itself collapsed. See Paterson *Evening News*, 15 July 1913, p. 1; 16 July 1913, p. 1; 19 July 1913, p. 1; 23 July 1913, p. 1; also Newark *News*, 26 July 1913. See also Flynn, *Rebel Girl*, 169–70.

81. Richard Brazier, "The Mass I.W.W. Trial of 1918: A Retrospect," *Labor History* 7 (Spring 1966): 188, Conlin, *Big Bill Haywood*, 237.

82. Conlin, *Big Bill Haywood*, 171.

83. Patrick M. Lynch, "Pennsylvania Anthracite: A Forgotten Venture, 1906–1916" (master's thesis, Bloomsburg State College, Bloomsburg, Penna., 1974), 93–97, 123–24, 132.

84. Flynn, "The Truth about the Paterson Strike," 226.

85. For a Wobbly version see Ben H. Williams, "Saga of the One Big Union—American Labor in the Jungle," (manuscript in IWW Collection, Box 146, Folder 15, Archives of Labor History), 51. See also Robert H. Zeiger, "Robin Hood in the Silk City: The I.W.W. and the Paterson Silk Strike of 1913," *Proceedings of the New Jersey Historical Society*, 84 (1966): 193; David J. Saposs, *Left-Wing Unionism: A Study of Radical Politics and Tactics* (New York, 1926), 172–74; James E. Wood, "History of Labor in the Broad-Silk Industry of Paterson, New Jersey, 1872–1940," (doctoral diss., University of California, Berkeley, 1941), 204; Philip S. Foner, *Women and the American Labor Movement: From Colonial Times to the Eve of World War I*

(New York, 1979), 456; Dubofsky, *We Shall Be All*, 345. For a minority view, suspicious of blaming the IWW's decline on its organizational weaknesses, see William Preston, "Shall This Be All? U.S. Historians versus William D. Haywood et al.," *Labor History* 12 (Summer 1971): 445; see also Mike Davis, "The Stop Watch and Wooden Shoe: Scientific Management and the Industrial Workers of the World," *Radical America* 4 (January–February 1975): 80.

86. Morris Hillquit, *Loose Leaves from A Busy Life* (New York, 1934), 28–29. On the similar experience of those who organized Jewish women, see Nancy Schrom Dye, *As Equals and as Sisters: Feminism, the Labor Movement, and the Woman's Trade Union League of New York* (Columbia, Mo., 1980), 114; Meredith Tax, *The Rising of the Women: Feminist Solidarity and Class Conflict, 1880–1917* (New York, 1980), 236.

87. Testimony of James Starr, *Report of C.I.R.*, 2614.

88. Ebert, *Trial of a New Society*, 96–97. On the one-day general strike, see also *Solidarity*, 5 October 1912, p. 2; Flynn, *Rebel Girl*, 148–49.

89. David Montgomery, *Workers' Control in America: Studies in the History of Work, Technology, and Labor Struggles* (Cambridge, 1979), 105.

CONCLUSION

1. On the 1912 resolution as decisive, see Ira Kipnis, *The American Socialist Movement: 1897–1912* (New York, 1952), 335–420; Joseph Robert Conlin, *Bread and Roses Too: Studies of the Wobblies* (Westport, Conn., 1969), 124–32; Joseph R. Conlin, *Big Bill Haywood and the Radical Union Movement* (Syracuse, N.Y., 1969), 166–69; and—in a somewhat more qualified form—David A. Shannon, *The Socialist Party of America: A History* (New York, 1955), 70–80. Studies of the decline of the left that emphasize the role of repression in 1917–19 include Daniel R. Fustfeld, *The Rise and Repression of Radical Labor, U.S.A., 1877–1918* (Chicago, 1980), 39–40; Robert Justin Goldstein, *Political Repression in Modern America: From 1870 to the Present* (Cambridge, Mass., 1978), 99, 105–63. Studies that emphasize, in addition, the role of the Soviet Revolution include John P. Diggins, *The American Left in the Twentieth Century* (New York, 1973), 81–105; Daniel Aaron, *Writers on the Left* (New York, 1961), 47; James Weinstein, *The Decline of Socialism in America, 1912–1925* (New York, 1967), 162–233.

2. Paul Buhle, "Italian-American Radicals and Labor in Rhode Island, 1905–1930," *Radical History Review*, no. 17 (Spring 1978): 133.

3. Robert E. Snyder, "Women, Wobblies, and Workers' Rights: The 1912 Textile Strike in Little Falls, New York," *New York History* 60 (January 1979): 36–41.

4. David Goldberg, review of Conlin, *At the Point of Production*, and of Philip S. Foner, ed., *Fellow Workers and Friends*, in *International Labor and Working-Class History*, no. 23 (Spring 1983): 107.

5. Fred Thompson, *The I.W.W.: Its First Fifty Years* (Chicago, 1955), 61; Robert J. Wheeler, "The Allentown Silk Dyers' Strike," *International Socialist Review* 13 (April 1913): 820–21; New York *Call*, 25 March 1913, p. 1.

6. Robert J. Wheeler, "Pennsylvania Federation of Labor," *International Socialist Review* 14 (July 1913): 41 (Wheeler is quoting Executive Officer Hall). See also Weinstein, *Decline of Socialism*, 41.

7. Alexander Scott, "What the Reds Are Doing in Paterson," *International Socialist Review* 13 (June 1913): 852.

8. Richard Perin, letter to the editor, New York *Call*, 18 July 1913, p. 6.

9. Patrick Quinlan, "The Paterson Strike and After," *New Review* 2 (January 1914): 31–32; Patrick Quinlan, "Glorious Paterson," *International Socialist Review* 14 (December 1913): 356–57. See also Conlin, *Bread and Roses Too*, 34.

10. New York *Call*, 27 February 1913, p. 1; for similar ironies, see 10 March 1913, p. 1, and 25 March 1913, p. 3.

11. *Solidarity*, 15 March 1913, p. 2.

12. See Jessie Ashley, letter to the editor, New York *Globe*, 21 April 1913, p. 8.

13. Paterson *Evening News*, 5 March 1913, p. 9.

14. Conlin, *Bread and Roses Too*, 149.

15. Ibid., 132; Conlin, *Big Bill Haywood*, 167–68.

16. Weinstein, *Decline of Socialism*, 204; for his dismissal of the IWW, see p. 1; also James Weinstein, "A Reply," *Radical America* 2 (January–February 1968): 52–53.

17. Paul Buhle, "Debsian Socialism and the 'New Immigrant' Worker," in William O'Neill, ed., *Insights and Parallels: Problems and Issues in American Social History* (Minneapolis, Minn., 1973), 263–64.

18. Conlin, *Bread and Roses Too*, 146.

19. On the Seattle general strike, see Jeremy Brecher, *Strike!* (Boston, 1972), 104–14.

20. See Max Eastman, *Heroes I Have Known* (New York, 1942), 33, 38; Elizabeth Gurley Flynn, *The Rebel Girl: An Autobiography* (New York, 1973), 333.

21. Rose Pastor Stokes, "Paterson," *The Masses* 4 (November 1913), in William L. O'Neill, ed., *Echoes of Revolt: THE MASSES, 1911–1917* (Chicago, 1966), 89.

22. Art Shields, *My Shaping-up Years: The Early Life of Labor's Great Reporter* (New York, 1982), 164.

23. Newark *News*, 21 January 1916, p. 22.

24. "Do You Believe in Patriotism?" *The Masses* 8 (March 1916): 12.

25. New York *Sun*, 12 March 1914, quoted in Mabel Dodge Luhan, *Movers and Shakers*, vol. 3 of *Intimate Memories* (New York, 1936), 122. On Dodge's turn away from politics, see *Movers and Shakers*, 116, 303; Hutchins Hapgood, *A Victorian in the Modern World* (New York, 1939), 391; Lois Palken Rudnick, *Mabel Dodge Luhan: New Woman, New Worlds* (Albuquerque, N.M., 1984), 106, 121.

26. "Money Is Needed," *The Masses* 5 (October 1913): 4.

27. Hapgood, *Victorian in the Modern World*, 385–86, 390–91. On Boyd's desperation and despair in 1914–15, see Granville Hicks, *John Reed: The Making of a Revolutionary* (New York, 1936), 150, 155, 181. Many Villagers regularly summered in Provincetown, and Wobblies were increasingly joining them there; in 1914, Flynn and Tresca were expected. See Elizabeth Gurley Flynn, letter to Mary Heaton Vorse, 17 July 1914, in Vorse Collection, Box 53, Archives of Labor History.

28. Mary Heaton Vorse, *A Footnote to Folly: Reminiscences of Mary Heaton Vorse* (New York, 1935), 73–74.

29. Max Eastman, *Enjoyment of Living* (New York, 1948), 548. See also Floyd Dell, *Homecoming* (New York, 1933), 251–52; Arthur F. Wertheim, *The New York Little Renaissance: Iconoclasm, Modernism, and Nationalism in American Culture, 1906–1917* (New York, 1976), 43–44.

30. On Sloan's subsequent political career and artistic decline, see Richard Fitzgerald, *Art and Politics: Cartoonists of the Masses and Liberator* (Westport, Conn., 1973), 153; Milton W. Brown, "The Two John Sloans," *Art News* 50 (January 1952):

26–27, 57. On Eastman's bewilderment, see *Enjoyment of Living*, 549. And on what was lost, see Harvey Swados, "Echoes of Revolt," *Massachusetts Review* (Spring 1967), 383; Genevieve Taggard, ed., *May Days: An Anthology of Verse from Masses-Liberator* (New York, 1925), 13.

31. Joseph Freeman, *An American Testament: A Narrative of Rebels and Romantics* (New York, 1936), 310. On the political despair behind the artistic appeal of Europe, see James Burkhart Gilbert, *Writers and Partisans: A History of Literary Radicalism in America* (New York, 1968), 40.

32. Freeman, *American Testament*, 307–8; Fitzgerald, *Art and Politics*, 109.

33. John Dos Passos, "They Want Ritzy Art," *New Masses* 4 (June 1928): 8.

34. Freeman, *American Testament*, 401; Mary Heaton Vorse, "Elizabeth Gurley Flynn," (Vorse Collection, Box 19, Archives of Labor History), 4. On the division of social and personal categories in modern culture, see Raymond Williams, *Modern Tragedy* (Stanford, Calif., 1966), 121–22, 138.

35. Margaret Sanger, *Margaret Sanger: An Autobiography* (New York, 1971), 84–85.

36. Alexander Campbell Sanger, "Margaret Sanger: The Early Years" (senior thesis, Princeton University, 1969), 46. On 1914, see David M. Kennedy, *Birth Control in America: The Career of Margaret Sanger* (New Haven, Conn., 1970), 30–31.

37. Sanger, quoted in ibid., 112; see also 113, 126.

38. Mari Jo Buhle, *Women and American Socialism, 1870–1920* (Urbana, Ill., 1981), 283.

39. Linda Gordon, *Woman's Body, Woman's Right: A Social History of Birth Control in America* (Middlesex, Eng., 1977), 207.

40. Meredith Tax, *The Rising of the Women: Feminist Solidarity and Class Conflict, 1880–1917* (New York, 1980), 163.

41. Ibid., 160; Gordon, *Woman's Body*, 222–23.

42. Linda Moerbeck Fuhr, quoted in Gordon, *Woman's Body*, 322. Fuhr, the speaker from the American Birth Control League, had worked in the Paterson mills as a child: p. 454 n.91.

43. John Reed, letter to Walter Lippmann, 18 September 1913, quoted in Robert Rosenstone, *Romantic Revolutionary: A Biography of John Reed* (New York, 1975), 119.

44. John Reed, "Almost Thirty," *The New Republic Anthology: 1915–1935*, ed. Groff Conklin (New York, 1936), 71. On Reed's emphasis on the "collapse of the I.W.W." (which he dated *before* 1917), see also his 1920 sketch for an autobiographical novel, quoted in Hicks, *Reed*, 384.

45. Note Hicks's subtitle: *The Making of a Revolutionary*; see also *Reed*, 106–7, 248, 357, 395, 402.

46. See, e.g., Rosenstone, *Romantic Revolutionary*, 256–57, 341, 347–56.

47. Mel Most, "The 1913 Silk Strike Terror: The Hoax That Killed Silk City," *Sunday Record* (New Jersey), 30 September 1973, p. 12.

48. See ibid., 6–7, 9, 11, 13.

49. *U.S.A. v. W. D. Haywood et al.*, no. 2721 (7th Cir. 1918) *Transcript of Record* (IWW Collection, Box 117, Folder 6, Archives of Labor History), 166. The weaver, Charles Frattinger, had been called as a witness for the defense in this trial, in Chicago.

50. Sophie Cohen, interview by Deborah Shaffer and Stewart Bird, 17 December

1977 (typescript, Program on Women and Work, University of Michigan/Wayne State University), pt. 1, 19.

51. Rudolph J. Vecoli, *The People of New Jersey* (Princeton, N.J., 1965), 198–99; Nancy Fogelson, "They Paved the Streets with Silk: Paterson, New Jersey, Silk Workers, 1913–1924," *New Jersey History* 97 (Autumn 1979): 145.

52. David J. Goldberg, "The Battle for Labor Supremacy in Paterson, 1916–22," in *Silk City: Studies of the Paterson Silk Industry, 1860–1940*, ed. Philip B. Scranton (Newark, N.J., 1985), 127.

53. George Shea, interview with author, New York City, 23 May 1983. Shea is Mayor Brueckmann's grandson.

54. Martin Russak, "Poems of a Silk Weaver," *New Masses* 4 (June 1928): 9. On the lost dream of 1913, see also Buhle, "Italian-American Radicals," 144–46.

55. See, e.g., Minnie Keller, interview with author, Paterson, N.J., 18 June 1982. See also Emilia Perrone, interview by Robert Kirkman, Haledon, N.J., 11 May 1981. Note that after the IWW declined in Rhode Island, the Sons of Italy fell increasingly under right-wing, pro-Mussolini influence: Buhle, "Italian-American Radicals," 141–43.

56. Tax, *The Rising of the Women*, 275.

57. Jack and Mona Mandell, interview with author, Wayne, N.J., 4 January 1984. Jack is Hannah Silverman's son.

58. Ernest Poole, *The Harbor* (New York, 1915), 319.

59. See also Ernest Poole, *The Bridge: My Own Story* (New York, 1940), 210; Truman Frederick Keefer, *Ernest Poole* (New York, 1966), 42–45. Many passages in *The Harbor* derive directly from Paterson; e.g., cf. *The Harbor*, 336, with *The Bridge*, 198.

60. Poole, *The Harbor*, 323. Note that because of what has been lost, college students in 1966 could not understand *The Harbor* without help: Keefer, *Ernest Poole*, 53–54.

61. Max Eastman, *Venture* (New York, 1927), 192, 244; Harry Kemp, *More Miles: An Autobiographical Novel* (New York, 1926), 352–53, 407–8.

62. See, e.g., Flynn, *Rebel Girl*, 155–73, 332–35; Dodge Luhan, *Movers and Shakers*, 141, 234, 249. (On the changes in Dodge after 1913, which are reflected in her memoirs, see Rudnick, *Mabel Dodge Luhan*, 93, 138.) To see what was lost, contrast these memoirs with a contemporary document like John Sloan, *John Sloan's New York Scene: From the Diaries, Notes, and Correspondence, 1906–1913*, ed. Bruce St. John (New York, 1965). Flynn shows a changing world, Dodge a changing self, Sloan a changing self in a changing world.

63. Christopher Lasch, *The Agony of the American Left* (New York, 1969), viii.

64. John Reed, "The Social Revolution in Court," *Liberator*, September 1918, reprinted as "The I.W.W. in Court" in John Reed, *The Education of John Reed*, ed. John Stuart (New York, 1955), 182; on the IWW as singing movement and intellectual center, see pp. 180–81.

65. William Preston, "Shall This Be All? U.S. Historians versus William D. Haywood et al.," *Labor History* 12 (Summer 1971): 436–37.

INDEX

Aaron, Daniel, 176
AFL (American Federation of Labor): in 1913
  strike, 44, 51, 82–84, 86–90, 139, 144,
  262 n.143; in Pa., 44, 198, 219, 223; and
  silk manufacturers, 75, 78, 87, 194; and silk
  weavers, 33, 75, 84–86, 198, 199; and
  women, 84, 122. *See also* Golden, John;
  Gompers, Samuel; United Textile Workers
Akron, Ohio, rubber strike in, 41, 102, 223,
  246 n.117
Aldermen, the: and police force, in 19th
  century, 20; powerlessness of, 27
Allentown, Pa.: silk dyeing in, 78; silk strike
  in, 43–44
Amalgamated Textile Workers of America,
  199, 201, 202
Anarchists: decline of, 27, 28; in 1894 and
  1902 strikes, 20, 27; and Italians, 26, 27;
  and IWW, 115, 118, 170, 207–8, 209; in
  1913 strike, 116, 274 n.107; and violence,
  26–27, 170, 207–8
Antunuccia, Fedela, 92
Antunuccia, Tony, 92
Armenians, in strike, 56
Armory Show of 1913, 7, 10
Ashley, Jessie: as feminist, 267 n.66; and
  IWW, 129–30, 171, 219, 267 n.66; in
  Lawrence strike, 133; as member of middle
  class, 267 n.66; in 1913 strike, 129–30,
  133–34, 144, 164, 186
Ashley and Bailey Silk Manufacturers, 73
Associated Press, 113, 148
Astoria, N.Y., 45, 173

Baldwin, Roger, 201
Bamford, Joseph, 74
Bamford Ribbon Mill, 65–67, 130, 196,
  286 n.77
Becker, Maurice, 115
Belasco, David, 55
Bellows, George, 116
Bialystok, Poland, 30, 285 n.75
Biella, Italy, 2, 3
Bimson, Chief John: assumption of, concern-
  ing strikers, 12–13, 39; and meeting halls,
  12, 38, 106; and 1907 reform of government,
  27, 79; as patrolman and captain, 27;
  reliance of, on force, 12–13, 37–39,
  50–51, 53, 80–81, 104–5, 152. *See also*
  Police
Birth control: and Paterson women, 64–65,
  142, 231; as workers' control, 230–31
Blacks, 145, 146, 256–57 n.37, 274 n.102
Boston, Mass., 45, 277 n.11
Botto, Adele, 192, 251 n.100
Botto, Eva, 192
Botto, Maria, 155
Botto, Pietro, 153, 192, 275 n.136
Botto house, 153, 154, 155, 192, 232,
  275 n.135
Bourne, Randolph, 9, 175
Boyd, Frederick Sumner: arrest of, 180, 227;
  on Pageant Executive Committee, 164; after
  Paterson, 212–13, 217, 227; on sabotage,
  143, 181, 212; as Socialist, 212, 218; as
  speaker, 104, 132, 145, 181
Boyd, Mrs. Frederick Sumner, 142, 212